D0936983

# Dynamics of Stress

## Physiological, Psychological, and Social Perspectives

# The Plenum Series on Stress and Coping

*Series Editor:*
**Donald Meichenbaum,** *University of Waterloo, Waterloo, Ontario, Canada*

*Editorial Board:* Bruce P. Dohrenwend, *Columbia University*
Marianne Frankenhaeuser, *University of Stockholm*
Norman Garmezy, *University of Minnesota*
Mardi J. Horowitz, *University of California Medical School,*
*San Francisco*
Richard S. Lazarus, *University of California, Berkeley*
Michael Rutter, *University of London*
Dennis C. Turk, *University of Pittsburgh*
Camille Wortman, *University of Michigan*

---

COPING WITH LIFE CRISES
An Integrated Approach
Edited by Rudolf H. Moos

DYNAMICS OF STRESS
Physiological, Psychological, and Social Perspectives
Edited by Mortimer H. Appley and Richard Trumbull

*Forthcoming*
COPING WITH NEGATIVE LIFE EVENTS
Clinical and Social Psychological Perspectives
Edited by C. R. Snyder and Carol E. Ford

---

A Continuation Order Plan is available for this series. A continuation order will bring delivery of each new volume immediately upon publication. Volumes are billed only upon actual shipment. For further information please contact the publisher.

# Dynamics
# of Stress
## Physiological, Psychological, and Social Perspectives

Edited by

## MORTIMER H. APPLEY
*Harvard University*
*Cambridge, Massachusetts*

and

## RICHARD TRUMBULL
*Former Research Director, Office of Naval Research*
*Washington, D.C.*

Plenum Press • New York and London

Library of Congress Cataloging in Publication Data

Dynamics of stress.

(The Plenum series on stress and coping)
Consists of updated papers presented at the Conference on Psychological Stress Theory, held Apr. 2–6, 1984 in Luxembourg and sponsored by Clark University and the Government of Luxembourg.
1. Stress (Psychology)—Congresses. 2. Stress (Physiology)—Congresses. 3. Stress (Psychology)—Social aspects—Congresses. I. Appley, Mortimer H. (Mortimer Herbert) II. Trumbull, Richard III. Conference on Psychological Stress Theory (1984: Luxembourg, Luxembourg) IV. Clark University (Worcester, Mass.) V. Luxembourg. VI. Series. [DNLM: 1. Stress, Psychological—congresses. WM 172 D997]
BF575.S75D96   1986                            155.9                            86-25175
ISBN 0-306-42252-2

© 1986 Plenum Press, New York
A Division of Plenum Publishing Corporation
233 Spring Street, New York, N.Y. 10013

All rights reserved

No part of this book may be reproduced, stored in a retrieval system, or transmitted in any form or by any means, electronic, mechanical, photocopying, microfilming, recording, or otherwise, without written permission from the Publisher

Printed in the United States of America

BF
575
.S75
O96
1986

To Henry J. Leir, whose generous support made
the Clark–Luxembourg conference series possible

# Contributors

**Bernice Andrews,** Department of Social Policy and Social Science, Royal Holloway and Bedford New College, University of London, London, England

**Mortimer H. Appley,** Department of Psychology, Harvard University, Cambridge, Massachusetts, and Clark University, Worcester, Massachusetts

**Shlomo Breznitz,** Roy D. Wolf Center for Study of Psychological Stress, University of Haifa, Haifa, Israel

**George W. Brown,** Department of Social Policy and Social Science, Royal Holloway and Bedford New College, University of London, London, England

**Laura M. Davidson,** Medical Psychology, Uniformed Services University of the Health Sciences, Bethesda, Maryland

**Bruce P. Dohrenwend,** New York State Psychiatric Institute, and Social Psychiatry Research Unit, College of Physicians and Surgeons, Columbia University, New York

**Susan Folkman,** Stress and Coping Project, Department of Psychology, University of California, Berkeley, California

**Marianne Frankenhaeuser,** Psychology Division, Department of Psychiatry and Psychology, Karolinska Institutet, Stockholm, Sweden

**Michael Frese,** Institut für Psychologie, Universität München, München, Federal Republic of Germany

**Giselher Guttmann,** Psychologisches Institut, Universität Wien, Wien, Austria

**Heinz W. Krohne,** Psychologisches Institut, Johannes-Gutenberg Universität, Mainz, Federal Republic of Germany

**Lothar Laux,** Lehrstuhl Personlichkeitspsychologie, Universität Bamberg, Bamberg, Federal Republic of Germany

**Richard S. Lazarus,** Stress and Coping Project, Department of Psychology, University of California, Berkeley, California

**Klaus R. Scherer,** Section de Psychologie, Université de Genève, Geneva, Switzerland, and Justus Liebig Universität, Giessen, Federal Republic of Germany

**Klaus Scheuch,** Institut für Arbeitshygiene, Medizinische Akademie "Carl Gustav Carus," Dresden, German Democratic Republic

**Wolfgang Schönpflug,** Institut für Psychologie, Freie Universität Berlin, Berlin, Federal Republic of Germany

**Jerome E. Singer,** Medical Psychology, Uniformed Services University of the Health Sciences, Bethesda, Maryland

**Richard Trumbull,** Former Research Director, Office of Naval Research, Washington, D.C., and 4708N. Chelsea Lane, Bethesda, Maryland

# Preface

It was our privilege, some twenty years ago, to assemble a group of Canadian and American investigators to examine the status of research in the then newly burgeoning field of psychological stress (Appley & Trumbull, 1967). As noted, in Chapter 1 of the present volume, there has been rapid development of the area since then. The conference on which the current volume is based was designed to do three things:

1. to further update the field,
2. to bring European and other perspectives to the subject, and
3. to focus on the status of *theory* of stress.

We believe the reader will agree that all three objectives were accomplished, though in so vast and active a field, one can never be totally satisfied.

The authors included in this volume are among the leading investigators in the field. They represent active research centers and programs in Austria, East and West Germany, Great Britain, Israel, Sweden, and the United States. Their chapters make contributions to stress theory and methodology, inform us meaningfully of the perspectives of the various research programs they represent, and provide, collectively, a description of the dynamics of the stress process as currently emerging.

Early versions of most of the chapters that compose this volume were presented and discussed at an invitational Conference on Psychological Stress Theory, held in Luxembourg during the week of April 2–6, 1984. The Conference was the tenth in a series, on various subjects, hosted by the Institut Pédagogique at its facilities in Walferdange, Luxembourg, under joint sponsorship of Clark University and the Government of Luxembourg.

Costs of the Clark-Luxembourg Conferences, and of editing the several volumes that have resulted from them, were underwritten by several grants from Mr. and Mrs. Henry J. Leir to Clark University. We are deeply grateful to Mr. and Mrs. Leir for the encouragement of the use of Luxembourg as a meeting place for international scholars and for their generous support of Clark University in its partnership in the Luxembourg conference programs.

One of us (MHA) is particularly indebted further to the Leirs for their personal friendship of many years and for their support of his transition from academic administration back to full-time involvement in scholarly work. A postpresidential sabbatical leave from Clark University, spent as Visiting Scholar in Psychology at Harvard University, was likewise extremely valuable in this regard.

We are grateful to the distinguished group of investigators who interrupted busy schedules to join us for a most provocative week of discussions, and for the care with which they (and their collaborators) undertook revisions and improvements in their papers, based on feedback from both formal and informal dialogue among the conference participants and with the editors.

Dr. Frankenhaeuser, originally scheduled to be with us in Luxembourg, was unable to attend at the last minute, but graciously submitted her paper for inclusion in this volume, to which it makes a fine contribution. Drs. Lazarus and Folkman combined efforts, subsequent to the Conference, to provide a single joint paper in place of the two they presented in Luxembourg: and Drs. Brown and Singer both added collaborators to help revise and extend their respective conference presentations.

Our thanks are extended to Dr. Gaston Schaber and his staff at the Institut Pédagogique for the Conference support arrangements and to Maripol and Véronique Schaber for their gracious hospitality. We especially appreciated the assistance, during and after the conference, of Mariann Hundahl Appley, as hostess, translator, and critic-in-residence.

We are pleased that this volume is appearing in the new Plenum Series on Stress and Coping, and look forward to subsequent volumes to contribute further clarification of issues in this vital field.

MORTIMER H. APPLEY
RICHARD TRUMBULL

# Contents

CHAPTER 3

CHAPTER 4

CHAPTER 8

*Ergopsychometric Testing: Predicting and Actualizing Optimum
Performance under Load* ...................................... 141
GISELHER GUTTMANN

CHAPTER 9

*Voice, Stress, and Emotion* ................................... 157
KLAUS R. SCHERER

PART IV. COPING AND STRESS .......................... 181

CHAPTER 10

*Coping as a Moderator and Mediator between Stress at Work and
Psychosomatic Complaints* .................................... 183
MICHAEL FRESE

CHAPTER 11

*Coping with Stress: Dispositions, Strategies, and the
Problem of Measurement* ..................................... 207
HEINZ W. KROHNE

CHAPTER 12

*A Self-Presentational View of Coping with Stress* ................... 233
LOTHAR LAUX

# PART I

# *Introduction*

# CHAPTER 1

# Development of the Stress Concept

## MORTIMER H. APPLEY and RICHARD TRUMBULL

## Introduction

Studies of stress, and particularly of psychological stress, have shifted focus and become considerably more sophisticated since the mid-1960s, when we assembled an interdisciplinary group of American and Canadian investigators at York University in Toronto, for an assessment of issues in stress research (Appley & Trumbull, 1967). Some of the same fundamental problems remain today, it seems to us, though their dimensions have been sharpened in many respects by nearly two decades of research and theory development that have occurred since that early conference took place. (We like to think that the seminal papers and discussions of that conference were a stimulus to changes in the field, cf. McGrath, 1970, but we know that there were many other influences as well.)

This chapter begins with a brief retrospective examination of the context in which our earlier conference took place, a review of some of the issues raised then that we believe have not been given enough attention by stress researchers, observations on development in the field in the past two decades, and some comment on current theory. In a separate chapter, we make some suggestions as to what, in our view,

MORTIMER H. APPLEY ● Department of Psychology, Harvard University, Cambridge, MA 02138, and Clark University, Worcester, MA 01610. RICHARD TRUMBULL ● Former Research Director, Office of Naval Research, Washington, DC and 4708 N. Chelsea Lane, Bethesda, MD 20814.

needs to be done to allow/encourage the development of a unified theory of psychological stress and discuss some of the elements that we believe need to be conceptualized as functioning simultaneously if we are to comprehend the dynamics of the stress process. These thoughts are offered in the way of developing a common conceptual framework *for* stress rather than suggesting a formal model *of* stress.

## Stress Research in the 1960s

A conference on a subject provides a means of sampling what is going on in a particular field at a particular time. It is likely also to reflect influences—fads, trends, dominant ideas, and so forth—that are prevalent at that time and that determine which aspects of a subject are explored, which instruments of measurement are employed, and which theoretical orientations govern the questions to be asked. Ideas inconsistent with the trends of the time tend to be ignored or minimized, though after a trend has gone on for a while, receptivity for a contrary or otherwise new position may suddenly develop. Our 1965 conference was no exception. We note briefly several influences that were consistent with the ethos of the times and that thus developed, and others that were not.

1. The term *stress* itself had limited previous use in psychology. Its early appearance, in human factors research, derived from the engineering use of the concept, as in *stress-producing strain.* Such work tended to focus on stimulus characteristics, attention, vigilance (in signal detection), and performance change (primarily decrement) under unusual input load and environmental conditions. Such useful concepts as system and system capacity, introduced in human factors research, were not widely adopted in general psychology at the time, though they appear to be coming into greater use now. Human factors research led to some interesting findings in regard to load capacities in man–machine systems, through research in sensory psychology, learning theory, and information processing, but had little direct impact on theory or practice in clinical or social psychology. The parallels between man–machine system organization and limits and those in personality organization and abnormal psychology were recognized but were not generally pursued.

2. At the same time, many physiological psychologists, and investigators in related fields, came under the influence of Hans Selye's (1936, 1946, 1950, 1955) proselyting use of the term *stress*, and were adopting it. One can trace the infiltration of Selye's concept through increasing listings in *Psychological Abstracts,* as it was substituted systematically and inexorably for earlier labels, like anxiety, tension, conflict, and so forth

(Appley, 1959; Appley & Trumbull, 1967; Cofer & Appley, 1964), and with good reason.

Selye's work extended, as he was wont to emphasize, the earlier insightful descriptions by Claude Bernard (1859) of the maintenance of vital balance in the "millieu intérieur" and by Walter Cannon (1932) of homeostatic processes. Selye pointed to his and his colleagues' consistent findings that, in addition to any specific, source-related systemic responses to traumatic input to the body, a *non*specific pituitary-adrenal reaction was also, and inevitably, involved. If the stimulus source did not abate, a stress response—the *General Adaptation Syndrome* (*G-A-S*)—would result, producing damage in the form of gastric ulcers, thymus involution, and/or adrenal atrophy—the *diseases of adaptation*—and, ultimately, exhaustion and death.

Because psychologists had long included Bernard's and Cannon's explanations in descriptions of the operation of biological motivational systems (cf. Cofer & Appley, 1964, Chapter 7), it is easy to see why Selye's elegant further development of these basic notions gained ready acceptance. Following Selye's 1955 invited address to the American Psychological Association, both his term and straightforward model were applied widely, though largely uncritically, by clinical and experimental psychologists alike. Such applications tended to define stress in terms of bodily response and to look for those conditions that would trigger this common, unitary, systemic reaction.

As with many matters, once looked at carefully enough, the simple relationships that Selye predicted tended not to be so simple or predictable at all. Mason (1975), among others, raised serious questions about both the unitary, all-or-none nature of the physiological response itself and whether, indeed, it occurs in the absence of psychological factors (see also Selye's response, 1975, and Singer & Davidson, this volume). Even by the time of our 1965 conference, it was becoming clear that stress—and certainly psychological stress—was neither a unitary nor an all-or-nothing phenomenon, and the applicability of Selye's elegantly simple model was beginning to be challenged in physiology and even more so in psychology (Appley & Trumbull, 1967; Lazarus, 1966; McGrath, 1970).

3. Yet another influence on our 1965 conference was its occurrence at a time when interest in *brain-washing* and the impact of isolation on cognition and behavior had been heightened by a war in which the technique was being employed more than ever before (cf. Solomon, Kubzansky, Leiderman, Mendelson, Trumbull, & Wexler, 1961). The parallel development of observation stations in arctic and antarctic environments (cf. Sells, 1970), of the manned space flights (cf. Ruff & Korchin, 1964), and of the prospect of long-term submersion in the then

new nuclear submarines (cf. Appley, 1957) gave further impetus to studies of the effects of sensory deprivation and/or social isolation on behavior (cf. Haythorn, 1970).

Human factors interests in sensory system overload (mentioned earlier) likewise led to studies of performance degradation under extreme conditions (cf. Miller, 1953; Sells, 1970). Natural disasters, laboratory simulations, and varieties of field studies were explored (cf. Baker & Chapman, 1962) to ascertain what factors would precipitate stress reactions and how stress impacted decisions and performance. No sensory system remained unassailed in controlled experiments in psychophysical and psychophysiological laboratories; and social psychologists likewise found their challenges in studies of changes in patterns of social interaction under conditions (natural or contrived) of isolation or reduced social contact.

In the main, performance degradation was the dependent variable measured in such studies, with biochemical or physiological (and even psychophysiological) measures used only to index the presence or absence of stress. As a result of this widespread interest in the effects of extreme environments, considerable attention in the mid-1960s conference was directed to studies of real or simulated environments where such stressors had been or were likely to be encountered. As might be expected, little standardization of methods or communality of criteria of stressfulness was found to exist across studies or reports. Despite the confusion—if not because of it—certain conclusions could be drawn from our conference, as from many that were to follow.

It continues to be clear that not all events that were presumed to be stressful turn out to be so; that even those that are in some manner demonstrably stressful are not necessarily so—or at least not uniformly so—for all individuals exposed to them; and that even the same individual exposed to the ostensibly same environmental stressor could react and/or be affected differently at different times or under different *sets*. In short, *there can be little generalization across categories of stressors—or even the same stressor exposure at different times—as to extent, intensity, direction, duration, or permanence of effect such stressors could be expected to have on individuals or their responses.* Thus, a model like the one Selye originally introduced and developed (1936, 1950), whether systemic or behavioral, would appear to be too inflexible to be able to handle the complexity of interaction of factors ordinarily found in all but the most extreme and overwhelming situations.

Recognizing the new directions that followed his earlier concept, Selye (1973) took occasion to report further research on the pathological front, where three essentially distinct stress adaptors had been identified: nervous, immunologic and phagocytic, and hormonal mechanisms. Further, these mechanisms could act syntoxically (tolerating) or catatoxically (fighting) toward the stressor. These multiple systems, then, introduced *heterostasis,* which Selye was to adopt in formulating his own "philosophy of life." (In his later work, he also denied that he had ever claimed that the objective of adaptation was to remove stress from one's life, arguing that "complete freedom from stress is death" [Selye, 1973, p. 693]).

## The Changing Face of Stress

Even during the early days of dominance of the physiological systemic orientation, psychologists began to introduce the tools of their trade in an effort to ascertain *who* was under stress and by how much. Individual differences had to be recognized even in studies using the criteria employed by Selye and others of a greater medical orientation. Why such differences obtained under seemingly similar conditions or in similar situations needed to be answered. This was true even if only to provide greater selectivity in individuals to be studied. Further, such information would provide the first suggestions for possible lessening of the impact of stressors in, if not eliminating them from, situations over which some control could be exercised. And, finally, for situations over which control could not be properly exercised, there would be a basis for selection of those individuals who could be assigned responsibilities with least jeopardy to them or to their mission.

It is understandable, then, that the personality questionnaire and the research methodology that sought to control for sociopsychological factors were brought into the study of stress. The tests that were readily available were tried, in efforts to identify relations between their established entities and evidence of stress from the physiological world as well as from performance deterioration. The Rorschach anxiety indices, Minnesota Multiphasic Personality Inventory, Taylor Manifest Anxiety Scale, Thematic Apperception Test, California Psychological Inventory anxiety scale, Mood Adjective Check List, and Necker Cube Test were among those from which some cue of correlation or predisposition was sought. The world of the psychologist was experiencing some difficulty in deciding just what trait or emotional base could be established for stress susceptibility (cf. Miller, 1953).

One notes that the editors of *Psychological Abstracts* experienced difficulty, in the early years (from 1927 to 1960), in determining a classification for stress. Their early volumes included Stress, Conflict, Emotion, Tension, Danger, and Disaster. From 1961 to 1965, Anxiety, Fear, and Frustration were added, with a physiological entry reflecting the more common laboratory stressors and systemic changes. A short period (1966–1968) found accelerated research on sensory deprivation gaining its own listing under Deprivation (sensory). Beginning in 1972, the categories of Stress referred readers to Environmental Stress, Occupational Stress, Physiological Stress, Social Stress, and Stress Reactions. This was a marked shift to various environments. Conflict now became associated with arguments, riots, violence, and war.

Emotions were to be treated under Emotional Adjustment and Coping Behavior; Emotional Control and Identity Crises; Emotional Security; Emotional Stability; Emotional Trauma; Emotionality (Personality), and Emotionally Disturbed.

Further evidence of the confusion that resulted from problems (and change) of definition, as well as determination of the scope of the concept, was found in the other categories under which it was being reported. Thus, a number of items that were listed under stress could be traced to such classifications as Behavior Correlates, Personality, Neurology and Physiology, Mental Disorders, and Psychophysiology.

The same story was found in the *Cumulated Index Medicus*, where the 1960 classification of Stress included complications, experiments, in infancy, childhood, in pregnancy, pathology, physiology, psychology, and therapy. Reflecting wider interest, as well as improved knowledge over the next two decades, the 1980 version acknowledged Stress, Mechanical and Psychological, as major headings for blood, chemically induced, complicators, diagnosis, drug therapy, enzymology, etiology, familial and genetic, immunology, metabolism, microbiology, mortality, pathology, physiopathology, prevention and control, psychology, radionuclide imaging, therapy, urine, and veterinary.

Articles were to appear in journals of nursing, teaching, medicine, dentistry, and a variety of professions that were experiencing some of the effects of stress as well as being in a position to provide treatment. In 1975, stress in humans was defined to the satisfaction of a limited number of individuals sufficiently to establish a journal, *Human Stress*, which continues to confine itself to its own definition of the term. Another journal was devoted to the interesting process of biofeedback, with all of its potential for producing stress as well as serving as a means of control. The *Biofeedback and Self Regulation* journal appeared in 1970, and *Psychosomatic Medicine, Clinical Psychology, Applied Psychology, Pharmacology, Motivation and Emotion*, and other journals published stress papers as well, reflecting the fractionation as well as the expansion of interest in the field.

Recognition of the important role to be played by cognitive processes, personality correlates and precursers, genetic determinants, and coping, stimulated the appearance of conferences, books, and journal articles in ever-increasing numbers. The shift from laboratory studies and interpretations of catastrophic events to the full life spectrum—through newly classified Life Events—brought new meaning to concepts like intensity, duration, and *normal* (cf. Dohrenwend & Dohrenwend, 1974).

Laboratory studies continued to pose many problems. Many stressors were identified *post facto*, after physiological and performance changes were established. Other stressors were identified as such primarily because the *experimenter* assumed that they would be stressful. Still other stressors were employed because certain equipment was available or because some interest of a sponsoring agency could be satisfied. Further, questions of how much, how intense, or for how long had to be answered, and such parameters were often set quite arbitrarily.

Certain shock, acceleration, noise, and deprivation studies raised issues of an ethical nature when even a few subjects were stressed beyond a level acceptable in an academic setting. The issue was not quite so pressing in the military service or in other situations where the stress could be more related to potential exposures in the line of duty. The earlier pressures for performance in demanding environments abated, however, and the time came to control the exposure of subjects more completely while the search for correlates and predetermining factors went on. The turn to broader, more *natural* environments, and particularly to the study of life events, took stress research farther toward the world of sociology, though still maintaining some links to psychology and to systemic physiology, with emphasis on illness. Research drew more on the capability for observation (including self observation) and inference, as the events under study were controlled by the vagaries of life itself. The new approach shared some of the problems of laboratory studies, as, once again, stressfulness often was attributed to the event *post facto*, following the appearance of depression, emotional change, or some few physiological criteria.

As this research was reported, we find the *Psychological Abstracts* reflecting the change. *Emotions*, in addition to the previously noted seven categories, was expanded to include separate new classifications for Emotional Content, Emotional Development, Emotional Disorders, Emotional Maturity, and Emotional Response. *Anxiety* was reduced to categories of Anxiety Neurosis; Castration Anxiety; Death Anxiety; and Separation Anxiety. *Fear* was allowed one subcategory, that of Fear of Success. *Frustration* remained a single category; while *Tension* dwindled to referencing premenstrual events. It was quite evident that interest in the field of stress had shifted to the clinical and social arenas.

The change in point of regard also introduced an array of new measures—Life Events Inventories, Social Readjustment Rating Scales,

Cultural Readjustment Rating Questionnaires—and studies on validation. There were Children's Life Events, Adolescent Life Changes, College Coping, and similar samplings of every stage and age to be undertaken in the 1970s. Type A and Type B personalities enjoyed popularity, especially in attempts to correlate patterns with cardiac and circulatory criteria for stressfulness.

Fortunately, the emphasis on life events also stimulated interest in the broader nature and implications of stress. Although earlier research often treated subjects with little regard for individual differences, and took refuge in average or gross scores, the newer approach helped bring those same differences into a prominence that could not be denied. The earlier history of each subject *did* matter, as did the total context of the stressful situation which was of momentary interest or concern. The sociologists' different perspective and experience in building case histories was of value.

Expansion into a broader context, via the study of Life Events, demanded a clearer understanding of coping and what are now conceived to be the many processes of cognition (cf. Lazarus, 1966). In 1967, *Psychological Abstracts* listed Coping Behavior with a reference to Adjustment/Personal and Social. Although Coping Behavior had fewer than 20 references, the Adjustment listing included 145. By 1975, Adjustment was incorporated under the heading of Coping Behavior, a practice which continues. As might be expected, the present listing includes the wide range of adjustments demanded during the entire life span under the single category of Coping. (It is important that this concept be more clearly defined and that the integration as well as the differentiation of coping processes over time—from the initiation of stress to the end product of its influence—become better understood.)

Unlike coping, the bibliographic story of cognitive processes was quite similar to what had happened to the original classification of stress. As various disciplines became interested in it, and found some utility in the concept, it was adapted, like stress, to cover a range of meanings as noun and verb. In 1960, the *Psychological Abstracts* listed Cognition (Thinking and Reasoning) and Cognitive Style. By 1980, a reader of the literature was confronted with 11 main categories and 27 subcategories of Cognition.

This explosion, coupled with that of Life Events studies, could not help but bring the concept of Stress to the attention of a much wider audience. It also compounded the problem or problems of those who were still attempting to structure or model the research entity of stress. As in early learning theory or in engineering psychology, explanations put forward merely in terms of labels on black boxes (e.g., boxes called *drive* or *operator* or, in this case *cognitive processes*) may be beguiling simplifications and not explanations at all. How drive functions in learning, what variability is to be expected of the operator, or, in the issue of interest here, how cognitive processes interact with stressor and/or coping responses need to be known if the dynamics of the stress process are to be understood or behavior in stress situations made predictable.

With this admonition in mind, let us continue our examination of the development of the stress concept, of models that have been proposed (along with their "black box" characteristics), and of attempts to describe, if not explain, what is happening within those boxes.

## Individual Susceptibility

The emphasis on differential individual susceptibility and differential response patterning was already clearly in evidence before the mid-1960s. There seemed then—and now—to be general agreement that the stressfulness of stimulus exposure or events is dependent on the "pattern of stimulus–organism interaction" at a particular time and in a particular place (Appley & Trumbull, 1967, p. 7).

Lazarus, Deese, and Osler (1952), in their excellent early analysis, concluded that (psychological) stress depended on "what the individual demands of himself" (p. 296). This would be determined, according to Pascal (1951) "in terms of a *perceived* [italics added] environmental situation which threatens the gratification of needs" (p. 177). Lazarus and his colleagues urged that we find ways to measure the "kinds and strengths of [the individual's] motivations . . . relating them to the characteristics of the situation in which he must perform." "The fulfillment of this aim," they prophetically concluded, "is, indeed, no simple affair." (Lazarus, Deese, & Osler, 1952, p. 314).

Vulnerability, or stress-proneness in different situations, according to Appley (1962), is mediated through "threat perception . . . [determined by] . . . the relative potencies of the motives being threatened in those situations" (see also Cofer & Appley, 1964, p. 459; Appley & Trumbull, 1967, pp. 10–11), and our ability to cope effectively with the perceived threat. (Lazarus [cf. Lazarus, 1966, Lazarus & Alfert, 1964] elaborated significantly on both the mediating cognitive appraisal and coping processes, as we know, and his and Folkman's contribution in this volume adds to this elaboration.)

Weitz (1966, 1970) and Sells (1970) likewise found stressfulness of any situation to be related *inversely* with the degree to which an individual in such a situation is able to respond effectively, and *directly* with the degree to which the consequences are significant to that individual. Sells further agreed to the interactional nature of stress, the importance of individual differences, and the critical role of the cognitive system (rather than emotion) in controlling stress reactions.

> The onset of stress is to be determined and understood . . . not in terms of stimulus parameters . . . , or of the personality profiles of the participants, although these are relevant, but in every case in terms of the individual's ability to make an effective response and his assessment of the consequences of failure. (p. 138)

Another extension was proposed by Teichner (1968), recognizing the requirement for interaction between "physiological and behavioral compensatory reactions to physical and symbolic stressors" (p. 217). He postulated "inter-regulatory controls among activating mechanisms and data-processing mechanisms with corresponding changes in the strength and direction of physiological and behavioral reactions" in an attempt to integrate the "effects of the information overloads, emotion-provoking stimuli, and the effects of the physical environment into one psychophysiological context" (p. 217). (See the discussion of similar concepts in the next chapter.)

Consolidation also was an objective of Lehman (1972) in introducing his "Transaction Model" to establish that presence or absence of stress reaction was "a multiplicative function of both situational and individual characteristics" (p. 484).

Both the range of interest and the factors now recognized as being in the stress arena far exceeded the earlier simplistic association of stressor and General Adaptation Syndrome, which had held sway so long since its introduction by Selye in the mid-1930s.


## Current Theories of Stress

Baum, Singer, and Baum (1981), in a rather comprehensive recent review of stress and the environment, further emphasized the interactive nature of stress source, transmission processes, and recipient. They agreed with Jenkins (1979) and Lazarus (1966) that transmission variables, such as adaptive capacity and appraisal, are essential to an understanding of the "one persistent and for the most part unanswered question [namely] why some people are more susceptible to stress-related disorders than others" (Baum, Singer & Baum, 1981, p. 28). They identified at least five groups of factors that mediate interpretation of stressors:

1. Wealth and availability of resources for coping (including social support systems)
2. Attitudes toward the sources of stress (e.g., perceived degree of harmfulness and/or controllability

3. Prior experience with the stress source
4. Risk assessment (including threat *and* danger assessment)
5. Stress vulnerability

Although we agree fully with their observations, we would have carried their analysis of *dispositional variables* one step further, namely, to the recognition of vulnerability *not* as a generalized state, as in the high-risk personalities implied by earlier investigators (e.g., Grinker & Spiegel, 1945; Cobb, 1976) or types (e.g., Friedman & Rosenman, 1959), but as highly individualized. In our view, individual *stress vulnerability profiles* (cf. Appley, 1962) are determined by underlying motivational patterns that identify particular areas of relatively greater or lesser susceptibility, thus influencing the appraisal processes in different ways for different individuals. An emphasis on motivational patterns was made earlier by Lazarus *et al.* (1952), as was noted.

Chalmers (1981) and Pearlin, Menaghan, Lieberman, and Mullan (1981), in two detailed and extensive recent reviews, pointed to the enormous scope of what is now included under the rubric "stress," and to the fact that "the range of issues normally encompassed by single investigations is too truncated to observe the extended web of relationships that gives shape and substance to the [stress] process" (Pearlin *et al.*, p. 337). Reviewing the alternatives (see McGrath, 1970), Chalmers concluded that the now widely held view of "the environment-organism transaction approach appears to offer a realistic framework for stress research and theory" (p. 328). He reminds us that the focus of transaction "can be situated at any system level (e.g., intraorganismically, such as at the level of cells or organs) or in the individual as a total system, or interorganismically at the interpersonal group or organizational level" (p. 328). And even further, following Cox and Mackay (1981), Chalmers (1981) noted that

> the experience of stress is the balance or imbalance resulting from the interaction of four components: internal needs and values, external environmental demands and constraints, personal resources or capabilities, and external environmental supplies and supports. (p. 333)

(In the next chapter, we treat more extensively the interaction of physiological, psychological, and sociological levels of functioning in relation to the stress experience.)

Cox (1978; Cox & Mackay, 1981) accepted McGrath's (1970) description of the stress process as involving four stages:

1. *Demand* (encompassing the load or input or stress situation or environmental force acting on the focal organism)
2. *Reception, cognitive appraisal, perception,* or (subjective) *recognition of demand* (either conscious or unconscious)

3. *Response(s)* to the perception of the stress situation (physiological, psychological, behavioral, and/or social)
4. *Perceived consequences* of response(s) for the organism and his/her environment

Cox then added an important fifth process, *feedback,* which can occur at *any* stage.

Appley also emphasized feedback in his schema of the dynamics of the stress process (Appley, 1962; Appley & Trumbull, 1967; Cofer & Appley, 1964). He expanded Lazarus's concept of appraisal to envision a virtually continuous, multi-level monitoring process (of appraisal and *re*appraisal) through the entire perception and coping sequence. At each step, the result(s) of appraisal and/or action would conceivably change the nature of the challenge or threat and of the consequent coping requirement. Appley's schema included first, an appraisal of *task require-ments* when the individual is confronted with a challenge (What is being demanded?), and, almost immediately, appraisal of one's *competence* to handle the challenge (Is an appropriate response within one's behavior repertoire? Will it suffice?); second, but almost simultaneously, the in-dividual would be appraising two other elements of the challenge: (a) its *relevance* to the individual (i.e., the effect it might have on the person's *role* in the situation in which the challenge occurs), and (b) its *significance* (i.e., whether or not it challenges—or potentially challenges—the indi-vidual at a deeper level of ongoing ego development or ego sustenance). This last determination takes into account *baseline* levels at different physical, social, or psychological stages, as opposed to a more superficial task or role impact (to which one might be able to adapt temporarily or from which one might be able to escape).

In the process of assessing task requirements, one would necessarily also appraise any *perceived environmental constraints* (physical or social/cultural) that would affect the nature of a possible response. (Here one can see the potential interplay of constraints and level of threat—the greater the level of physical constraint, the greater the likelihood of the threat taking on more serious proportions—and conversely, perhaps, the greater the perceived *significance* [or even *relevance*] of the threat, the greater the likelihood of overcoming inhibitions derived from social and/or cultural constraints.)

Finally, but again serially throughout the monitoring process, an appraisal would occur of the *impact* of one's actions (coping responses)—taken or anticipated—on the changing task requirements and on any changes in the level of relevance or significance of the threat (as such levels are affected by ongoing coping responses). *It is in the process of experiencing a stress situation that its dimensions unfold* as a function of the sequential testing of perceptions through covert or overt coping, and the sequential changing of coping requirements as perceptions are modified.

Wild and Hanes (1976) emphasized yet another aspect of stressor evaluation. Although parallel processes arising from the interplay of internal psychological forces and external environmental factors had been supplemented by the concept of *feedback* loops to account for coping and adaptive behavior, there still was need, they pointed out, to emphasize the dynamic nature of adaptation, where feedback from *past* failures contributes to failure in new situations, even those with less stressful stimuli.

Adler (1977) added a further developmental perspective, emphasizing the sequential nature of adaptive processes. Using cardiovascular disease as an illustration, he traced "the effects of psychological stress, from the psychic/psychosocial stimulus to the psychic stress, to physiological and biochemical reactions, to forerunners of disease, and to disease itself" (p. 43). Development of understanding of the many elements related to reactions of many systems involved in stress, even in the case of disease etiology, has taken research quite a way from the original, fairly simple sequence in the General Adaptation Syndrome, as has already been noted.

Structuring a model that can encompass the new contributions from other disciplines, while dealing with their interactions as well as individual dynamics over time, is difficult. Veno and Davidson (1978) proposed one model comprised of five levels:

> (a) the internal mediating processing center, (b) the perceptual/cognitive filter, (c) relationships, (d) behavioral interactions with environmental stimuli that form the basis for relationships, and (e) environs around which relations can be grouped. It is proposed that the basic unit of analysis must be the individual and that the sum of an individual's experiences with his/her environment (social/physical/internal/external) at any given point in time (a relationship) is the dynamic construct around which varying responses to stress can be conceptualized. This model accounts for 3 properties of stress which previous models have left largely unresolved: (1) an individual's different response to the same stressor at different points in time (i.e., adaptation to stress); (2) a single stressor being perceived as a potentially positive or negative event; and (3) different perceptions of the same stressor by different individuals. (p. 75)

Redfield and Stone (1979) also noted that "important characteristics of [life] events may vary widely among individuals and that future assessment of the properties of life stress [must] be both multidimensional and specific for individuals" (p. 147). Toward this end, Hwang (1980), employing multidimensional scaling on the Social Readjustment Rating Scale, found three dimensions that constituted "the perceptual space for perceiving life events": *magnitude, uncontrollability,* and *stability.* Other perceptual and psychological modifiers of response to stress concerned Jenkins (1979), whose work relates to the earlier criterion of pathology. His expanded model "takes into account both the adaptive capacity of the organism before the stressor occurs and the defenses marshalled in response to the stressor" (p. 3). Emphasizing the need for a multidisciplinary approach to "begin to capture the wholeness of human experience," Jenkins offers a research paradigm that "anticipates that stressors, adaptive capacities, defenses, alarm reactions, and pathological end-states will take place at the biological, psychological, interpersonal, and sociocultural levels simultaneously and successively" (p. 3).

We come to the point, then, when the disciplines involved in the description, prediction, and control of adjustment to life events, to isolated stressors, and/or to incidental inconvenience or disruption of ongoing activity recognize their unique contributions as well as the interdependence required of them. As their new findings, whether in immunological systems or cultural determinants of cognitive processes, enter the picture, they should be able to build on the current consensus that seems to be developing about the nature of the stress process.

# References

Adler, R. (1977). Physiology and pathophysiology of psychic stress. *Schweizer Archiv für Neurologie, Neurochirurgie und Psychiatry, 121,* 33–46.

Appley, M. H. (1957, February). Psychological stress. (Appendix II of *A study of operational safety requirements in the submarine polaris missile system*). New London, CT: Electric Boat Division, General Dynamics.

Appley, M. H. (1959). *Psychological stress and related concepts: An indexed bibliography.* (ONR Contract 996 [02], Technical Report No. 7). New London: Connecticut College.

Appley, M. H. (1962). Motivation, threat perception, and the induction of psychological stress. *Proceedings, Sixteenth International Congress of Psychology, Bonn 1960* (pp. 880–881). Amsterdam: North Holland.

Appley, M. H., & Trumbull, R. (Eds.) (1967). *Psychological stress: Issues in research.* New York: Appleton-Century-Crofts.

Baker, G. W., & Chapman, D. W. (Eds.) (1962). *Man and society in disaster.* New York: Basic Books.

Baum, A., Singer, J. E., & Baum, D. S. (1981). Stress and the environment. *Journal of Social Issues, 37,* 4–35.

Bernard, C. (1859). *Leçons sur les propriétés physiologiques et les altérations pathologiques des liquides de l'organisme.* Vols. I and II. Paris: Ballière.

Cannon, W. B. (1932). *The wisdom of the body.* New York: W. W. Norton.

Chalmers, B. E. (1981). A selective review of stress: Some cognitive approaches taken a step further. *Current Psychological Reviews, 1,* 325–344.

Cobb, S. (1976). Social support as a moderator of life stress. *Psychosomatic Medicine*, *38*, 300–314.

Cofer, C. N., & Appley, M. H. (1964). *Motivation: Theory and research.* New York: Wiley.

Cox, T. (1978). *Stress.* London: Macmillan.

Cox, T., & Mackay, C. (1981). A transactional approach to occupational stress. In E. N. Corlett & J. Richardson (Eds.), *Stress, work design, and productivity* (pp. 91–113). New York: Wiley.

Dohrenwend, B. S., & Dohrenwend, B. P. (1974). *Stressful life events: Their nature and effects.* New York: Wiley.

Friedman, M., & Rosenman, R. H. (1959). Association of specific overt behavior pattern with blood and cardiovascular findings. *Journal of the American Medical Association, 169*, 1286–1296.

Grinker, R. R., & Spiegel, J. P. (1945). *Men under stress.* New York: McGraw-Hill.

Haythorn, W. W. (1970). Interpersonal stress in isolated groups. In J. E. McGrath (Ed.), *Social and psychological factors in stress* (pp. 159–176). New York: Holt, Rinehart & Winston.

Hwang, K-H. (1980). Perception of life events: The application of non-metric multi-dimensional scaling. *Acta Psychologica Taiwanica, 22*, 25–32.

Jenkins, C. D. (1979). Psychosocial modifiers of response to stress. *Journal of Human Stress, 5*, No. 4, 3–15.

Lazarus, R. S. (1966). *Psychological stress and the coping process.* New York: McGraw-Hill.

Lazarus, R. S., & Alfert, E. (1964). Short-circuiting of threat by experimentally altering cognitive appraisal. *Journal of Abnormal and Social Psychology, 69*, 195–205.

Lazarus, R. S., Deese, J., & Osler, S. F. (1952). The effects of psychological stress on performance. *Psychological Bulletin, 49*, 293–317.

Lehman, E. C., Jr. (1972). An empirical note on the transactional model of psychological stress. *The Sociological Quarterly, 13*, 484–495.

Mason, J. W. (1975). A historical view of the stress field. *Journal of Human Stress, 1*, 6–12, 22–36.

McGrath, J. E. (Ed.) (1970). *Social and psychological factors in stress.* New York: Holt, Rinehart & Winston.

Miller, J. G. (1953). *The development of experimental stress-sensitive tests for predicting performance in military tasks.* (PRB Technical Report 1079). Washington, DC: Psychological Research Associates.

Pascal, G. R. (1951). Psychological deficit as a function of stress and constitution. *Journal of Personality, 20*, 175–187.

Pearlin, L. I., Menaghan, E. G., Lieberman, M. A., & Mullan, J. T. (1981). The stress process. *Journal of Health and Social Behavior, 22*, 337–356.

Redfield, J., & Stone, A. (1979). Individual viewpoints of stressful life events. *Journal of Consulting and Clinical Psychology, 47*, 147–154.

Ruff, G. E., & Korchin, S. J. (1964). Psychological responses of the Mercury astronauts to stress. In G. H. Grosser, H. Wechsler, & M. Greenblatt (Eds.), *The threat of impending disaster: Contributions to the psychology of stress* (pp. 208–220). Cambridge, MA: M.I.T. Press.

Sells, S. B. (1970). On the nature of stress. In J. McGrath (Ed.), *Social and psychological factors in stress* (pp. 134–139). New York: Holt, Rinehart & Winston.

Selye, H. (1936). A syndrome produced by diverse nocuous agents. *Nature, 138,* 32.

Selye, H. (1946). The general adaptation syndrome and the diseases of adaptation. *Journal of Clinical Endocrinology and Metabolism, 2,* 117–130.

Selye, H. (1950). *The physiology and pathology of exposure to stress.* Montreal: Acta.

Selye, H. (1955). Stress and disease. *Science, 122,* 625–631.

Selye, H. (1973). The evolution of the stress concept. *American Scientist, 61,* 692–699.

Selye, H. (1975). Confusion and controversy in the stress field. *Journal of Human Stress, 1,* 37–44.

Solomon, P., Kubzansky, P. E., Leiderman, P. H., Mendelson, J. H., Trumbull, R., & Wexler, D. (Eds.) (1961). *Sensory deprivation. A symposium at Harvard Medical School.* Cambridge, MA: Harvard University Press.

Teichner, W. H. (1968). Interaction of behavioral and physiological stress reactions. *Psychological Review, 75,* 271–291.

Veno, A., & Davidson, M. J. (1978). A relational model of stress and adaptation. *Man Environment Systems, 8,* 75–89.

Weitz, J. (1966, April). *Stress.* (Research Paper P-251. Report IDA/HQ 66–4672). Washington, DC: Institute for Defense Analysis.

Weitz, J. (1970). Psychological research needs on the problem of human stress. In J. McGrath (Ed.), *Social and psychological factors in stress* (pp. 124–133). New York: Holt, Rinehart & Winston.

Wild, B. S., & Hanes, C. (1976). A dynamic conceptual framework of general adaptation to stressful stimuli. *Psychological Reports, 38,* 319–334.

# PART II

# Some Theoretical Approaches

*The four chapters that comprise this section were grouped here because they present more general models and/or deal with more generic issues in stress theory. However, all the contributions to this volume address issues relevant to stress theory, and it would be of value to examine each of the chapters in the book in relation to the assumptions and concepts they and others use in discussing the stress process.*

*Trumbull and Appley examine the dynamics of interaction of individuals and their environments, insisting that any comprehensive stress theory must take into account what happens* before *and during a stress experience, and of the alteration of the individual* after *stressor encounter. They offer a model involving simultaneous consideration of physiological, psychological, and social systems, each with its own subsystems, and all interfacing as a series of interlocking sheaths (or wires), each capable not only of* conductance *within its own sheath, or subsets within that sheath, but also of affecting each other via* inductance *from adjacent levels.*

*For these authors, the capability of each system (and/or subsystem) to sustain itself* over time *is affected by its own developmental history, the dynamics of system interaction (e.g., the "readiness" of each system for the impact or overflow from others, in both its circadian and life cycles), and the nature of the demands placed on the individual. Their model utilizes concepts of timeliness, feedback, vulnerability, anticipation, and predictability, among others, and defines stress as the* discrepancy between demand (stressor) characteristics and the carrying (resistance) capacity of the individual.

*Singer and Davidson likewise emphasize the importance of the connection between psychological and physiological aspects of behavior. They examine two broad models of stress: the reactive* physiological *(pathogen) model and the interactive* transactional *model, suggesting that the latter, in fact, incorporates the former as a special class. Recognizing the importance of human cognitive activities and the need for appraisal of what they call stressor "potential," Singer and Davidson review the ways in which the transactional model is (or is not, as yet, at least) able to account for individual differences in stress vulnerability and such particular phenomena as stress-seeking, choice of coping styles, and role of social support. Although they applaud the emergence of "an integrated biobehavioral perspective on stress," Singer and Davidson point to the difficulties that consideration of a broader range of variables introduces, and suggest ways in which research methodologies will have to be modified to accommodate "theoretical parsimony."*

*Lazarus and Folkman provide a spirited defense of "appraisal-centered" or cognitive stress theory against charges of methodological confounding or circularity. They argue for the validity of treating appraisal as different from the events and/or emotions being appraised, even while acknowledging a necessary partial overlap of the two types of variables. Only by the addition of appraisal, they point out, can the influence of antecedent variables on outcome of a stress situation be predicted.*

*Like the other authors in this section, Lazarus and Folkman consider "the rubric, stress" to be* dynamic *("appraisal and coping processes continuously change"), and* recursive *("outcomes can influence antecedent variables, depending on where in the flow of psychological events one chooses to begin and end the analysis"). And, like the other positions presented here, they see appraisal and coping as requiring consideration of "adjacent" physiological and social as well as psychological levels, and needing to take account of both immediate and long-term effects.*

*Finally, Schönpflug's behavior economics model likewise offers a dynamic view of stress, based on a* cost–benefit analysis *of stress situations. He considers the* process *(rather than the product) of problem orientation or appraisal (and control) as constituting the* psychic load *and defining the degree and temporal extension of stress. The efficiency of active problem solving and the adequacy of appraisals affect the* payoff, *which is the resultant of a comparison of benefits or savings (of costs) achieved by coping and the resources (or costs) invested. Thus, a coping response may be rejected or aborted if its (projected) costs exceed (potential) benefits.*

# CHAPTER 2

# A Conceptual Model for the Examination of Stress Dynamics

RICHARD TRUMBULL and MORTIMER H. APPLEY

## Introduction

The stress concept has proved to be an effective stimulus to reconsideration and redefinition of styles and strategies of coping as well as of life itself. The history of the stress concept, some of which has been presented in Chapter 1, has been an interesting one, as various disciplines found a way to relate to others and make some contribution to its development. As noted earlier, there have been many efforts at sketching or making a model of the stress concept in the tradition of Selye, who had stated "You must first have a concept derived from observation and symbolized by a name before you can even try to delimit it more precisely by a definition" (Selye, 1956, p. 61).

One step in that process is the making of a model that attempts to place all the pieces on the table before defining. Models tend to be simplistic abstractions with characteristic enhancement of the section representing the discipline of the author. This feature allows or assures enough space to include all that he or she believes will derive from that discipline (or specialty), but usually pays little homage to others, even in

RICHARD TRUMBULL • Former Research Director, Office of Naval Research, Washington, DC, and 4708 N. Chelsea Lane, Bethesda, MD 20814. MORTIMER H. APPLEY • Department of Psychology, Harvard University, Cambridge, MA 02138, and Clark University, Worcester, MA 01610.

an avowed interdisciplinary representation. Over the years, then, there has been a steady output of such limited aspects of the total picture with block diagrams, flow diagrams, systems analyses, and verbal rationalizations for utilization of the stress concept. Most block diagrams included various forms of "black boxes," in which vital and intricate functions were labeled *cognition* or *coping* at a point where something was supposed to occur. The delineation of activities associated with cognition or coping was left to others. In turn, new models appeared with adequate representation of *those* functions but, in turn, producing *other* black boxes that, for example, indicated where something of a physiological nature was to occur or where some social influence might make a difference. Some writers have recognized the difficulties involved in representing the total system by stating that the concept itself was no longer of use, although it might have served some heuristic function in the past.

Even with this discouraging picture before us, we would like to sketch a brief picture of the world of stress reaction systems with the objective of facilitating their study and understanding. The emphasis is on the dynamics of the interactions between the individual and his environment—to explain what is happening *before* a stressor is encountered, *during* the period of response, and—*following* stress experience—how the individual has been altered, for better or worse, to deal with stressors yet to come.

## Parallel Systems

Today, there is general acceptance of three parallel systems—physiological, psychological, and social—that function to maintain a person and provide whatever means there are for dealing with stressors over his or her lifetime. Each system, in turn, has subsystems. In the physiological system, for example, one can identify circulation, respiration, glandular, nervous, and digestive subsystems, all of which depend on biochemical and neurological functions for their activation and interactions. Our primary evidence of the efficiency of these systems and functions is in the state of health, work performed, and/or waste products. We must also be aware of the dynamic nature of such systems, their development, the underlying rhythms, and the ebb and flow of adjustments in their normal variations, from circardian to life cycles.

The psychological system also has subsystems of functions and traits, among which are perception, memory, emotion, and an ill-defined category of "needs." These, too, can develop and exhibit periodicities, many of which are associated with, if not determined by, underlying rhythms of physiological functions. Here we may recognize the psychological "pace" for walking, for working and for assumption of increasing difficulties and/or responsibilities, and the stress resulting from a *relative* increase or decrease imposed on such "natural" rhythms. The potential role of predisposition, or underlying background, has always been implicit in the psychologist's search for personality and problem-solving traits or characteristics.

Subsystems for functions in the social system include ethos, values, family, and culture, among others. These systems impose structure and provide support as the final veneer to the physiological and psychological components of the individual. Once again, we find evidence of developmental histories and of "normal" rhythms and periodic influence. Pearlin, Lieberman, Menaghan, & Mullan (1981) recognized an undercurrent or flow in social situations that influenced the process in stress resolution.

The interrelationships among physiological, psychological, and social systems are subtle and dramatic and demand a better comprehension of the ranges of adaptability, resilience, and recovery to be expected within each system before its influences on the activity of other systems can be understood. Individually and collectively, these three systems determine the resources available to an individual under stress. The dynamics of their development and interactions must be understood more fully to deal with stress reactions of the moment. Of greater promise is the role such understanding will play in providing guidance to the development of these systems, during an individual's lifetime, to assure the presence of appropriate resources when stressful life events are encountered.

## Physiological System Functioning

The physiological system of the new-born has a genetic and a prenatal history. At birth, there are on-going respiratory, circulatory, glandular, neural, and digestive processes. Early stimuli facilitate development of neurological connections, biochemical reactions, movement, and the first manifestations of stress reactions when elicited. Today, we have a general conception of how these systems extend their range, of their interrelationships, and of the nutritional factors that assure an orderly sequence in development as well as the ultimate utilization of the system's potential. We know that certain glands play their biochemical role on a largely predetermined schedule and then reduce their influence. We know that certain inherent weaknesses can be held in abeyance until some stress or prolonged drain on the systems allows them to surface. We know that the senses have far greater potential than any single in-

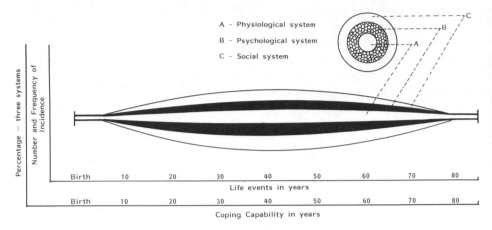

**Figure 1.** Developmental chart for life events and coping.

dividual will ever realize. Adequate testimony to this is found in the hearing and tactile senses of the blind and in the professionals who utilize olfaction, taste, and vision.

As we analyze the elements of life events that provide for stressfulness, we may recognize many of them as *natural* or *expected* at certain times during the life history of a particular physiological system. Then, we can ascertain whether the physiological system, with its many components, has developed appropriately to the point where it can be expected to provide the resources needed for a "normal" pattern of successful coping.

In the beginning, birth itself can provide the initial stressor or initiate strain in a system that will be predisposed to vulnerability later on.[1] As the physiological system develops through the life cycle, there is a natural diminution of function, adaptability, and interaction that serves to place the individual at greater risk with or without augmentation by apprehension or other psychological intervention. The final coping is left for the waning vital signs and basic reflexes. A schematic representation of such a history is shown in Figure 1 (A). Although a life-cycle scale is provided, accurate depiction of the first availability of certain capabilities and functions should be represented by a range that allows for individual differences. On such a scale, one should be able to indicate early sensorimotor coordination and glandular activity, as is often presented in

---

[1] It is important to recognize that this *beginning* can occur in a wide range of sociocultural settings with attendant differences in implications for scope and rate of development of all of the three systems being discussed here.

standard texts on development. The peak years—when the greatest amount of the physiological system is functioning and available for dealing with stress or life events—might be determined and/or altered by environmental, nutritional, and medical factors. At the same time, these years also can be enhanced or protracted by actions taken, at first, by parents and, later, by the individual to assure availability of the best resources possible over the longest span of life time. Even acknowledging the presence of inherent biological weaknesses, which may lie in wait through the years, we may accrue the information required to keep them in check to assure optimum physical health.

## Psychological System Functioning

The psychological system is not understood so well in its true composition or in what one might posit as a "natural" development of its parts and functions. We do not enjoy psychological parallels with other members of the animal kingdom who have served us well as prototypes for an understanding of circulatory, respiratory, digestive, muscular, glandular, and neurological elements of the physiological system. Another problem arises from a different aspect of the term "normal" when we move from physiological to psychological levels of functioning. In the former, there is a reasonable consensus as to what comprises a "healthy" state and function for every element in the system. This feature does not exist, however, except in very broad generalization, in the elements and functions of the personality or the psychological resources on which one draws when confronted with stressors. If we decide that "threat" is an important element in establishing the stressfulness of certain life events, and even if we can delineate the various types of "threat" involved, we still have a long way to go before we can say that the psychological base for dealing with that aspect of threat is laid at some particular time in life or through some particular sequence of experience through which the individual may go, either under normal circumstances or by design.

If *self-confidence* is deemed to be necessary for successful coping, we lack the knowledge of when and how that attribute is best established for either specific events or generalization. (This attribute is chosen deliberately because it demonstrates the necessary interaction with the physiological system and the sense of good health and physical competence to deal with the task.) Rahe and Arthur (1978) concentrated on this borderline in relating illness to incidence of stress. The model suggests that one can find a parallel between muscle development through increasingly heavier lifting and self-confidence development through feedback from successful coping with increasingly difficult situations. Further, the model would anticipate the parallel decrease in confidence associated with decrease in physiological capability in later years. Hence, the suggestion is that psychological resources have their optimum time for development and utilization, before a final waning, even as do the physiological resources (Wild & Hanes, 1976). Once again, we must admit the difficulty of the task before us as we delineate these psychological resources and establish their functional histories. The complexity in the total system should not deter us from further definition and the ultimate goal of assuring the timely appearance of such capabilities and their maintenance over the longest period possible in supporting the life cycle.

Figure 1 (B) depicts the relationship of the psychological system to the physiological system as a surrounding field (Mikhail, 1981). Insofar as psychological function depends on physiological efficiency or reflects its malfunction, we can expect the same predetermination of reaction to stressors. This relationship begins early in birth order, where the maturation of the physiological system sets a background against which the psychological system will develop. When talking about "overload" and "boredom" as stressors, we implicitly recognize the boundaries of the range of psychophysiological relationships in pacing or personal tempo that characterize the individual. There is an optimum that allows one's established rhythms to function smoothly. Attention span, rate for taking in new sensory material, rate of thinking, and other activities reflect the same interface and functional relationship between the physiological and psychological systems. Enough research has been done on sensory stimulation and the human counterpart to imprinting to establish that there is a very early formation of psychological patterns. The same early association capability extends into the social world and assures us that the beginnings of its influence, too, have a longer history than is generally acknowledged.

## Social System Functioning

The social (or sociological or sociocultural) system poses greater problems than those indicated for the psychological system. It is another step removed from the animal models and, more significantly, a greater step away from description, control, and modification. Although the psychological system can be set in operation as early as prenatal development through conditioning, the social system awaits the development of psychological mediators before any base can be established. Once again, order of birth is an early physiological determinant of later social stress. When the child reacts to others and when associations result in reactions to proximity and voice, have we the beginning of sociability as well as dependence? When we have delineated the sociological or psychosociological aspects of our life events, can we sketch out a life cycle of development for the traits or characteristics that will assure that *this* system will be "healthy" and ready to cope, when the time comes, with some "normal" demand of a life event?

Once again, the task before us is evident. As is true for the other two systems, this system, composed of psychosociological traits or attributes, has its own history, with appropriate periods for development of its various attributes, for their introduction into the life cycle, for their utilization, and for their waning. As life expectancy continues to be extended, we shall have a better understanding of those final attributes of this system, too, serving to cope in a transition to where no further coping will be demanded of it.

## Dynamics of System Interaction

Figure 1 shows the three systems in place. The life cycle is deliberately used as a base in order to break away from the usual time sample or resource slice that is subjected to observation in laboratory studies and, even, in some samplings of life events. The dynamic flow within and between these systems must be represented *over time*. We might think of them as streams (or currents) to assure recognition of the on-going flow from which we can draw only a sample at any particular time. It is inevitable that we revert to metaphor for ease of presentation and, it is hoped, understanding. Our stream, then, might alternatively be conceived of as a wire, representing the physiological system, surrounded by another wire for the psychological system and, in turn, another for the social system functions. These wires, through which the currents flow, are made of different materials, have different conducting rates, and include impurities or weak areas in which malfunctions can occur as predetermined by the original drawing of (or possible damage to) the wire. In such structures, current in the physiological wire can induce a current in the sheath of the psychological wire. An illustration of such a loop or feedback is found in expectancy, threat, or other mental appraisal process influencing physiological sensitivity. This process is followed by increased "feelings" and, ultimately, further physiological activity such as nausea. The same conductance and inductance can occur in and between the psychological and the social sheaths. Note that the placement of the psychological sheath assures that it is a moderator, interpreter, transducer, or mediator between the social and the physiological streams.

Earlier, we discussed the bridges between disciplines and the relationships between subsystems *within* each of the three systems. This variety is accommodated by proposing that each of the three systems of strands is composed of smaller wires that, in turn, have similar potential for conductance and inductance. Thus, biochemical and neurological systems experience such an interplay within the physiological stream. Different cognitive processes or personality traits will interact within the psychological stream. Ethics, values, family, and peer strands can be shown to have the same type of interaction within the social stream. (And, in fact, each of these smaller "fibers" is studied by a subset of investigators that develops its own disciplinary base and its own means of communication in journals, special meetings, and other formats. The interfaces or permeable membranes between them often are represented by additional disciplines. We can think of psychosomatic medicine as the study of the sheath between the physiological and the psychological streams. Things pertaining to psychosocial interactions are categorized in many forms, representing the sheath between the psychological and social streams.)

It is tempting to indicate the influence of the real world on the physiological system as the originator of a sequence of events, leading to psychological reaction and feedback, through inductance, until stress is evident. It is possible to consider such a situation in which the outer sheath of social operation never enters into the development of the reaction or process. Many models have represented such sequences: for example, the startle response in the newborn would be a sequence, from stimulus to reaction, entirely within the physiological stream. As indicated earlier, however, it is not very long before the psychological stream *does* become influenced by a flow in or from the physiological current, as memory and other processes influence both reception and perception of the stimulus and, in turn, feed back to the physiological level. Nor is it much later that association of a voice or touch of others brings the interaction of the social stream. And, in fact, culturally-determined feeding or holding patterns may well influence physiological as well as psychological levels very early on. The pattern is then set. The future of the developing organism will involve many different levels and degrees of interaction between and among systems and subsystems as stress is experienced, from excessive physical assault to ethnic pressure.

As the individual develops, the complexity or composition of the three major wires invites further extrapolation of the metaphor. We do not have all the information we would require to propose that some of the individual psychological or social strands, in turn, are built up by surrounding sheaths in the same way we have pictured the three major systems. Do certain characteristics build upon others and, once established, represent a sheathing interaction, or are they layered? Are higher ethical values similarly a layering or a sheathing? Do we consider our outer sheath or social stream to be more of a veneer of layers with the more sensitive and higher conducting strands closer to the psychological stream? Do later stresses that arise from within the social stream come down through that stream by influencing other *social* strands before inducing a current in the psychological stream? But, we are getting ahead of our story.

The observer, whether clinician or researcher, taking a small time sample of these three streams in passing, must recognize the developmental or transitional nature of *on-going* processes or functioning. Stress can result, for example, from a purely coincidental surge of current in one stream/wire at a parallel point of weakness or low resistance in another. This is a stressful event in the absence of an "outside" stimulus. Outside stimuli, of course, will exert their pressure on one or more of the streams, inducing broader involvement through the others. As one passes through the stages of life, each with its own associated physiological, psychological, and social cross-sections, one may also periodically enjoy nonstressful periods, with a balance or heterostasis existing (Selye, 1973).

## Symptoms and Sources

Imbalance in any one of the systems can result in symptoms produced by stress in that system alone, or by inductance through one or more of the remaining systems. In the latter instance, there is danger that treatment might be provided for the symptoms generated by the second or third level while the originating stream is overlooked. A majority of stress management programs place much emphasis on symptoms, and are thus potentially in danger of misdirecting corrective action.

An equally important point needs to be made for second- and third-order derivatives as they occur between subsystems within a single system. Thus, for example, in the physiological system, when a stressor influences respiration and circulation, as it invariably does, there will be changes in sensory systems and, ultimately, in performance, depending on the function. It should come as no surprise, for example, that high $g$ loading influences muscular performance. In a more widely studied area, that of stress as reflected in coronary arrest, one must recognize the primary role that may have been played by such factors as arterial pressure, hypertension, regional redistribution of blood, atherosclerosis, coagulation, platelet aggregation, lipid content, myocardium, and mitral valve status. Further, with circulation so altered, what is the trail to galvanic skin response (GSR) changes, neurodetermatitis, psoriasis, or acne vulgaris? The same circulatory changes can influence other areas where passage of blood, vessel dilation, and increased pressure are reflected in migraine. With changes also in the composition of blood now flowing, other cellular growth patterns will be altered. The point being made here is that there are certain sequences of events that take place entirely within a single stream of our model that, in their normal course, may have no effect, but that will produce evidence of stress where they impact on a latent predisposition or weakness.

This sequential history can be as easily demonstrated within the psychological or social streams. Such within-system as well as cross-system analyses can usefully direct our attention to the intermediaries as well as to the final "symptom."

## Life Events and Coping

It is evident that the sociologist's introduction of life events as stressors moved research a long way from the laboratory study of performance degradation under the influence of loud noise (Cleary, 1980; Dohrenwend & Dohrenwend, 1974; Lei & Skinner, 1980). It has taken us many years to appreciate all the ramifications of "loud," experimental setting, interaction with the experimenter, presence of peers, and other variables that denied us a simple, direct line between stimulus and effect. Before we knew it, we were studying motivation, emotion, personality, and sociology, almost all of which were foreign to the physiological psychologist or the human factors specialist with whom the study of psychological stress began. When the stimulus became something called a *life event*, the very scope of this stimulus assured us of a longer search for all the implications, the predispositions, and the full range of cognitive processes and coping mechanisms. The latter leads us further into those mechanisms *within* the systems as they seek their own homeostasis or interactive heterostasis. Many investigators seem to believe that coping begins and ends with cognitive processes. That is why we have emphasized the *history* of the systems and the *feedback* that keeps twining in and out, over time, even as the systems are undergoing changes within themselves. The stream keeps on flowing, and an impulse or conductance sent from one system to another feeds back onto the former at some later point in function as well as in time. Let us consider feedback for a moment on a larger scale.

## Feedback

Feedback is not peculiarly physiological, as in proprioception or delayed auditory return, as attractive as these loops might be in their relative simplicity. Feedback is a set of continuing processes within and between the three systems under consideration. The interplay between physiological and psychological and social is also demonstrable (Jenkins, 1979). When an individual is in a stress situation in the presence of peers (Friedman, 1981), for example, whether such peers are calmer or more agitated, his or her response will be influenced in a manner reflecting the psychological recognition of and/or need for peer approval. Indeed, a source and determinant of the stressfulness of the situation will be this feedback from and degree of sensitivity to social factors. Conflict between morals, codes and the example of others, and psychological or physiological needs plays an increasing role in stress during the adolescent years. Here, we can have an individual reacting to a stressor operating at all three levels.

Consider what happens when the loops or feedback on one of the three systems impact on a stressor already operative in another system: for example, the social stream and its feedback elements operative through the psychological stream. The conflict that occurs there can increase any physiological stress that is already under way or, if the social feedback reinforces an adaptive psychological response that is in process, then the stress would be lessened.

The nature of the social stream is emerging from correlations between life events and such factors as age, socioeconomic status, marital status, race, and location (cf. Goldberg & Comstock, 1980). Further, there are "the continuous problems" that make their contribution to compounding the impact of discrete events in the stress process (Pearlin *et al.*, 1981).

## Inter- and Intrasystem Manifestations of Stress

We would now like to address the measurement of stress as it becomes manifest in all three systems—physiological, psychological, and social—over time. Selye (1936) first employed three pathological conditions as end points, primarily because he was working with animals that could be sacrificed by running stress to such an extreme that it could be verified or validated by pathological analysis. There are similar end points in the other two systems, represented, for example, by emotional breakdown in the psychological system or divorce in the social system. In each instance, the "carrying" or "load capacity" of the system has been tested as far as possible.

By the time a system has been tested to such an extreme, however, there have been many previous manifestations of successful and/or unsuccessful coping efforts. As a system attempts to adjust or respond to a stressor, that response may have the potential for growing to the point that it impacts one of the other systems. An interaction might then occur such that the earlier or originating system response is decreased or augmented. The feedback can continue, off and on, over time and does not have to be a one-time-only affair. The second system might be thought of as not being responsive or susceptible at the moment because of its own state of health or homeostasis. When this occurs, the eddy in the first stream will be contained and move along only in its own system. It is possible that time alone will bring a reduction in the eddy or the early manifestation of coping, and the original system will return to homeostasis. When this does not take place, the same amount of eddy might stress the second system at a later point in time where or when susceptibility has been increased by changes within that system. An example might help at this point.

Suppose that one manifestation of physiological response to a stressor is tension. Within that system, a tic or twitching results. The area might be reflexly massaged, or other physiological changes might occur that prevent any impact on the psychological stream. On the other hand, its persistence, the interruption to an on-going task, or the presence of others may initiate a response in the psychological system. A scenario can be developed that includes turning the head to hide the tic from others, through a conviction that *everyone* is looking at it, to leaving the room or even to making some comment or striking someone. This induction of current from the physiological system through the psychological to disruption of social behavior depends on the personality structure and the flow that represents its functioning within the psychological stream or system.

Let us try inducing manifestations of stress arising in the social stream through the psychological to the physiological to establish the two-way flow of this system. Suppose we have a "healthy" individual who is quite satisfied, even happy, with present employment. On the surface, there is no reason to believe that life events associated with employment are apt to jeopardize the heterostasis we assume is being enjoyed by the three systems. However, let us now inform our subject that a co-worker has received an increase in salary to a point quite a bit above the subject's salary. The social milieu now undergoes a change. Performance of work might be degraded. The psychological system is now operating and, depending on the personality structure and its relationship to emotions, based on past experience and vulnerability in both psychological and physiological systems, a scenario can be developed that would include loss of appetite, loss of sleep, dissatisfaction with that same job, and generalized response widening into areas other than work. Ultimate physiological validation of stress can appear in alcoholism, ulcers, or simply weight loss. All three systems have played their role in the transfer of stress.

These scenarios have been negative, but we believe that positive transfer from one system to another is also possible. Certainly, if and when the intermediary psychological system is healthy, imposition or transfer of stress from either of the other systems through it can be denied or deferred long enough for the passing of time and concurrent changes in both streams to remove the stress. These interactions must be understood and appreciated more fully if we are to separate correlates from causes in our discussions of stress reactions. The sequence of events must also be recognized as being capable of dormancy in one stream until the right weakness appears in that adjoining. Over time, the dynamic nature of this stream concept becomes manifest as the physiological system undergoes a variety of changes in biochemical, endocrine, immunologic and other sectors, while the psychological development of the individual assures a similar ebb and flow of susceptibility in that stream. There is no need to emphasize the negative here because the ebb and flow in both systems also represents strengths and resistances as well. The veneer provided by our posited outer coating, or social wire, also represents a stream wherein the current may gain strength, thus lessening its ability to induce a flow into (or resist a flow out of) the psychological stream as the individual develops a social life.

Let us return to our discussion of the flow *within* the streams. We alluded to this earlier, in our consideration of the many elements in the circulatory system that are influenced by constriction of blood vessels, as one of the earliest physiological changes that takes place under stress. There are similar sequences in activation of the adrenal system, production of catecholamines, and the interference with the immune system function. There is, then, a chain of events that will take place within the physiological system once trigger mechanisms have been stimulated. This sequence can be stopped, slowed, maintained, or exaggerated by interplay from the psychological stream. The individual's sensitivity and response to somatic changes become part of the input for perception. At times, stress will be produced by conflicts between this input and that from other sensors, as in rotation-room experiments or amusement-park rides. At times, stress will arise from a conflict between these inputs or cues and those that are *expected* from previous experience, as found when skilled operators are confronted by simulators which lack validity in real world representation. Such conflict of cues from *within* the physiological system or stream can produce nausea or other responses that increase the individual's distress and/or vulnerability without any contribution from the psychological system. Alternatively, such responses can be precipitated by anxiety, presence of others, and similar interplay with both the psychological and social systems. Further, *anticipation* of an unwanted somatic response is capable of producing the same reaction in some individuals in the absence of physiological conflicts, evidencing the influence of the psychological system alone. To be sure, breakdowns in the psychological system need not necessarily impact on the physiological and/or social systems. However, in attempts to treat a psychological breakdown (or symptom), it is essential that appropriate consideration be given to physical well-being and life-style implications. There can also be breakdowns in the social system, as in antisocial behavior, retreating, or rebellion. Here, too, the interplay of psychological factors as an undercurrent must be recognized and dealt with. Psychiatry deals mainly with this psychosocial interface, even as psychosomatics tends to emphasize the interface between the physiological and the psychological. In time, both of these specialities must deal with all three streams, their conducting layers, and how they function.

## Stress as Discrepancy

*When the functioning of one or more of these systems results in a discrepancy between any stressor and the carrying or resistance capacity available, there is stress.* Stated otherwise, stress results from a demand, real or perceived, beyond the real or perceived carrying capacity of the individual's physiological, psychological, and/or social systems.[2] The demand may arise from eventful, chronic, or cumulative stressors, as well as change within the systems. The role of perception is acknowledged here as important but not necessary. Those who would require perception and/or cognitive processes in a definition of stress overlook the role of emergency reactions, such as reflex and conditioned responses, which are *followed* by "feelings" and appraisal. The same oversight is found in retrospective recall of life-events in which individuals might remember elements out of actual sequence. Let us now represent this interaction as total carrying capacity versus total demand at a given moment.

As noted in Figure 2, the normal vacillations of the cumulative or ambient demand level (A) and the carrying capacity (B) keep them within a range of tolerance (C–D), even when one is at its crest and the other is in its trough, as at point (E). Even an increase above normal in demand will be taken in stride or tolerated if the carrying capacity is at its crest

---

[2] The potential for stress arising from high carrying capacity in the absence of demand is recognized as a separate issue, but will not be discussed here.

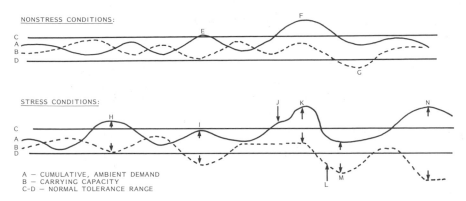

**Figure 2.** Dynamics of demand-carrying capacity relationships.

and restraining the distance (C–D), as at point (F). The tolerable spread also can be maintained when the carrying capacity is below normal if the demand at the time also is lower, as at (G).

Much research on stress has concerned itself only with situations wherein the distance (C–D) has been exceeded by additional demand from a precipitator stressor or demand, as at (H), at a time when the carrying capacity is not and cannot be raised enough to accommodate it (I). It is at this point that coping comes into play, according to such theory. The same discrepancy between demand and carrying capacity obtains, however, when the carrying capacity is caused to fall below normal while the level of demand remains normal. A precipitate demand (J) or a precipitate loss of carrying capacity (L) will also result in the discrepancy that produces stress, as indicated at (K) or (M), respectively. Finally, a major demand may occur at a time when carrying capacity has been lost and traumatic stress occurs (N).

In sum, we are suggesting that it is the exceeding of distance (C–D) which defines stress. That distance, as we have indicated, can be produced by change in either demand and/or carrying capacity. It must be remembered that carrying capacity, at any given moment, reflects activities within and interactions among the three systems: physiological, psychological, and social. Change in one or in any combination of these, over time, can alter resilience of one's carrying capacity and, thus, affect vulnerability. Perception, in the psychological system, may make its contribution to the determination of stressfulness (as represented by the discrepancy, C–D) through interpretation or misinterpretation of demand and/or estimation or misestimation of carrying capacity.

## Applicability of Neurological Descriptors

With the above representation of our three systems and the definition of stress, which calls upon their ability to cope at the introduction of some stressor, let us consider some of the mechanisms that will be brought into play. There is a remarkable parallel between the systems. Well-known concepts in the functioning neurological system are applicable to the psychological and social systems as well. Selye's original work (1936) recognized a common response to various stressors in his General Adaptation Syndrome. This pattern of activity is shared in neurological function in what is known as *the final common pathway*. No matter what earlier pathways have been utilized to reach a certain point or no matter what the nature of a stimulus might be, there is a common pathway shared in producing a common response. We shall consider sequences of events that take place within each of our three systems—physiological, psychological, and social—to establish later the presence of more such final pathways in each as well as in their interactions.

Another neurological term that has special significance in the triggering of stress is *just noticeable difference (jnd)*. Initiation of neural activity requires a change in or alteration of stimulus to a degree that relates to the present state of the system. This change must occur within a specific time to effect activation. If the change is introduced over time, a gradual adjustment will occur and accommodate a much larger change in stimulus than could have been imposed instantly at the beginning of the transition. The reason for this is that the base level is increasing throughout the transition, and increasingly larger increments would be required to induce activity. When we recognize the same principle in the psychological system, we introduce "perception of change" at a cognitive level. Here, too, major changes can be introduced in stressor magnitude if implemented *over time*. We attribute this to the development of tolerance at this level.

## Recovery Time

The basic neurological system also demonstrates the requirement for recovery time in what is called a *refractory period*. The firing across a synapse and the conduction along a nerve cell require the availability of certain chemicals whose depletion, through activity, can be reversed in a very small period of time; but that time is necessary. Similar to the period of recovery for the cell, a period is also required when psychological and/or social systems have undergone stress. We shall return to this fine balance of magnitude and time in our discussion of sequences and cumulation in stress-level production.

## Predisposing versus Precipitating

We return now to the concepts of *predisposing* and *precipitating*, already mentioned, to explain a variety of events in the stress process. *Predisposing* has two aspects in "making susceptible beforehand." The first involves the presence of a higher than normal state of stress that is on-going at the time of introduction of another stressor. The latter is called the *precipitating* stressor because it elicits the response that, in this case, will be exaggerated or be beyond the level that might have been expected from mere imposition of that stressor alone. The neurological system is quite capable of such responses when stimuli are introduced before a return to normal, following a previous stimulus. This example also applies to timing or sequential stimulation, which can be experienced in all three systems.

The second aspect of predisposing pertains to a predetermined weakness or lower resistance in a system that is not immediately evident but that may have its influence some place down the line or in the future. This aspect is like a trap set to spring when time alone will bring a previous level of stress not yet manifest to an area predisposed to failure. It illustrates nicely the relationship of level of stress to homeostatic balance or resistance of the system and also the dynamic, on-going process that can be triggered by summation of stimuli, sequence of stimuli, and/ or concurrence of stimuli, and one's available resources for coping. These stressor values, however derived, test the "carrying capacity" of the systems involved even as that same capacity is tested in bridge construction through loads at certain points or over the entire span. Stress exerts its influence at particular points in life as well as over the life span or cycle.

## Life Events and Life Cycles

Research on life events and their correlates has provided social scientists with a major technique for studying stress over a life time. However, the focus of many studies of life events is on relatively short time intervals, and this does not always allow sufficient consideration of the context in which such events occur—the flow of such events as well as the dynamic flow taking place within the three systems, which represent the resources available for the coping at any particular time. In such a concept, these life events are but peaks or valleys of basic cycles that run over the life-span cycles, which translate physiological needs, ego development, and societal pressures. As an example, let us use *marriage* as such an event, in and of itself neutral, but taking on greater significance, for better or worse, depending on the physiological state, the psychological readiness, and the social setting that already contributed their predisposing factors. (It will be remembered that some of those predisposing factors may not be evident at the time, but only become known later in life and play a role in a major period of stress.) The marriage ceremony, then, is an event of relatively short duration taken from a cycle already underway. It might be stated that its antecedents included falling in love. Freud would insist that an earlier section of the cycle was parental relationships. The psychological system, then, at the moment of marriage, already had an on-going cycle, one with a history, and one that will continue from now on. The event—or *cycle*—of marriage will provide a new dimension through interaction with a reproductive cycle, which also had some history before this moment. Other cycles, related to earning a living, being self-sufficient, increasing self-expression will also experience wider fluctuations as they interact with this new cycle of marriage. These interactions will continue through life past the possible event of divorce because "having been married" has a trace that remains to influence emotions and relationships.

The range of the cycle put into motion by the event of getting married will be influenced by the presence and amount of commitment, a separate factor, with its own cycle, which might have arisen earlier in the psychosocial interface. Discrepancies between the anticipated and the realized in marriage will be enhanced, off and on, by the cycle of commitment. (This same commitment has been recognized as a major contributor to "burn out" in professions in which safety and welfare of others is a primary concern, such as, nursing, teaching, and social work,— service-oriented work (Perlman & Hartman, 1982). In marriage, interactions will increase between a number of cycles, physiological and psychological, with the coming of children. Here the independence of cycles may become quite evident, as disparities occur between family size, desire for professional self-expression, and desire for self-sufficiency. Much of this stress is and can be avoided where psychosocial systems have no established cycles in which child bearing or the event of marriage has imposed urgency *at the time*. Living together in childless relationships seemingly has removed, for many young people, some of the major potentials for stressful events. Once again, the predispositions of a psychological and/or social nature established earlier in the development of the two individuals might have laid the background for some future loss of coping capability. For the present, however, they perceive marriage and childbearing as predominately negative and contributing to an undercurrent of stress. All these major cycles can potentially vacillate from an augmentation of stress to an equal contribution to the carrying capacity or coping through stabilization and satisfaction of other needs. Most individuals experience these variations in childbearing and marriage.

We have used the event of marriage as an illustration of the cyclical nature of major streams in one's life. As shown in Figure 2, the various cycles have different wave lengths or periods from crest to trough, from high to low, and their interactions are capable of reinforcing a stress, reinforcing the carrying capacity or coping ability, or contributing to an exaggerated disparity between stressor and coping and a resultant severe stress.

A person's final hours may bring a concurrence of such cycles so that the ultimate stress results from a disparity produced by loss of social support and psychological integrity at a time when health continues in a trough, precipated often by a skeletal failure in an environment unable to provide the support needed. For example, pneumonia can be a diagnosis that can also represent a capitulation (resignation) to stress.

A similar concurrence of cycles in one and more systems, cumulative and sequential at a rate depriving an individual of recovery time, often characterizes the case histories in clinics and hospitals. Once again, we must be reminded that *perception* of a load or sequence of events as being beyond a person's ability to cope is just as effective as an actual overload. The attitude that is brought into the situation is of vital importance in the determination of stress. As indicated by Breznitz (in this volume), *hope* may well add a new dimension to a person's *carrying capacity.*

## The Disparity Model

The emphasis that our model places on disparity between demand and carrying capacity extends our appreciation of the various ways in which this disparity can be produced (see Figure 2). It also provides insights into the inversion of roles that occurs when demand, assault, or trauma *do not* arise from the outside world. The majority of research on stress has started with this as an assumption, with the requirement for adjustment or coping on the part of the individual. Inasmuch as we are concerning outselves with the perception of disparity, we must recognize the potential for stress arising from needs within the individual not being met by the outer world, family, or society. Among these are physiological needs, including nutrition, water, vitamins, minerals, and exercise, that are capable of producing predisposing as well as precipitating stress. Also included are psychological needs for attention, affection, expression, and so forth that can play the same traumatic or long-term role in stress. Similarly, a variety of social needs may arise from psychological interactions. When the appropriate part of the environment fails to meet these needs, the disparity between demand and coping capacity appears and stress results. The failure to cope or possess adequate carrying capacity in such situations does not depend on the individual's awareness or, in fact, produce awareness of the nature of the disparity. The cry for help, in the absence of recognizable external stressors, goes unnoticed until we belatedly find a biochemical or other malfunction, often after providing a label and assigning the individual to our concept of a support clinic, agency, or institution.

These few examples serve to illustrate the dynamics in stress reactions as recent research has contributed various elements for the paradigm that has been presented. Table 1 provides a summary of the premises on which the paradigm was constructed.

## Control of Stress

Much of the early research on stress was concerned either with the characteristics of the environment that were likely to produce stress or the nature of the stress response itself. Studies of extreme environments, of laboratory-induced stress conditions, and even the more recent emphasis on life events, as experienced by patients in clinical settings, the always available college population, and various community groups, have tended to be descriptive and correlative in nature.

Control or *management* of stress, in the first instance, was concentrated on changing environmental conditions and monitoring consequent performance improvement, especially in military and industrial settings in which a premium was and is necessarily placed on the quality and quantity of output. The clinical world began its "management" with the assistance of tranquilizers, which appeared at the same time as awareness of the personal cost of stress. Once again, it was the physical and physiological system on which attention was focused.

Later, largely in clinical and social psychological settings, it became clear that personality structure played a role in stress development, that experiences provided feedback and subsequent encounters were influenced, that each age had its own type of events with which to deal and so forth. Notwithstanding, few questions were asked as to how a person came into these situations or faced these events. What were the individual histories which separated those who were more vulnerable from the less

**Table 1.** Paradigm Premises

1.  We are dealing with three systems: physiological, psychological, and social.
2.  The psychological system is the intermediary between the other two systems, capable of simple conduction, distortion, amplification and/or damping of stressor input as well as subsequent reaction.
3.  Each system has its own developmental cycle.
4.  Within each system there are components, each with its own developmental history.
5.  There is a rhythm or tempo to each system with a synchrony producing homeostasis within itself and heterostasis with other systems.
6.  These systems have extensive potential for interaction.
7.  The systems are dynamic and represent a flow with eddies or feedback.
8.  While a time sample might be isolated and used for study, the developmental history of the flows before and during any given study must be recognized.
9.  Stress susceptibility of the individual varies over one's life time as a function of the momentary status of these systems and their interactions.
10. Stress can be induced in one system alone or in a combination of systems.
11. The stress can remain (be conducted) within a system and/or transfer (be induced) across systems.
12. At any given moment of consideration, the three systems may be in different states of stress or stress susceptibility.
13. Interactions between or among systems might serve to exaggerate, maintain, or lessen the stressfulness of the initial system of impact or origin.
14. When system equilibrium or balance is not achieved, that system, itself, can fail, resulting in removal of the individual from the situation.
15. Whether system equilibrium is achieved or not, feedback brings that system into the next situation at a different level of susceptibility.
16. The majority of activities within and between these systems takes place daily, where a low level of stress is always present in the individual, reflecting the ebb and flow of equilibrating mechanisms in the three systems. Sensitivity and reactivity to additional load, then, will be influenced by this underlying stress level, as derived from past experience.
17. The experiencing of stress and consequent development of appropriate adaptive or coping responses can be positive and utilized to the advantage of the individual.
18. Stress is a major component in both initiation and maintenance of motivation.

vulnerable? What were the data telling us about dealing with *vulnerability* before the fact? There were no *answers* in hypothetical prospect or retrospect. This does not deny us some inferences, however, about control.

There are certain extreme traumatic events involving individuals in which control is neither expected nor possible. Acts of God, such as earthquakes, tornadoes, and accidents, are among these. Even in these circumstances, however, or in their aftermaths, to be more accurate, *the sense of control* or of having some influence over such events reduces stress (Miller, 1979). Even in quasi-controllable circumstances this appears to be the case. *Accurate anticipation* of an event reduces stress. *Accurate information* about the substance of, the reasons for, and/or the likely results of an event reduces stress. An *awareness of the means for reducing the stress or of escaping from it* reduces stress. A person's insight into his or her reactions, physiological and psychological, reduces stress. These are not major findings but critical determinants of the stressfulness of events a person faces during life. Let us consider our three systems and note what has been done and what might be done through them for better control of stress situations.

Control of the physiological system has received much attention in the form of successful symptom reduction through the use of drugs. Drugs can ease muscle tension, reduce heart rate, reduce blood pressure, decrease neural activity, and treat ulcers. The symptoms of stress, evident in every section of the physiological system, have their own pharmacological "control." Although drugs alter the feeling of stress and the feeling of competence to deal with it, they do not, in fact, alter the situation. Fortunately, there are instances in which the inevitable flow of life and the changes in the physiological system can bring a person to a later point in time when the situation has changed or he or she is better able to deal with it. This gamble is like Russian roulette, however, because the same flow of events and changes in the system might bring a concurrence of more stress from another source and a decreased carrying capacity. Once tranquilizers have been prescribed, their subtle influence on the sense of control must also be considered. Other treatments of symptoms include biofeedback from blood pressure, electromyograph (EMG), heart rate, and respiration (Credido, 1980).

With the psychological system playing so dominant a role as mediator, it was inevitable that self-relaxation, yoga, autohypnosis, and transcendental meditation would be used to effect a change in the physiological response. Reducing the perceived threat of the stressor has been attempted through selective perception and even the denial of its existence. The perceived threat can also be reduced by familiarization and practice to reduce the impact of the new, the strange, and/or the unexpected.

The social system has also been studied for its contribution to dealing with stress through family support, the mere presence of others, religiosity, spiritualism, moral and ethical values, and support groups and hot lines to others who share or have experienced the same event or stress. Most of these studies have pertained to stress situations experienced in later years, however.

If we believe in feedback, habituation, the building of personality, the development of coping strategies, and a general development of invulnerability to stress, there must be a more orderly way to go about the business of research that will establish their feasibility and implementation. In Figure 1, we provided a schematic illustration of the three systems of concern, their cyclical development and functioning, and their potential for interaction. There is a need for better understanding of how these systems are aided in their development to bring all of them into a heterostatic balance that supports the individual as various life events are encountered. Just what *does* constitute the best "state of health" for these systems? We have our clearest understanding of that concept as it pertains to the physiological system, and yet we have not advanced as far as we should have from the data available to us.

There is evidence that dealing with life events at the "expected" time is less stressful and contributes to the resources available on the next occasion. We must recognize that "expected" will have different meanings for the three systems, and whereas one system might be "ready" for an event, the others might incur greater stress if that event should occur. Pregnancy is a good example in which physiological readiness may not be concurrent with psychological or social readiness. The conflicts between these systems, then, can be a source of stress in themselves. The reverse will be found when, for example, a child is psychologically ready to undertake some physical event but the rate of growth and coordination in the physical and physiological system deny success if not rewarding efforts. The concept that there are such optimum times for testing the readiness of the systems is not new but does lack attention as a research entity, especially if we consider the problems of "cross-system" readiness, as noted in an example such as this. The price a child pays for too early an attempt at ice skating or the delay in trying to skate while peers are becoming proficient illustrates the problems inherent in the interactions of the three systems. We need a chronological scaling of events that can build confidence in *physical* ability to cope, a sense of self-actualization in the *psychological* realm, and a sense of belonging and contributing in the *social* setting. Although studies of stress have underscored these requirements, they have not stimulated the developmental training to bring these resources into the stream of life. Among other needs is a listing of events that are the testers or trials at early ages, events that can show just what is still lacking at a time when "normal" stress reactions should have been established through previous exposure (Newman, 1979).

The dynamics indicated in Figures 1 and 2 may also provide guidance for dealing with stress in later years. They indicate that there are a number of things that an individual can understand and do to reduce the stresses in life. An action that reduces the vacillations in the three systems also reduces the potential for their separation to the point where stress occurs. A person's familiarization with his or her physiological cycles can result in the favorable timing of new undertakings. It also can make a person more aware of the way that a system's capability can be decreased through poor health practices and the use of various drugs. Many life events are, or can be, placed more firmly under a person's control. Although procrastination is ordinarily not the best way to deal with life, there are occasions when deferral of an activity until a person *feels* more like it, or some previous stressor has run its course, is advisable. Some individuals undertake too many things within too short a time period and the summation of stress can be as critical as a major stress event that is imposed (Justice, McBee, & Allen, 1977). At issue is the determination of events or actions that are *appropriate* for the stage of life and the extent to which the three systems can provide the resources to meet the demands made upon them. In later years, the physiological support can be expected to diminish, as might the family and other social supports (Holahan & Moos, 1981). The desire to undertake something new "to prove one's self," with only the remaining psychological system as a resource for coping, does not promise well. These later years test the systems just as surely as did the formative years, but now a person has to look at the resources and coping strategies that were developed over the years. Have they been well enough established to provide the support needed? Have earlier social ties been replaced with new ones? Have the physiological and psychological systems also had enough "exercising" of their attributes to keep them in "good health" and ready to be utilized in times of stress? Or is the individual reliant on support that is no longer available or, if available, no longer useful?

This possibility, too, emphasizes the need to improve our understanding of the genesis and ongoing nature of coping as it pertains to the three systems called upon for their appropriate resources in times of stress at different stages of the life cycle.

We believe that the model presented here provides a useful means of representation of the complex interactions of the systems available to individuals for dealing with stress. It underscores the requirement for better understanding and provision of developmental histories of the several systems to establish the availability of resources and the way they may be expected to interact. Finally, it graphically demonstrates possible cyclical factors—at physiological, psychological, and social levels—that may determine stress vulnerability and/or provide insights into the timing of responses to permit some control over, or successful coping with, stressful life events.

# References

Cleary, P. J. (1980). A checklist for life events research. *Journal of Psychosomatic Research, 24,* 199–207.

Credido, S. G. (1980). Stress management with a psychophysiological profile, biofeedback, and relaxation training. *American Journal of Feedback, 3,* 130–136.

Dohrenwend, B. S., & Dohrenwend, B. P. (1974). *Stressful life events: Their nature and effects.* New York: Wiley.

Friedman, I.. (1981). How affiliation affects stress in fear and anxiety situations. *Journal of Personality and Social Psychology, 40,* 1102–1117.

Goldberg, E. L., & Comstock G. W. (1980). Epidemiology of life events: Frequency in general populations. *American Journal of Epidemiology, 111,* 736–750

Holahan, C. J., & Moos, R. H. (1981). Social support and psychological distress: A longitudinal analysis. *Journal of Abnormal Psychology, 90,* 365–370.

Jenkins, C. D. (1979). Psychological modifiers of response to stress. *Journal of Human Stress, 5,* 3–15.

Justice, B., McBee, G., & Allen, R. (1977). Life events, psychological distress and social functioning. *Psychological Reports, 40,* 467–473.

Lei, H., & Skinner, H. A. (1980). A psychometric study of life events and social readjustment. *Journal of Psychosomatic Research, 24,* 57–65.

Mikhail, A., (1981). Stress: A psychophysiological conception. *Journal of Human Stress, 7,* 9–15.

Miller, S. M. (1979). Controllability and human stress: Method, evidence and theory. *Behavioral Research and Therapy, 17,* 287–304

Newman, B. M. (1979). Coping and adaptation in adolescence. *Human Development, 22,* 255–262.

Pearlin, L. I., Lieberman, M. A., Menaghan, E. G., & Mullan, J. T. (1981). The stress processs. *Journal of Health and Social Behavior, 22,* 337–356.

Perlman, B., & Hartman, E. A. (1982). Burnout: Summary and future research. *Human Relations, 35,* 283–305.

Rahe, R. H., & Arthur, R. J. (1978). Life change and illness studies: Past history and future directions. *Journal of Human Stress, 4,* 3–15.

Selye, H. (1936). A syndrome produced by diverse nocuous agents. *Nature, 138,* 32.

Selye, H. (1956). *The stress of life.* N.Y.: McGraw-Hill.

Selye, H. (1973). Homeostasis and heterostasis. *Perspectives in Biological Medicine, 16,* 441–445.

Wild, B. S., & Hanes, C. (1976). A dynamic conceptual framework of general adaptation to stressful stimuli. *Psychological Reports, 38,* 319–334.

# CHAPTER 3

# Specificity and Stress Research

## JEROME E. SINGER and LAURA M. DAVIDSON

## Introduction

There are a number of different ways in which the psychological and physiological aspects of behavior have been interrelated. The connection between the two domains is fundamental. It is the distinction between them that is artificial. Yet there is some administrative virtue in partitioning the unitary responses of a human being or an animal into components that follow disciplinary lines. Each discipline—physiology, endocrinology, psychology, anthropology, and so forth—tends to focus on its aspect of the integrated biobehavioral response with its own set of questions and investigative concepts and techniques. This chapter discusses one of the most common and important of the biobehavioral responses, namely, stress. The perspective will be psychological, and the question to be examined will be the source of individual differences in the diverse factors believed to enter into the stress system.

The term *stress* has evolved, over the past several decades, to encompass a large variety of phenomena and is used in a number of different ways. In general, however, research on stress falls into one of two broad categories. The first of these categories is essentially *physiologically* defined. It is the original notion of stress formulated by Selye (1936) in his paper in *Nature*. *Stress here is defined as the reaction of the organism to some sort of outside threat.* The organism is reactive and little cognition is involved in the model. In later formulations, Selye attempted to build

JEROME E. SINGER AND LAURA M. DAVIDSON • Medical Psychology, Uniformed Services University of the Health Sciences, Bethesda, MD 20814.

in a broader concept of stress, making it applicable to a wider range of human situations, but at heart it remained a reactive model. Research done with this conceptualization was of the sort that followed the medical tradition of animal models, using physical or physiological stressors, and measuring physiological and endocrinological changes as indications of stress.

In contradistinction, a second tradition of stress research can be considered to be *transactional;* that is, *stress is defined as the outcome of interactions between the organism and the environment.* The general approaches taken by Lazarus (1966) and Leventhal (1970) are examples of this type of work. In the transactional model, an event in the environment is considered to be a stressor only if the organism's appraisals of it, and of its own resources, suggest that it is threatening or disturbing. Research done in this tradition tends to be human oriented and uses psychological measures, both for how the subject evaluates the stress and in terms of the subject's reactions to it. Although the model is said explicitly to apply to physiological and physical stimuli as well as to psychological ones, most of the work done within this framework has been on psychological or nonphysical environmental stimuli.

## Pathogen Reaction Model

Selye (1956, 1976) outlined the nature of the pathogen reaction model in a number of different publications. His description of the General Adaptation Syndrome, with three stages of alarm, resistance, and exhaustion, is now well known. The emphasis throughout his explication of the system is that stress consists of the nonspecific consequences of any stressor. In this context (although Selye goes to great pains to make clear what he means), the term *nonspecific* is slightly confusing. Selye means that every stressor produces certain reactions specific to that stressor as well as nonspecific changes that result from all stressors. In the pathogen reaction model, if an organism or an animal were to break a leg, the consequence of the leg breaking would be specific and local—the fracture of the bone, the tissue damage in that area, the disruption of the blood supply, the edema, and all other consequences brought about precisely by the breaking of the leg would be the specific reaction. The nonspecific reaction to the leg breaking would be the increased output of the adrenal cortical steroids and a variety of other endocrine changes that precede and react to the increased adrenal output (Mason, 1968, 1975; Selye, 1956, 1976). Although it is possible to be precise about these nonspecific changes, they are called nonspecific because the same steroid output occurs in response to each stressor or pathogen. If the same organism or animal at some later time, after the leg had healed, were to acquire a dose of food poisoning, it would have specific effects of the food poisoning in the gastrointestinal (GI) tract. In addition, it would have the same nonspecific effects from the food poisoning that occurred from the broken leg—primarily increased cortical steroid output. Because the more or less precisely defined neuroendocrinological changes occur to any stressor or pathogen, they acquired the name nonspecific. Some confusion can be avoided if it is realized that nonspecific does not mean unspecified but rather occurring in response to every stressor.

## Cumulative Stress Effects

There are several implications of this notion of nonspecificity. First, it implies that the effects of stress are cumulative, such that each episode leaves behind a residue that may add up across stressful exposures. Such consequences are relatively easy to see when the stress is chronic. Daily hassles, for example, are chronic low-intensity threats that may accumulate over time (Lazarus & Cohen, 1977). Each exposure to such a stressor poses little threat to the individual, but severe consequences may ensue if the stressor persists or if adaptive abilities are low. When animals are chronically exposed to noise, heat, crowding, hemorrhagic shock, or blood loss, they will continue to suffer the debilitation of nonspecific stress effects. Indeed, Selye's formulation of the general adaptation syndrome suggests that the model is best tested with a chronic stressor. The stress is ever present; the animal continually reacts to it and, after a certain amount of continued resistance, exhaustion ensues. When exhaustion is reached, the animal can no longer cope with the stress and ultimately expires. The model is less explicit and more ambiguous when the stressor is cyclic or episodic. If the stressor occurs at intervals (and at this point it does not matter whether it occurs cyclically at regular intervals or episodically at irregular ones), the effects can be considered the same as for a chronic stressor if the new stressor begins before the organism has returned to baseline from previous stress responses.

The model is unclear, and the research is equivocal about what happens when periodic stressors occur far enough apart so that the nonspecific responses of the organism do return to baseline. For example, there are any number of things that create stress in human beings and that are toxic in large doses, but are tolerated, and in many cases sought after, in small doses. Throughout life, many individuals ingest caffeine, nicotine, or alcohol. These substances have specific effects that are cumulative. For example, damage to the lung tissue from ingesting cigarette smoke, damage to the cardiovascular system from caffeine, and damage to the liver from alcohol are cumulative and specific effects of those stressors. But the extent to which any of those agents or toxins has nonspecific stress components that accumulate is unknown. In addition, there are other substances that have specific toxic effects in large amounts, but, taken cyclically, seem to have no specific debilitating effects. For example, spinach contains oxalic acid, a chemical that could be lethal if sufficient quantities were ingested. It is not known if there are nonspecific stress effects from small amounts of spinach or how much spinach one would have to eat at a sitting in order for it to be a toxicant. Whether everything that needs to be detoxified is a stressor remains to be explored for episodic and cyclic stressors. Also, the circumstances under which nonspecific cyclic or episodic stress reactions cumulate, and the relationships between the cumulation of the specific effects and the nonspecific effects, need to be explored.

Selye's model, in which all stressors have the same nonspecific effects, or in which stress is the nonspecific effect common to all stressors, implies that stress cumulates over stressors. Thus, the pathogen reaction model would argue that if an animal breaks a leg and, a short time later, eats contaminated food, the nonspecific effects of both of these stressors would be additive. The leg break or the contaminated food alone would not cause the animal to go from resistance to exhaustion, but both together could deplete the resistive powers. It is an unsolved question whether a potential stressor may be potentiated by occurring along with another stressful event. For example, a person who eats spinach before getting in a traffic jam might find that a previously nonbothersome dose of spinach now has a stressful consequence.

## Counting the Cumulative Effects of Stress

Considerations of both cumulation over periodic stressors and cumulation across different stressors raise a set of questions and generate research issues. One question concerns how the organism keeps track of stressors. Thus, if some of the nonspecific stress effects are irreversible, the organism must have some mechanism to keep track of the dosage level and the cumulation of stress effects. For example, it is possible that after an organism successfully resists a nonchronic stressor and returns to baseline, there will be no apparent damage or permanent harm caused by the stressor. But, when stressors occur repeatedly, the organism may develop harmful consequences, even though nonspecific responses have returned to baseline after each stressor occurs.

Counting mechanisms do seem to exist in other systems of the body, and, by using adipose tissue to draw an analogy, it becomes more clear how such a mechanism may exist for stress. Hirsch and his colleagues (Hirsch & Knittle, 1970) have suggested that the number of adipocytes remains constant, even though the person's weight may fluctuate and the amount of fat stored in each cell may change. The curious aspect of this is that although lipectomy (the surgical removal of fatty tissue) decreases the number of adipocytes by mechanical excision, new adipocytes grow, bringing the number present back to the baseline or the number that existed before the lipectomy. There is no way to determine whether "back to baseline" means the exact same number of adipose cells, but roughly the same magnitude will return. This growth occurs even though that same person would probably not generate new adipose cells without the lipectomy. Also, since the storage capacity of each adipocyte varies greatly, the new cells would not, strictly speaking, be necessary in order to return to the baseline levels of fat deposits. The point is that somewhere within the system something must be keeping count of the number of adipocytes, the adipocyte activity, the amount of product that each adipocyte puts out, or some other indicator to suggest what this baseline number should be. In the same way, if multiple stressors, each of which does not appear to be toxic, result in some kind of cumulation of toxicity, then some mechanism may exist in order for the body of the human to keep track of what is happening.

## Causal Stress Models

Not knowing the counting mechanisms for stressors may compound the establishment of retrospective causal stress models. Thus, although it is common to hear clinical statements such as "this is a stress-related disorder," it becomes impossible, in the absence of knowing the counting or cumulation mechanism, to discern what stressors were responsible for the disorder. Even though research indicates that clusters of life changes may be associated with illness episodes in the following year (e.g., Rahe, 1975), many of the so-called stress disorders develop over a time span, perhaps up to 20 years. Such diseases as atherosclerosis or several of the types of cancer require at least 20 years for incubation (Herbst, Robboy, Scully & Poskanzer, 1974; Julius, 1977). The logical, let alone empirical, task of stating what stressors, toxicants, or irritants may have initiated or facilitated the pathophysiology of these diseases is very difficult.

The difficulty in establishing causal models may be illustrated by considering noise as a stressor. There is some evidence that noise has cardiovascular effects and that continued exposure to it, chronically or cyclically, may bring about an elevation in blood pressure (Cohen, Evans, Krantz, Stokols, & Kelly, 1981; Peterson, 1979; Welch, 1979). These findings come from both epidemiological studies and from animal models. Nevertheless, the research is not conclusive about the circumstances under which noise will produce such effects, but suggests that, under some circumstances, the effects will be of clinical significance. Consider the situation of a person suffering from cardiovascular disease who has been exposed to a noxious and noisy environment. The question is whether it is possible to claim that the noise in the person's immediate environment caused the cardiovascular changes; the answer is not simple. Such a question is often the basis for court cases, and it turns out that it is impossible to prove that cardiovascular disease has been caused by a noise stressor. It could have been a response to any number of other cardiovascular irritants. On the other hand, it is impossible to prove that the noise was not at least a precipitating factor in the development of the disease. In short, the problem is one of the burden of proof, and the side of the issue that has the burden of proof is at a disadvantage, because the mechanisms of cumulation of stress and of its specificity cannot be established.

## Transactional Model

The transactional model is not so much in opposition to the pathogen reaction model but addresses different issues or incorporates the reaction model as a special subclass. Thus, in the transactional model, a stressor is any potential threat in the environment. The emphasis is on the word *potential* because in the transactional model nothing by itself is considered to be a stressor. Rather, any stimulus, no matter how noxious or how pleasant, can be viewed as either desired, interesting, nonthreatening, or nonharmful and, if it is so appraised, it will not be considered a stressor (e.g., Lazarus, 1966). For the transactional model, physical or physiological stressors will only produce stress responses after they have been defined as threatening by human beings. Unlike the pathogen reaction model, the transactional model does not assume that life threat or harm are inevitably stressful.

## Appraisal

Indeed, the key issue in the transactional model is appraisal, which may occur repeatedly following introduction of a stressor. First, the potential stressor is evaluated in terms of its capacity to do harm. Subevaluations are then made about novelty, certainty, and predictability. Importantly, the stressor is construed as a threat or challenge. Having appraised a stressor, the individual appraises its own ability to handle this stress or challenge and the strategy most likely to reduce the potential harm (e.g., Appley, 1967). These appraisals are not unitary judgments but rather are like iterative computer programs. It is as if the organism were to handle a stressor by the use of an algorithm: for example, appraise the stressor, appraise own capacities, decide on coping strategy, meet the stressor, reevaluate stressor, reevaluate own capacities, decide on coping strategy again, and so forth. This procedure suggests that circumstances once thought of as benign or challenging may become stressful as appraisals and coping are modified. Similarly, threatening stressors can become merely challenges, or even can become sought after, as the individual has experience with them and modified appraisals of both its own capabilities and the environmental challenges.

The transactional models are very important because they bring into play a full panoply of human cognitive activities. Also, they enable stress researchers to understand and explain a number of situations that are difficult to comprehend in the pathogen reaction model. For example, in physiological studies of the pathogen reaction model, one of the laboratory techniques is hemorrhagic shock. An experimental animal, such as a dog, will be placed on an operating table and have 10% of its blood supply withdrawn. Aside from the specific effects of withdrawing the blood, this induces a nonspecific stress response. The animal's reactions, in terms of cardiovascular, kidney, and gastrointestinal functioning, can all be assessed during the stress to see what the nonspecific consequences are. One prominent physiological researcher has reported that although stress reactions to hemorrhagic shock are as large and significant as stress reactions to any other physiological stressor, the single largest reaction ever obtained from an experimental dog occurred after the dog had been strapped to the operating table and a new dog was brought into the room. This was done prior to anesthetization and blood withdrawal. The stress reaction to the threat of a strange dog under these circumstances was more potent than the hemorrhagic shock. Although it would be difficult to explain this situation using the pathogen reaction model, the transactional model can more adequately handle such kinds of stressors.

## Individual Differences

Although the transactional model does take account of more situations and handles a number of issues, such as the ability of people to withstand stress under seemingly heavy physical loads and how a person escalates a minor physical demand into a rather stressful environment, there are problems inherent to the system. Chief among these problems is the price that the transactional model exacts for being able to handle a number of situations and to impose several layers of human cognitive appraisal on the environment. The price is that it raises a host of individual difference measures that need not be considered in the stress pathogen model. For example, individuals may be exposed to different amounts of stress. This difference may occur in terms of the number, the frequency, or the patterning of stress exposures.

Second, when stress is examined using the transactional model, people may be viewed as differing in the extent to which they are stress-seeking. Almost all who study stress do not regard it as unalloyed harm in the environment but, rather consider it as a natural and unavoidable consequence of the real world. To some extent, people may view stress as providing relief from what would be humdrum monotony. Indeed, there are a number of people who seem to seek stress exposure (Zuckerman, 1979). Participation in sports, such as race car driving, ski jumping, parachuting, and the like, indicates that people may seek what could be regarded as extremely potent stressors. Often, sport parachutists or ski jumpers report that they appraise their activity as stressful, particularly at the beginning of the season or at the start of a new exposure to it. Nevertheless, their enjoyment eventually overshadows the stress that they feel. Therefore, this is not a question of people necessarily regarding something as pleasurable, which others regard as stressful, but rather acknowledging the stress and still seeking it out. Clearly, there are individual differences in the extent to which this occurs.

The third individual difference variable, which results from the transactional perspective, is that people differ greatly in their interpretation of stressful situations. This interpretation can determine whether the potential stressor is viewed as a threat or as a challenge. Lazarus (1966; Lazarus & Launier, 1978), among others, argued that stressful consequences are engendered only if the potential threat is perceived as such. If, on the other hand, it is perceived as a challenge, those same circumstances will evoke a different kind of response and have different consequences. In addition, people will differ not just in how they appraise the stressor, but in how they appraise their own resources and capabilities. Whether these differences in appraisals are based on differences in actual experience, knowledge, and practice, or whether they are due to individual differences in self-esteem and perceived self-competence, is not known. Cognitive mediation comes into play in handling other aspects of the stress response. There is a large literature, and considerable debate, on the extent to which a person can have cognitive mediation of physiological consequence, that is, the extent to which emotion, mood, and their physiological and neuroendocrine concomitants can be influenced by, or determined by, the cognitions and labels that are attached to them (Schachter & Singer, 1962). Rather than view cognitive manipulations of physiological states as an all-or-nothing phenomenon, it is perhaps best to think of that as yet one other individual difference barrier.

Fourth, people differ in their choice of coping styles, and there are any number of ways to categorize coping styles. Lazarus (1966) described problem and emotional forms of coping. Using problem-focused coping, the person tries to manipulate the environment, confront the source of stress, and change the potential stressor itself. For example, coming in out of the rain is problem-focused coping. This form can be contrasted to a style that attempts to work on the emotional or the physiological responses directly. Tap dancing and whistling in the rain are emotion-focused coping. Even within these two broad categories, there are any number of other subvarieties of coping styles, like denial, meditation, and avoidance. All of these coping styles will be used differentially by people.

Fifth, people are placed in different circumstances, and the circumstances will determine how stress is moderated. For example, studies have shown that stressors that are predictable have less of an impact than stressors that are unpredictable (Glass & Singer, 1972). The predictability can come about either because of a signal that indicates the stressor is going to occur or because of a timing or a periodicity that enables one to predict when the stressor is going to occur. Similarly, perceived control (i.e., a person's perception that he or she can modify a stressor) has also been shown to be a potent moderator of the stressor response (Baron & Rodin, 1978; Glass & Singer, 1972). The extent to which people differ in their ability or their willingness to attribute causality to controllable events, to infer predictability, or to be in circumstances that confer either predictability or controllability upon them will determine the amount of stress that they experience.

The sixth and final class of individual differences comes about from ancillary measures that are not present on a firm theoretical basis. Nevertheless, these differences have been shown to be of importance in stress reduction; social support is a suitable example of this. There has been a long debate about whether social support is a mediator or a moderator of stress. As a mediator, social support would be a benefit under all circumstances. Unstressed people with social support would be in better shape than unstressed people without social support, and stressed people with social support would be in better shape than stressed people without social support. Research in this area indicates that better health is associated with social support (Cassel, 1976). In conceiving of it as a moderator, social support is viewed as a factor that ameliorates the effects of stress, although it has no effect when stress is not present (Cohen &

McKay, 1984). The evidence for social support either mediating or moderating stress is confusing at best. In studying social support, it is difficult to determine whether social support should be measured objectively or subjectively. If measured objectively, it would be assessed by counting the number of support groups, like groups of people, spouses, children, and the like (e.g., Berkman & Syme, 1979). If measured subjectively, social support should be viewed as a perceived variable, irrespective of how many groups, family members, or friends a person has (e.g., Caplan, Cobb, & French, 1975). The perception of support when needed is counted as the major consideration.

## Some Additional Considerations

Overall, the net effect of these models has been to keep two different sets of variables separated. The pathogen reaction model deals primarily with physiological endocrine measures. The transactional model deals primarily with cognitive personality factors. In recent years, there have been a number of studies that have sought to view stress as an integrated biosocial phenomenon. Such research groups as Frankenhaeuser and her colleagues (Frankenhaeuser, 1975; Frankenhaeuser, Nordhedin, Myrsten, & Post, 1971); Mason (1975), in differentiating endocrinological patterns to different stress responses; Baum and his associates, in studies of Three Mile Island (Baum, Gatchel, & Schaeffer, 1983; Davidson, Baum, & Collins, 1982); and many others have sought to look at stress from a transactional perspective while taking biological indicators and markers to see to what extent the neuroendocrine system correlates and covaries with the psychological cognitive system. Increasingly, these studies have shown that the two systems are really aspects of the same unitary process.

The further importance of combining physiological and psychological approaches may be illustrated using coronary heart disease (CHD) as an example. Traditional risk factors for CHD, such as age, diet, serum cholesterol, obesity, and so forth, are mainly physiological determinants of the disorder (Krantz, Glass, Contrada, & Miller, 1981). But, the majority of new cases of heart disease cannot be predicted using these factors alone (e.g., Mann, 1977). Psychological factors, including threat perceptions and coping styles, may also play key roles in the pathogenesis of CHD. By combining physiological and psychological perspectives, researchers have been better able to understand a disorder that accounts for almost half of all deaths in the United States (Krantz *et al.*, 1981). Unfortunately, in areas of study like stress and heart disease, physiological and psychological theories have evolved separately. But it is becoming clear that the two perspectives cannot be separated and that an integrative approach provides the most information.

## Implications and Problems

The recent emergence of an integrated biobehavioral perspective on stress has increased the number of variables under study at any given time (e.g., Baum, Singer, & Baum, 1981; Frankenhaeuser, 1975). Despite the spate of articles and books written about stress, so much remains to be examined and explained that even those investigations attempting to be integrative are rather preliminary. As these studies develop, they will undoubtedly broaden the range of variables and factors implicated in the stress process. The result of this enlargement will be a number of new problems.

First, the number of individual difference variables will be compounded because of the simultaneous consideration of both physiological (broadly defined) and psychological variables (equally broadly defined). Not only will the integrative investigator now consider the variability in two sets of factors, but he or she must also consider their interactions as well. For example, a researcher who studies the effect of threat appraisal and coping style on productivity and absenteeism in the work place might include cardiovascular reactivity or rate of increase of catecholamines to a challenge as part of the investigation. It is quite possible that appraisal of threat might interact with these physiological mechanisms (see Schachter & Singer, 1962, for a perspective on the relationship of autonomic arousal to self-labeling of state), and that different coping styles will be effective, depending on the mutually moderating effects of these variables. Thus, the underlying model for absenteeism is a more complicated one than would be expected from a mere addition of a physiological model to a transactional one.

Second, the use of an integrated investigative format has brought about the collection of physiological data in field settings (Baum *et al.*, 1983; Singer, Lundberg, & Frankenhaeuser, 1978). The transport of neuroendocrine collections from laboratory to field presents a series of problems, none insurmountable, but which do increase sources of variation. For example, if urine samples are taken for epinephrine and norepinephrine, the investigator must take account of circadian and subcircadian cycles in secretion of these hormones. Methodological choices, such as whether to take 24-hour samples or use a double voiding technique, before and after a critical incident, all raise a number of interpretive issues (see Baum, Grunberg, & Singer, 1982, for a fuller discussion of these points). As psychophysiological apparatus becomes more portable, we can expect to see it used in field settings also. It will probably be the case that choices and decisions that did not occur in the more controlled laboratory settings will arise to complicate the field environment.

Third, one of the paradoxical effects of an integrative approach to the study of stress will be to fragment the study of the phenomenon into smaller and more manageable units. Each aspect of stress has grown so complex that integration produces a monster—a study with so many variables that no scholar can keep them distinct in any one project. As a result, investigators will have to focus on one or another subarea, such as arousability, resistance, coping, or social support. This restriction of focus, to problems of workable size, in order to reduce overly complex phenomena reflects what has already transpired in the stress community. The hope is that when these subareas are studied, they will be examined from a biobehavioral approach. If, for instance, coping was the dependent variable, then not just self-reports or psychiatric check lists but performance data and physiologic measures would also be included in the study.

Fourth, the inclusion of a larger number of variables will necessitate the incorporation of new research techniques and strategies. The use of a large variable set puts a burden of cognitive management on the investigator; it also makes things more difficult for the subjects. There is a limit to how many questionnaires, scales, report forms, and ratings people will tolerate. Although our recent history suggests that, over time, experimenter ingenuity will extend those limits, it is still not logistically feasible to give all subjects every measure of interest in a stress study. One possible way of handling this difficulty is to adapt methods used in other fields with analogous problems. For example, human factors research can be faced with complex situations and too many independent variables to study fully. This problem is often solved by using experimental designs that are incomplete factorials. That is, by appropriately confounding the arrangement of the independent variables, many main effects and simple interactions can be evaluated. The price paid is the inability to assess, or to separate out, the higher order interactions. The net result is an interpretation closer to the individual variable and farther from the more complex models. In a field such as stress, where the complexities of the models often far outstrip the reliability of the basic observations, techniques that advance the breadth of data collection, while simultaneously encouraging theoretical parsimony, seem salutory. As an illustration, one can imagine an investigator with 16 pencil-and-paper inventories assigning groups of 4 of the inventories to subjects in an incomplete block design. All the main effects could be assessed (with a partial number of subjects), and the assessment of first-order interactions could also be designed. But the higher order interactions could not be evaluated. Although each subject fills out 4 forms, 16 forms are used in the study; the use of all 16 forms is accomplished without requiring an inordinate increase in the number of requisite subjects.

## Conclusion

The study of stress has been benefited by two separate approaches: a physiologically oriented reactive one and a psychologically oriented transactional one. There has emerged an integrative, biobehavioral approach to the field that builds on the physiological and the psychological contributions. The integrative view has been hindered, to some extent, by confusion over terminology. Although there has come to be some shared definition of the meaning of stress and stressor, terms such as variability, reactivity, and specificity have been confusing. We have explored the issues that are presented to a biobehavioral perspective by consideration of the phenomena encompassed by those terms, and speculated on the effects they will have on the study of stress.[1]

## References

Appley, M. H. (1967). Invited commentary. In M. H. Appley & R. Trumbull (Eds.), *Psychological stress: Issues in research* (pp. 169–172). New York: Appleton-Century-Crofts.

Baron, R., & Rodin, J. (1978). Personal control as a mediator of crowding. In A. Baum, J. E. Singer, & S. Valins (Eds.), *Advances in environmental psychology: Vol. 1. The urban environment* (pp. 145–192). Hillsdale, NJ: Erlbaum.

Baum, A., Singer, J. E., & Baum, C. S. (1981). Stress and the environment. *Journal of Social Issues, 37,* 4–35.

Baum, A., Grunberg, N. E., & Singer, J. E. (1982). The use of psychological and neuroendocrinological measurements in the study of stress. *Health Psychology, 1,* 217–236.

Baum, A., Gatchel, R. J., & Schaeffer, M. A. (1983). Emotional, behavioral and physiological effects of chronic stress at Three Mile Island. *Journal of Consulting and Clinical Psychology, 51,* 562–572.

Berkman, L. F., & Syme, S. L. (1979). Social networks, host resistance, and mortality: A nine-year follow-up study of Alameda County residents. *American Journal of Epidemiology, 109,* 186–204.

---

[1] The opinions or assertions contained in this chapter are the private ones of the authors and are not to be construed as official or reflecting the views of the Department of Defense or the Uniformed Services University of the Health Sciences.

Caplan, R. D., Cobb, S., & French, J. R. (1975). Job demands and worker health. *Journal of Applied Psychology, 60,* 211–219.

Cassel, J. (1976). The contribution of social environment to host resistance. *American Journal of Epidemiology, 104,* 107–123.

Cohen, S., & McKay, G. (1984). Social support, stress and the buffering hypothesis: A theoretical analysis. In A. Baum, J. E. Singer, & S. E. Taylor (Eds.), *Handbook of psychology and health: Vol. 4. Social psychological aspects of health* (pp. 253–267). Hillsdale, NJ: Erlbaum.

Cohen, S., Evans, G. W., Krantz, D. S., Stokols, D., & Kelly, S. (1981). Psychological, motivational, and cognitive effects of aircraft noise on children: Moving from the laboratory to the field. *American Psychologist, 35,* 231–243.

Davidson, L. M., Baum, A., & Collins, D. L. (1982). Stress and control-related problems at Three Mile Island. *Journal of Applied Social Psychology, 12,* 349–359.

Frankenhaeuser, M. (1975). Experimental approaches to the study of catecholamines and emotion. In L. Levi (Ed.), *Emotions: Their parameters and measurements* (pp. 209–234). New York: McGraw-Hill.

Frankenhaeuser, M., Nordhedin, B., Myrsten, A. L., & Post, B. (1971). Psychophysiological reactions to understimulation and overstimulation. *Acta Psychologia, 35,* 298–308.

Glass, D. C., & Singer, J. E. (1972). *Urban stress: Experiments on noise and social stressors.* New York: Academic.

Herbst, A. L., Robboy, S. J., Scully, R. E., & Poskanzer, D. C. (1974). Clear-cell adenocarcinoma of the vagina and cervix in girls: Analysis of 170 registry cases. *American Journal of Obstetrics and Gynecology, 119,* 713–724.

Hirsch, J., & Knittle, J. L. (1970). Cellularity of obese and nonobese adipose tissue. *Federation Proceedings, 29,* 1516–1521.

Julius, S. A. (1977). Borderline hypertension: Epidemiologic and clinical implication. In J. Genest, E. Koiw, & O. Kuchel (Eds.), *Hypertension physiopathology and treatment* (pp. 630–640). New York: McGraw-Hill.

Krantz, D. S., Glass, D. C., Contrada, R., & Miller, N. E. (1981). Behavior and health. In *National Science Foundation's second five-year outlook on science and technology.* Washington, DC: U. S. Government Printing Office.

Lazarus, R. S. (1966). *Psychological stress and the coping process.* New York: McGraw-Hill.

Lazarus, R. S., & Cohen, J. B. (1977). Environmental stress. In I. Altman & J. F. Wohlwill (Eds.), *Human behavior and the environment: Current theory and research* (Vol. 2, pp. 89–128). New York: Plenum Press.

Lazarus, R. S., & Launier, R. (1978). Stress-related transactions between person and environment. In L. A. Pervin & M. Lewis (Eds.), *Perspectives in interactional psychology* (pp. 287–327). New York: Plenum Press.

Leventhal, H. (1970). Findings and theory in the study of fear communications. In L. Berkowitz (Ed.), *Advances in experimental social psychology: Vol. 5* (pp. 120–186). New York: Academic Press.

Mann, G. V. (1977). Diet-heart: End of an era. *New England Journal of Medicine, 297,* 646–650.

Mason, J. W. (1968). Organization of psychoendocrine mechanisms. *Psychosomatic Medicine, 30,* 565–791.

Mason, J. W. (1975). Emotion as reflected in patterns of endocrine integration. In L. Levi (Ed.), *Emotions: Their parameters and measurement* (pp. 143–181). New York: Raven Press.

Peterson, E. A. (1979, August). *Some issues and investigations concerning extraauditory effects of noise.* Paper presented at the annual meeting of the American Psychological Association, New York, NY.

Rahe, R. H. (1975). Life changes and near-future illness reports. In L. Levi (Ed.), *Emotion: Their parameters and measurements* (pp. 511–529). New York: Raven Press.

Schachter, S., & Singer, J. E. (1962). Cognitive, social, and physiological determinants of emotional state. *Psychological Review, 69,* 379–399.

Selye, H. (1936). A syndrome produced by diverse nocuous agents. *Nature, 138,* 32.

Selye, H. (1956). *The stress of life.* New York: McGraw-Hill.

Selye, H. (1976). *Stress in health and disease.* Reading, MA: Buttersworth.

Singer, J. E., Lundberg, U., & Frankenhaeuser, M. (1978). Stress on the train: A study of urban commuting. In A. Baum, J. E. Singer, & S. Valins (Eds.), *Advances in environmental psychology: Vol. 1. The urban environment* (pp. 21–57). Hillsdale, NJ: Erlbaum.

Welch, B. L. (1979). *Extra-auditory health effects of industrial noise: Survey of foreign literature.* Dayton: Wright-Patterson, Aerospace Medical Research Division, Air Force Systems Command.

Zuckerman, M. (1979). *Sensation seeking: Beyond the optimal level of arousal.* Hillsdale, NJ: Erlbaum.

# CHAPTER 4

# Cognitive Theories of Stress and the Issue of Circularity

RICHARD S. LAZARUS and SUSAN FOLKMAN

## Introduction

No issue in the psychology of health is of greater interest and importance than whether and how stress influences adaptational outcomes, such as well-being, social functioning, and somatic health. This issue has generated extensive research on stressful life events (see Thoits, 1983, for a recent review). More recently, researchers have been interested in the stressful events of day-to-day living, variously referred to as microstressors (McLean, 1976; Monroe, 1983), chronic role strains (Pearlin, 1983), and daily hassles (DeLongis, Coyne, Dakof, Folkman, & Lazarus, 1982; Kanner, Coyne, Schaefer, & Lazarus, 1981; Lazarus, 1984; Lazarus & DeLongis, 1983).

The importance of the relationship between stress and health also helps to account for continued interest in the theory of psychological stress and coping that we have expanded in recent years (Lazarus & Folkman, 1984a,b) from earlier, more modest beginnings (Lazarus, 1966). *In this theory, psychological stress refers to a relationship with the environment that the person appraises as significant for his or her well-being and in which the demands tax or exceed available coping resources.*

---

**RICHARD S. LAZARUS** AND **SUSAN FOLKMAN** • Stress and Coping Project, Department of Psychology, University of California, Berkeley, CA 94720. Portions of this chapter are based on an article by Richard S. Lazarus, Anita DeLongis, Susan Folkman, and Rand Gruen entitled "Stress and Adaptational Outcomes: The Problem of Confounded Measures," *American Psychologist*, 1985, *40*, 770–779.

One of the searching questions that appraisal-centered stress theorists must deal with is the extent to which cognitive or subjective formulations force us into circular reasoning when doing empirical research on the effects of stress on adaptational outcomes. There have been a number of recent challenges to such formulations (e.g., Dohrenwend & Dohrenwend, 1978; Thoits, 1985), including the following comment by Kasl (1978):

> Unfortunately, this convergence of theoretical formulations [about the role of individual differences in appraisal] has led to a self-serving methodological trap which has tended to trivialize a good deal of the research on work stress or role stress: the measurement of the "independent" variable (e.g., role ambiguity, role conflict, quantitative overload, etc.) and the measurement of the "dependent" variable (work strain, distress, dissatisfaction) are sometimes so close operationally that they appear to be simply two similar measures of a single concept. (p. 13)

The issue can be confronted by examining this claim of circularity in close detail. At stake is the viability of all cognitive, relational conceptualizations of stress.

Circularity occurs when there is total redundancy among the variables being correlated: "The causes contain all that is contained in the effect; the effect contains nothing that is not contained in the causes" (*OED*, 1970, Vol. II, p. 116). Circularity occurs for at least two reasons. First, the components making up the variables themselves can be similar or identical. It might be even better to speak of *overlapping measures* (see Nicholls, Licht, & Pearl, 1982). Second, the variables as measured can reflect some third, underlying process in common, even without explicit redundancy in the form of duplicated or similar items.

That circularity is indeed a problem in present-day research is illustrated in a recent article by Cohen, Kamarck, and Mermelstein (1983). The authors present a "global measure of perceived stress" and report that their global measure correlates well with outcome measures of symptomatology. However, the 14 items of their scale appear to assess general, negative feelings and reactions *over the previous month*, suggesting that it is yet another measure of psychopathology or distress. The items describe being upset, having or lacking control over things, feeling nervous and stressed, feeling or not feeling effective, and being overwhelmed by difficulties. In this scale, the antecedent and consequent measures seem to overlap entirely, making it questionable whether the correlation offers any gain in understanding. (However, see Cohen, 1986.)

Scientists have been debating the problem of circular or tautological reasoning for a long time. Some argue that circularity is inevitable in any specific explanation. For example, Pratt (1939) says:

The aversion to circular arguments is the last stronghold of that faith which believes that science can furnish for any given array of well-established facts a *why* which is more than a mere statement of how the facts go together. In certain quarters the faith still lingers on that the laws of nature are something more than the events in nature themselves. The events *obey* the laws, which cannot be the same as saying that the events obey themselves. If the statement that nature is subject to law really means that nature is subject to nature, then the so-called laws of science explain nothing. They are pompous tautologies, vicious circles.

The majority of present-day scientists, particularly the correlationists, have indeed come to realize that a scientific *why* can be no more than an exact *how*, but the corollary is frequently overlooked, namely, that all arguments in support of any given hypothesis must of necessity be circular. (pp. 149–150)

Pratt provides a well-known historical example of how circular concepts can have value. Shortly after the discovery of the planet Uranus, it became evident that its orbit could not be accounted for by the known motions of Jupiter and Saturn. After inaccurate observation was ruled out as an explanation, the suggestion was made that the deviations in orbit must be due to the action of a still more distant, as yet undiscovered, planet. Calculations were made of the orbit such a new planet would have to produce the positions observed for Uranus. This hypothesized planet came to be accepted as a reasonable explanation for the perplexing behavior of Uranus, an explanation that is, as Pratt states, a perfect illustration of circularity: "The formal properties of the calculated planet were derived from the material properties, that is, the observed positions of Uranus, and then these same formal properties were used to explain the behavior of Uranus" (p. 153). However, this circular reasoning led to the discovery of a material object, now called Neptune, a discovery that might have been long delayed without knowing where in the heavens to look.

The concept of instinct has had a similar history. Countless patterns of behavior in animals had long been attributed to wired-in mechanisms called *instincts*. Instincts, in turn, were used to explain these behaviors. In this sense, the concept was of little value; however, it ultimately led to important work, such as Lehrman's (1964) study on the role of environmental and hormonal variables in the ring dove's reproductive behavior.

These historical examples help us to understand that circularity is not only inevitable in exploratory research, but that it can also prove valuable in advancing knowledge and understanding in the long run (see also formulations by Carnap, 1936; Kant, 1956; Putnam, 1962; Quine, 1951, 1953). The value can come from a concept's capacity to point to hitherto only suspected material objects and characteristics, as in the case of Uranus, or to organize a search for more complete descriptive knowledge, as when the vague concept of instinct was later transformed into a rich understanding of the internal (e.g., hormonal) and external (e.g., behavior of a ring dove's mate) conditions that shape an animal's behavior. As we show below, these points are relevant to criticisms of our Hassles Scale, with which we have attempted to assess the degree and sources of daily stress in living, as well as the relational, cognitive conceptions of stress on which the scale is based.

## Psychopathology and Confounding in the Hassles Scale

Monroe (1983) writes that

> while at face value the Hassles Scale developed by Kanner et al. (1981) appears to contain relatively minor everyday difficulties (e.g., traffic noise, preparing meals, having to wait, etc.), closer inspection of the scale reveals numerous items that may be more directly related to psychological problems or symptoms. (p. 191)

A study reported by Dohrenwend, Dohrenwend, Dodson, and Shrout (1984) assessed confounding in the Hassles Scale and two other measures, the Life Events Scale (Holmes & Rahe, 1967) and the Instrumental-Expressive Social Support Scale (Lin, Dean, & Ensel, 1981). Clinical psychologists rated each item on a scale ranging from 1 ("almost certainly a symptom of psychological disorder") to 5 ("almost certainly not a symptom of psychological disorder"). Ratings on all three tests varied from a low value of 1.8 to a high value of 4.6. For the Hassles Scale, the average rating was 3.17, whereas for the Holmes and Rahe life events measure, it was 3.52, and for the Instrumental-Expressive Social Support Scale, it was 2.72. A rating of 3 was defined as meaning that the item was "about as likely as not to be a symptom of psychological disorder" (p. 8).[1]

---

[1]In the Dohrenwend et al. study, the Hassles Scale items were reworded, though usually in minor ways. Nonetheless, such changes might well have affected the ratings of items with respect to psychopathology. For example, an item that appears in our version of the scale as "gossip" was rewritten as "You have been concerned about gossip." "Unexpected company" was changed to "You have had unexpected company." All the items in our original scale were changed in similar ways, and it is difficult to ascertain whether and how such changes might have affected the ratings of clinicians, although, if it did have an effect, it would have added to any confounding with psychopathological content, since being "concerned" is now explicitly rather than implicitly stated in the item. Ironically, Dohrenwend et al. point out that "some hassles such as 'having unexpected

On the basis of their findings, Dohrenwend *et al.* (1984) wrote:

> The use of measures such as these almost guarantees positive correlations between "stress" and illness outcomes, but contributes little but confusion to our understanding of the role of environmentally induced stress in psychological stress and disorder. Nor is this problem of confounding measures of stress with measures of psychological symptoms limited to studies of psychopathology. It interferes as well with our understanding of the role of environmentally induced stress and physical illnesses which tend to be strongly related to psychological distress and disorders. (p. 15)

Those of us who are involved in stress theory and measurement need to evaluate the conclusion that psychopathology is a source of confounding in the Hassles Scale and that analytic confusion results from this. We have already addressed some of these issues in a previous article (Lazarus, DeLongis, Folkman, & Gruen, 1985). We concluded that, both theoretically and empirically, psychopathology could not have accounted for our findings. Aside from the vague, noncontextual, and inadequate concept of psychopathology inherent in the judgments of the clinical psychologists used by Dohrenwend *et al.*, when we reanalyzed our data on the basis of their ratings—for example, by comparing the so-called highly confounded items with the unconfounded—the correlations between Hassles scores and psychological symptoms remained unchanged. Therefore, confounding via psychopathology is not an explanation for our previous findings about hassles and psychological symptoms, though other unidentified forms of confounding could still be present.

Psychopathology remains one of the very vague concepts of the field of mental health. Thoits (1985) has argued that affective criteria are at the core of most assessments of psychopathology. She states that

> an examination of the criteria for mental disorders in the most recent Diagnostic and Statistical Manual of Mental Disorders, DSM III (American Psychiatric Association, 1980) indicates that excessive or inappropriate affect and affect displays are important indicators for several types of disorder. My informal analyses of the diagnostic criteria in DSM III reveal that inappropriate, usually negative, emotional states or emotional displays are an essential defining feature of 81 out of a total of 228 disorders (35.5%) and an "associated feature" of 64.9% of these disorders. These percentages

---

company' or 'having to care for a pet' are highly unlikely to be confounded with symptoms and others could probably be made so by avoiding the use of terms like 'concerned with' in their description." Our view of the psychodynamics of hassles (cf. Lazarus, 1984) is that the mere endorsement of an item implies both "concern" and a negative reaction to a previous experience. Nevertheless, it is not clear to what extent the findings of Dohrenwend *et al.* are specific to *their* version of the Hassles Scale.

would be even higher if disorders due to genetic or organic causes (e.g., mental retardation, substance abuse, organic disorder) were excluded. These observations suggest that socially inappropriate or undesirable feelings and feeling displays play an important part in the recognition and labelling of disturbance. Psychological disturbance might usefully be conceptualized as, then, persistent or recurrent *emotional deviance*. (pp. 55)

Thoits is not the only writer to say that the diagnosis of psycho-pathology is based on evidence of emotional distress. Gotlib (1984), for example, reviews evidence that a wide variety of measures of depression, dysfunctional attitudes, anxiety, nonassertiveness, and the Hopkins Symptom Checklist (the SCL-90) are highly intercorrelated. The overlap suggests that they tap, at least with subclinical samples, some kind of general psychopathology, dysphoria, or malaise involving the experience of multiple forms of emotional distress.

Distress *per se* should *not* be regarded as tantamount to psychopath-ology (cf. Lazarus, 1985). A person who experiences anxiety or fear is not necessarily disturbed or neurotic. Before making a judgment of its pathological significance, we need to know the type of distress, the cir-cumstances under which it is manifested, and the processes that explain it. Other concepts of psychopathology are also possible, such as the rigidly self-defeating cognitions described by Beck (1976) and Ellis (1962), or the ego-psychology formulations of defensive processes (e.g., Haan, 1977; Loevinger, 1976; Menninger, 1963; Vaillant, 1977). These latter all hinge on a failure of reality-testing and inflexible, inner-determined, and de-velopmentally primitive defensive styles.

Putting aside the empirical case, if we look carefully at the findings of Dohrenwend *et al.*, and we examine the Hassles Scale items rated highest and lowest in psychopathology, the argument that hassles reflect psychopathology becomes subject to grave doubt on conceptual grounds. The Hassles Scale item rated by clinical psychologists as having the most psychopathological content was, "You have had sexual problems other than those resulting from physical problems"; also rated as having high psychopathological content were, "You are concerned about your use of alcohol," "You have had trouble making decisions," and "You have had a fear of rejection." In contrast, the four Hassles Scale items rated as having the least psychopathological content were, "You have had un-expected company," "You have had to care for a pet," "You have been financing your children's education," and "You have had to plan meals."

Clinicians who view these items as indicators of psychopathology probably assume that they express *chronic* concerns. Nevertheless, by what reasoning are concerns with sexual problems, use of alcohol or drugs, making decisions, and rejection signs of mental illness or disturbance? Why is being bothered by such matters more psychopathological than being bothered by having to care for a pet, having had to plan meals, or having had unexpected company?

Fear of rejection, for example, which is the basis of most advertisements of soap, shampoo, and mouthwash, is often rather mundane. The critical and unstated question, of course, is when is such a fear a sign of illness and when is it not? Drinking is common among perfectly well-functioning people, and unless drinking *per se* in our society is psychopathological, it could be an indication of wisdom to be concerned about drinking too much. Furthermore, worrying about such matters might be far less deviant than worrying about unexpected company and planning meals; one could argue that anyone who gets upset about these routine matters is the more troubled person. In any case, without reference to the actual context of a person's life, hassles such as these reveal little about the psychological soundness of the person who endorses them. No reputable clinician would offer a diagnosis of psychopathology without understanding the context of a difficulty, yet this is exactly what the clinicians in the Dohrenwend *et al.* study were asked to do.

## Psychological Stress: Rubric or Variable?

In the name of scientific rigor—that is, to eliminate redundancy—researchers are often urged to measure stress by means of pure environmental events, uncontaminated by perceptions, appraisals, or reactions (cf. Dohrenwend *et al.*, 1984). This would mean abandoning the hard-won insight that there are no environmental stressors without vulnerable people whose agendas and resources influence whether or not there will be stress, the form it will take, and its short- and long-term outcomes. Those who press the demand for purely objective measures of stress present a classic catch-22 to those of us who say that no environmental event can be identified fruitfully as a stressor independently of its appraised significance to the person, even when such an event is normatively stressful. To speak of stressors in an objective and normative sense is to ignore the inevitable and extensive individual differences in response to similar environmental conditions.

It is difficult to see how social scientists can argue against a relational approach to stress, considering the acceptance of a relational view of disease itself (Dubos, 1959). Disease is no longer thought of as the result of environmental agents, such as bacteria and viruses alone, but of multiple factors. The concept of "host resistance" (Cassel, 1976; Syme, 1984), which states that many conditions influencing infection lie in the organism itself, illustrates the relational view of disease. Stress, too, cannot be defined as an environmental agent but represents a particular kind of relationship between a stimulus and a vulnerable person.

The core issue concerns the degree of overlap and its meaning in relational approaches. Cognitive theories of emotion, for example, state that fear is a consequence of an appraisal that one is not able to neutralize danger. Although this appraisal is an essential component of fear in a specific context, *it is not the same as fear*. In effect, the overlap between appraisal and fear is not total. Similarly, stress (viewed relationally) and distress overlap, but they are not the same. To follow the recommendations of those who worry about confounding due to a common appraisal term would require that Bandura's research on self-efficacy and fear (e.g., Bandura, Adams, Hardy, & Howells, 1980) be regarded as tautological. One would have to argue that to expect to be inefficacious is the same as to be actually fearful. Efficacy expectations and appraisals refer to cognitions; fear and distress refer to emotional states that include cognitions. These are part–whole relationships. We must be careful to avoid whole–whole relationships, where the independent and dependent variables are mutually and totally inclusive. Part–whole relationships have some redundancy, yet leave room for additional understanding and new knowledge.

Where, then, does this leave us with respect to the question of stress as rubric or variable? We have consistently argued (cf. Lazarus, 1966; Lazarus & Folkman, (1984a,b) that stress is best regarded as a complex *rubric*, like emotion, motivation, or cognition, rather than as a simple variable. This does not mean, however, that it is merely a chapter heading. The meaning sphere of stress is defined by many variables and processes that are reflected in the person's appraisal of a relationship with the environment as *relevant to well-being* and *taxing or exceeding his or her resources*. Changes in the relationship and how it is appraised by the person explain the flux observed in the short-term emotional reactions and behavior that flow from any person–environment encounter (Folkman & Lazarus, 1985).

The solution, which is proposed by those who argue for cleaning up the independent variable by eliminating its overlap with perceptions, appraisals, and other reactions, is to return to an older mode of thought that in its extremes can be identified as S-R and behavioristic. This style of thinking dies hard. It still dominates current empirical research as illustrated by the plethora of studies of life events as stressors without concern for personal meaning. An exception is the effort of Brown and Harris (1978), whose work on life events centers on such meaning.

We can trace the evolution of relational, cognitive theories by a series of figures, beginning with Figure 1.

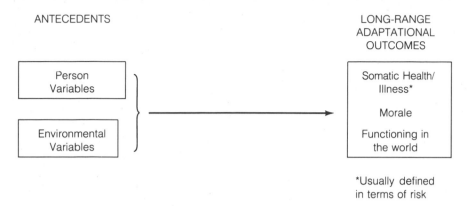

**Figure 1.** Traditional cause-and-effect research. From *Stress, Appraisal, and Coping* (p. 303) by R. S. Lazarus and S. Folkman, 1984. New York: Springer. Reproduced by permission.

Figure 1 illustrates how one or more antecedent variables can be examined as possible causes of long-range adaptational outcomes such as illness or impaired functioning. The research style can be experimental or correlational, and in its most sophisticated form includes the possibility of interaction between antecedent person and environment variables. Variables are typically assessed once, and large $N$'s are preferred in order to obtain representative samples and statistical significance. Much of life events research falls into this category; subjects are divided into high and low stress to predict rates of illness. Our initial work on daily hassles is similar, in that Hassles Scale (stress) scores were used to explain psychological symptoms (Kanner *et al.*, 1980) and somatic illness (DeLongis *et al.*, 1982). However, in the latter cases, a characteristic degree of stress was generated by aggregating nine monthly assessments of daily hassles.

In the traditional research design of Figure 1, nothing can be learned directly about the processes by which the antecedent variables affect the outcome variables. If one is interested in these processes, they must be inferred, usually by reference to the personality variables being studied as antecedents. For example, Kobasa (1979) says that hardy people, defined by personality assessments, are said to react differently to stressful encounters, thereby being protected against the ravages of stress on health. The problem is that in such antecedent–consequent research, the appraisal or coping processes whereby the subjects manage stressful encounters are never actually assessed. This research style can be interactional, as when both person and environment variables are combined in the research, but not transactional or process-centered, because the person is not studied across time or in a variety of stressful encounters.

In Kobasa's research, the interaction is between high and low stress, as the environmental variable, and high and low hardiness, as the personality variable.

Research such as that of Kobasa is not radical behaviorism, because its premise is that numerous processes, such as appraisal and coping, intervene or mediate between environmental stressors and adaptational outcomes. It is neobehavioral; the model is S-O-R rather than S-R, the "O" standing for personality dispositions that lead the person to think and act under stressful encounters in ways that make a difference in outcome. However, because only dispositions are measured, and not the mediating thoughts and acts that presumably flow from them, they might better be referred to as moderator rather than mediating variables (cf. Frese, this volume).

Moderators are usually used to divide a heterogeneous population into homogeneous subgroups that affect the relationship between a predictor and a criterion in order to increase the correlation or to locate a suppressor variable (see, for example, Zedeck, 1971). When Johnson and Sarason (1979a,b) use social support or perceived control as variables that interact with an environmental condition, such as high life events scores, to improve the prediction of health outcomes, they are dealing with moderator variables, strictly speaking, not mediation, however they interpret the effects. Such variables increase the sheer number of antecedent variables rather than throw light on the ways processes (such as appraisal and coping) work when they affect short- and long-range adaptational outcomes.

Therefore, the next step is to specify and try to observe the processes that transform antecedent variables into various response states and thereby affect outcomes. Figure 2 identifies a set of variables—antecedent, process, and outcome—that comprise the rubric of stress as we see it.

Person and environment antecedent variables interact to produce divergent appraisals that reflect whether the encounter is irrelevant, benign, or stressful, and, if stressful, what might be done to cope. The concept of appraisal integrates person variables, such as values and commitments, with the environmental conditions being faced and provides the bases of individual differences in reaction. Appraisal shapes the coping process, which, in turn, affects the immediate outcome of the encounter, and probably also the long-term adaptational outcomes of multiple encounters.

Although it is not shown in Figure 2, the system is dynamic, in that appraisal and coping processes continuously change, and it is recursive, in that outcomes can influence antecedent variables, depending on where in the flow of psychological events one chooses to begin and end the analysis (Coyne & Lazarus, 1980). For example, psychological symptoms or distress can, themselves, be sources of stress. The point applies also

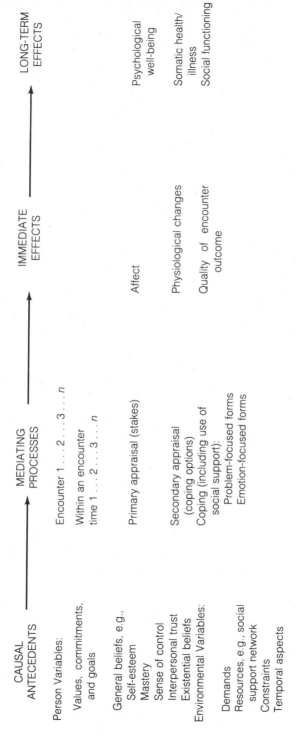

**Figure 2.** Illustrative system variables for the stress rubric. (Although not shown here, the model is recursive.)

to health concerns, such as headaches or not getting enough sleep; for many people, sleeplessness and health problems are a source of stress in daily living as well as a reaction. Thoits (1983) has recognized this dilemma of recursive conceptualizations of stress and symptoms in her review of research connecting life events with psychological distress.

Figure 3 merely enlarges the portion of Figure 2 that deals with process. The same persons are shown repeatedly over time (Time 1, 2, 3 and $n$) and/or across different encounters (Encounter 1, 2, 3, and $n$). Only by repeatedly observing the individual's reactions in slices of time within a complex stressful encounter, or across encounters that are connected as to theme (e.g., bereavement), can we obtain a picture of changes in the stress and coping process. Change is what process means. In effect, we must examine primary and secondary appraisal as it changes over time, as well as coping, as the encounter unfolds or as the person moves from one encounter to another (Folkman & Lazarus, 1985).

Therefore, what is important in Figures 2 and 3 is twofold. First, these analyses direct attention to the processes that transform what is happening in the static sense of a person–environment interaction, and move the person toward outcomes; second, they divide outcomes into immediate end states of the diverse appraisal and coping processes in a given stressful encounter, and long-range outcomes that result from multiple stressful encounters over a long time. The encounter outcome, or immediate effects, including physiological changes, feeling states, and coping effectiveness, are paralleled in the long run by health, morale or well-being, and social functioning. These long-range outcomes cannot, in the ordinary course of events, be the result of a single stressful encounter but reflect an aggregate of how the person handles many stressful encounters. We can examine the dynamics of a specific stressful en-

MEDIATING PROCESSES

| Time 1 | Time 2 | Time 3 | . . . Time N |
| Encounter 1 | Encounter 2 | Encounter 3 | . . . Encounter N |

Appraisal-Reappraisal
Coping:
    problem-focused
    emotion-focused
    seeking, obtaining
      and using social
      support

**Figure 3.** A transactional model: ipsative-normative arrangement (Box 2 of Figure 2). From *Stress, Appraisal, and Coping* (p. 307) by R. S. Lazarus and S. Folkman, 1984. New York: Springer. Reproduced by permission.

counter and try to understand how they work, but to understand the long-run effects of psychosocial variables and processes, we must examine such dynamics in any given person or set of persons again and again, in short, over many such encounters and over a long time.

Finally, if one wishes to be complete, it is necessary to move from the psychological level of analysis to two other adjacent levels, namely, the social and the physiological levels (see Trumbull & Appley, this volume). Many important theoretical and practical issues reside in the interface between levels. Thus, behavioral or psychosomatic medicine operates at the borderline where psychological processes influence the physiological, and vice versa. Similarly, to fully understand stress at the psychological level requires that we embed the individual in a social system. In Figure 4 we have provided a version of the social and physiological levels, along with the psychological level illustrated in Figures 1, 2, and 3; this version uses the same array of variables on the horizontal axis as before, namely, antecedents, processes, immediate or short-term effects, and long-range effects. Our choice of variables at the social and physiological levels is illustrative, and other researchers might make different choices depending on interest or theoretical predilections.

## Conclusions

With this multivariate, multiprocess system, one can easily see that *no single variable,* whether in the environment or within the person, whether a structural, causal antecedent variable, a process, or an outcome, can stand for stress. *All* the variables in the system can contribute to the immediate appraisal of stress and its emotional effects, and perhaps to long-term effects, too, if a given process is stable or recurrent over time or across encounters. If we consider the system as a whole, what it means to speak of stress as a *rubric* rather than a variable can be more easily understood. We can recognize that none of the variables individually is capable of explaining the emotional response. Therefore, stress is just a handy term to refer to the operation of many variables and processes when demands *tax or exceed the person's resources* and the person *appraises* the encounter as relevant to well-being, engages in *coping* processes, and responds cognitively, affectively, and behaviorally to *feedback* about what is happening.

Once this principle is well understood, the term *environmentally induced stress,* or *environmental stress* loses its usefulness. To one person a traffic jam is simply a condition of life to be managed philosophically or negotiated with minimum stress and distress; such a person may not report the traffic jam on the Hassles Scale. To another, however, a traffic jam is an additional pressure on an already pressured existence, or a

**Figure 4.** Three levels of analysis. From *Stress, Appraisal, and Coping* (p. 308) by R. S. Lazarus and S. Folkman, 1984. New York: Springer. Reproduced by permission.

| | ANTECEDENTS | MEDIATING PROCESSES | IMMEDIATE EFFECTS | LONG-TERM EFFECTS |
|---|---|---|---|---|
| SOCIAL | Socio economic status<br>Cultural templates<br>Institutional systems<br>Group structures (e.g., role patterns)<br>Social networks | Social supports as proffered<br>Available social/institutional means of ameliorating problems | Social disturbances<br>Government responses<br>Sociopolitical pressures<br>Group alienation | Social failure<br>Revolution<br>Social change<br>Structural changes |
| PSYCHOLOGICAL | Person variables:<br>values-commitments<br>beliefs-assumptions, e.g., personal control<br>cognitive coping styles<br><br>Environmental (Situational) variables:<br>situational demands<br>imminence<br>timing<br>ambiguity<br>social and material resources | Vulnerabilites<br>Appraisal-<br>Reappraisal<br><br>Coping:<br>problem-focused<br>emotion-focused<br>cultivating, seeking & using social support<br>Perceived social support:<br>emotional<br>tangible<br>informational | Positive or negative feelings<br><br>Quality of outcome of stressful encounters | Morale<br><br>Functioning in the world |
| PHYSIOLOGICAL | Genetic or constitutional factors<br>Physiological conditioning-- individual response steriotypy (e.g., Lacey, 1967)<br>Illness risk factors--<br>Physiological conditioning-- e.g., smoking | Immune resources<br>Species vulnerability<br>Temporary vulnerability<br>Acquired defects | Somatic changes (precursors of illness)<br><br>Acute illness | Chronic illness<br>Impaired physiological functioning<br>Recover from illness<br>Longevity |

personal affront by the social system; such a person is very likely to remember the traffic jam and to endorse it as a severe hassle.

Let us further test the traditional environmental stressor concept. Is an insult a stressor? Often, but not always. An insult may not be perceived as such if it is subtle, or if it is directed at a person who regards it as without the potential for doing damage. Even major events, such as the death of a loved one, divorce, loss of job, illness, or incapacitation, elicit wide individual variation in the degree to which they are experienced as stressful. And what about stressful conditions that are characterized by the absence of an identifiable stimulus, as when a person who needs approval from a loved one is ignored and reacts with great distress? It would take a considerable expansion and distortion to regard the absence of a response by another—a non-event—as a stimulus. But more to the point, there is simply no way to define an event as a stressor without referring to the properties of persons that make their well-being in some way vulnerable to that event. If one accepts this reasoning, it is counterproductive to keep trying to reify the environmental input as a stressor, and it is essential to find principles for predicting the stress response from the person-environment relationship, and from the rest of the variables and processes that influence the outcome.

It would be better to ask, instead, what it is about the person and the situational context that produces appraisals of harm and threat or appraisals that some benefit is possible or probable. The discovery of these antecedents of appraisal would be of greater informational and research value than merely comparing people in the *amount of stress,* as identified by the frequency and/or the intensity of daily hassles. To take this important further step requires examination of individual differences in the *content of stress,* as measured, say, by hassles' patterns observed over time for both individuals and groups of people chosen on the basis of vulnerabilities they share. These individual differences could be the result both of stable environmental factors, such as a continuing marriage, neighborhood or conditions of work, and of stable personal agendas, such as patterns of commitment (e.g., Type A, perfectionism, ambition, insatiable needs for approval, etc.), beliefs about one's capabilities or lack of them, and skill (or its lack) in coping with important ongoing sources of stress. Predicting the nature and type of response on the basis of these or other variables would do much to overcome any problems of circularity in the study of stress processes.

One must acknowledge that stress is an "unclean" concept in that it depends on the interaction, over time, of two complex systems, the environment and the person. There is no way to separate them without destroying the concept of stress as a relational and cognitively mediated phenomenon. One should not treat stress as static when it is a complex process involving constant change. To suggest that the independent variable be cleaned up, so to speak, is not useful, because stress does not exist in the absence of a special person–environment relationship and the processes that explain this relationship. The environment affects the person, the person affects the environment; this recursive arrangement is going on in all adaptational encounters, in a fashion also implied by Bandura's (1978) term *reciprocal determinism*. The only way these interlocking variables or systems can be separated is by studying their temporal relations cross-sectionally in slices of time, as one variable and then another takes on the role of antecedent (see also Coyne & Lazarus, 1980; Lazarus, Coyne, & Folkman, 1982; and Phillips & Orton, 1983).

Much of the confounding that we have been speaking about reflects the fusion of variables in nature rather than being merely the result of measurement errors of researchers. If we try to delete the overlap in variables of genuine importance, we will be distorting nature to fit a simpler, mythical metatheory of separable antecedent and consequent variables. We urge researchers who are tempted to objectify stress as an event in the environment to consider these consequences carefully.

# References

American Psychiatric Association. (1980). *Diagnostic and statistical manual of mental disorders* (3rd ed.). Washington, DC: Author.

Bandura, A. (1978). The self-system in reciprocal determinism. *American Psychologist, 33*, 344–358.

Bandura, A., Adams, N. E., Hardy, A. B., & Howells, G. N. (1980). Tests of the generality of self-efficacy theory. *Cognitive Therapy and Research, 4*, 39–66.

Beck, A. T. (1976). *Cognitive therapy and the emotional disorders.* New York: International Universities Press.

Brown, G. W., & Harris, T. (1978). *Social origins of depression: A study of psychiatric disorder in women.* New York: The Free Press.

Carnap, R. (1936). Testability and meaning. *Philosophy of Science, 3*, 419–471.

Cassel, J. (1976). The contribution of the social environment to host resistance. *American Journal of Epidemiology, 104*, 107–123.

Cohen, S. (1986). Contrasting the Hassles Scale and the Perceived Stress Scale: Who's really measuring appraised stress? *American Psychologist, 41*, 716–718.

Cohen, S., Kamarck, T., & Mermelstein, R. (1983). A global measure of perceived stress. *Journal of Health and Social Behavior, 24*, 385–396.

Coyne, J. C., & Lazarus, R. S. (1980). Cognitive style, stress perception, and coping. In I. L. Kutash & L. B. Schlesinger (Eds.), *Handbook on stress and anxiety: Contemporary knowledge, theory, and treatment* (pp. 144–158). San Francisco: Jossey-Bass.

DeLongis, A., Coyne, J. C., Dakof, G., Folkman, S., & Lazarus, R. S. (1982). Relationship of daily hassles, uplifts, and major life events to health status. *Health Psychology, 1*, 119–136.

Dohrenwend, B. S., & Dohrenwend, B. P. (1978). Some issues in research on stressful life events. *Journal of Nervous and Mental Disease, 166*, 7–15.

Dohrenwend, B. S., Dohrenwend, B. P., Dodson, M., & Shrout, P. E. (1984). Symptoms, hassles, social supports, and life events: The problem of confounded measures. *Journal of Abnormal Psychology, 93,* 222–230.

Dubos, R. (1959). *Mirage of health: Utopias, progress, and biological change.* New York: Harper & Row (Perennial paperback).

Ellis, A. (1962). *Reason and emotion in psychotherapy.* New York: Lyle Stuart.

Folkman, S., & Lazarus, R. S. (1985). If it changes it must be a process: A study of emotion and coping during three stages of a college examination. *Journal of Personality and Social Psychology, 48,* 150–170.

Gotlib, I. H. (1984). Depression and general psychopathology in university students. *Journal of Abnormal Psychology, 93,* 19–30.

Haan, N. (1977). *Coping and defending: Processes of self-environment organization.* New York: Academic Press.

Holmes, T. H., & Rahe, R. H. (1967). The social readjustment rating scale. *Journal of Psychosomatic Research, 11* 213–218.

Johnson, J. H., & Sarason, I. G. (1979a). Moderator variables in life stress research. In I. G. Sarason & C. D. Spielberger (Eds.), *Stress and anxiety* (Vol. 6, pp. 151–167). Washington, DC: Hemisphere.

Johnson, J. H., & Sarason, I. G. (1979b). Recent developments in research on life stress. In V. Hamilton & D. M. Warburton (Eds.), *Human stress and cognition: An information processing approach* (pp. 265–298). London: Wiley.

Kanner, A. D., Coyne, J. C., Schaefer, C., & Lazarus, R. S. (1981). Comparisons of two modes of stress measurement: Daily hassles and uplifts versus major life events. *Journal of Behavioral Medicine, 4,* 1–39.

Kant, I. (1956). *Critique of practical reason* (trans. by L. W. Beck). New York:Bobbs-Merrill.

Kasl, S. V. (1978). Epidemiological contributions to the study of work stress. In C. L. Cooper & R. Payne (Eds.), *Stress at work* (pp. 3–48). New York: Wiley.

Kobasa, S. C. (1979). Stressful life events, personality, and health: An inquiry into hardiness. *Journal of Personality and Social Psychology, 37,* 1–11.

Lacey, J. I. (1967). Somatic response patterning and stress: Some revisions of activation theory. In M. H. Appley & R. Trumbull (Eds.), *Psychological stress: Issues in Research* (pp. 14–37). New York: Appleton-Century-Crofts.

Lazarus, R. S. (1966). *Psychological stress and the coping process.* New York: McGraw-Hill.

Lazarus, R. S. (1984). Puzzles in the study of daily hassles. *Journal of Behavioral Medicine, 7,* 375–389.

Lazarus, R. S. (1985). The trivialization of distress. In J. C. Rosen & L. J. Solomon (Eds.), *Preventing health risk behaviors and promoting coping with illness Vol. 8. Vermont Conference on the Primary Prevention of Psychopathology* (pp. 279–298). Hanover, NH: University Press of New England.

Lazarus, R. S., & DeLongis, A. (1983). Psychological stress and coping in aging. *American Psychologist, 38,* 245–254.

Lazarus, R. S., & Folkman, S. (1984a). Coping and adaptation. In W. D. Gentry (Ed.), *The handbook of behavioral medicine* (pp. 282–325). New York: Guilford.

Lazarus, R. S., & Folkman, S. (1984b). *Stress, appraisal, and coping.* New York: Springer.

Lazarus, R. S., Coyne, J. C., & Folkman, S. (1982). Cognition, emotion, and motivation: The doctoring of Humpty-Dumpty. In R. W. J. Neufeld (Ed.), *Psychological stress and psychopathology* (pp. 218–239). New York: McGraw-Hill.

Lazarus, R. S., DeLongis, A., Folkman, S., & Gruen, R. (1985). Stress and adaptational outcomes: The problem of confounded measures. *American Psychologist, 40,* 770–779.

Lehrman, D. S. (1964). The reproductive behavior of ring doves. *Scientific American, 211,* 48–54.

Lin, N., Dean, A., & Ensel, W. M. (1981). Social support scales: A methodological note. *Schizophrenia Bulletin, 7,* 73–87.

Loevinger, J. (1976). *Ego development.* San Francisco: Jossey-Bass.

McLean, P. (1976). Depression as a specific response to stress. In I. G. Sarason & C. D. Spielberger (Eds.), *Stress and anxiety* (Vol. 3, pp. 297–323). Washington, DC: Hemisphere.

Menninger, K. (1963). *The vital balance: The life process in mental health and illness.* New York: Viking.

Monroe, S. M. (1983). Major and minor life events as predictors of psychological distress: Further issues and findings. *Journal of Behavioral Medicine, 6,* 189–205.

Nicholls, J. G., Licht, B. G., & Pearl, R. A. (1982). Some dangers of using personality questionnaires to study personality. *Psychological Bulletin, 92,* 572–580.

Oxford English Dictionary (1970). Oxford, Clarendon Press.

Pearlin, L. I. (1983). Role strains and personal stress. In H. B. Kaplan (Ed.), *Psychosocial stress: Trends in theory and research* (pp. 3–32). New York: Academic Press.

Phillips, D. C., & Orton, R. (1983). The new causal principle of cognitive learning theory: Perspectives on Bandura's "reciprocal determinism." *Psychological Review, 90,* 158–165.

Pratt, C. C. (1939). *The logic of modern psychology.* New York: Macmillan.

Putnam, H. (1962). The analytic and the synthetic. In H. Feigl & G. Maxwell (Eds.), *Minnesota studies in the philosophy of science, Vol. 3.* Minneapolis: University of Minnesota Press.

Quine, W. V. O. (1951). Two dogmas of empiricism. *Philosophical Review, 60,* 20–43.

Quine, W. V. O. (1953). *From a logical point of view.* Cambridge: Harvard University Press.

Syme, S. L. (1984). Sociocultural factors and disease etiology. In D. W. Gentry (Ed.), *The handbook of behavioral medicine* (pp. 13–37). New York: Guilford.

Thoits, P. A. (1983). Dimensions of life events that influence psychological distress: An evaluation and synthesis of the literature. In H. B. Kaplan (Ed.), *Psychosocial stress: Trends in theory and research* (pp. 51–72). New York: Academic Press.

Thoits, P. A. (1985). Social support processes and psychological well-being: Theoretical possibilities. In I. G. Sarason & B. R. Sarason (Eds.), *Social support: Theory, research, and application.* The Hague: Martinus Nijhof.

Vaillant, G. E. (1977). *Adaptation to life.* Boston: Little, Brown.

Zedeck, S. (1971). Problem with the use of "moderator" variables. *Psychological Bulletin, 76,* 295–310.

# CHAPTER 5

# Behavior Economics as an Approach to Stress Theory

## WOLFGANG SCHÖNPFLUG

### Benefits and Costs of Coping: Theoretical Considerations

The behavior economics approach (Schönpflug, 1979, 1983) has been developed as an extension and partial reformulation of earlier *cognitive stress theories* (Appley, 1967; French & Kahn, 1962; Kahn, Wolfe, Quinn, Snoek, & Rosenthal, 1964; Lazarus, 1966; Lazarus & Launier, 1978; McGrath, 1976). Cognitive stress theories deal with problem states as sources of stress, that is, with task demands and threats that heavily tax or even overcharge an individual's abilities and resources. Attempts have been made to assess demands and threats, and abilities and resources objectively, as features of a person's environment or as characteristics of the person. However, cognitive theorists rely more on subjective appraisal than on objective problem states. Subjective appraisals establish mental representations of problem states, yielding large interindividual differences in representations of the same objective situation; veridical representations, as well as biased, incomplete, and illusionary versions can be observed. Cognitive theorists then relate emotional and physiological stress reactions to these subjective representations rather than to objective problem states.

Three modes of coping with states of stress are described: (a) direct palliation of adverse emotional states; (b) reappraisal of subjective rep-

**WOLFGANG SCHÖNPFLUG** ● Institut für Psychologie, Freie Universität Berlin, 1000 Berlin 33, Federal Republic of Germany.

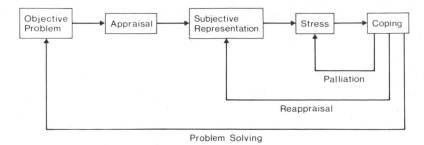

**Figure 1.** Synopsis of cognitive stress theories.

resentations of problems that instigate stress responses; and (c) solution of the objective problems on which appraisals and stress reactions are based. The resulting model is illustrated in Figure 1.

Cognitive theorists, in general, explicitly emphasize the strategies of effective coping, thereby introducing an *optimistic bias.* They show less concern for the factors contributing to the prolongation and aggravation of stress states, thereby avoiding a more pessimistic perspective. If one examines the *pessimistic perspective,* however, three issues become clear:

1.  Coping attempts may fail (cf. Kahn *et al.,* 1964; Lumsden, 1975; Neufeld, 1976; Schulz, 1979). Despite problem-solving efforts, and despite attempts at reappraisal and palliation, the objective problem states, the internal representations of problems, and the emotional states may remain unchanged.
2.  Coping attempts may (a) even make old problems worse and/or (b) create new problems (cf. Kahn *et al.,* 1964). Often, problem-solving procedures have adverse side- or after-effects: for example, hitting a pedestrian while driving to the hospital; offending a friend by making a joke in order to cheer him up. Also, attempts at reappraisal may lead to still more critical views of a situation. For instance, the search for arguments against the danger of nuclear arms may lead to evidence for the additional threat from conventional weapons.
3.  All modes of coping require mental, emotional, and motor involvement. They consume external and internal resources, and thereby are costly (cf. Glass, Singer, & Friedman, 1969). This is most evident in problem solving but can also be demonstrated for appraisal or reappraisal.

Problem solving consists of two components: (a) *orientation* to the problem and strategies for modifying the problem state; and (b) *control* operations, which aim at performing the desired modification. Control operations usually are implemented by motor and speech movements (e.g., pulling a lever, giving a command); but they also require mental activity, since they have to be planned and monitored (e.g., work sequences have to be decided upon, discourse strategies have to be selected). These mental and motor activities consume resources. The same is true for orientation during problem solving. Orientation is basically a mental process; however, it may call for quite a few motor acts, ranging from eye movements to more global processes of information retrieval (e.g., purchasing and carrying a book, visiting a friend and asking him for advice). What can be stated for orientation during problem solving is also true for appraisal or reappraisal. Appraisal processes cannot be distinguished from orienting processes in problem solving, and therefore encompass the same mental and motor operations. In addition to costs from mental and motor processes, as described above, control and orientation are likely to evoke or include emotional responses (e.g., fear, excitement, disappointment) as well; the involvement in these responses may be interpreted as emotional costs.

It is assumed that it is the amount of mental, emotional, and motor activity aiming at control and orientation that determines the psychic load in a situation and defines the degree of stress. From this assumption then, it follows that: Neither the objective problem state *per se* nor its mental representation *per se* affects the state of stress in a direct manner. They are, rather, only the basis on which mental, emotional, and motor

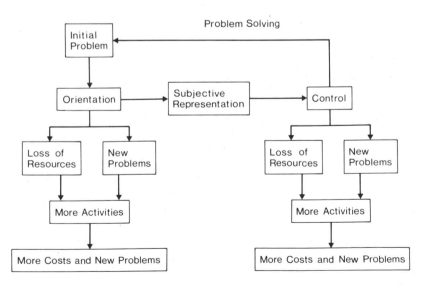

**Figure 2.** Outline of the behavior economics approach to stress.

activities operate. However, the quantity and quality of objective and subjective problem states will have an impact on the extent of activity engaged in by an individual in a given situation. For this reason, the degree and the temporal extension of stress depend on the efficiency of active problem solving and on the adequacy of appraisal.

The state of stress can be terminated if active coping indeed leads to the elimination of the problem followed by a recognition of the solution achieved. Then, control activity also can be terminated, and the psychic load from coping discontinues. Of course, the problem-solving activity and the psychic load discontinue, as well, if only the representation of the problem is altered, indicating that the initial problem has been solved or no longer can be structured as a severe problem. On the other hand, new problems, generated in the course of orientation and control, are likely to necessitate more activities, raising the level of stress.

Another consequence should be mentioned: Because new problems lead to more activities, which also can turn out to be dysfunctional, they increase the risk of creating further problems. Thus, a dynamic system can be conceptualized in which a broad spectrum of problems emerges as a result of coping efforts. In a similar way, loss of resources calls for compensation, and is likely to induce further, possibly dysfunctional, activities (e.g., traveling to a resort to recover from exhaustion, accepting a second job in order to repay debts).

Figure 2 illustrates the model as advocated here. Comparison with Figure 1 shows the similarities with the now classical cognitive approach, but three major differences are also apparent. First, in Figure 2, it is the *process* rather than the product of orientation or appraisal that constitutes the psychic load; the threatening or challenging features of the subjective representation of the problem are not described as stressing, whereas the efforts and difficulties associated with the perceptual, inferential, and evaluative process of structuring the problem are described this way. Second, control or active coping is not only treated as a reaction to a stressful antecedent but also as an antecedent of stress itself; this follows from the interpretation of stress as the loss of resources or psychic costs associated with control. Third, it is also illustrated that not only is the initial problem taken into account but also subsequent problems that arise as after-effects of reactions to the initial problem; activities instigated by the loss of resources are considered as well.

*Costs* is a concept from economics. It is introduced here to allow an interpretation of stress in terms of established theories of economics. Since the logic of economics is applied to behavior regulation, the approach presented here has been called *behavior economics*. As already expressed above, the total costs, or resources consumed, are represented in the lower portion of Figure 2. They are assumed to result from a reaction to the initial problem and to new problems generated in the course of orientation and control. There are also *benefits* of coping in the form of *savings of costs*. They result from effective problem solving, as represented in the upper portion of Figure 2 by the control loop. Also, the orientation process will contribute to saving costs, if it succeeds in eliminating threatening and challenging features from internal representations and thus reduces the need for further acts of orientation and control; this is expressed in the upper portion of Figure 2, as well.

The general presupposition underlying this model is as follows: *States of stress are states of limited and overcharged resources, and individuals involved in stressful encounters operate toward savings of resources.* If savings can be achieved, the state of stress will be attenuated, otherwise the stress will be augmented. Under these conditions, *payoff* refers to the comparison between the benefits or savings achieved by a coping procedure and the resources or costs invested for this procedure. If the benefits or savings exceed the costs, the procedure can be evaluated as paying off. Cost/benefit ratios, however, have to be estimated for a longer period of time. During the course of active coping, the resources invested may generally be considerable, and not be balanced by immediate benefits. But even high, short-term expenses of coping may be justified in the long run, if compared with costs saved during a longer interval after effective coping. An example would be helping efforts in emergency situations. The load from rescue work during a fire or a hurricane will be heavy but will be more than balanced if lives and valuables are saved. Also, different coping strategies can be compared on the basis of their cost/benefit ratio, as, for instance, individual and social actions in cases of emergency.

Even an abstract description of the model will serve to demonstrate some qualitative economical evaluations (see Table 1):

*Case 1:* An initial problem arises, but there is no (or only minimal) involvement in the problem. Therefore, there is no loss of resources and no self-generated problems.

*Case 2:* There is an initial problem that is attended to. But the problem disappears for external reasons and without further involvement. In this case, there will also be no costs and no new problems. But this case is mostly wishful thinking.

*Case 3:* Compared to Case 2, successful involvement is more realistic. Successful involvement is effective in eradicating the initial problem without creating an additional one. In this case, however, loss of resources has to be taken into account.

*Case 4:* A coping attempt ends with a failure. Aside from the failure that has occurred, expenses arise, and these expenses continue because the initial problem persists and calls for further coping attempts.

**Table 1.** Combination of Costs, Initial (old) Problems and Self-Generated (new) Problems

|                                    | Initial problem | Costs of coping with initial problem | New problems |
|------------------------------------|-----------------|--------------------------------------|--------------|
| 1. Initial state                   | unsolved        | none                                 | none         |
| 2. Wishful thinking                | solved          | none                                 | none         |
| 3. Success                         | solved          | yes                                  | none         |
| 4. Failure                         | unsolved        | yes                                  | none         |
| 5. Success and problem generation  | solved          | yes                                  | yes          |
| 6. Failure and problem generation  | unsolved        | yes                                  | yes          |

*Case 5:* Success in coping with the initial problem may coincide with the generation of a new one. Then the costs of coping with the old problem are followed by additional costs from involvement in the new problem.

*Case 6:* Finally, failure and problem generation can go together. This combines involvement in old problems and new problems, and expenses from dealing with both sets of problems accumulate.

If saving of resources or costs is regarded as the dominant tendency in stress situations, it can intuitively be assumed that failure is less economical and more stressful than success, and problem generation in association with failure is the most stressful combination. But one has to be careful with intuition. Economic evaluation requires quantification and the assessment of time allocation. Precise quantification may show that costs of success were higher than were expenses for tolerating the initial problem. This is termed the Pyrrhus-effect, after the King of Macedonia, who is said to have exclaimed, after seeing his casualties: "Another such victory and we have lost!" An analysis of time allocation may show that new problems are less severe because they have a long latency and individuals have time to prepare for their occurrence. Because quantification and balancing over time are so important, static and global models are only helpful in demonstrating general principles. They have to be adjusted and tested under specified conditions, and this is what we are doing in our research.

In our research group at the Freie Universität in Berlin, we conduct field and laboratory work and, where possible, link the two together (cf.

Mündelein & Schönpflug, 1984; Schönpflug, 1979). At best, we start out with an exploratory study in the field, specify relevant conditions, and simulate the field situation in our laboratory. After finishing the laboratory experiment, we return to the field to evaluate our findings. Two levels of analysis have been attempted: analyses of complex problem situations, and analyses of specific task situations.

The more specific the situation, the more differentiated are behavior descriptions as far as individual style and temporal structure are concerned. In order to exemplify and to elaborate the behavior economics approach, two studies will be reported: one dealing with behavior in a fairly complex situation—involvement in health advancement measures; the second with behavior in a task-specific situation—planning and keeping appointments. The first is a field study, the second a laboratory study.

## Reduction and Induction of Stress by Health Advancement Measures: A Field Study

The health study was conducted in collaboration with Petra Sange (for further details see Schönpflug, 1984). We had no special theoretical interest in the domain of health; we just selected health as one example of a larger problem area in modern life. If the model in Figure 2 is applied to this area, how should one define the initial problem? Obviously, there is no single problem in this area to be represented, but a network of interrelated problems. Within this network three *classes of problems* can be identified:

1. Prototypical problems, which in the field of health refer to the incidence of diseases.
2. Origins of prototypical problems: usually risk factors that are not necessarily medical in nature, for example, air pollution or fast driving.
3. Consequences of prototypical problems: effects of diseases that need not be medical, such as loss of job or social isolation.

All these problems can be classified as externally generated, and they persist unless an individual intervenes. Thus, our block "initial problem" splits into three blocks of externally generated problems.

Also, the terms *orientation* and *control* had to be related to the three kinds of problems. Orientation as related to the prototypical problem "incidence of a disease" was to be interpreted as diagnostic activity as performed by medical personnel (e.g., X-raying, taking and testing blood samples) or by the persons under treatment (e.g., measuring one's own body temperature, discussing body symptoms with family members). Orientation is further related to risk factors and consequences as exhibited in other types of behavior (e.g., inquiring about hazards in a job, testing the loyalty of friends after a contagious disease). In a similar way, the meaning of the term *control* is specified in relation to the three types of problems. Control with regard to the incidence of diseases takes the special form of medical treatment (e.g., surgery, medication); with regard to risk factors, it is prevention (e.g., environmental protection, vaccination); with consecutive problems, it takes the form of aftercare or rehabilitation (e.g., training in case of invalidism, compensation for social isolation).

Combining the three classes of problems and the two types of activities yields a 3 × 2 schedule. Each field in the schedule represents a source of costs and a potential origin of self-generated problems. Costs may be defined as loss of internal resources, like energy, optimism, or abilities. Also, the loss of external resources, like money or social support, may be taken into account. Typical examples of self-generated problems in the area of health are malpractice or the side-effects of drugs. In this way, the concepts of the behavior economics approach have been specified for the area of health, as illustrated in Figure 3.

The amount of stress experienced in this system will depend on the number and difficulty of external problems. A substantial variable will be *efficiency*. The higher the individual's skills of orientation and control,

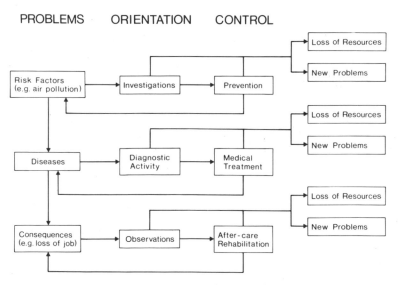

**Figure 3.** The behavior economics approach as specified for the area of health.

the lower will be the consumption of resources and the probability of problem generation. Within the system, there are several ways of operating toward *economy*. One strategy is emphasis on prevention. If all risk factors are controlled, no prototypical and sequential problems will arise. However, if the number of risk factors is high, and their impact is difficult to determine, the prevention strategy may become highly demanding. People involved in it may feel a considerable load of health problems even if never becoming ill. So, waiting for diseases to appear may be the more economical strategy. It is similar to reacting to alarms— as has been investigated by Breznitz (1984).

What is the psychological reality of such economic reasoning? We had never validated our model for such a complex situation as the problem of health, and we thought we should design a questionnaire that could determine whether our concepts and our logic could be communicated to a larger population. We could have asked questions like: How many diseases are there in our city? How are they prevented? How effective are the medical measures taken? Such questions would have required absolute judgments as answers. However, economics or quality of life, as we tried to assess it, is not just a matter of absolute judgment; it is also a matter of comparison. One option is social comparison, another is historical comparison. As we were more interested in historical change, we decided to ask for relative judgments, comparing two epochs of German history: the time before World War I—the year 1910, and the present—the year 1980. So we asked questions in the format: Were there more diseases in 1910? Or do we have more diseases in 1980?

We constructed a questionnaire and interviewed subjects who could actually recall and compare experiences during the years 1910 and 1980. This group of subjects consisted of 43 senior citizens, 80 years of age or older, the oldest two being 96. As we suspected that our senior sample responded not only on the basis of personal memories but also on the basis of general historical knowledge, we included two additional samples without personal experience with the time before the first World War: 45 high school students, of about 16 years of age, and 30 university students, with a median age of 23 years.

The responses that are most significant for the theoretical model can be summarized, as follows:

1. All samples agree that modern life produces more hazards for human health.
2. They also agree that nowadays there are more diseases.
3. Health protection measures are rated as increasing.
4. An increment in medical treatment of diseases is indicated as well.

5. Modern biotechnology is described as highly effective, much more effective than in the beginning of the century.
6. Despite considerable advancements in medical diagnosis and medical treatment, an increasing number of unintended after- and side effects is indicated in the ratings.
7. The number of false alarms, resulting from wrong diagnostic judgments, is said to rise.
8. A rising number of errors in medical treatment is stated as well.
9. Financial problems as a consequence of the expanding health service are mentioned; these problems, however, appear to be socialized, thanks to the compulsory insurance system in Germany.
10. Older people, but not younger ones, also mention an increase in nonfinancial problems related to medical treatment and health protection, especially more inconveniences associated with visiting the doctor, prolonged waiting times, and trouble with insurance companies and state health agencies.

The exact distribution of responses relating to statements one to six is given in Table 2. The data are pooled over the three samples (total $n = 118$). There were no significant differences between samples, as indicated by chi-square tests. The differences between the years 1910 and 1980 are significant, as indicated by $t$ = tests. (For more details, see Schönpflug, 1984.)

For our purposes, it does not matter whether or not these statements are true, or whether or not they are representative of any population; what matters here is that they can be interpreted neatly in the frame of our economic model. The central issue is the increase of health advancement measures, which can be assumed to cause more psychic costs. Also, the reported augmentation of false alarms, extra loads, and medical errors point to self-generated problems that attract an increasing amount of attention. Due to rising concern, the problem area of health also calls for more activity—according to our subjects' judgments, and—as can be concluded—it has at the same time become more stressful.

Highly significant, from the economic point of view, is the contrast between efficiency of health advancement measures and emergence of diseases and risk factors. In closed systems, rising efficiency of orientation and control should mean reduction of problems. In the area of health, as described, problems rise despite progress achieved in recognizing and coping with them. More problems despite more activity and more efficiency—this can only be the characteristic of an emotionally frustrating and cognitively overcharging situation. The Greeks had a special symbol for such situations: Hydra, the Lernaen snake; if a bold hero arrived and chopped off one of her heads, two new ones grew in its place.

**Table 2.** Comparisons between Incidence of Problems, Control Activity, Efficiency and Problem Generation in the Years 1910 and 1980 (Percentage of undecided answers omitted)

|  | Percentage | |
| --- | --- | --- |
|  | 1910 | 1980 |
| *Incidence of problems* | | |
| more hazards | 11 | 53 |
| more diseases | 4 | 62 |
| *Control activity* | | |
| more prevention | 4 | 93 |
| more treatment | 4 | 92 |
| *Efficiency* | | |
| higher success of treatment | 3 | 81 |
| *Problem generation* | | |
| more negative side-effects of treatment | 11 | 61 |

It is quite clear that this is not the forum in which to argue about the decay of health and happiness in modern life, or the futility of biotechnology. Social and political issues that are touched by our results should not be discussed here. What can be demonstrated, however, is that concepts from our economics model can be applied successfully to complex situations, that the model can guide the investigator during empirical assessments, and that the data collected on the basis of the model can be submitted to economic evaluations, yielding estimates of psychic load and indications of the origins and the structure of the load.

## Stress-inducing and Stress-reducing Effects of Planning: An Experimental Study

Field investigations, like our interviews on health advancement measures, have their merits, but they also have their shortcomings. Because hard data are lacking, there is no detailed assessment of temporal sequences of behavior and no reliable discrimination of individual patterns. For a process analysis, which also takes individual strategies into account, one has to go to the laboratory in order to utilize advanced methods of behavior registration. And, in order to control the situation, the task situation has to be specified. On the other hand, the task situation must not be too restricted, in order to permit the subject some choice of strategy and to utilize his or her routines and skills.

A study conducted by Wolfgang Battmann has been selected for presentation here because it meets these requirements and offers an example of application of economic reasoning to *individual processes of coping* with demands (for further details see Battmann, 1984).

The subjects in Battmann's experiment had to play the role of the supervisor of a chain of department stores. Within an experimental day, the supervisor had to visit twelve stores that were scattered over the city. In each store, two problems waited for the subject's decision: hiring personnel and accounting or marketing. Of course, the subjects did not actually travel through Berlin. The entire task environment was simulated on a display, which was connected to a DEC 11/40 laboratory computer. A plan of the city could be exposed, where both the locations of stores and of the subject were indicated. Once a store was reached, the local problems were presented, and the subjects could order additional information which they might need for a rational decision. Since the whole environment was simulated, and the subjects communicated with the task system by means of a keyboard, when they made a decision, ordered information, or indicated a change of location, the complete stream of their behavior could be registered on-line. Not only were performance data collected automatically, but subjective data were processed on-line as well. Questions concerning emotional state, causal attribution of failures, and so forth, were exposed on the screen, and answers were given by pointing to defined fields on the monitor. In addition, physiological measures—heart rate and electrodermal activity among them—were registered as indices of load.

For a laboratory setup, this is a rather complex design. Only one detail will be reported, in order to illustrate our main theoretical issue in another domain, the impact of *planning*. Planning is a favorite topic in cognitive psychology (cf. Wilensky, 1983). Good plans lead to efficient performance. Good plans give confidence and drive anxiety away. So, good plans reduce stress. This is what one reads in the literature. It is the bright side of planning. We wondered about the dark side. Constructing a good plan may be hard work. Does it pay off? Constructing a plan goes along with confrontation with high demands and one's own insufficiencies. Would that not evoke anxiety? Again, asking these questions means playing our old game of balancing benefits and costs, of estimating economy. A chance for planning was offered in the supervisor environment in arranging the route through the city and fixing appointments at the different shops. By saving time and keeping appointments, subjects could earn extra money. If they came too early, they either lost time in waiting or they had to visit another shop first and then return again. If they came too late, they found the shop closed. In order to avoid delays, each appointment could be changed; but a change became effective only after half an hour of system time; it thus had to be made well in advance.

All subjects were familiarized with the task before the experiment was started. But one half of the subjects received special planning instructions. They were explicitly told to plan extensively, to think about intermediate goals, and to enter their time schedule, at the beginning of each trial, on the screen beside the city map. The city map and their schedule were not exposed permanently. However, the subjects were free to expose them whenever they had finished their tasks at a local shop, to check whether they were still on schedule, and to change appointments, if necessary. The other half of the subjects was not instructed to plan, although they were free to do so. These subjects could not enter their schedule beside the map, but they could memorize their schedule if they had one, and the map was also available to them on request.

Individual capacity, or competence, is an important factor in calculating trade-offs and estimating stress. We had no special technique for measuring planning competence. But we administered a verbal intelligence test (Amthauer, 1971) to the subjects, and both groups, with and without planning instructions, were divided into two subgroups by the overall median of intelligence. In this way, a 2 × 2 design resulted, and, from a total of 72 subjects, 18 were assigned to each cell.

Again, a small selection of the theoretically most illustrative data:

1. One of the *performance* measures related to planning is driving time. Driving time corresponds to the length of the route taken. Figure 1 presents the scores for three consecutive trials. All subjects improve over time. Subjects with planning instructions are faster throughout, and higher intelligence is correlated with higher speed in both conditions. The same effect of planning instructions was found with another performance measure, not reported here in detail, punctuality, that is, the number of appointments kept. This is, again, the bright side of planning. Planning, as demonstrated in these data, aids efficiency.

2. What about *costs?* Figure 5 shows an indicator of involvement—the number of appointments changed over the three trials. Evidently, groups with planning instructions are more active in organizing their way. They control their time schedules more often—as can be seen from other data, such as the frequency of exposing the city map—and initiate more changes. It should be noted that the lower intelligence subjects are less active, especially if they did not receive planning instructions. These

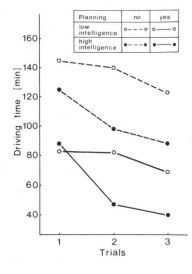

**Figure 4.** Total driving time as index of efficiency (planning factor: $F$ (1,60) = 14.98, $p < .01$, intelligence factor: $F$ (1,60) = 4.92, $p < .05$, interaction intelligence/planning: n.s.).

data give evidence for the amount of required planning that has to be traded in for higher efficiency.

3. How is the *tradeoff* between planning efforts and gain in performance? We asked the subjects themselves. One subjective indicator of stress was the experience of time pressure. Presented in Figure 6 are subjective statements, averaged over trials, in which we find an interaction effect. A similar tendency is exhibited in other subjective estimates as well. Higher intelligence subjects feel more at ease if they are involved in planning, but lower intelligence subjects feel more relaxed if they are not.

4. Is this just a subjective illusion? Probably not. Figure 7 shows a *physiological measure of involvement,* or relaxation, respectively, by measuring heart period changes. Decreases in heart period, that is, the reductions of interbeat intervals, are complementary to increases in heart rate, and indicate a rising level of psychophysiological activation. In this study, scores during planning activity were contrasted to scores during the execution of the other experimental tasks; thus, the data given in Figure 7 are differences in heart periods during planning time, on the one hand, and during the residual testing time, on the other, separated for the three consecutive trials.

More intelligent subjects start on a higher level of activation, if planning, and then relax as time goes by. Those more intelligent subjects who do not plan start from a lower level and become more activated

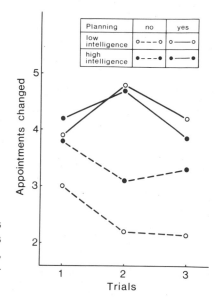

**Figure 5.** Number of appointments changed as index of operational costs (planning factor: $F$ (1,60) = 11.60, $p < .01$), intelligence factor and interaction planning/intelligence: n.s.).

over trials. The contrary is true for subjects lower in intelligence—they become more activated if they engage in planning, and relax if they do not.

What is the conclusion? Organizing and controlling one's work schedule is an extra task. Coping with this task constitutes an extra load.

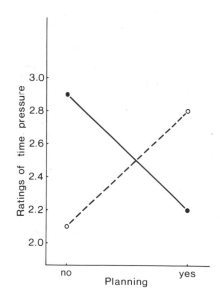

**Figure 6.** Attribution of failures to time pressure as index of experienced stress (ratings on 4-point scales, interaction planning/intelligence: $F$ (1,60) = 4.59, $p < .05$). Low intelligence (o---o) High intelligence (●——●).

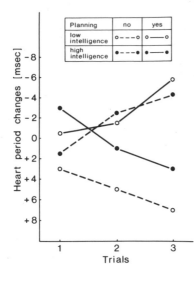

**Figure 7.** Heart period changes during planning operations as indices of objective strain (differences between scores during planning time and during the residual test trial; negative heart period changes equivalent to increases in heart rate; interaction planning/intelligence: $F(1,60) = 5.29$, $p < .05$, interaction planning/intelligence/trials: $F(2,112) = 3.99$, $p < .05$).

Not coping results in continued confrontation with disorganization and frustration. To carry the extra load of coping may well pay off as compared to suffering from disorganization. But this is only true for those who are strong enough to carry the extra load; these are the more intelligent subjects. It is not true for the less capable subjects. By planning, they gain performance efficiency and satisfaction from improved outcome, but they lose personal comfort. Better outcome for more strain—this is a debatable tradeoff. Possibly, lower capacity individuals are better off if they do not engage in planning; they give up the benefits of good organization but also save the costs of organizing, which are so difficult for them to tolerate.

Of course, such interpretations depend on the time perspective, the impact of performance outcomes, and the evaluation of resources invested. Organizing a fictitious working day in a laboratory offers intermediate incentives and has hardly any long-term consequences; so there are no persuasive reasons for trading personal comfort during the experiment for performance efficiency. There are other situations where most people would agree that extreme efforts are justified in face of highly salient long-term consequences—for example, saving a child's life. However, it can be argued that economic principles have been operating in the individual decisions on the level of effort. In general, it was intended to demonstrate that theories of stress can be promoted by taking such economic principles into account.

# References

Amthauer, R. (1971). *Der Intelligenz-Struktur-Test 70* [Test for the structure of intelligence 70]. Göttingen: Hogrefe.

Appley, M. H. (1967). Invited commentary. In M. H. Appley & R. Trumbull (Eds.), *Psychological stress: Issues in research* (pp. 169–172). New York: Appleton-Century-Crofts.

Battmann, W. (1984). Regulation und Fehlregulation im Verhalten. IX. Entlastung und Belastung durch Planung. IX.[Behavioral regulation and disregulation. Load reduction and load enforcement by planning]. *Psychologische Beiträge, 26,* 672–691.

Breznitz, S. (1984). *Cry wolf: The psychology of false alarms.* Hillsdale, NJ: Erlbaum.

French, J. R. P., & Kahn, R. L. (1962). A programmatic approach to studying the industrial environment and mental health. *Journal of Social Issues, 18,* 1–47.

Glass, D. C., Singer, J. E., & Friedman, L. N. (1969). Psychic costs of adaptation to an environmental stressor. *Journal of Personality and Social Psychology, 12,* 200–210.

Kahn, R. L., Wolfe, D. M., Quinn, R. P., Snoek, J. D., & Rosenthal, R. A. (1964). *Organizational stress: Studies in role conflict and ambiguity.* New York: Wiley.

Lazarus, R. S. (1966). *Psychological stress and the coping process.* New York: McGraw-Hill.

Lazarus, R. S., & Launier, R. (1978). Stress-related transactions between person and environment. In L. A. Pervin & M. Lewis (Eds.), *Perspectives in interactional psychology* (pp. 287–327). New York: Plenum Press.

Lumsden, D. P. (1975). Towards a systems model of stress: Feedback from an anthropological study of the impact of Ghana's Volta River project. In I. G. Sarason & C. D. Spielberger (Eds.), *Stress and anxiety* (Vol. 2, pp. 191–228). New York: Wiley.

McGrath, J. E. (1976). Stress and behavior in organizations. In M. D. Dunette (Ed.), *Handbook of industrial and organizational psychology* (pp. 1351–1395). Chicago: Rand McNally.

Mündelein, H., & Schönpflug, W. (1984). Okologische Validierung eines im Laboratorium nachgebildeten Arbeitsplatzes mit Hilfe des Fragebogens zur Arbeitsanalyse (FAA) [Ecological validity of a laboratory setting that simulates an office—an application of the Position-Analysis-Questionnaire]. *Psychologie und Praxis/Zeitschrift für Organisationspsychologie, 28,* 2–10.

Neufeld, R. W. (1976). Evidence of stress as a function of experimentally altered appraisal of stimulus aversiveness and coping adequacy. *Journal of Personality and Social Psychology, 33,* 632–646.

Schönpflug, W. (1979). Regulation und Fehlregulation im Verhalten. I. Verhaltensstruktur, Effizienz und Belastung—theoretische Grundlagen eines Untersuchungsprogramms [Behavioral regulation and disregulation. I. Structure of behavior, efficiency and stress—a theoretical conception for a research program]. *Psychologische Beiträge, 21,* 174–202.

Schönpflug, W. (1983). Coping efficiency and situational demands. In R. Hockey (Ed.), *Stress and fatigue in human performance* (pp. 299–330). Chichester: Wiley.

Schönpflug, W. (1984). Regulation und Fehlregulation im Verhalten. X. Entlastung und Belastung durch gesundheitsfördernde Maßnahmen [Behavioral regulation and disregulation. X. Reduction and induction of load by health advancement measures]. *Psychologische Beiträge, 26,* 692–721.

Schulz, P. (1979). Regulation und Fehlregulation im Verhalten. II. Stress durch Fehlregulation. [Behavioral regulation and disregulation. II. Stress following disregulation]. *Psychologische Beiträge, 21,* 579–621.

Wilensky, R. (1983). *Planning and understanding.* Reading, MA: Addison-Wesley.

# PART III

# Psychophysiological Considerations

*The introduction of psychological considerations in the study of stress has contributed to its identification, its definition of cause/effect relationships, and its potential for control. The early pioneers had determined the pathological end points of severe stress and, then, the involvement of glandular systems in the reaction process. Refinement was to come in the definition of stressor in lesser degree and the mechanisms through which "fight" or "flight" was to be achieved. Further, the interpretation of stressfulness and reactions short of "fight" or "flight" were open invitations to the interests and applications of psychologists. The transition from pathological analysis to control of stressors as well as stress reactions is represented by the chapters that follow.*

*Frankenhaeuser reports further delineation of catecholamine and corticosteroid production in response to cognitive appraisal of stressor vis-à-vis coping resources, convinced that the* psychological *characteristics are primary determinants of the response. Her separation of* mental *stress from* physical *stress and establishment of correlated secretion production begin "identifying the psychological characteristics of different environmental demands." They also assist in determining where the "buffering effects of control" are to be introduced.*

*Scheuch reminds us of the role that "needs" play in setting the stage for stress and the reactions elicited by "interpretation-specific causes" and "somato-specific causes." Promise of control arises from the development of coping strategies for the former and conditioning somatic processes for the latter. A cluster analysis of 13 traits, action-oriented versus demand-specific, shows relationships to somatic parameters and to experience parameters. Differential* level *and* time *courses also establish independence of the physiological and psychological processes. He finds promise in these correlations for control of stress and development of the individual.*

*Another expression of stress does not require laboratory analyses or personality profiles. Scherer discusses the relationships between the elements of vocalization*

**99**

*and the physiological changes produced by emotion and stress. This example of juxtaposition of "various functions of emotions with different bodily systems" emphasizes the phylogenetic developmental patterns of response. However, these vocal expressions are influenced by the perception of a situation and the amount of conscious control exercised through the emotion that has been aroused. To this end, he would treat stress as another negative emotion.*

*Recognizing another expression of stress—through performance—Guttmann uses laboratory and field studies to ascertain the predictability of performance under stress and the selection of performers through laboratory studies. Both the interpretation of the task and of a person's own level of activation play significant roles in his "ergopsychometry"—the determination of discrepancies between performance under neutral versus load conditions. His concept of "Training Champion" will stimulate further research and application in many performance settings. The promise of overcoming stress through "attributional style" and the introduction of voluntary control of cortical negativity underscore the emphasis of the section on emerging techniques for the control of stress through an understanding of the psychophysiological mechanisms involved.*

# CHAPTER 6

# A Psychobiological Framework for Research on Human Stress and Coping

## MARIANNE FRANKENHAEUSER

## Endocrine Markers of Stressful Person–Environment Interactions

This chapter is based on research carried out in the author's laboratory during the past decades. The central theme is the experimental study of how environmental factors influence human health and behavior. Special attention is given to the health hazards associated with demands on human adaptation to the rapid rate of change in modern society. The approach is multidisciplinary, focusing on the dynamics of stressful person–environment interactions, viewed from social, psychological, and biological perspectives.

One of the key notions in our approach to stress is that neuroendocrine responses to the psychosocial environment reflect its emotional impact on the individual. The emotional impact, in turn, is determined by the person's cognitive appraisal of the severity of the demands in relation to his or her own coping resources.

MARIANNE FRANKENHAEUSER ● Psychology Division, Department of Psychiatry and Psychology, Karolinska Institutet, Stockholm S-10691, Sweden. The research reported in this chapter has been supported by grants to the author from the John D. and Catherine T. MacArthur Foundation, the Swedish Work Environment Fund, and the Swedish Medical Research Council.

**101**

Advances in biomedical techniques have made it possible to obtain blood samples from human subjects engaged in their daily activities and, thus, to monitor how hormones and other neuroactive compounds change during exposure to various demands (e.g., Dimsdale & Moss, 1980). Other new ambulatory recording techniques enable monitoring of nearly all organs in the body, including the brain, from subjects moving freely while exposed to stressors of different kinds. Thus, the individuals themselves serve as measuring rods, that is, sensitive instruments, which help to identify factors in the environment which increase bodily wear and tear.

An important feature of our research strategy is the combination of laboratory and field studies. In the former type of study, specific problems are extracted from natural settings and brought into the laboratory for systematic examination. The latter takes our laboratory-based experimental techniques into the field and applies them to persons engaged in their daily activities. Both approaches involve examining individual response patterns under controlled environmental conditions, securing concurrent measures of responses at the psychological and biological levels, and relating these to more enduring characteristics of the person, including susceptibility to disease. In this context, techniques for measuring endocrine and other bodily responses are seen as tools by which new insights can be gained into the dynamics of person–environment interactions.

Recent advances in neuroendocrinology pertinent to behavior have brought about a reorientation of research in the stress field. Until recently, the brain and the endocrine system were generally viewed as separate entities. The brain was seen as mediating the organism's relation to the external environment via behavior. The endocrine system, on the other hand, was seen as oriented toward the body's internal environment. Thanks to the contributions of Nobel laureates Roger Guillemin (1978) and Andrew Schally (1978), new insights have been gained into the pathways and neuroendocrine mechanisms by which the brain controls the endocrine system. We are now beginning to grasp the coordinated functioning of the nervous and endocrine systems in the adaptation of the whole organism to environmental conditions (cf. Hamburg, Elliott, & Parron, 1982).

In the early days of psychoendocrinology, the common strategy was to study the response of a single hormone to a variety of laboratory and natural stressors. As techniques for assessing different hormones have become available, approaches are gradually changing to studying the patterning of a broad spectrum of endocrine responses. These developments have occurred during the past two decades. In addition to the adrenal-medullary and the adrenal-cortical hormones, a number of pituitary and hypothalamic hormones have been found to be responsive to psychological demands (cf. Rose, 1985). Techniques for their assessment have been developed (e.g., radioimmunologic, enzymatic, mass-spectrometric, gaschromatographic and fluorimetric techniques) and have opened up an array of new research possibilities.

Research in our laboratory has focused on the psychological significance of the two adrenal systems. We will consider each of the systems separately, and, then, discuss the balance between them under different psychosocial conditions.

## Adrenal Hormones: Cornerstones in Stress Research

Already, much has been learned about the role of the sympathetic-adrenal-medullary system, with the secretion of catecholamines, and the pituitary-adrenal-cortical system, with the secretion of corticosteroids, in mediating human responses to changing circumstances. Catecholamines and corticosteroids are of key importance in several ways: as sensitive indicators of the stressfulness of person–environment interactions, as regulators of vital bodily functions and, under some circumstances, as mediators of bodily reactions leading to pathological states. In short, the effects of the hormones may be adaptive, but they may also be harmful, particularly in promoting cardiovascular pathology.

An issue of current interest is whether the two systems do, in fact, respond selectively to different emotional and behavioral demands and, if so, which activators are critical for each of the systems. Since most of the psychoendocrinologists engaged in stress research have restricted their work to one of the two adrenal systems, knowledge about their relative sensitivity to different demands has been meager until recently.

Figure 1 gives a schematic representation of the pathways from the brain to the adrenal medulla and cortex. Any threat or challenge that a person perceives in the environment triggers a chain of neuroendocrine events. Messages are sent from the brain via the sympathetic nervous system to the adrenal medulla, which secretes two catecholamines—adrenaline and noradrenaline. Another route takes messages to the adrenal cortex, which secretes corticosteroids, e.g., cortisol. This route is more complex, involving secretion of the adrenal corticotropic hormone (ACTH) from the pituitary gland and the corticotropin releasing factor (CRF) from the hypothalamus.

Catecholamines and cortisol can be measured in blood and in urine. Estimates in urine are particularly useful when studying people under naturalistic circumstances. Urine samples can be obtained under field conditions—for example, in the factory, in the office, at the day-care center—without interfering with the person's daily routines. Urinary measurements do not reflect momentary changes, but they are useful

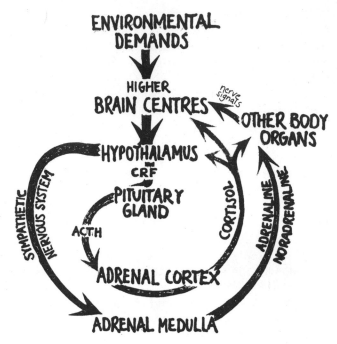

**Figure 1.** Schematic representation of pathways from the brain to the adrenal systems involved in stress: (1) the sympathetic-adrenal medullary system and (2) the pituitary-adrenal cortical system.

for assessing the total load, integrated over one or several hours, that a particular environmental setting exerts on an individual.

## Activation of the Adrenal-Medullary Response

The susceptibility of the sympathetic-adrenal system to both psychological and physical factors was first demonstrated by Walter B. Cannon in the early 1930s. His emergency function theory of adrenal-medullary activity, states that many of the physiological effects of adrenal-medullary secretion serve to prepare the organism for fight or flight by speeding up the heart and increasing blood pressure and the availability of glucose. These changes, which evolved from the fight or flight response which helped our ancestors to survive, are involved in the human body's response to the psychosocial demands in modern society, too.

Our experiments show increased catecholamine output in subjects exposed to a variety of stressors, including noise, electric shock, parachute jumping, radial acceleration, crowded trains, performance tasks involving time pressure or cognitive conflict, and so forth (see review by Frankenhaeuser, 1979). Analysis of the "critical elements" in these diverse situations has made it clear that it is the emotional experience, whether pleasant or unpleasant, evoked by these different situations, that induces the catecholamine increase. In other words, the psychological characteristics of the situation, rather than the physical conditions *per se*, determine the adrenal-medullary response. For example, conditions of overload and underload, although each others' opposite in terms of physical characteristics, are similar in that both are experienced as disturbing deviations from the level of stimulation to which the person is cognitively set and emotionally tuned. Accordingly, both underload and overload trigger the adrenal-medullary response (Frankenhaeuser, Nordheden, Myrsten, & Post, 1971).

Of the two amines, adrenaline is more sensitive than noradrenaline to mental stress. Noradrenaline, too, may increase under mental stress, but only when stress is intense. In other words, the threshold for noradrenaline release in response to psychological demands is generally much higher than that for adrenaline. In contrast, noradrenaline is more sensitive to physical stressors, such as exercise or the cold-pressor test. These conclusions are based on a series of experiments in our laboratory, where both subjective responses and catecholamine secretion have been measured (reviewed by Frankenhaeuser, 1975, 1979).

A hypothesis, put forward in the early days of psychoendocrinology, was that adrenaline and noradrenaline were released selectively under different emotional experiences. Adrenaline was considered to be specifically related to anxious reactions and noradrenaline to aggressive reactions (Ax, 1953; Funkenstein, 1956). Later studies, however (Levi, 1965; Pátkai, 1971), which were specifically designed to test this hypothesis, failed to confirm it. Instead, adrenaline secretion was shown to increase in a number of emotional states, not only anger and fear, but also elation and amusement.

## Activation of the Corticosteroid Response

The sensitivity of the pituitary-adrenal system to adverse conditions, such as immobilization, heat and cold, was established already in the pioneering animal studies of Hans Selye in the late 1930s (Selye, 1950). As underscored by John Mason (1975), the situations activating the adrenal-cortical system in animals had some common denominators: they were novel, strange, and unfamiliar to the animal. The animal's state could be described in terms of helplessness, uncertainty, and lack of adequate responses for controlling adverse influences. These conclusions were supported by experiments where the psychological element of uncertainty had been eliminated. Under these circumstances, there was no increase in adrenal-cortical activity.

Results from more recent human studies are consistent with the early animal data. Thus, cortisol generally increases in human subjects exposed to novel and unfamiliar situations, which evoke feelings of uncertainty and anxiety (Frankenhaeuser, 1980, 1983; Rose, 1985). This was the case in a study in our laboratory (Lundberg, de Chateau, Winberg, & Frankenhaeuser, 1981) of a group of three-year-old children who spent the day in the hospital with their parents for a medical checkup. A subgroup of children responded with anxiety when told that they would be separated from their parents for a brief period of psychological testing. Although these anxious children were allowed to remain with their parents, the threat of separation induced a significantly greater increase in cortisol in these children than in the other children in the group. These results are in agreement with those of Rose (1985) in showing that anticipation is a very provocative stimulus for cortisol release.

Studies of psychiatric patients have established that cortisol levels tend to be high in states of anxiety and depression (Sachar, 1975). Phobics, too, respond with increased cortisol secretion when exposed to pictures of the objects that they fear (e.g., spiders, snakes, blood), as shown in experiments in our laboratory (Fredrikson, Sundin, & Frankenhaeuser, 1985).

A point of special interest is that environmental circumstances characterized by predictability and controllability can *suppress* the secretion of corticosteroids. This was first demonstrated in animal studies (Coover, Goldman, & Levine, 1971; Levine, Goldman, & Coover, 1972). In essence, unpredictability was shown to activate the pituitary-adrenal system, a change from predictable to unpredictable events being sufficient to increase corticosteroid secretion. Conversely, when expectancies were fulfilled and the situation was predictable, pituitary-adrenal activity was suppressed. Recent studies of human subjects in low-control versus high-control situations demonstrate a principally similar bidirectional pituitary-adrenal response.

## Patterns of Endocrine Stress Responses

As already pointed out, the pattern of adrenaline and noradrenaline secretion from the adrenal medulla tends to be rather similar, irrespective of the quality or nature of the emotional experience. In other words, intense positive and negative experiences evoke essentially the same response. However, the balance between sympathetic-adrenal and pituitary-adrenal activity varies predictably with the different emotions elicited by different environmental demands. It is an exciting task for modern psychoendocrinology to identify the psychological characteristics of environmental and psychological factors that selectively activate either the sympathetic-adrenal or the pituitary-adrenal system.

Studies in our laboratory, based on factor analyses of self-reports obtained from subjects in a large number of different situations, point to two major components of the stress experience: effort and distress (Lundberg & Frankenhaeuser, 1980). The effort factor involves elements of interest, engagement, and determination. In short, effort implies an active way of coping, a striving to gain and maintain control. The distress factor involves elements of dissatisfaction, boredom, uncertainty, and anxiety. It is associated with a passive attitude and feelings of helplessness.

Effort and distress may be experienced either one at a time, or they may occur together in one and the same situation. The interesting point is that these two aspects of the stress experience seem to be differentially associated with catecholamine and cortisol release. The psychoendocrine relationships can be conceptualized as shown in Figure 2.

*Effort with distress* tends to be accompanied by an increase of both catecholamine *and* cortisol secretion. This is the state typical of daily hassles, that of striving to gain and maintain control. In working life, it commonly occurs among people engaged in repetitious, machine-paced jobs on the assembly line or in highly routinized work as, for example, at a computer terminal.

*Effort without distress* is a joyous state, characterized by active and successful coping, high job involvement, and a high degree of personal control. It is accompanied by increased catecholamine secretion, whereas cortisol secretion may be suppressed.

*Distress without effort* implies feeling helpless, losing control, giving up. It is generally accompanied by increased cortisol secretion, but catecholamines may be elevated, too. This is the endocrine profile typical of depressed patients, and it commonly occurs also in other states characterized by passivity and learned helplessness (Seligman, 1975).

To summarize, Figure 2 tells us *first* that the endocrine profile varies with the psychological significance of the situation, and *second* that adrenaline is a more general (less specific) response than cortisol to situational demands which are perceived differently. Thus, adrenaline, but not cortisol, increases in pleasantly engaging as well as in distressing situations.

A key question is how to facilitate achieving a state of effort without distress. Our hypothesis is that personal control is an important modu-

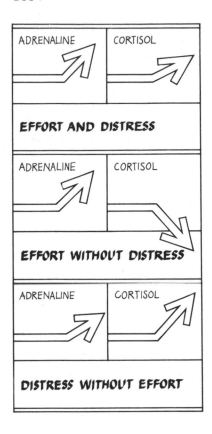

**Figure 2.** Schematic representation of adrenal-medullary and adrenal-cortical responses to effort and distress.

lating factor in this regard. A lack of control is almost invariably associated with feelings of distress, whereas personal control tends to stimulate effort and reduce negative emotions. Insofar as control versus lack of control changes the balance between effort and distress experience, it is likely to change the balance between sympathetic-adrenal and pituitary-adrenal activity as well.

The modulating influence of personal control on the endocrine profile will be illustrated by data from two laboratory experiments. One was a low-control situation, designed to induce both effort and distress (Lundberg & Forsman, 1979). The other was a high-control situation, designed to induce effort without distress (Frankenhaeuser, Lundberg, & Forsman, 1980).

In the low-control situation, a group of students performed a vigilance task, which consisted of pressing a key in response to each randomly occurring intensity change in a weak light signal. The situation was characterized by monotony and unpredictability.

In the high-control situation, the same subjects performed a choice–reaction task. Great care was taken to create a situation characterized by a high degree of personal control and feelings of competence and mastery. This was achieved by giving each subject the opportunity to choose and to modify the stimulus rate so as to maintain an optimal pace throughout the session. According to self-reports, experimental arrangements were successful in creating a work situation where all subjects felt pleasantly challenged, perceived themselves as being in complete control, and felt motivated to perform at their best.

The results (Figure 3) showed that the low-control task induced both effort and distress. The high-control task induced effort, whereas distress fell below the "baseline" ratings obtained in a nonwork situation.

The neuroendocrine pattern, too, differed in the two situations. During the low-control task, which induced both effort and distress,

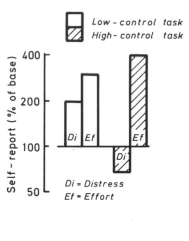

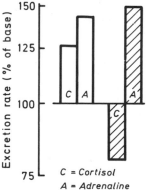

**Figure 3.** Mean values for self-reports of distress and effort (upper diagram) and cortisol and adrenaline excretion (lower diagram). Values obtained during a low-control task and a high-control task are expressed as percentages of values obtained during a baseline condition. (From Frankenhaeuser, 1983.)

adrenaline as well as cortisol increased. During the high-control task, the effort invested in performance was accompanied by adrenaline increase, whereas the lack of distress was reflected in the decrease of cortisol. Thus, in this high-control situation, the sympathetic-adrenal system was activated, while the pituitary-adrenal system was "put to rest."

A similar difference in neuroendocrine profile was found in a study (Johansson & Sandén, 1982) of control-room operators, who were engaged in low-control and high-control tasks in a steel factory. The results are also consistent with those of Ursin, Baade, and Levine (1978), who identified a "cortisol factor" and a "catecholamine factor" in a study of parachute trainees.

There is general agreement between these results from human studies and studies of animals in controllable and uncontrollable situations (e.g., Seligman, 1975; Weiss, 1970), as well as studies of dominant and submissive animals (Henry & Stephens, 1977). According to the animal model proposed by Henry, the sympathetic-adrenal system is activated when the organism is challenged in its control of the environment, whereas the pituitary-adrenal system is associated with the conservation–withdrawal response. Recent evidence in support of this model has been presented by von Holst, Fuchs, and Stöhr (1983) in studies of tree shrews. They found that dominant animals, in control of their territory, were high in catecholamines and low in corticosteroids. In submissive, anxious animals, the hormone balance was reversed, that is, corticosteroid levels were high and catecholamine levels low.

## Personal Control and Health Outcomes

The beneficial effects of personal control on well-being, efficiency, and health have been amply documented, but the mechanisms by which control exerts its buffering effects are poorly understood. Speculation on this issue generally involves catecholamine and cortisol release. Insofar as the ability to exert control counteracts excessive release of catecholamines, this might protect the cardiovascular system from damage (cf. Krantz, Lundberg, & Frankenhaeuser, in press). Similarly, a control-mediated change in balance between catecholamines and cortisol could have a bearing on health. It has been suggested (Steptoe, 1981) that damage to the myocardium may require the simultaneous release of catecholamines and cortisol. Hence, the fact that,—as previously discussed,—cortisol tends to be low in highly controllable situations could account for some of the buffering effects of personal control. Such a neuroendocrine mechanism could, in fact, explain the epidemiological data (Karasek, 1979; Theorell, Lind, Lundberg, Christensson, & Edhag,

1981) showing that high job demands have adverse health consequences *only when combined with* low decision latitude, that is, low control over job-related decisions.

## The "Unwinding" Process

Yet another mechanism by which personal control might exert its positive influence on health outcomes has to do with the ability to "unwind" after stressful encounters. Results indicate (cf. Frankenhaeuser, 1981) that being able to exercise control facilitates the process of unwinding, thereby reducing the aftereffects of short-term stress.

The speed at which a person unwinds after, for example, a day at work, will influence the total load on the organism. A quick return to neuroendocrine and physiological baselines implies an "economic" response, in the sense that physiological resources are "demobilized" as soon as they are no longer needed. Conditions shown to slow down the unwinding process include repetitive, uncontrollable work situations, such as prevail on the assembly line and at the computer terminal (Frankenhaeuser, 1981). Such aftereffects mean that stress at work is carried over into leisure time. It may also mean a greater total load on the cardiovascular system.

## Who Benefits from Personal Control?

The study of interindividual differences in stress responses to controllable and uncontrollable conditions may throw light on the mechanisms by which control exerts its actions on the organism. For instance, there is an interesting association between the benefits of control and the rushed, competitive, aggressive Type A behavior, which is considered a risk factor in coronary heart disease. The factors linking this behavior pattern to coronary heart disease have not yet been identified, but high catecholamine levels are assumed to play a significant role. On the psychological level, the issue of control has been emphasized by David Glass (1977), who points to fear of losing control as a major threat in the life of Type A persons. Conversely, as shown in our laboratory, Type A persons excel in achievement situations when given complete control over work pace (Frankenhaeuser *et al.*, 1980). Their physiological stress responses, however, were no more intense than those of their Type B counterparts, although the latter performed less effectively. These experimental results may be interpreted as showing that the Type A person, when in control of the situation, sets his or her standards high, copes

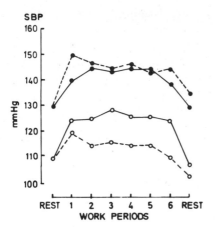

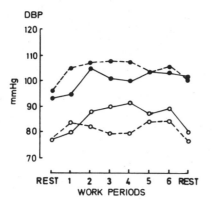

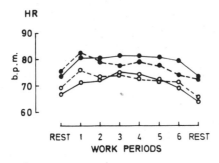

**Figure 4.** Systolic blood pressure (SBP), diastolic blood pressure (DBP) and heart rate (HR) in normotensives (open circles) and borderline hypertensives (closed circles) at rest and while performing a task under externally paced (solid lines) and self-paced (dotted lines) conditions. *Note.* From "Personal control over work pace—circulatory, neuroendocrine and subjective responses in borderline hypertension" by G. Bohlin, K. Eliasson, P. Hjemdahl, K. Klein, M. Fredrikson, and M. Frankenhaeuser(1986), *Journal of Hypertension, 4,* 295–305. Copyright 1986 by Gower Medical Publishing Limited. Reprinted by permission.

effectively with the self-selected heavy load, and does so without mobilizing excessive physiological resources.

These conclusions are consistent with those drawn by Margaret Chesney (1983), who studied white-collar workers in an aerospace plant. Her results indicated that Type A workers, who rated themselves as having a high degree of autonomy on the job, had lower systolic and diastolic pressures than Type Bs. When, on the other hand, autonomy in the work place was rated as low, Type As were found to have higher blood pressure than Type Bs.

Although relationships between personal control and coronary-prone behavior have been extensively studied, less is known about other vulnerable groups, for example, hypertensives, in this regard. In a recent study (Bohlin, Eliasson, Hjemdahl, Klein, Fredrikson, & Frankenhaeuser, in press), we compared cardiovascular responses of borderline hypertensives and normotensives while they performed a task under two different conditions: self-pacing or external pacing. As expected, both groups responded to the task by increased systolic and diastolic blood pressure and heart rate (Figure 4). There was, however, an interesting difference between the groups with regard to the influence of personal control. In the normotensive group, the rise in systolic blood pressure was significantly greater when the task was externally paced than when it was self-paced. In contrast, personal control did not influence the circulatory response of the borderline hypertensives; their blood-pressure rise was of the same magnitude regardless of the pacing condition. It is also noteworthy that, irrespective of pacing condition, the diastolic pressure remained elevated for a prolonged period after the task session in the borderline group but not in the normotensive group.

Borderline hypertensives, as a group, run an increased risk of developing established hypertension. On the basis of our results, one could argue that the vulnerability of borderline hypertensives might be due in part to their inability to benefit from conditions allowing personal control over achievement demands.

# References

Ax, A. (1953). The physiological differentiation between fear and anger in humans. *Psychosomatic Medicine, 15*, 433–442.

Bohlin, G., Eliasson, K., Hjemdahl, P., Klein, K., Fredrikson, M., & Frankenhaeuser, M. (1986). Personal control over work pace—circulatory, neuroendocrine and subjective responses in borderline hypertension. *Journal of Hypertension, 4*, 295–305.

Chesney, M. A. (1983). Occupational setting and coronary-prone behavior in men and women. In T. M. Dembroski, T. H. Schmidt, & G. Blumchen (Eds.), *Biobehavioral bases of coronary heart disease* (pp. 79–90). Basel: Karger.

Coover, G. D., Goldman, L., & Levine, S. (1971). Plasma corticosterone increases produced by extinction of operant behavior in rats. *Physiology and Behavior, 6,* 261–263.

Dimsdale, J. E., & Moss, J. (1980). Short-term catecholamine response to psychological stress. *Psychosomatic Medicine, 42,* 493–497.

Frankenhaeuser, M. (1975). Experimental approaches to the study of catecholamines and emotion. In L. Levi (Ed.), *Emotions—Their parameters and measurement* (pp. 209–234). New York: Raven Press.

Frankenhaeuser, M. (1979). Psychoneuroendocrine approaches to the study of emotion as related to stress and coping. In H. E. Howe & R. A. Dienstbier (Eds.), *Nebraska Symposium on Motivation 1978* (pp. 123–161). Lincoln: University of Nebraska Press.

Frankenhaeuser, M. (1980). Psychobiological aspects of life stress. In S. Levine & H. Ursin (Eds.), *Coping and health* (pp. 203–223). New York: Plenum Press.

Frankenhaeuser, M. (1981). Coping with stress at work. *International Journal of Health Services, 11,* 491–510.

Frankenhaeuser, M. (1983). The sympathetic-adrenal and pituitary-adrenal response to challenge: Comparison between the sexes. In T. M. Dembroski, T. H. Schmidt & G. Blinchen, (Eds.), *Biobehavioral bases of coronary heart disease* (pp. 91–105). Basel: Karger.

Frankenhaeuser, M., Nordheden, B., Myrsten, A-L., & Post, B. (1971). Psychophysiological reactions to understimulation and overstimulation. *Acta Psychologica, 35,* 298–308.

Frankenhaeuser, M., Lundberg, U., & Forsman, L. (1980). Dissociation between sympathetic-adrenal and pituitary-adrenal responses to an achievement situation characterized by high controllability: Comparison between Type A and Type B males and females. *Biological Psychology, 10,* 79–91.

Fredrikson, M., Sundin, Ö., & Frankenhaeuser, M. (1985). Cortisol excretion during the defense reaction in humans. *Psychosomatic Medicine, 47,* 313–319.

Funkenstein, D. H. (1956). Nor-epinephrine-like and epinephrine-like substances in relation to human behavior. *Journal of Mental Disease, 124,* 58–68.

Glass, D. C. (1977). *Behavior patterns, stress, and coronary disease.* Hillsdale, NJ.: Erlbaum.

Guillemin, R. (1978). Peptides in the brain: The new endocrinology of the neuron. *Science, 202,* 390–402.

Hamburg, D. A., Elliott, G. R., & Parron, D. L. (1982). *Health and behavior: Frontiers of research in the biobehavioral sciences.* Washington, DC: National Academy Press.

Henry, J. P., & Stephens, P. M. (1977). *Stress, health, and the social environment. A sociobiologic approach to medicine.* New York, Heidelberg & Berlin: Springer-Verlag.

Holst, von. D., Fuchs, E., & Ströhr, W. (1983). Physiological changes in male Tupaia belangeri under different types of social stress. In T. M. Dembroski, T. H. Schmidt, & G. Blumchen (Eds.), *Biobehavioral bases of coronary heart disease* (pp. 382–390). Basel, New York: Karger.

Johansson, G., & Sandén, P. -O. (1982).*Mental belastning och arbetstillfredsställelse i kontrollrumsarbete. (Mental load and job satisfaction of control room operators.) (Rep. No. 40). Stockholm: University of Stockholm, Department of Psychology.*

Karasek, R. A. (1979). Job demands, job decision latitude and mental strain: Implications for job redesign. *Administrative Science Quarterly, 24,* 285–308.

Krantz, D. S., Lundberg, U., & Frankenhaeuser, M. (in press). Stress and Type A behavior. Interactions between environmental and biological factors. In A. Baum & J. E. Singer (Eds.), *Handbook of psychology and health (Volume 5): Stress and coping.* Hillsdale, NJ: Erlbaum.

Levi, L. (1965). The urinary output of adrenaline and noradrenaline during pleasant and unpleasant emotional states. *Psychosomatic Medicine, 27,* 80–85.

Levine, S., Goldman, L., & Coover, G. D. (1972). Expectancy and the pituitary-adrenal system. In R. Porter & J. Knight (Eds.), *Physiology, emotion and psychosomatic illness* (pp. 281–296). Amsterdam: Elsevier.

Lundberg, U., & Forsman, L. (1979). Adrenal-medullary and adrenal-cortical responses to understimulation and overstimulation: comparison between Type A and Type B persons. *Biological Psychology, 9,* 79–89.

Lundberg, U., & Frankenhaeuser, M. (1980). Pituitary-adrenal and sympathetic-adrenal correlates of distress and effort. *Journal of Psychosomatic Research, 24,* 125–130.

Lundberg, U., de Chateau, P., Winberg, J., & Frankenhaeuser, M. (1981). Catecholamine and cortisol excretion patterns in three year old children and their parents. *Journal of Human Stress, 7,* 3–11.

Mason, J. (1975). Emotion as reflected in patterns of endocrine integration. In L. Levi (Ed.), *Emotions. Their parameters and measurement* (pp. 143–187). New York: Raven.

Pátkai, P. (1971). Catecholamine excretion in pleasant and unpleasant situations. *Acta Psychologica, 35,* 352–363.

Rose, R. M. (1985). Psychoendocrinology. In Williams *Textbook of Endocrinology,* 7th ed. Philadelphia: Saunders.

Sachar, E. J. (1975). Neuroendocrine abnormalities in depressive illness. In E. J. Sachar (Ed.), *Topics in psychoendocrinology (pp. 135–156).* New York: Grune & Stratton.

Schally, A. V. (1978). Aspects of hypothalamic regulation of the pituitary gland. *Science, 202,* 18–28.

Seligman, M. (1975). *Helplessness.* San Francisco: W. H. Freeman.

Selye, H. (1950). *The physiology and pathology of exposure to stress.* Montreal: Acta.

Steptoe, A. (1981). *Psychological factors in cardiovascular disorders.* London: Academic Press.

Theorell, T., Lind, E., Lundberg, U., Christensson, T., & Edhag, O. (1981). The individual and his work in relation to myocardial infarction. In L. Levi (Ed.),

*Society, stress and disease. Vol. IV: Working life* (pp. 191–200). New York and Toronto: Oxford University Press.

Ursin, H., Baade, E., & Levine, S. (1978). *Psychobiology of stress. A study of coping men.* New York, San Francisco, and London: Academic Press.

Weiss, J. M. (1970). Somatic effects of predictable and unpredictable shock. *Psychosomatic Medicine, 32,* 408.

# CHAPTER 7

# Theoretical and Empirical Considerations in the Theory of Stress from a Psychophysiological Point of View

KLAUS SCHEUCH

## Theoretical Considerations

Although various disciplines attempt in part to explain stress as *one* form of interaction of the living being with its environment, the complexity of the stress process can be explained only at an interdisciplinary level.

It is impossible for me to provide here a survey of the extensive stress research done in socialist countries. Such research has become quite multifarious and is little known in western countries. However, I must state, that there is no agreement about stress in our countries either (see Rudow & Scheuch, 1982; Scheuch & Schreinicke, 1983).

In the first part of this chapter, a rough outline of my views on a number of issues in stress research are presented, because the main problem in such research arises from the obscurity of the terms used in relating to stress. I make no claim to presenting a complete concept of

KLAUS SCHEUCH ● Institut für Arbeitshygiene, Medizinische Akademie "Carl Gustav Carus", 8019 Dresden, German Democratic Republic.

stress here, but I have singled out three problem areas that are closely connected with one another.

## The Problem of the Origin of Stress

I am among those scientists who view stress from an interactional point of view, based on a theory of action (Leontjew, 1979). From this viewpoint, stress is not a state but a process, in which the person appears as an acting and reacting being, a changing and self-changing one. This does not mean that from the interactional point of view (Nitsch, 1981), the term stress completely disappears in classifications of the several stress theories. Stress maintains a state of a living being. It arises from, and is changed and mastered in, the interaction between concrete abilities and a concrete environment. In our view, impulses that prompt the individual to act must be seen as needs. Owing to humankind's double character, these needs are biological and social. A discrepancy between demands and the individual's opportunities to meet those demands (McGrath, 1970) is not enough alone to cause stress. The satisfaction of needs must be endangered. We think that stress arises when the satisfaction of needs is endangered, and it is necessary, and difficult, for the individual to act.

Thus, the process of appraisal takes account not only of demands and the individual's opportunities to meet them but also of the existing need structure. It is difficult, methodologically, to determine needs. Since needs manifest themselves through goals, we believe that goals acquire ever greater importance in psychological stress research (Hacker, 1983). In the interaction with demands, goals are moulded largely by needs. However, what matters in the origin of stress is not only the goal but also the individual's possibilities for action, in other words, the way to goal attainment. Thus, the existence of a need that has not been satisfied, a goal that has not yet been attained, is not enough to cause a state of stress.

By emphasizing both biological and social needs, we want to counteract a one-sided conception of stress in psychological terms only and to call attention to the original view of stress, in terms of a general adaptation syndrome. This syndrome serves not only the restoration of a previous state but also the development of the individual. Needs arise and develop by the process of satisfaction. Just as a human being cannot be subdivided into a biological and a social being, it is also impossible to set biological and social needs in opposition to each other. Concerning the origin of stress, needs can be regarded as biological-centered, subject-centered, action-centered, social communication-centered, and emotion-centered.

Stress arises not only through the individual's process of evaluation but can also arise when biological needs cannot be satisfied, in the absence of conscious evaluation, as is the case, for example, with the needs for activity, for optimal stimulus level, and for biological recovery. In contrast to Maslow's classification (1977), I think that both his lower and higher needs represent deficiency needs *as well as* growth needs. To conclude this point, I should emphasize (and not just because I am an occupational physician) the important role of *work* in people's need satisfaction and need development.

## The Problem of the Characterization of Stress

Stress is a psychophysical process, in which I subsume "social" under "psychic", since social conditions operate only through the individual psychic regulation of behavior. Any reductionism, whether to the psychological or the biological level, does not take adequate account of the complex nature of stress. The point is that one must recognize not only the interaction between these two levels but also the fact that the two have relative autonomy. To reduce one to the other means limiting our capacity to identify, to influence, and to predict the consequences of stress.

The *psychic characteristic* of stress is to be seen in (a) the individual's experience of a threat to the satisfaction of essential needs, with the feeling qualities that have been so aptly described by psychologists (see Appley and Trumbull, 1967; Lazarus, 1966; McGrath, 1970), and/or in (b) the ineffectiveness and destruction of the individual's action and behavior, on the output side. This subdivision is a methodological one and should not deny the character of process and interaction.

The *somatic characteristic* of stress lies in the disturbance of the homeostasis of the organism's regulatory systems. If demands that arise during an interaction lead to responses *within* the organismic scope for homeostasis, this does not constitute stress. Stress is linked to compensatory mechanisms that lie *outside* the compass of homeostasis, and that have both quantitative and qualitative characteristics. From this point of view, we regard stress as a *form of compensation*.

In this stress context, we should not leave the "nonspecific" term out of consideration, even though criticism has been voiced of it recently (e.g., Mason, 1975), because without such a characteristic, the basic idea of stress would be abandoned. The criticism centers upon the nonspecificity of *responses*, a view we partly share. One disadvantage of the Selye concept (Selye, 1974) is its *separate* consideration of the nonspecific and specific, although he emphasized, over and over again, the occurrence

of both reactions. Another direction of criticism concerns the nonspecificity of *demands* resulting in stress. We think that the nonspecific feature
should be dealt with at another level, and that nonspecificity should be
seen *independently* of the kind of endangered need satisfaction.

Stress reactions are individually caused, their dynamics influenced,
their reactions specified, and their consequences determined by (a) *interpretation-specific causes*, that is, by the objectively real or subjectively altered
reflection of environmental demands in relation to needs and the individual's opportunities to meet them, by subsequent action, and by the
individual and social interpretation of results; and (b) *somato-specific causes*,
that is, by the differential responsiveness—either genetically determined
or formed in the course of individual development—of organismic functional systems, by characteristics of impaired responsiveness in the form
of disease, or by the demand-specific responsiveness of functional systems.

We think of stress, conceived as a state in the process of one's interaction with one's environment, as something *negative* because a pathological disorder can develop. If coping and compensation fail, it interferes with action and behavior.

The dialectic nature of this process lies in the fact that, by overcoming this state, through the acquisition of coping strategies, and by conditioning somatic processes, the individual is able to develop lasting response mechanisms that serve the development and represent the positive
facet of the stress mechanism.

In this consideration, there is no room for such terms as "eustress"
and "distress" (Levi, 1972; Selye, 1974), which, although widely used in
medicine, are elusive and thus not available to methodological study.
They result from pure cause–effect thinking, which takes no account of
interaction and the individual's process of transaction with his environment. In our opinion, those terms should no longer be used.

In this context, I will make an observation on the phylogenetically
old response pattern, which supposedly is so dangerous because, in today's world, a person cannot consume the produced energy for fight or
flight. I think such a biological view—that one is at the mercy of the old
response pattern—is erroneous and dangerous. It leads to recommendations of entirely wrong strategies for prevention of the negative consequences of stress. The problem we face today is not just that a change
in the demand structure is occurring at an unprecedented rate, nor the
phylogenetically old response pattern, but the necessity for a change in
the way we structure needs and the way in which they are satisfied. It is
the process of adaptation (which, in turn, must be seen as an expression
of one's interaction with the environment), that gives rise to today's
problems associated with stress. One implication of these remarks is that

the basic strategy for preventing the unfavorable consequences of stress does *not* suggest that the individual is in agreement with his environment. Moreover, this basic strategy does not involve treating the state of stress by means of medication or autosuggestion, but in developing conditions of performance, as well as a broad structure of needs and provision of wide individual and social opportunities to meet them. In this way, we emphasize the importance of change in the situation, rather than the role of possible stressors.

We think that more attention should be focussed on the distinction between *acute and chronic stress*. Not only is duration of the state of stress important, but chronic stress is a new, qualitative state, which we consider pathological because the individual's physical and psychic well-being and ability to act are disturbed. (It is possible that the physical and psychic well-being is disturbed but the performance, the "ability to act" is not restricted.) In our view, acute stress develops in a concrete action situation, when attainment of a concrete goal is endangered. Chronic stress is mainly a result of frustrated satisfaction of essential needs, which continue for a long time and which do not require immediate action.

From the viewpoint of occupational physiology, we consider acute stress—just like fatigue (e.g., the fatiguelike state of monotony, and the stresslike state of psychic saturation)—to be a negative consequence of strain. Such states represent various forms of adaptation, differing from one another in the process of interaction with demands, in somatic changes, and in feeling (Scheuch & Schreinicke, 1983). It follows, from this exposition of our interactionist view of stress, that we do not think highly of a subdivision in terms of a "strain/stress" concept, as used by a number of occupational physiologists (see Rutenfranz, 1981). We consider strain as the reactions of a living being to demands (in German: Beanspruchung). In this sense, stress represents one form of strain.

## The Problem of the Relationship of Stress and Disease

We regard stress reactions as risk reactions, which we deliberately distinguish from static risk factors. Here, we mean risk not only in terms of pathological development but also in the sense of danger to an individual's performance. To conclude these sketchy theoretical observations, I want to elaborate a little on the relation between stress and disease, from the physician's point of view. I feel that the idea of a simple cause–effect relationship should be abandoned. Stress is able to act as a factor causing disease, predisposing to disease, or preventing disease. In fact, we consider chronic stress *as* disease. On the other hand, disease is able to result in stress, to act as a factor predisposing to stress, or as a factor preventing stress. In my opinion, health consists not only of well-being, or the absence of complaints, but also in the range of abilities and of opportunities for action and for self-development. This conception has consequences for the diagnosis of stress and its sequela, as well as of the health status.

The causes of stress reactions can be reduced to the individual's interaction with his environment and to the somatically specific responsiveness of the organism's functional systems. These causes are at the same time the circumstances in which a risk can become a manifest disturbance.

To generalize, we may say that we do not see the causality of diseases as an etiological factor acting *on* the individual *from* his environment. Rather, this causality lies in the *interaction* of environmental factors with the biosocial individual.

## Empirical Results of Psychophysiological Investigations

I would like to present some examples that illustrate the limits and the advantages of complementary psychophysiological views in connection with the topic of this volume. The aim of our investigations was to describe factors influencing strain reactions and strain consequences. For this purpose, we felt that examinations would be suitable as real demand situations.

Let me start with some remarks on the methods underlying the results to be presented. The load model used consisted of final medical examinations and a three-month period containing 14 other examinations. Sixty-nine medical health students, selected from 190 students in terms of low and high (demand-specific) test anxiety, participated in the study.

Complex investigations were carried out at the start of the academic year in September, and after the students' next-to-last examination in August of the following year. The investigations consisted of analyses of a number of hormonal and vegetative parameters, lipid metabolism and trace elements, as well as psychophysiological measurements, and a maximum ergometry. The same investigations were undertaken with a control group composed of 20 students who did not take examinations during that academic year.

The students' 14 medical examinations took place from May to August (examination period). The students were subjected to extensive physiological and psychological diagnostic scrutiny (Scheuch, 1983). Based on the above-mentioned theoretical remarks, we primarily considered habitual action-oriented personality traits of healthy persons and not

**Table 1.** Psychological Measures of Personality and Abilities

---

1. Test Anxiety Inventory (Alt & Kraus, 1980)
2. Interpersonal Anxiety (Tai al Deen, Mehl, & Wolfram, 1977)[a]
3. Selection of Information (avoidance or sensitization) (Döhler, 1978)[a]
4. Tolerance of insecurity (Döhler, 1978)[a]
5. Readiness for communication (self-concept) ⎱ (Seidel, 1978)[a]
6. Ability to mold communication (self-concept) ⎰
7. Awareness of self-concept ⎱ (Hartung &
8. Awareness of control of one's environment ⎰ Rössler, 1978)
9. Ability to combine ⎫
10. Ability to abstract ⎪
11. Retention ⎬ (Amthauer, 1969)
12. Imagination ⎪
13. Inductive reasoning ⎪
14. General level of intelligence ⎭
15. Concentration (Brickenkamp, 1968)
16. Future-related achievement motivation ⎱
17. Performance-inhibiting anxiety ⎬ (Modick, 1977)
18. Performance-facilitating tension ⎰
19. Decentering (Szustrowa, 1976)
20. 470-F-TEST (modified MMPI)
21. Neurotic tendencies with BFB or VFB (Höck & Hess, 1976)
22. Jenkins activity scale

---

[a]Developed at the Section of Psychology, Karl-Marx-University of Leipzig, GDR, unpublished dissertations.

global psychopathological ones (see Table 1). Among the measures we used were a modification of the Minnesota Multiphasic Personality Inventory (MMPI) and the neurosis screening questionnaires Beschwerdefragebogen (BFB) and Verhaltensfreteagebogen (VFB).[1] The psychological investigations were carried out with H. Schröder (1984), in Leipzig.

All subjects who took examinations were tested in at least two of them, one that all students of the course rated as easy and another which they rated as difficult. Five minutes before and 5 minutes after the examination, parameters of metabolism and immunology, including hemograms and trace elements, as well as specific stress and fatigue feelings, were analyzed. During the examinations, heart rate, arterial blood pressure, and acral microcirculation were measured. Nineteen of the 69 students were investigated in two examinations under standardized conditions (as far as possible). This included hospital admissions one day

---

[1] Questionnaire of complaints (BFB), questionnaire of behavior (VFB).

prior to the examination, for the same duration and under the same conditions as the examinations of the others.

Based on the physiological tests used, we reject one-parameter physiological descriptions of the strain-including stress state, especially for prognostic assessment of consequences for health. Such descriptions are not supported for methodological reasons either, because rarely are continuous investigations of a time course possible.

I will now focus on two problems.

## Problem One: Action-oriented Personality Traits and Psychophysiological Activation

The relations between personality traits and strain parameters have often been investigated. The basis of our considerations was action-correlated aspects of personality (Schröder, 1984), in contrast to demand-unspecific personality traits, as *one* possibility of explanation of individual strain reactions.

The results of investigations on 44 students are shown in Table 2, (only significant and near-significant findings are presented). They indicate that:

1. Under rest conditions, no significant relations were found between the personality traits measured and the somatic parameters. Under load (i.e., *in* examinations), the correlative relations became closer, but remained small. It should be emphasized that these action-oriented personality traits show far stronger relations to the experience parameters than to the somatic ones. Unspecific psychopathological measures (e.g., MMPI, BFB, VFB) showed no essential connections in these subjects.

2. Situative feelings and complaints show closer relations to the somatic parameters than do the habitual personality traits. In this connection, the occurring psychosomatic complaints are not to be underestimated in their influence on somatic changes over time. This is an important issue for medicine.

3. Some somatic parameters (e.g., the fotopulsamplitude, cholesterol, and, partly, heart rate) appear to be more closely related to *personality* traits. This was also found for the respiration parameters in other psychophysiological investigations (Scheuch & Schreinicke, 1978). Connections between action-oriented personality traits and somatic parameters also show a time course. As a consequence, the *recovery period* plays a special role. This applies to coronary-prone behavior and to the selection of information, but not to the several forms of anxiety.

4. Also, the demand-specific habitual test anxiety individuals are only slightly higher in somatic strain in the real (final) examination, and show

**Table 2.** Significant Correlations between Habitual Personality Traits as Well as Situational Psychic Factors and Psychic Strain Parameters (n = 44)[a]

| | Strain parameters | | | | | | | | | | | | | |
| --- | --- | --- | --- | --- | --- | --- | --- | --- | --- | --- | --- | --- | --- | --- |
| | Vegetative parameters | | | | Situational psychic parameters | | Lipid metabolism | | | Hormones | | | Hemogram | |
| Personality traits[b] | HR | BP$_s$ | BP$_d$ | FPA | Stress feeling | Complaints | Chol. | $\dfrac{\text{LDL}}{\text{HDL}}$ | TG | Cort. n = 19 | Vaso. n = 19 | c-AMP n = 19 | Lympho after | Eosin. after |
| 1. Test anxiety | + | | | – – – | + + + | + + + | + | | | + | + | + | – | |
| 2. Interpersonal anxiety | + + | | | – – – | + + + | + + | + + | | + | + | + | | | |
| 3. Selection of information | | | | – | + + | + + + | + | + | | | | | | – |
| 4. Tolerance for insecurity | | | – | + + | – – | – – – | | | | | | | – | |
| 16. Future-related achievement motivation | | | | | | + + | | | | | | | | |

(continued)

**Table 2.** *(Continued)*

| Personality traits[b] | Strain parameters | | | | | | | | | | | | | |
|---|---|---|---|---|---|---|---|---|---|---|---|---|---|---|
| | Vegetative parameters | | | | Situational psychic parameters | | Lipid metabolism | | | Hormones | | | Hemogram | |
| | HR | $BP_s$ | $BP_d$ | FPA | Stress feeling | Complaints | Chol. | LDL/HDL | TG | Cort. | Vaso. $n = 19$ | c-AMP $n = 19$ | Lympho after $n = 19$ | Eosin. after |
| 17. Performance-inhibiting anxiety | | | | − | ++ | +++ | + | | | | | | | |
| 18. Performance-facilitating tension | − − | | + | | ++ | | − | | − | | | | | |
| 22. Coronary prone behavior | | ++ (post) | | − | | | | | | − | | | | |
| 20. MMPI | | | | | | | | − | | | | | | |
| 21. Neurotic tendencies (BFB) | | | | − | + | ++ | | | | | | | | |
| Stress feelings | ++ | | | − − | | | +++ | + | − (post) | ++ | + | − | − | − − |
| Complaints | +++ | | | − − − | | | ++ | | | ++ | | | − | − |

*Note.* + = positive correlation; − = negative correlation; +/− = $p < 0.1$; + + +/− − − = $p < 0.05$; + + + +/− − − − = $p < 0.01$; BP = blood pressure; HR = heart rate; TG = triglyceride; FPA = fotopulsamplitude; post = after the examination; chol. = cholesterol; cort. = cortisol.

[a] Correlations represented in this table occurred in at least two examinations.

[b] The numbers of the personality traits correspond to those in Table 1.

no marked effects after 14 examinations (examination period), in comparison with persons with little test anxiety.

We also found further that a cluster analysis of 13 personality traits (based on 61 subjects) can improve the correlations with psychophysiological strain parameters. It would appear that such psychological profiles correspond better to the complex character of the interaction between the person and his environment. Grouping subjects into 5 clusters seemed suitable for our interpretation (see Table 3). Although the other three clusters show specific, partly compensatory patterns, attention should be directed to the *extreme* clusters III and IV. The personality structures of these clusters are characterized in an opposite way. Cluster IV, called neurotic anxiety type, is characterized by high performance-inhibiting anxiety, low control expectation, high interpersonal anxiety, sensitive selection of information, low tolerance to insecurity, and high egocentrism. These, taken together, lead to a very high test anxiety. The performance results of this group (grades of all final examinations) are very poor and the actual stress feeling (before the examination) is very high. Such a profile of personality traits clearly represents an unfavorable promise for coping with examinations. The somatic parameters of this group, in a real examination, are at the upper limit of all investigations. However, although this extreme personality structure influences the coping process, it does not also lead to extreme somatic activation *during* examination. On the other hand, when one looks at somatic changes *after* the period of examinations, this cluster (IV) is the most remarkable, in showing the greatest decline in physical performance, a negative development in fat metabolism, and a decreased hormonal adaptive reaction.

For the analysis of load effects and of coping in a medical sense, the psychology of personality is surely important, but—as these results have shown—they are limited, on the one hand, and not yet exhausted, on the other. Dysregulation connected with stress cannot be explained by consistent personality traits alone (Schröder, 1984), even if they are action-oriented and demand-specific. For this purpose, further processing variables connected with the situation need to be taken into account, as well as the peculiarities of somatic regulation.

# Problem Two: Importance of and Influencing Factors in Psychophysiological Strain Reactions

The importance of actual strain reactions for long-term consequences is still an unsolved question, and not only for medicine. We found it interesting that the correlations of actual strain parameters were

**Table 3.** Results of Classification after Profile A Cluster Analysis (Späth, 1977)

| | Characterization of personality traits | Denotation | Test anxiety (habitual) | Marks of all exams | Actual feeling (before exam) | Actual somatic activation (in exam) | Somatic changes (after 14 exams) |
|---|---|---|---|---|---|---|---|
| Cluster I n = 13 | Environmental control ↑<br>Self-control ↑<br>Sensitive selection of information ↑<br>Control expectation ↑<br>Performance motivation ↑ | High-motivated | Moderate | Good | Moderate | Moderate to high | Small to moderate |
| Cluster II n = 10 | Environmental control ↑<br>Self-control ↑<br>Tolerance to insecurity ↑<br>Egocentrism ↑<br>Control expectation ↔ | Outwardly "composed" | Moderate | Good | Moderate | Small to moderate | Small |

| Cluster | Traits | | | | | | |
|---|---|---|---|---|---|---|---|
| Cluster III<br>n = 16 | Environmental control ↑<br>Self-control ↑<br>Control expectation ↑<br>Egocentrism ↓<br>Interpersonal anxiety ↓<br>Tolerance to insecurity ↑<br>Intellectual level ↑ | "Competent" | Extremely low | Very good | Very small | Small to moderate | Small |
| Cluster IV<br>n = 6 | Performance inhibition anxiety ↑<br>Control expectation ↓<br>Interpers. anxiety ↑<br>Sensitive selection of information ↓<br>Tolerance to insecurity ↑<br>Egocentrism ↓ | Neurotic "anxiety type" | Extremely high | Very poor | High | Moderate to high | Moderate to high |
| Cluster V<br>n = 16 | Interpersonal anxiety ↑<br>Environmental control ↓<br>Tolerance to insecurity ↑<br>Sensitive selection of information ↓<br>Intellectual level ↑ | Situational "failure-fear-type" | Moderate | Poor | Moderate to high | Moderate | Moderate |

*Note:* ↑ high level of personality traits; ↓ low level of personality traits; italicized personality traits—unfavorable feature.

closer in the rest stage *after* 14 examinations than in the rest *before* the period of examination. This is illustrated in Figure 1 for various parameters.

An indirect example of the importance of actual changes can be shown by comparing somatic reaction specificities in women and men. Women, in this investigated age, show significantly smaller changes in blood pressure and a faster recovery to initial level than do men (see Figure 2). Likewise, women exhibit a significantly lower high-density lipoprotein (HDL)-cholesterol decrease ($p < 0.01$) under standardized examinations, too. HDL is considered to be a protective factor against arteriosclerosis. The question arises, whether the lower morbidity of ischemic heart diseases in women can also be explained by means of these reaction specificities. This notion is supported for other diseases, too; for example, by the more extended reactions under examination of thyroid hormone $T_3$ in women (see Figure 3). Greater thyroid morbidity in women is generally well recognized.

The importance of these changes can also be seen when not only somatic but also psychological aspects are taken into account. We have compared students showing a high stress feeling in both examinations with those showing a low one (see Figure 4). The group with a high stress feeling shows extensive negative changes in fat metabolism *during* actual examinations, whereas differences did not occur in the period *before* examinations ("rest"). In addition, we observed a higher (LDL/HDL)-quotient level and a lower HDL *after* the period of examination, normally indicative of high atherogenic risk. This underlines our observation that actual psychic, as well as somatic, changes can influence long-term somatic consequences. Looking at the regression lines between the values of fat metabolism before and after a period of examinations, it can be seen that only in the group with high stress feeling is there a significant positive correlation for cholesterol ($r = .58$, $p < 0.01$), LDL-cholesterol ($r = .76$, $p < 0.001$), and triglyceride ($r = .52$, $p < 0.01$). We found no significant correlations in the group without stress feeling. Likewise, no significant correlations existed in either group for the HDL-cholesterol (see Scheuch, Pietruschka, & Eckhardt, 1984). If a negative initial somatic state is connected with an extended, ever-present, actual negative feeling, this would appear to be an especially unfavorable constellation. Thus, the estimation of actual somatic changes can be improved by knowledge of situation-specific feeling parameters. These examples demonstrate that the importance of actual somatic and psychic strain reactions should not be underestimated.

It may be noted that the level of changes of psychophysiological parameters *and* the time characteristic of those changes play roles in a demand situation. This can be illustrated by blood pressure reactions

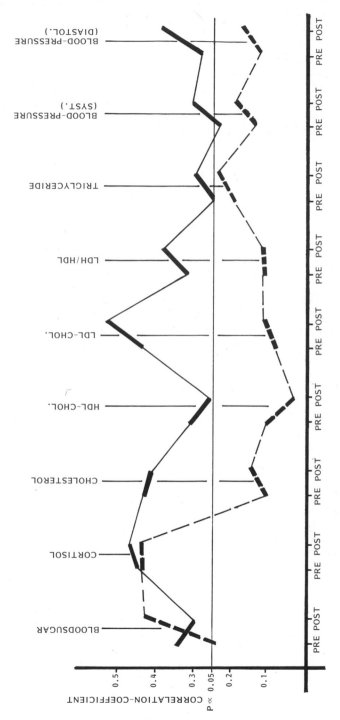

**Figure 1.** Linear correlation coefficients of various somatic parameters between a real "difficult" examination and the level before the examination (---) and after the examination (———). Measurement taken 5 min before (pre) and 5 min after (post) the examinations.

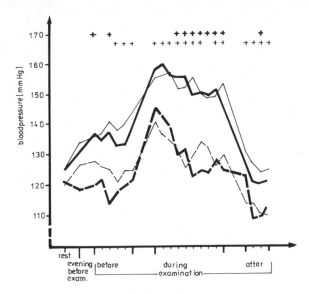

**Figure 2.** Systolic blood pressures of men and women in two examinations. + = significant differences (at least $p < 0.05$) for the internal medicine examination (dark +) and work hygiene examination (light +). Internal medicine examination (—) males, (— —) females. Work hygiene examination (——) males, (– –) females. Duration of measurements: before the examination, 150 minutes; during the examination, 30 minutes; after the examination, 90 minutes.

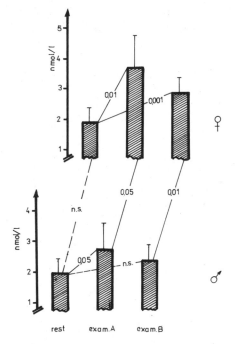

**Figure 3.** Trijodothyronin of men and women in rest (3 months before examinations) and in two real examinations.

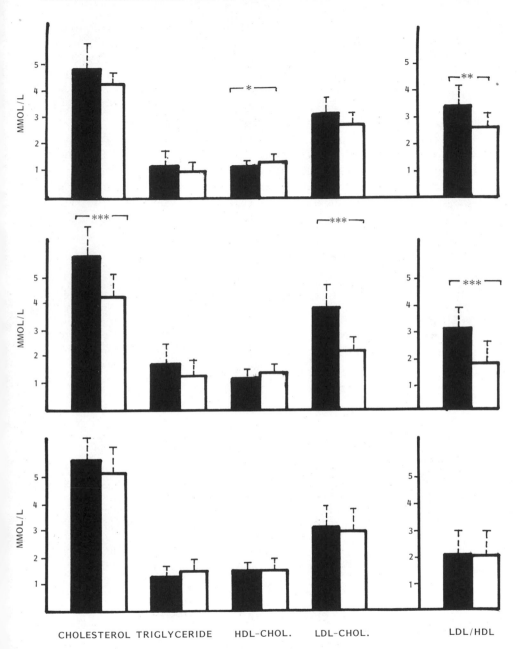

**Figure 4.** Parameters of lipid metabolism of a group with high (dark column) and low (white column) stress feeling before the period of examination (A), before a real examination (B) and after the period of examination (C) * = $p < 0.05$; ** = $p < 0.01$; *** = $p < 0.001$.

(Figure 5). Three groups were studied, one without essential changes of blood pressure, a second showing extensive changes before and during the examinations, with a rapid recovery afterward, and a third, exhibiting a delayed recovery of blood pressure after the examination. It is interesting to note that there were no significant differences among the groups on any of the psychological diagnostics (see also Table 1). The third group showed only marginal coronary-prone behavior ($p < 0.1$). Also, the rest level of vegetative parameters before the period of examinations did not differ. All groups achieved the same results on all examinations. As shown in Figure 6, there are some interesting differences among these three groups *after* the period of examination, especially in metabolic measures (e.g., the increase of blood sugar), as well as the (LDL/HDL) quotient and the stronger decrease of HDL. In group 3 (with delayed

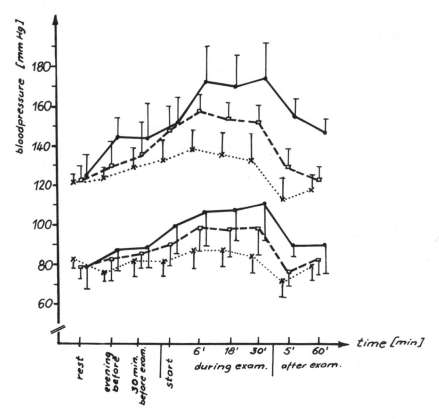

**Figure 5.** Group characteristics of various time courses of blood pressure (see text): (•——•) delayed readaptation; (□——□) good readaptation; (x · · · x) no marked changes of blood pressure.

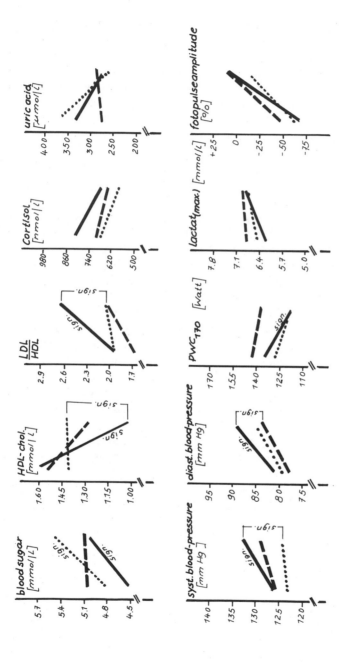

**Figure 6.** Level of various vegetative and metabolic parameters before (beginning of lines) and after a period of 14 examinations (end of lines): sign. = significant differences (at least $p < 0.05$); (—) delayed readaptation; (——) good readaptation; (···) no marked changes of blood pressure. For explanation, see text.

recovery), blood pressure was significantly higher, and the drop in physical performance, assessed with maximal ergometry, was more pronounced and was connected with an increase of blood lactate level. The changes of peripheral blood circulation under psychic load in the laboratory were also more marked in this group after the period of examinations, indicating changed functional adaptation. These findings illustrate the importance of the time dynamic of somatic parameters for the prognosis of effects of actual parameters, as well as the importance of the recovery course.

The complementary consideration of somatic and psychological processes and factors can improve the explanation of causes and the prognosis of strain reactions. However, it cannot explain all aspects of this complex interaction between people and their environment in a comprehensive way. I will therefore conclude by noting a case analysis (of which many could be given), that provides an example of psychophysiological strain profiles or strain patterns (Scheuch, 1984). Mason (1975) has suggested hormonal patterns for the strain diagnostic. Our psychophysiological strain profiles include the somatic activation of several physiological and biochemical parameters, experience in a demanding situation, performance, and such usual indicators of action (abilities) as personality traits. In Figure 7 are shown test results on several parameters for a young male student, compared to means and standard deviations for all students in our investigation in real examinations (shown in box form). It is evident immediately which of the parameters are outside of the statistical normal range. This student shows an extended vegetative activation, with heart rates to 170/min and blood pressure of 210/125 mm/Hg. In the other strain parameters, there is an elevated level of vanylmandelic acid (VMA) and of vasopressin, and a decline of lymphocytes. The low specific stress feeling in topical examination is surprising. However, with the addition of a psychological diagnostic, we can suggest the cause of the possible discrepancy. This student is characterized by an avoidance selection of information and by a high self-concept.

Another example, that of a female student (not illustrated here), showed an extremely high stress feeling, which did not reflect in heart rate or blood pressure, but in occurrence of extrasystoles, high cortisol and VMS levels, and a large decline in lymphocytes (see Scheuch, 1983). Psychologically, she was characterized by a sensitized selection of information, a low self-concept with high future-related achievement motivation and high interpersonal anxiety.

Both students showed the same grades, averaged over all examinations.

On the basis of our findings, we deny that there is a universality of

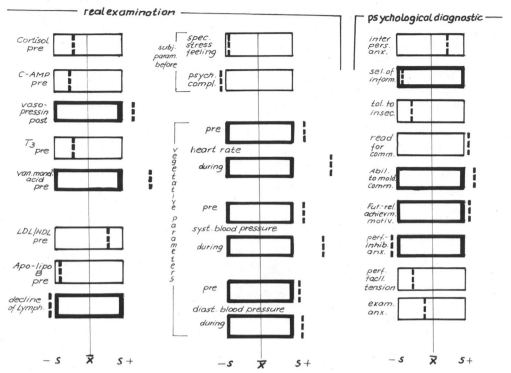

**Figure 7.** Example of a strain profile (male student, age 24). For explanation, see text.

mental and somatic activation parameters. The reasons, we think, are the relative independence of physiological and psychological processes, as well as the different time courses these parameters follow. Thus, we must always recognize, in strain investigations, that in most instances we are assessing only a portion of the functional systems of the organism. The usual comparisons of *group* levels of parameters obscures the interesting individual differences in reactions. The next task will be to progress from such individual strain patterns to the identification of general processes of regulation and their consequences.

The main purposes of our stress research are to improve our ability to diagnose persons with stress-sensitivity as a feature of reduced emotional stability and to further explore the importance of actual strain reactions in the prognosis of health and performance. As has been shown in this chapter, the problem represents a wide and largely uncharted field.

# References

Alt, M., & Kraus, R. (1980). Bedingungsanalyse der Prüfungsangst [Analysis of conditions of test anxiety]. *Dissertation A*, Karl-Marx-University of Leipzig.

Amthauer, R. (1969). I-S-T. *Intelligenz-Struktur-Test 2. Auflage.* Verlag für Psychologie. Göttingen: Dr. C. J. Hogrefe.

Appley, M. H., & Trumbull, R. (1967). On the concept of psychological stress. In M. H. Appley & R. Trumbull (Eds.), *Psychological stress: Issues in research* (pp. 1–13). New York: Appleton-Century-Crofts.

Brickenkamp, R. (1968). *Test d 2. Aufmerksamkeits-Belastungs-test,* Verlag für Psychologie. Göttingen: Dr. C. J. Hogrefe.

Döhler, J. (1978). Entwicklung eines Verfahrens zur Messung der personalen Abwehrstrategien Angstvermeidung und Angstsensibilisierung. *Diplomarbeit*, Leipzig.

Hacker, W. (1983). Ziele—eine vergessene psychologische Schlüsselvariable? Zur antriebsregulatorischen Potenz von Tätigkeitsinhalten. *Psychologische Praxis 1*, 5–26.

Hartung, R., & Rössler, K. (1978). Zur Messung von Dimensionen des Selbstbildes. *Diplomarbeit*, Leipzig.

Höck, K., & Hess, H. (1976). *Der Beschwerdefragebogen (BFB)* Berlin: Verlag der Wissenschaften.

Lazarus, R. S. (1966). *Psychological stress and the coping process.* New York: McGraw-Hill.

Leontjew, A. N. (1979). *Tätigkeit, Bewusstsein, Persönlichkeit.* Berlin: Volk and Wissen Volkseigener Verlag.

Levi, L. (1972). *Stress and distress in response to psychosocial stimuli.* Oxford: Pergamon Press.

Maslow, A. H. (1977). *Motivation and Persönlichkeit.* Olten: Olten-Verlag.

Mason, J. W. (1975). A historical view of the "stress" field. *Journal of Human Stress, 1*, 6–12, 22–36.

McGrath, J. E. (Ed.). (1970). *Social and psychological factors in stress.* New York: Holt, Rinehart & Winston.

Modick, H.-E. (1977). Ein dreiskaliger Fragebogen zur Erfassung des Leistungsmotivs—Bericht über eine deutschsprachige Weiterentwicklung des Prestatie Motivatie Test. *Diagnostica, 23* (4), 298–321.

Nitsch, J. R. (Ed.) (1981). *Stress.* Bern, Stuttgart, Wien: Huber Verlag.

Rudow, B., & Scheuch, K. (1982). Konzepte und Begriffe in der psychologischen Stressforschung—eine kritische Betrachtung aus tätigkeitstheoretischer Sicht. *Nederlands Tijdschrift voor de Psychologie, 37*, 361–382.

Rutenfranz, J. (1981). Arbeitsmedizinische Aspekte des Stressproblems. In J. R. Nitsch (Ed.) *Stress* (pp. 379–390). Bern, Stuttgart, Wien: Huber Verlag.

Scheuch, K. (1983). Untersuchungen zur Abhängigkeit von psychophysiologischen, biochemischen und immunologischen Veränderungen unter Examensbedingungen und im Verlaufe einer mehrmonatigen Prüfungsperiode unter dem Aspekt der Stresssensibilität. *Forschungsbericht* Dresden/Leipzig, 125 Seiten, 50 Abbildungen.

Scheuch, K., & Schreinicke, G. (1978). Psychophysiologische Untersuchungen zur Erfassung der Stresssensibilität—experimentelle Studie als ein Beitrag zur Eignungsdiagnostik. *Promotion B,* Leipzig.

Scheuch, K., & Schreinicke, G. (1983). *Stress, Gedanken—Theorien—Probleme.* Berlin: Verlag Volk und Gesundheit.

Scheuch, K., Pietruschka, W., & Eckhardt, G. (1984). HDL- und LDL-Cholesterolveränderungen bein psychischen Belastungen in Abhängigkeit vom Streßerleben. *Zeitschrift für die gesamte Innere Medizin, 39,* 273–277.

Schröder, H. (1984). Persönlichkeitspsychologische Komponenten des Stressverhaltens. *Wissenschaftliche Zeitschrift der Karl-Marx-Universität Leipzig, Mathematisch-Naturwissenschaftliche Reihe, 33,* (5), 560–568.

Seidel, W. (1978). Entwicklung von Skalenzur Erfassung von Variablen des Bereiches "Effektbezogene Verhaltensqualitäten" [Development of scales for assessment of "effect behavior qualities"]. Unpublished dissertation, Karl-Marx-University of Leipzig.

Selye, H. (1974). *Stress without distress.* Philadelphia, New York: Lippincott.

Späth, H. (1977). *Fallstudien Cluster Analyse.* München: Oldenburg.

Szustrowa, T. (1976). Test of egocentric association (TES). *Polish Psychological Bulletin, 4,* 12–21.

Tai Al Deen, H., Mehl, I., & Wolfram H. (1977). Die Validierung eines Furchtfragebogens für Neurotiker. In I. Helm, E. Kasielke, & I. Mehl (Eds.), *Neurosendiagnostik.* Berlin: Deutscher Verlag der Wissenschaften.

# CHAPTER 8

# Ergopsychometric Testing

## Predicting and Actualizing Optimum Performance under Load

GISELHER GUTTMANN

## Introduction

The question of human performance in stressful situations has long been of interest to psychologists, and the literature abounds with data stemming from carefully planned empirical investigations. However, the limited prognostic power of the findings has always been recognized. Wherever one tries to predict performance under stress, for example in sports, the discrepancy between experimental and real-life situations becomes obvious, and great caution must be exercised in the predictions of actual performance and in the endeavor to select promising talent on the basis of studies carried out in the laboratory.

Doubtlessly, one of the causes lies in the fact that *genuine* stress, as experienced in *real* competition, can be only poorly approximated in the laboratory. Therefore, years ago we moved out of the laboratory into real-life critical situations that were carefully chosen for their paradigmatic characteristics, in the hope of gaining practice-relevant insights into the mechanisms of performance under load. As a consequence, we were able to obtain a number of highly interesting findings, which were valuable not only for use in the psychology of sports, but also for psychologists in work and management settings, who make predictions about the qualifications of applicants.

GISELHER GUTTMANN ● Psychologisches Institut, Universität Wien, A-1010 Wien, Austria. This work was supported by the Ludwig Boltzmann Institut für Lernforschung.

## Real Load versus Laboratory Simulation

The first studies that eventually were to lead us on the road to ergopsychometric testing were done with the participants in an elective rock-climbing course offered by the University of Vienna (Heitzlhofer, 1978; Lackner, 1979).

The experimental group consisted of 33 students between 18 and 25 years of age, the number of male and female subjects being approximately equal. Only subjects who had no previous experience in rock-climbing were chosen, that is, who had never before attempted to do any rock-climbing whatsoever. They were briefly informed that, as part of their course in rock-climbing, they were also going to participate in a scientific study that would test their performance and motivation. Then they were trained to rate the extent of certain attitudes, such as approach, avoidance, subjectively experienced fear, and so forth, on a scale from 0 to 100. This was of importance with regard to the subsequent self-rating, which was demanded of them in the actual climbing situation.

All 33 subjects were tested extensively in the psychological laboratory. The test battery was comprised of tests measuring intelligence and personality, as well as a number of specialized tests to measure sensorimotor coordination, spatial imagination, and risk taking. All subjects were tested individually.

A few days after this testing, the group was confronted with its first climbing task in the mountains. Their behavior as they approached the Peilstein (a popular climbers' cliff along a bouldery limestone massif near Vienna) was observed. The actual climbing behavior was recorded by two suitably positioned videocameras as the novices worked their way up a 10-meter chimney. This made subsequent detailed analysis of the subjects' movements possible.

During this initiation into rock-climbing, the students were secured by a top rope. Care was taken to ensure that each of the climbers was alone when undertaking this first attempt at rock-climbing, and only the investigating team was present. Thus, group effects due to the presence of other climbers were eliminated to a large extent.

Several hours later on that same day, the students were confronted with the second climbing task. The same crack had to be mastered, but this time the students were not secured by a top rope. This approach, which was unusual for rock-climbing courses in Austria, was based on a particular training strategy. The students were to learn to become self-reliant on the face of the mountain as early as possible, to make necessary decisions themselves, and at the same time to cope with the load of not being secured by a top rope.

This intensification of the demands on the novices was perfectly suited to our purposes for, despite the objective safety (even in the worst case, the climber could only slip down a couple of feet), the subjective stress on performance was especially high under such conditions.

The evaluation of the videotapes provided us with a very exact picture of actual climbing behavior, which was objectified into more than 80 scores by Lackner (1979), for example, the number of purposive grips, number and duration of balanced and unbalanced phases, number and duration of purposive and nonpurposive steps, and so forth. A factor analysis of these data revealed a clear-cut 3-factor structure, which has served as a valuable basis for understanding climbing behavior and preparing optimal didactic concepts.

From those individual scores that seemed most suitable on the basis of the factor loads, a composite total score was determined, which served as external criterion. The external criterion was thus the performance in the real-life climbing situation. The test scores obtained in the psychological laboratory were correlated with this criterion and the resultant correlations were at first found to be surprisingly low.

## The Typology "Load-Stable" and "Load-Instable"

The decisive input that guided our further studies came from one of our tests which we had included on the basis of everyday observations. The subjects were first asked to perform a pursuit–rotor task under usual (i.e., unhampered, neutral) test conditions. Later, the same test was repeated, this time, however, the subjects were asked to operate the pursuit rotor with one hand, while pulling an expander at maximum strength with the other.

The results of these complementary test situations were surprising. The correlations of the pursuit–rotor task administered under neutral conditions with the external criterion (actual climbing) were very low, whereas the correlations for the test under load showed a considerable and significant increase. Apparently the performance of the subjects while under load had been altered so substantially that the load scores covaried to a much higher degree with those of the criterion in which we were interested!

We continued to pursue this course in several further projects, again choosing as a model sports situations in which demanding and clearly delineated cognitive operations must be executed under physical load. Table tennis and judo were the next modes chosen to study performance under exacting conditions (Weingarten, 1980). Two simple tests were used to quantify the efficiency of optical information processing (two-dimensional channel capacity) and decision speed. Both tests were administered under neutral conditions (N), that is, under such conditions as are customary in a psychodiagnostic situation, and then again, subsequently, under physical load (L), specifically, while pedaling a bicycle ergometer at a work load of 70 watts.

The results showed that although some subjects experienced distinct *decreases* in performance under the load testing condition, others actually *improved* (see Figure 1)! Thus, one group was able to cope with the stressful situation, whereas the other experienced it as an excessive strain that they were unable to handle (Guttmann, 1982). This is a key finding, highly significant not only for prognoses in sports performance, but in psychological testing in general, whenever the objective is to predict human performance in critical situations. For this strategy, that is, the testing of a person under neutral conditions as well as under load, we have subsequently, in analogy to the medical term ergometry, suggested the term *ergopsychometry*.

## Approach and Avoidance Types

Another important aspect, which Lazarus (1966, 1977) has pointed out in his fundamental work, is that a load situation is decisively characterized by the manner in which it is experienced by the person con-

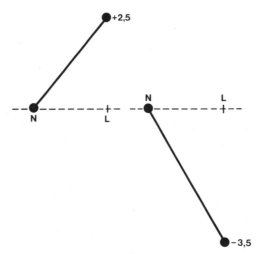

**Figure 1.** Optical information processing as one example of performance change under physical load; $N$ = value for testing under neutral conditions, standardized at "zero," $L$ = performance during bicycle ergometer load. Left section: average of all subjects who showed a performance increase under load; right section: average of all subjects who showed a decrease in performance under load. (Total population $n$ = 28.) The scale shows the raw scores; the difference is significant at the 0.05 level.

cerned. One and the same event can be interpreted quite differently by two people. Moreover, an individual will be expected to modify his or her interpretation of one and the same event as the circumstances sur-'rounding it vary. In order to gain insight into the significance of certain attitudinal patterns for long-run motivation, we endeavored to ascertain (and measure) the course of approach and avoidance motivation, as well as fear, not only in anticipation of a forthcoming performance—as Epstein and Fenz (1962) had done in their fundamental studies as well as Epstein (1973) in his later work—but also *after* the subjects had (in whatever way) mastered the load situation. We first studied such transitions of attitudes, as the critical situation nears (Heitzlhofer, 1978), with the rock-climbing model. Based on the above-mentioned training for individuals in expressing their momentary attitudes, direct ratings were obtained for approach and avoidance motivation as well as for the level of fear.

These ratings were requested at various intervals both prior to, and twice after the critical load situation (in this case, the first actual attempt at rock-climbing). The intervals in relation to the first climb were: one hour before, 5 minutes before, at the beginning of the ascent, 5 minutes afterward, and one hour afterward.

As had been discussed and practiced several days prior to the main test, the subjects had to rate approach, avoidance, and fear on a scale between 0 and 100. These ratings were obtained in individual tests and recorded during the climbing activity itself with the help of a directional microphone. In this way it was possible to observe the course of these three dimensions during the climb up the crack and in certain cases, where the subject fell, to follow the ratings even up to that point. In the following analysis, however, one rating, which turned out to be significant for the real climbing situation, namely, the self-rated approach motivation, is used (Figure 2).

Long before the actual beginning of the stressful event (1) the self-ratings of the two groups are almost identical. Interestingly, it is only when the critical event is more and more imminent that the two groups differ, and one of them shows an increase in approach motivation while the other displays a marked decrease (2).

During the actual critical situation (3) approach motivation is relatively equal for all individuals. The intense confrontation completely evens out the previously observable differences, and all subjects registered similar (near the initial level) approach motivation. This results in a V-curve for the one group—the "Vanishing motivation type"—and an A-curve for the "Approach type."

Despite the fact that no differences were observable during the stressful situation itself, it appears that the *direction* of change in level of preload

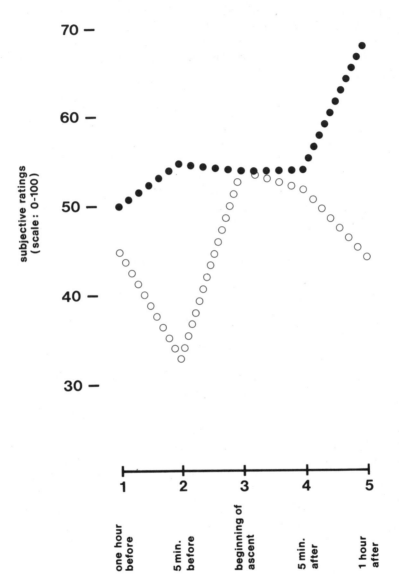

**Figure 2.** The changes in approach motivation before, during, and after the first actual rock-climbing attempt ($n = 33$). Discriminant analysis revealed two groups, an A-type (solid circles) and a V-type (open circles), whose approach motivation is plotted here.

approach motivation was able to predict postload ratings (4, 5). The V-types, whose motivation already tended to diminish in the prestress period, also displayed a clear *decrease* in approach motivation *after* having overcome the critical situation, whereas the A-types' motivation *increased* considerably in the aftermath.

This typology was also found applicable in a further study with parachuting novices by Schwarzinger (1980), who took the first parachute jump as the model for a natural load situation and used analogous ratings for quantification.

The individual's interpretation of his own level of activation and the degree to which his activation in fact varies, contribute to determining the effects of a stressful situation on the individual's performance. This is of primary signficance when one is interested in preparing individuals to cope with load situations. In addition to controlling activation—on which our own attention is focused—modifying of attributional style can also be a highly effective form of intervention. If it is possible for an individual to learn that an initially seemingly frightening situation can be approached with a positive attitude, such a strategy can be used as an alternative to physiological self-control, especially in those situations that evoke extreme arousal.

## The Diagnosis of "Training Champion"

Beyond giving indications for the typology of load-stable and load-instable persons, these studies alerted us to another promising application. According to the evaluations of their coaches, athletes whose test scores were clearly lower during load seemed to be "training champions," that is, individuals who are talented, who train diligently and also as a rule perform superbly during practice, but who are not able to realize their full potential in actual, competitive situations.

This topic deserves more detailed investigation, for it is not exclusive to sports—a domain in which one is, if need be, able to forego elaborate psychometric designs, and can simply wait for the actual competition as a model for real load. Prognoses about certain kinds of professional qualifications—as, for example, in pilot selection—demand, that the training champion be recognized in good time.

We chose orienteering as an especially appropriate model (Bischof, 1984; Beiglböck, 1984). This sport requires that a cross-country runner navigate difficult terrain with the aid of a map and a compass. He must pass several check-points in a defined order but may choose the path taken in-between: he can opt to tackle a steep incline directly, thus taking the shorter but more taxing route, or elect to run diagonally across a longer, but less steep course.

Experienced orienteerers have recounted that occasionally during competition, a runner realizes that the chosen course is completely wrong. Instead of correcting this mistake immediately, he or she sometimes continues in the wrong direction, although aware of the error, before finally finding the energy to invoke the strenuous process of deciding and correcting his or her course.

These casual observations seemed to us to indicate that orienteering could serve as an especially informative model for the interplay between physical and cognitive load. We therefore asked the coaches of Austria's orienteering elite to name likely candidates for such a study, that is, to differentiate between the most successful and, in contrast, the most promising but disappointing competitors. Of the 31 clearly classified athletes thus identified, 5 were named as training champions and 26, in fact, as successful contestants.

The entire group was examined ergopsychometrically, again allowing for a comparison of performance under neutral against load conditions (bicycle ergometer set at 90% of the value found to be each individual's maximum load). Two tests were used that seemed typical of the demands made on physical and cognitive performance in the real competitive sports situation: (1) A choice reaction time measurement, requiring a button-press response to certain light–sound stimulus patterns, and (2) a test of spatial orientation that was especially constructed for this purpose. The subjects were handed five small sections cut out from larger maps, with a point in the center of each section clearly marked. Then a group of four slides was projected onto a screen showing the actual views to the North, South, East, and West photographed from one of the locations indicated on the map sections. These views had to be matched with the correct map section. Pretests with experienced orienteerers had confirmed that this test situation does actually take into account those variables that were of central interest.

The results fully substantiated those previously found regarding load-stable or load-instable types. Furthermore, the relationship between the reaction tendency and competitive performance was convincing, as improved performance under test load was characteristic of the successful contestant. If we look only at the performance on the spatial orientation test, the training champions showed a marked decrease in performance under load (24%), whereas the successful athletes showed on average an equally good performance.

A combination score (unweighted sum of the standard values of the spatial orientation and reaction time tests) showed a very marked tendency on the part of the training champions to experience a decrease

**Table 1.** Changes in Test Performance of Orienteerers Under Load

| Test performance under load | Training champions | Successful competitors |
|---|---|---|
| Increased or unchanged | 0 | 25 |
| Decreased | 5 | 1 |

in performance under load, whereas almost all (25 out of 26!) of the really successful contestants showed either the same or a better performance level under load (Table 1).

We are quite aware of the limited size of the sample—and of the fact that these remarkably clear findings may not stand up to the stringent requirements of cross-validation. Nevertheless, the putative relationship between the reaction tendency of the training champion and an ergopsychometric decrease in performance is exceedingly convincingly borne out, and our subjects were a carefully selected group of clearly defined and highly motivated sportsmen.

## Ergopsychometry—Testing under Load

These results form the basis of different applications in the sense of "sports as a model of reality". As one example, a test battery developed by us for the selection of aircraft pilots may be mentioned, whereby both the test situation and the form of load were designed to match the requirements of the actual flying situation (Guttmann, Bauer, & Trimmel, 1981):

1. All tasks shown to be essential to the demands of the profession in question were singled out. Included were—in addition to certain basic qualities—the ability to integrate demanding sensorimotor coordination skills with cognitive decision processes while abiding by given priorities, and, further, the correct assimilation and extrapolation of movements.

None of these functions could be satisfactorily tested conventionally at the time. Therefore, their objectification required the use of sophisticated computer systems capable of handling the presentation of tests via a monitor for all necessary behavioral dimensions.

2. Applicable simulations of suitable load conditions were devised. This was a difficult problem in the case of psychic load. Our solution was to administer tasks whose critical attribute was a notable discrepancy

between apparent and real difficulty, whereby a considerable amount of load can fairly easily be induced in performance-oriented individuals.

3. Also, certain physiological variables were recorded, in particular, one which represents a sensitive indicator of activation: the slow cortical potential shifts, which are a measure of cortical excitability and, consequently, of the actual fluctuations in capability.

## Physiological Indicators of Activation

Slow cortical potential shifts have been considered an expression of local cortical activation ever since the earliest days of electroencephalogram (EEG) investigations. Securing proof of this relationship has, however, been a difficult undertaking. Quite aside from the particular difficulties of DC-registration (the relevant shifts occur within a range of only a few millionths of a volt), longer-term observations are subject to an especially persistent problem, namely, baseline drift.

During the course of an investigation lasting over longer time-periods, the baseline value of the DC-potential can deviate from the initial value by several dozen millivolts (whereby, again, we are interested in DC-shifts of a mere few microvolts). If the signal is adjusted manually in an endeavor to keep it within the working range of the amplifier, it is not long before the information regarding the real baseline value is hopelessly lost, and with it, the ability to detect enhanced or decreased negativity relative to the baseline as initially registered.

This problem of slow cortical potential research has been mastered at our Institute by Bauer (1980), who succeeded in developing an automatic baseline-reset-system that employs compensation voltage to maintain the signal within the range of the amplifier. The computer simultaneously processes the information concerning each reset procedure online, and can, therefore, reliably take the *actual* shifts into account at any given time. (Having this system at our disposal, we are in a position to register a one microvolt change in the signal even after the baseline has risen or fallen as much as one full volt!)

Our ensuing longitudinal observations revealed surprisingly high correlations between shifts toward negativity and performance, in particular, learning capability. These associations can be quite clearly demonstrated by making use of an experimental design developed at our Institute, in which the behavior under study, for example, learning performance, is demanded exclusively when the appropriate change in cortical functioning has taken place.

In order to examine the significance of the actual state of cortical negativity for learning performance, we carried out online computer analyses, registering the cortical DC-potential and its spontaneous shifts continuously. Exactly when a sufficiently large negative shift occurred, the computer presented a learning item on the monitor. In this experimental design, the subject's learning was directed by his own brain, the items being presented exclusively after the onset of phases of enhanced cortical negativity, followed by control runs with presentations during reduced negativity.

Using this *brain trigger design,* as we have called it (Guttmann & Bauer, 1982, 1984), we have secured unexpectedly large differences in performance dependent on the momentary state of cortical negativity. Time and again we have found the difference in learning performance to hover around 25% when the trigger-criterion is defined as + or − 25 microvolts. The state of enhanced negativity was not only efficacious for the learning of simple material (trigrams) but also for complex learning and decision processes (concept learning) (Bauer & Nirnberger, 1980).

The possibility of inducing states of increased or decreased cortical negativity voluntarily by means of suitable biofeedback training gives rise to a number of very practice-oriented applications which, however, cannot be described in detail here (see Bauer & Lauber, 1979). What is decisive with regard to the main problem discussed here is the connection between activation and performance, this connection also being reflected in electrical activities of the brain which indicate changes in activation level. On the basis of our data we assume that the decisive factor for the quality of performance at any given moment is the extent to which a person is able to increase his or her level of activation (i.e., local cortical negativity) at the moment of performance. From too high a level of activation, however—as seen from the point of view of the cortical DC-potential—the readiness for a further increase in activation lessens noticeably. We were able to show this with the help of a brain trigger design, by means of which a contingent variation was evoked at different stages of cortical negativity. Thereby the amplitude of an expectancy wave was dramatically reduced with increasing spontaneous negativity (Guttmann, Trimmel, & Bauer, 1983).

The amplitudes and frequencies of spontaneous DC-shifts, as well as the examinations of functional processes by way of the brain trigger design, proved to be valuable diagnostic aids in our ergopsychometric studies. In this way reliable objective indicators of the peculiarities of each individual's activation and activating mechanisms can be obtained. The inclusion of physiological observations provides us with valuable supplemental data for predictions about a person's performance under load.

# Therapy for the Training Champion

Is the diagnosis *training champion* equivalent to a life-sentence? Does it mean that the person concerned will always be unable to cope with a particular stress situation, or that this stress situation is experienced as an excessive strain that cannot be mastered, although for another person the very same situation represents a challenge that can still be mastered positively? Or is there perhaps a simple therapy that can translate the diagnosis into a positive beginning? The long-recognized (albeit often critically discussed) relationship between activation and performance suggests an unpretentious hypothesis. If our level of activation shifts too high—as can certainly be expected in the case of decisive competitive situations—we leave the range of optimal activation and may even have to anticipate losses in performance.

If this idea is correct, then it suggests an obvious expedient: by instructing the training champion in the techniques of self-control we should be able to put him in control of his level of activation and provide him with an efficacious method of holding it in rein during stressful situations. We first tested this strategy with a group of 31 orienteerers, 15 of whom practiced relaxation techniques over a period of six weeks (Beiglböck, 1984). We chose a modification of the Jacobson technique, one we had worked out using our ample experience with schoolchildren within the framework of a program aimed at "Learning under Self-Control." The success of this type of program is known to depend on the willingness of its intended recipients to keep to its regimens. For the program to be used in schools and sports, it must neither noticeably upset the routine of the main activity (curriculum, training schedule) nor make conspicuous demands on the participants' time. The variation we developed had precisely this advantage: it could be executed easily and quickly.

By random selection, an experimental and a control group were formed. The subjects in the first group were taught to induce a state of increased relaxation by means of an interplay of strong isometric contraction and relaxation, beginning with their facial muscles and continuing with the muscles of the shoulders, arms, trunk, and legs.

A comparison of this group with the control group, using the ergopsychometric complementary double-testing technique described above, revealed a distinct and statistically significant effect attributable to the six-week training program. Some of our subjects were even shown to have completely reversed their performance behavior so that they were now performing better under load than under neutral conditions; but even those whose performance still declined under load evidenced a substantially lesser impairment of performance.

A comparison of the changes in the experimental group and the controls showed an average improvement on the orientation test of the self-control group by 18% (significant at the 0.05 level).

In conclusion, a cautionary note is warranted: self-control is *not* identical with relaxation. Self-control denotes the conscious and intentional management of activation processes. In actual load situations this often is purposive relaxation. However, there are some persons with habitually low arousal levels, who still fall short of their optimum performance, even under load. These are the ones who must learn to *elevate* their level of activation according to the demands for performance made upon them.

Our technique provides for the alternation of enhanced and reduced activation, which can be accomplished by the use of verbal bywords (i.e., self-instructions) appropriate to each of the states to be induced. After sufficient training, these bywords can be used to induce the desired state, whether it be one of lowered or of enhanced activation.

The crux of the matter lies in objectifying the naturally operating and the optimal states of each individual and in providing him with methods by which he can learn to adjust his level of activation as appropriately as possible to the demands of the moment.

## Discussion

Our results are derived, on the one hand, from real-life stress situations, which provide us with results not easily obtained in the laboratory, and, on the other hand, from brain research, where we find extremely sensitive indicators of the momentary level of activation or the change in the activation level in the cortical DC-potentials and their shifts.

The comparative interpretation encourages us to take up a very simple and matter-of-fact position, which is also supported by Ursin in his excellent work on the hormonal correlates of stress (Ursin, Baade, & Levine, 1978). Stress in its most basic sense should be regarded as excessive strain, and we should exclude all other load situations with which a person believes he can cope and that he experiences as surmountable. Thus, load as such need not always be a stressor; one and the same load situation may be either conducive to or inhibiting for performance, depending entirely on the person exposed to it.

Whenever the activation level exceeds a certain critical value, capability decreases, and even the cortical DC-potentials seem to confirm the somewhat controversial Yerkes–Dodson Law. Therefore, we venture the hypothesis that different activation reactions are responsible for the observed differences in performance under load, despite the fact that

EEG controls of our training champions are still missing. If, in a load situation, a person's activation level rises too high, then that person's performance will decline; if we give him or her the means to purposefully decrease his or her activation level, then this decline in performance can be avoided.

Thus, these simple self-control techniques become an extremely effective coping strategy. We have been able to prove their usefulness, taking as models of reality various sports situations that supply us with data that could not be simulated in any laboratory.

However, I venture to demand one thing: psychodiagnostics must never be limited to the traditional neutral test situations; only the comparison of results obtained in a neutral situation with suitably designed tests under load, that is, ergopsychometric testing, provides us with valid data.

ACKNOWLEDGMENTS

We would like to thank Ms. M. E. Clay and Ms. S. Etlinger for advice and help.

# References

Bauer, H. & Lauber, W. (1979). Operant conditioning of brain steady potential shifts in man. *Biofeedback and Self-Regulation, 4,* 145–153.

Bauer, H., Steinringer, H., & Schock, P. (1980). A new highly sensitive DC-amplifier for steady biopotential recording. *Archiv für Psychologie, 133,* 333–337.

Bauer, H., & Nirnberger, G. (1980). Paired-associate learning with feedback of DC potential shifts of the cerebral cortex. *Archives of Psychology, 132,* 237–239.

Bauer, H., Guttmann, G., & Trimmel, M. (1983). *The Brain-Triggered CNV.* In F. Denoth (Ed.), 7th International Conference on Event Related Potentials of the Brain, (September 4–10, 1983, pp. 74–75). Florence, Italy.

Beiglböck, W. (1984). *Ergopsychometrische Diagnostik in der Sportpsychologie.* [Ergopsychometric diagnostics in sports psychology]. Unpublished doctoral dissertation, University of Vienna.

Bischof, B. (1984). *Psychologische und psychophysiologische Moderatorvariablen in der Belastungsdiagnostik.* [Psychological and psychophysiological moderator variables in testing under load]. Unpublished doctoral dissertation, University of Vienna.

Epstein, S. (1973). Versuch einer Theorie der Angst [An attempt towards a theory of anxiety]. In N. Birbaumer (Ed.), *Neuropsychologie der Angst.* [Neuropsychology of anxiety] (pp. 184–241). München-Berlin-Wien: Urban & Schwarzenberg.

Epstein S., & Fenz, W. D. (1962). Theory and experiment on the measurement of approach–avoidance conflict. *Journal of Abnormal and Social Psychology, 64*, 97–112.

Guttmann, G. (1982). Ergopsychometry—Testing under physical or psychological load. *The German Journal of Psychology, 6*, 141–144.

Guttmann, G. (1984). Ergopsychometry. In R. J. Corsini (Ed.), *Encyclopedia of Psychology*, (pp. 446& 447). New York: John Wiley & Sons.

Guttmann, G., & Bauer, H. (1982). Learning and information processing in dependence on cortical DC-potentials. In M. Rosenzweig & R. Sinz (Eds.), *Psychophysiology 1980*, (pp. 141–149). Jena, Fischer und Elsevier.

Guttmann, G. & Bauer, H. (1984). The brain trigger design: A powerful tool to investigate brain behavior relations. *Annals New York Academy of Sciences*, New York.

Guttman, G. Bauer, H., & Trimmel, M. (1981). *A computer-supported psychological and psychophysiological test-battery for aircraft-pilot selection*. In K. Brändli (Ed.), Aviation Psychological Research. Reports of the 14th Conference for Aviation Psychology (pp. 45–70). Bürgenstock, Switzerland.

Heitzlhofer, K. (1978). *Der Appetenz-Aversions-Konfliktverlauf beim Klettern. Eine Typenanalyse*. [The approach—avoidance conflict in rock climbing] Unpublished doctoral dissertation, University of Vienna.

Lackner, E. (1979). *Experimentelle Untersuchung über den Einfluß psychischer und motorischer Fähigkeiten auf die Kletterleistung von Anfängern*. [An experimental study of the influence of psychological and motor capabilities on the climbing performance of beginners.] Unpublished doctoral dissertation, University of Vienna.

Lazarus, R. S. (1966). *Psychological stress and the coping process*. New York: McGraw-Hill.

Lazarus, R. S. (1977). Cognitive and coping processes in emotion. In A. Monat & R. S. Lazarus (Eds.) *Stress and coping: An anthology* (pp. 145–159). New York: Columbia University Press.

Schwarzinger, G. (1980). *Konfliktabhängige Situationsbewältigung und-verarbeitung*. [Conflict—dependent coping]. Unpublished doctoral dissertation, University of Vienna.

Ursin, H., Baade, E. & Levine, S. (Eds.) (1978). *Psychobiology of stress: A study of coping men*. New York: Academic Press.

Weingarten, P. (1980). *Leistungsverhalten jugendlicher Sportler unter Berücksichtigung der Ergopsychometrie*. [The performance of young athletes based on ergopsychometry] Research report of the Austrian Ministry of Education, Vienna.

# CHAPTER 9

# Voice, Stress, and Emotion

## KLAUS R. SCHERER

## Introduction

There are two major points that I would like to make in this chapter: first, that voice and speech cues are important yet neglected indicators of stress, and second, that stress should be studied within the general framework of a comprehensive theory of emotion. The order of these two points also reflects the development of research interests and theoretical inclinations in my research group during the past decade. Consequently, in addition to developing arguments for these points, I use the opportunity to describe a series of studies conducted in our laboratory. In doing so, I stress the historical development of this research, since it may illustrate how we came to hold the theoretical views that are presented in this chapter.

## The Voice as an Indicator of Speaker State

The vocal-auditory modality is the most important channel for the expression and communication of motivational states for many species

KLAUS R. SCHERER ● Section de Psychologie, Université de Genève, Ch-1211 Genève 4, Switzerland, and Justus Liebig Universität, D-6300 Giessen, Federal Republic of Germany. The research reported herein has been supported by grants from the Deutsche Forschungsygemeinschaft and has been conducted in collaboration with Günther Bergmann, Ilse Höfer, Reiner Standke, Frank Tolkmitt, and Harald Wallbott. Preparation of the chapter has been greatly facilitated by a resident fellowship at the Netherlands Institute for Advanced Study in the Humanities and Social Sciences (N.I.A.S.).

of animals. One of its major advantages is that it allows for very subtly graded shadings of emotional meaning (Scherer, 1985). At least in primate species, these calls can be elicited by electrical stimulation of highly emotion-relevant areas in the limbic system of the brain (Jürgens, 1979). Although there is little experimental evidence, neurological examination of brain-damaged patients seems to indicate that human affect vocalizations also originate in subcortical areas and, particularly, in the limbic system (Lamendella, 1977; Robinson, 1972).

Given the intricate connection between the subcortical substratum of both emotion and motivation, on the one hand, and vocalization, on the other, the study of a variety of vocal parameters would appear to be a very promising area for the discovery of indicators of emotional state, including stress. A closer look at the process of voice production reveals why this is so. Simply put, vocalization consists of pulses of air produced by vibrations of the vocal folds and modified by the supralaryngeal vocal tract that acts as an acoustic filter. The major determinants of vocalization are the respiration pattern and the changing tension states of the muscle groups involved in phonation and articulation.

Respiration and muscle tone have always been considered to be prime correlates of emotional tension (Gellhorn, 1970; Malmo, 1975). It is highly probable that stress-related changes in these processes will affect vocalization in such a way that the tension state will become detectable in the acoustic sound wave of a concomitant vocalization. Furthermore, these vocal changes should be more easily accessible to human observers than are changes in respiration pattern and, particularly, muscle-tension changes, which can often only be observed by the use of highly sophisticated methodology and fairly obtrusive procedures. It is not surprising then, that the voice, ever since antiquity, has been considered to be one of the most powerful indicators of emotional states (see Görlitz, 1972; Laver, 1975).

Early psychologists, too, were impressed with the potential of voice as an emotion indicator; and German Expression psychology, a popular and powerful subdiscipline until the second World War, devoted much research to discovering the role of the voice in signalling emotional states (Görlitz, 1972; Rudert, 1965). The orientation of the scholars in this area was highly phenomenological in nature. Because this approach was considered to be outdated and objectionable by many modern psychologists, this tradition came to an abrupt end in the 1950s, to be revived in the 1960s, in a more modern form, under the term *nonverbal communication*. Although the study of facial expression has enjoyed a fairly high degree of popularity in nonverbal communication research, vocal phenomena have been rather neglected. As I have argued elsewhere (Scherer, 1982), the fleeting nature of sound (which cannot be easily reproduced on paper for study except by using highly sophisticated apparatus to produce fairly abstract representations of acoustic variables) may account for this neglect of the voice as a potential stress indicator. In addition, the study of vocal parameters often requires interdisciplinary research, and thus a heavy investment by the investigator in acquiring concepts and methods from acoustics and phonetics.

Having had some exposure to acoustics and phonetics, I started in the early 1970s to build a research group and a laboratory aimed at the investigation of the potential of vocal parameters as indicators of speaker states, particularly motivation, emotion, and stress. I will not dwell on the time-consuming and often frustrating efforts to develop a computer-based analysis system with the appropriate software to analyze a variety of vocal parameters. May it suffice to say that we have now developed a procedure whereby speech (coming either directly from a microphone or from magnetic tape) is digitized and then analyzed for a number of parameters, such as fundamental frequency of the voice (i.e., the vibration rate of the glottal folds heard as pitch) and various measures of the energy distribution in the spectrum (for a more detailed description, see Scherer, 1982).

*Fundamental frequency* ($F_0$) is a particularly interesting parameter, because one can make a theoretical argument that it should reliably increase with increases in stress or emotional tension (Scherer, 1979, 1981a,b). Using the tools we had developed, we set out to investigate the diagnostic valence of vocal parameters as indicators of emotional states. We particularly focussed on the possibility of using vocal cues as stress indicators, because it seemed easy to produce stress in the laboratory under conditions that would also allow obtaining clean tape recordings of voices.

## Individual Differences in Vocal Indicators of Stress

For a first attempt, in 1972, I collaborated with a research group headed by Paul Ekman at the University of California in San Francisco, who had done a naturalistic stress–deception study using nursing students. Under the pretext of wanting to see how well these students might be able to perform in trying to hide unpleasant affect from patients, these investigators showed pleasant films in an "honest baseline" condition, in which subjects were asked to report their true feelings, and rather unpleasant surgery films in a "deception stress" condition, in which they were asked to lie about their feelings. The subjects, who were exposed to both conditions in a repeated measures design, were questioned by an interviewer who first asked them about the nature of the film, then challenged their truthfulness, and finally asked them to report their reactions and feelings. (For further details of the methods used in this study, see Ekman & Friesen, 1974.)

The fundamental frequency ($F_0$) of the subjects' voice during the interviews was analyzed, and the honest, pleasant film condition and the stress–deception condition compared. Although we were not interested in deception *per se*, the joint operation of the unpleasant movie and the need to deceive was actually of particular interest, because we expected the stress level to be especially high in this condition. The results showed, as predicted, a significant increase in $F_0$ from the baseline to the stress condition. This finding was quite consistent with what we expected on the basis of some of the considerations mentioned above. In a study modelled very closely after the approach of Ekman, Friesen, and Scherer (1976), Streeter, Krauss, Geller, Olson, and Apple (1977) were able to replicate the finding that average $F_0$ for a group of speakers increases under stress.

Although the aggregate results were clear enough, I was puzzled by a fairly high degree of variance in the data, showing that for some subjects there was very little or no increase for $F_0$ in the stress condition. Correlations of the change scores with personality inventory data (California Personality Inventory, CPI) indicated that the response might be related to personality characteristics of the subject. Specifically, as shown in Figure 1, subjects with High Achievement via Independence (described as nonconforming, independent, active, dominant, demanding, and flexible) showed a very high increase in $F_0$, whereas there was almost no change for subjects low on this trait. It seemed probable that some kind of coping mechanism related to this personality dimension had to be responsible for these individual differences in vocal response structure (Scherer, 1981a).

These results had a strong impact on our further research procedure. We were quite convinced that it was not sufficient to investigate the potential diagnostic value of vocal parameters as stress indicators on an aggregate level of group mean comparisons, but that individual styles of coping with stress needed to be systematically controlled. We were reinforced in this belief by the results of two student thesis projects (Asendorpf, 1978; Müller, 1978), in which fairly strong differences were found for repressors and sensitizers (see Byrne, 1964) in responding vocally and nonverbally to a series of stressors.

Assuming that the *type* of stressor might also have an effect on the response, we designed a major study to investigate the relative effects of cognitive versus emotional stressors, on repressors and sensitizers. We used the repression–sensitization scale to select eighteen "sensitizers" and nineteen "repressors" from a group of 200 female medical assistant stu-

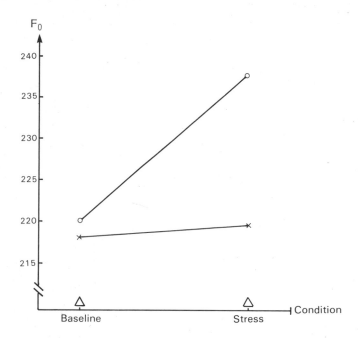

**Figure 1.** $F_0$ changes under stress in relation to personality differences. o——o = high achievement via independence, x——x = low achievement by independence. Source: Scherer, 1981a, p. 181.

dents. The stressors were either easy versus difficult arithmetic tasks (cognitive stressors) or a neutral movie on pottery versus an unpleasant surgery movie (emotional stress). In addition to the usual set of vocal measures, we also obtained measures on a variety of other dependent variables, such as verbal affect report, variability in skin resistance, and facial expression activity. We hypothesized that the repressors should show very little stress response in verbal report and possibly also in facial expressiveness, but fairly marked changes in vocal and physiological indicators, whereas sensitizers should show high scores in all modalities.

This hypothesis was not confirmed. In general, the patterns of the data were highly confusing. Although we were able once again to demonstrate the usefulness of vocal measures, particularly $F_0$, as indicators of degree of stress on an aggregate level, we were unable to obtain clear-cut response patterns in terms of either individual differences between coping groups or clear correlational patterns between the various response domains (Höfer, Wallbott & Scherer 1985). What had been particularly worrisome in this study was that quite a number of the subjects did not seem to experience much stress at all. For example, several of the subjects actually demanded to see more of the surgery film, which most of the research staff had firmly declined to see more than once, if at all.

We decided that our inability to confirm our hypothesis might have been due to a number of methodological problems in the study, as well as to the fact that the repression–sensitization scale might not be very useful as a coping style inventory because it is highly correlated with straight anxiety scales (Asendorpf & Scherer, 1983; Weinberger, Schwartz, & Davidson, 1979). For the next study, we used a two-dimensional approach for the operation of the coping style variable, using both an anxiety scale, in this case the Taylor Manifest Anxiety Scale (MAS), and the Crowne-Marlowe Social Desirability (SD) Scale (Crowne & Marlowe, 1960; Taylor, 1953). Using these scales with tercile cut-off levels for extremes, we obtained four extreme groups from a pool of 374 students: anxiety-deniers (low MAS, high SD), high-anxiety subjects (high MAS, low SD), defensive high-anxiety subjects (high MAS, high SD), and low-anxiety subjects (low MAS, low SD) (Scherer, Wallbott, Tolkmitt, & Bergmann, 1985).

We decided to add the sex of the subjects as a factor to the design as most of the studies so far had been done with male students. As in the earlier study, both cognitive and emotional stressors were used, in this case presented in the form of slides. The cognitive stressors consisted of slides with items from the Raven Progressive Matrices Test (easy versus difficult, i.e., low versus high cognitive stress), the emotional stressors of slides showing minor skin blemishes (low emotional stress) or very severe accident wounds (high emotional stress). The design of the study is shown

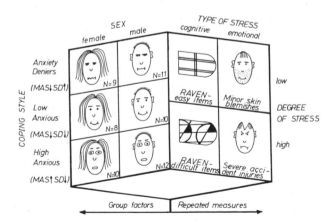

**Figure 2.** Design of the slide stress study. Source: Scherer, Wallbott, Tolkmitt, & Bergmann, 1985.

in Figure 2. Again, a large number of variables in many response domains were measured (see list of dependent variables in Table 1).

The results are very complex indeed and require a major monograph for their detailed description (see Scherer *et al.,* 1985). For the purpose of the present exposition, I will focus on two major aspects. One is the validity and usefulness of the vocal measures. Mean fundamental frequency (i.e., the fundamental frequency average over a complete utterance or episode of the experiment), did not perform as well as an indicator of stress as in the earlier studies. This is possibly because of the rather different nature of the speech material in this study that consisted of half standardized response sentences to the slides. We did find, however, that when we used an estimate of $F_0$ floor (i.e., the lowest $F_0$ value in an utterance which is possibly the best indicator of the physiologically determined mode of vibration of the vocal folds), we again were able to show a significant effect of stress on this parameter.

Another acoustic parameter, which had looked very promising in the previous study, but had seemed such an unlikely candidate that we did not pay much attention to it, was *formant frequency.* We had assumed that formant frequency (i.e., the specific areas of energy concentrations in the spectrum that mark specific vowels and that are produced by different vocal tract configurations), would be heavily bound up with the phonological system of the language and would not be free to vary with the emotional states. Figure 3 shows the results separately for cognitive and emotional stressors, for the difference between mean frequency of the first three formants averaged over three vowels (a, e, i), and the expected values of these formants for a "neutral" vocal tract shape with all articulators in rest position (schwa vowel). The analysis of variance of the data shows a very significant ($p = .0001$) four-way interaction among coping style, sex, degree of stress, and type of stress. As inspection of

**Table 1.** List of Dependent Measures Used in the Slide Stress Study

| | |
|---|---|
| Voice | Fundamental frequency (mean, floor) |
| | Energy distribution |
| | Formant frequencies |
| | Intensity |
| Face | Action units of the Facial Action Coding System |
| | Blink rate |
| Physiology | Pulse rate |
| | Breath rate |
| | EMG (frontalis, lower arm) |
| | Skin conductance level |
| Verbal report | Reported arousal |

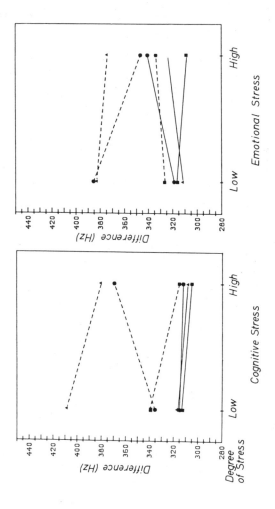

**Figure 3.** Stress-induced changes in the difference between neutral vocal tract and obtained vowel formant frequencies (averaged across several instances of the vowels A,E,I): ● = anxiety deniers; ■ = low anxious; ▲ = high anxious; (---)females; (—)males. Source: Scherer, Wallbott, Tolkmitt, & Bergman, 1985.

the figure shows, however, much of the effect is due to the response pattern for the female anxiety deniers. For this group, the differences between the neutral frequencies and the actually found vowel frequencies increase in the situation of cognitive stress and decrease under emotional stress.

How can this result be interpreted? The variable "difference between neutral and obtained frequencies" can be linked to precision of articulation, because the frequencies are farther away from the neutral position when the articulatory movements reach their targets rather precisely. The difference is likely to be smaller when the articulatory movements are imprecise or very weak. Thus, female anxiety deniers seem to have increased their precision of articulation in the case of a high cognitive stressor, whereas they decreased it (always compared to the other groups as well as absolutely) in the case of the high emotional stressor. The interpretation for this finding that we currently favor, even though it is highly speculative, is that the difference between neutral and obtained formant values is a potentially important indicator of emotional tension. We presume that the precision of articulation will decrease under stress. On the other hand, precision of articulation is, to some extent, a highly controllable behavioral modality. We can force ourselves to speak precisely if we turn our attention to this parameter.

The reason why we find differential effects for the two kinds of stressors for the group of female anxiety deniers might then be related to psychosocial factors, for example, the perception of the importance of the stress reaction and its differential visibility in these two cases. Anxiety deniers, after all, are characterized by their strong desire to present a socially desirable image of themselves. It seems possible that for female anxiety deniers, it is particularly important not to show stress in a cognitive condition, as compared to the emotional condition, because the cultural stereotype seems to allow women to be affected by emotional stimuli more strongly than men. This, in combination with the fact that the present set of subjects had chosen an academic career, may strongly orient them toward not showing signs of stress in the face of being exposed to very difficult intellectual tasks. If this is correct, we might expect the opposite tendency for male anxiety deniers. As the figure shows, there is indeed a tendency in this direction, but it is not nearly as strong as the opposite was for the female subjects. Although these conclusions are partly supported by the results for other variables, further research is needed to determine the viability of this interpretation.

The results reported above illustrate why we believe that vocal cues are valid and powerful indicators of stress and other emotional states. A large number of studies done in our laboratory, as well as elsewhere, provide additional justification for this assumption. Voice changes have been found in a large number of emotional situations, ranging from a variety of laboratory stress experiments to natural settings, such as dangerous aviation incidents and other situations (see Scherer, 1981a, for a review). Furthermore, there is evidence for the effect of emotion (see Scherer 1981b, 1986 for reviews), of psychotherapy (Tolkmitt, Helfrich, Standke, & Scherer, 1982), of psychoactive drugs (Helfrich, Standke, & Scherer, 1984), of life-stressors in old-age home inmates (Scherer, Helfrich, & Scherer, 1980), and of emotional tension in civil servant–client interactions (Scherer & Scherer, 1980). In many of these studies, however, it has become quite clear that vocal indicators are not easy, foolproof indices that can be routinely obtained and interpreted on an aggregate level. Just as for the psychophysiological variables studied in stress and emotion research, we find a high degree of individual differences in response patterns that need to be examined rather carefully in each case. Furthermore, with a number of voice variables, it is very important to check the relationship with language-based determinants because the purpose of vocalization is, in most cases, the production of speech within the inherent constraints of the language system.

Vocal variables vary greatly with respect to the amount of conscious control that can be exerted. This liability is, at the same time, a potential advantage. If we are able to determine more clearly which aspects of voice production are more or less involuntary—and can be seen as valid indicators of emotional state independent of coping attempts—and which (such as precision of articulation) are highly subject to control and self-presentation attempts, we might be able to differentiate better between a biological reaction pattern, produced by the stressful situation, and the coping attempts that set in to deal with this reaction. If this differentiation were available, we might be able to better comprehend the thorny issue of distinguishing those coping attempts that are *part of* the stimulus evaluation and interpretation (for example, perceptual defense strategies) from those that are directed toward covering up or adjusting to an emotional reaction *after* an evaluation has taken place.

Our ability to deal with this issue will have *major* consequences for progress in this research area. This brings us up to the second point raised above. One of the most serious problems in stress and emotion research is our inability to deal with the huge amount of variance due to individual differences in response measures, and with the apparent lack of relationships among different response modalities. So far, we have been singularly unsuccessful in predicting either patterns of responses for individuals or lawful relationships between response channels (both within and between response domains, such as autonomic system response, vocal and/or nonverbal behaviors). As mentioned earlier, in both of the multivariate stress studies, which we conducted in our laboratory (attempting to measure as many response domains as possible), we were unable to discover clearly interpretable change patterns, a finding that has been true for a number of other investigators as well (*cf.* Fahrenberg, Walschburger, Förster, Myrtek, & Müller, 1979; van Heck, 1981).

I have come to believe that this failure to find predictable patterns may not be so much because of the lack of lawfulness in nature but rather our inability to specify what we are actually manipulating in our stress experiments. I feel that the same laboratory stimulation may produce a variety of very different emotional states, with different response patterns, in the individuals we study. Although we use the label *stress* to refer to all those situations and responses, there can be no assurance that lumping together a large number of potentially very different emotional states under this very abstract term means that these emotional states share common response dimensions.

Thus, in the studies that we have done, different subjects may have reacted with very different emotional states to the same stressor. For example, in the study with the Ekman group, using nursing students (Ekman *et al.*, 1976), it may be that some of the subjects reacted primarily to the ugly content of the surgery movie, resulting in disgust. Others (particularly those with High Scores on Achievement via Independence) may have been much more affected by the evaluation apprehension contained in this situation, that is, the knowledge that they were being tested for their ability to deal competently with patients in their future careers. Still others may have been affected by the moral issue of deception, and the guilt that this may have engendered.

Similarly, in the experiments we ran in our Giessen laboratory, it is possible that a variety of different emotional states may have occurred, depending on the characteristics of the person and the nature of the evaluation. The differences in male and female role perceptions, for example, could be one determinant of these different evaluations and consequent differences in emotional state. Other differences could be due to self-esteem, or social desirability concerns, which might explain the differences in coping style variables. Additionally, achievement motivation could be the basis for differences in emotional states resulting from the very same stressor, as illustrated by medical assistant students who wanted to see more of the very unpleasant surgery movie.

These examples show that, although it may be true that there was some degree of "stress" involved for all of the subjects, the *type* of emotional tension may have been very different indeed. This point is forcefully made by "transactional" models (see Lazarus & Folkman, this volume) that argue that the type of appraisal and the coping potential of the individual co-determine the type of stress response. As indicated above, there seems to be no good reason to assume that these differences are limited to the evaluation of a situation (i.e., the cognitive aspect of the stress process) and do not extend to the resulting physiological and behavioral reactions. On the contrary, given the fact that physiological and behavioral reactivity have evolved phylogenetically to serve adaptation, it would seem more realistic to assume that differences in the evaluation of an event should also result in different physiological and behavioral response patterns to deal with it in an optimal fashion.

I believe that we will have to relinquish the type of "general impact" model of stress that assumes that organisms respond in a uniform manner to a particular type of stressor. Although this model may be applicable to highly noxious physical stressors of the kind used by Selye (1936) in his early work, it seems much less useful to explain the response patterning in the case of social or psychological stressors. As the empirical results reported in this chapter show, it seems impossible to save the general impact model even by introducing grouping factors for persons and situations. Consequently, we need to change radically the classical paradigm and focus on the appraisal mechanisms of individuals in trying to understand physiological and motor expression responses to stressful events.

## Stress and Emotion: Toward an Integrated Model

In the remainder of this chapter, I will attempt to show how differential stress responses can be integrated into a general model of emotion, which I have proposed elsewhere (Scherer, 1981c, 1984a,b). In this functional approach, the important adaptive role of emotion in preparing the organism to deal with environmental contingencies is reasserted. More specifically, I have argued that emotions have "decoupled" stimulus response chains in the course of evolution, thereby freeing organisms from rigid reflex control of behavior and allowing for much greater flexibility of behavioral responses. Emotions provide a latency time between the evaluation of an event and the execution of a behavioral response. This time period can be used for the reevaluation of the event and for choosing between different response alternatives. This is particularly useful for social-living species, for whom emotion also provides an important signalling mechanism in the form of emotional expression. Facial and vocal signals of reaction and intention allow prediction of the behavior tendencies of others in social interaction. Because of the predictability of others' reactions, one can better gauge the likely consequences of one's own behavior.

It is possible to link these functions of emotions to subsystems of the organism and to the different components of the emotion construct that are postulated by modern emotion theorists. Table 2 shows the way in which one might conceive of the specialization of particular components for specific functions of emotion. The theory also emphasizes the dynamic nature of emotion. Emotions can change very rapidly on the basis of new stimuli, new patterns of evaluation, or even the recall of a prior emotion. I have suggested, therefore, that emotion be studied in terms of a *component process model* (Scherer, 1981c, 1984a,b) in order to establish how the various components of emotion (representing states of subsystems of the organism) change over time.

The major part of the model is an attempt to predict the differentiation of various emotional states. I have argued that organisms constantly scan their environment and evaluate events, including internal stimulation. Although this approach is highly indebted to earlier evaluation or appraisal theories (Arnold, 1960; Lazarus, 1966, Wallon, 1969), I have attempted to add a specification of the *criteria* used and the nature of the evaluative process. I postulate the existence of a sequence of stimulus evaluation checks (SECs), and predict that the pattern of outcomes of these checks determines the resulting emotion, conceptualized as the state changes in all of the subsystems of the organism (*sequence theory of emotional differentiation*). Table 3 contains a list of the SECs, which are assumed to always occur in this order (for a more detailed discussion, see Scherer, 1984a).

How can this model account for the occurrence of specific discrete emotions? Table 4 shows a hypothetical listing of the SEC outcomes that may be expected to precede a number of frequently studied emotions. For example, hot anger or rage is expected to appear in situations in

**Table 2.** Relationships between Organismic Subsystems and the Functions and Components of Emotion

| Function | Subsystem | Component |
|---|---|---|
| Evaluation of stimulation | Information processing | Cognitive |
| System regulation | Support | Neurophysiological |
| Preparation and direction of action | Executive | Motivational |
| Communication of reaction and intent | Action | Expressive |
| Reflection and monitoring | Monitor | Subjective feeling |

which a novel event occurs that has high relevance for the organism's goals or plans but that is quite discrepant from expectation and obstructs reaching those goals. Furthermore, for the emotion to occur, there would have to be some urgency, as well as controllability of the event or its consequences, combined with a high degree of perceived power and/or adjustment capability of the individual. Although these hypothetical assumptions will require empirical testing, they do seem to have some face validity in terms of the way people experience emotionally relevant events (Scherer, 1984a,b).

One of the hotly debated issues in the psychology of emotion is the existence of differentiated responses in the physiological and expressive domains. I have proposed to approach this issue from the vantage point of SEC outcome effects rather than of discrete emotion patterns. This approach, which I call a *componential patterning model*, attempts to predict the patterns of changes in the autonomic nervous system, as well as in the motor expressive systems. The assumption is that each outcome of SEC will produce an adaptive response in one or several subsystems. A highly speculative set of predictions concerning such changes is shown in Table 5.

This kind of model can account very easily for individual differences in response patterning across several systems. It assumes that the differences in the SEC outcomes, depending on individual evaluation patterns, will have a differential effect on various other subsystems. This is due to the fact that the SECs use criteria that are specific for individuals, either as habitual characteristics (power and control attributions) or momentary states (need state, goal priorities). Because these criteria will differ widely across individuals, even for objectively equivalent stimulus events, one can expect widely varying emotional outcomes. For example, the very same event will be evaluated very differently by two individuals who differ in terms of their perceived power to cope with the event. This will lead to different emotional states, to be labelled with different emotional terms (such as fear, when there is very little or no perceived power, or anger, when there is perceived power in the case of an obstructive event), and characterized by different autonomic and expressive response patterns. However, even if the resulting emotions should be roughly similar, and be labelled the same way by use of broad emotion terms, it is still possible that subtle differences in SEC outcome, including differences in gradation or extent, will differentially affect the response domains.

We can now return to the problem of individual response tendencies in stress. First, I would argue that stress can be treated very much like most other negative emotions, in terms of the forementioned model. The appraisal or evaluation process should be characterized by SEC outcomes

**Table 3.** Sequence of Stimulus Evaluation Checks (SECs)

1. *Novelty check*
   Determines whether there is a change in the pattern of external or internal stimulation, particularly whether a novel event occurred or is to be expected.
2. *Intrinsic pleasantness check*
   Determines whether a stimulus event is pleasant, inducing approach tendencies, or unpleasant, inducing avoidance tendencies; based on innate feature detectors or on learned associations.
3. *Goal/need significance check*
   Determines whether a stimulus event is relevant to important goals or needs of the organism (relevance subcheck), whether the outcome is consistent with or discrepant from the state expected for this point in the goal/plan sequence (expectation subcheck), and whether it is conducive or obstructive to reaching the respective goals or satisfying the relevant needs (conduciveness subcheck), and how urgently some kind of behavioral response is required (urgency subcheck).
4. *Coping potential check*
   Determines the causation of a stimulus event (causation subcheck) and the coping potential available to the organism, particularly the degree of control over the event or its consequences (control subcheck), the relative power of the organism to change or avoid the outcome through fight or flight (power subcheck), and the potential for adjustment to the final outcome via internal restructuring (adjustment subcheck).
5. *Norm/self compatibility check*
   Determines whether the event, particularly an action, conforms to social norms, cultural conventions, or expectations of significant others (external standards subcheck), and whether it is consistent with internalized norms or standards as part of the self concept or ideal self (internal standards subcheck).

representing novelty, unpleasantness, goal discrepancy and obstructiveness, and, in many cases, low controllability and low power. Second, the componential patterning model should account for the individual differences found in terms of subjective feelings, physiological response, and motor expression. If subjects differ in terms of their self-esteem or perceived power, for example, their response to a stressor should vary greatly in terms of the various response measures. Often, particularly in laboratory experiments, it may be questionable if the term *stress* is not too broad a label to use for the many different negative affect states provoked by stimuli or events that commonly affect individuals. In many cases, one might more profitably talk about various specific negative emotions, such as anger, fear, or anxiety. If there is to be a use for the

**Table 4.** Hypothetical Outcomes of Stimulus Evaluation Checks for Selected Emotional States[a]

| | Novelty | Pleasantness | Goal/need significance | | | | Coping potential | | | Norm compatibility | |
|---|---|---|---|---|---|---|---|---|---|---|---|
| | | | Relevance | Expectation | Conducive | Urgency | Control | Power | Adjust | External | Internal |
| Enjoyment Happiness | low | high | medium | consistent | high | very low | —[b] | — | high | high | high |
| Elation Joy | high | high | high | discrepant | high | low | — | — | medium | high | high |
| Displeasure Disgust | open | very low | low | discrepant | low | medium | open | open | high | low | — |
| Contempt Scorn | open | low | low | discrepant | low | low | open | high | high | low | — |
| Sadness Dejection | low | low | high | discrepant | obstruct | low | none | — | medium | — | — |
| Grief Desperation | high | low | high | discrepant | obstruct | high | low | low | low | — | — |

| Emotion | | | | | | | | | | | |
|---|---|---|---|---|---|---|---|---|---|---|---|
| Anxiety / Worry | low | open | medium | discrepant | obstruct | medium | open | low | medium | — | — |
| Fear / Terror | high | low | high | discrepant | obstruct | very high | open | very low | medium | — | — |
| Irritation / Anger | low | open | medium | discrepant | obstruct | medium | high | medium | high | low | low |
| Rage / Hot Anger | high | open | high | discrepant | obstruct | high | high | high | high | low | low |
| Boredom / Indifference | very low | open | low | consistent | obstruct | low | medium | medium | high | — | — |
| Shame / Guilt | low | open | high | discrepant | obstruct | medium | high | open | medium | very low | very low |

[a] Source: From Scherer, 1984c.
[b] — = not applicable.

**Table 5.** Component Patterning Theory Predictions of SEC Outcome Effects on Subsystems[a]

| SEC outcome | Organismic functions | Social functions | Support system | Action system | | | | | |
|---|---|---|---|---|---|---|---|---|---|
| | | | | Muscle tone | Face | Voice | Instrumental | Posture | Locomotion |
| *Novelty* | | | | | | | | | |
| Novel | Orienting Focussing | Alerting | Orienting response | Local changes | Brows/lids up Open orifices | Interruption Inhalation | Interruption | Straightening Raising head | Interruption |
| Old | Homeostasis | Reassuring | No change | No change | No change | No change | No change | No change | No change |
| *Intrinsic pleasantness* | | | | | | | | | |
| Pleasant | Incorporation | Recommending | Sensitization of sensorium | Slight decrease | Expanding orifices "sweet face" | Wide voice | Centripetal movement | Expanding Opening | Approach |
| Unpleasant | Expulsion Rejection | Warning Recommending | Defense response, desensitization | Increase | Closing orifices "sour face" | Narrow voice | Centrifugal movement | Shrinking Closing in | Avoidance Distancing |
| *Goal/Need Significance* | | | | | | | | | |
| Consistent | Relaxation | Announcing stability | Trophotropic shift | Decrease | Relaxed tone | Relaxed voice | Comfort position | Comfort position | Rest position |

| Discrepant | Activation | Announcing activity | Ergotropic dominance | Increase | Corrugator | Tense voice | Task-dependent | Task-dependent | Task-dependent |
|---|---|---|---|---|---|---|---|---|---|
| *Coping Potential* | | | | | | | | | |
| No control | Readjustment | Indicating withdrawal | Trophotropic dominance | Hypotonus | Lowered eyelids | Lax voice | No activity or slowing | Slump | No movement or slowing |
| High power/ control | Goal assertion | Dominance assertion | Ergo-tropho balance, Noradrenaline, Respiration volume up | Slight decrease, Tension in head and neck | Baring teeth, Tensing mouth | Full voice | Agonistic movement | Anchoring body, lean forward | Approach |
| Low power/ control | Protection | Indicating submission | Ergotropic dominance, Adrenaline, Peripheral vaso-constriction, Respiration rate up | Hypertonus, Tension in locomotor areas | Open mouth | Thin voice | Protective movement | Readiness for locomotion | Fast locomotion or freezing |

Source: From Scherer, 1985[a]

term stress over and above the various negative emotions, it would need to be defined more carefully, within a comprehensive theory of emotion.

I will conclude by suggesting such a definition. It would seem to be the case that emotion, in contrast to long-lasting mood states, for example, is a short-term phenomenon. As mentioned above, one can argue that emotions have developed phylogenetically to provide flexible, yet partially preprogrammed, preparatory adaptation mechanisms for unusual events, particularly emergency situations. The task of the mechanism is to support intra-organismic or behavioral responses that bring about short-term resolution of a problem. Thus, the subsystem changes brought about by the various SEC outcomes, while producing a disequilibrium, can be expected generally to return to baseline rather quickly. The amount of time necessary for this return to baseline may of course be different for different emotions. For example, there is some evidence that this time is longer for sadness than for anger (Scherer, Wallbott, & Summerfield, 1986). Yet, in the main, emotion is a short-term, emergency response. Stress, on the other hand, could be defined as those changes in various subsystem states that maintain a disequilibrium for a long period of time without returning to baseline or without the establishment of a new equilibrium at a different level.

A return to baseline may be impossible because of (a) continuous aversive stimulation, requiring persisting coping attempts, (b) lack of coping or adjustment capability, or (c) cognitive perseveration about past or expected events. Again, these different factors might account for differences in response patterning of the individual's stress reaction. Although the organism is built to accommodate to short-term perturbations in emergency situations (the emotions), the system gets "stressed" when recovery fails to take place and a particular emotional state, with all concomitant subsystem changes, persists over a long period of time. As mentioned before, the nature of "stress" is likely to be determined by the type of emotion that persists beyond the "normal" recovery period. In other words, we should be able to differentiate between anger-stress, fear-stress, disgust-stress, and so forth.

If this conceptualization of stress seems reasonable, and it does seem to be compatible with a number of stress theories in the literature, it is evident that stress needs to be studied in the context of a general model of emotion—in terms of antecedents, reactions, and regulation. An important first step in the direction of such a paradigm would consist in conducting a number of ideographically oriented case studies—using both real-life and laboratory stressors—to carefully study the details of the relationships between evaluation check outcomes and subsystem changes. Clearly, it will be necessary to develop new instruments to get at the fine-grained structure of the subjective evaluation process. Careful case studies could help to revise and correct the prediction concerning subsystem changes in response to specific check outcomes and pave the way for experimental studies, nomothetically oriented, in which information about individuals' evaluative criteria is used to manipulate evaluation outcomes and to test empirically the componential patterning predictions.

In conclusion, I argue that we have little to lose and much to gain by an increasing rapprochement and possibly convergence of research on stress and emotion.

ACKNOWLEDGEMENTS

The author thanks Mortimer Appley and Richard Trumbull for helpful suggestions.

# References

Arnold, M. B. (1960). *Emotion and personality. (Vol. I) Psychological aspects.* New York: Columbia University Press.

Asendorpf, J. (1978). *Bewegung and Erregung* [Movement and Arousal]. Unpublished diploma thesis, University of Giessen.

Asendorpf, J., & Scherer, K. R. (1983). The discrepant repressor: Differentiation between low anxiety, high anxiety, and repression of anxiety by autonomic-facial-verbal patterns of behavior. *Journal of Personality and Social Psychology, 45,* 1334–1346.

Byrne, D. (1964). Repression-sensitization as a dimension of personality. In B. Maher (Ed.), *Progress in experimental personality research* (Vol. 1, pp. 169–219). New York: Academic Press.

Crowne, D. P., & Marlowe, D. (1960). A new scale of social desirability independent of psychopathology. *Journal of Consulting Psychology, 66,* 547–555.

Ekman, P., & Friesen, W. V. (1974). Detecting deception from the body or face. *Journal of Personality and Social Psychology, 29,* 288–298.

Ekman, P., Friesen, W. V., & Scherer, K. R. (1976). Body movement and voice pitch in deceptive interaction. *Semiotica, 16,* 23–27.

Fahrenberg, J., Walschburger, P., Förster, F., Myrtek, M., & Müller, W. (1979). *Psychophysiologische Aktivierungsforschung.* [Research on Psychological Activation]. München: Minerva.

Gellhorn, E. (1970). The emotions and the ergotropic and trophotropic systems. *Psychologische Forschung, 34,* 48–94.

Görlitz, D. (1972). *Ergebnisse und Probleme der ausdruckspsychologischen Sprechstimmforschung.* Meisenheim: Hain.

Helfrich, H., Standke, R., & Scherer, K. R. (1984). Psychoactive drug effects on vocal characteristics. *Speech Communication, 3,* 245–252.

Höfer, I., Wallbott, H. G., & Scherer, K. R. (1985). Messung multimodaler Stress-indikatoren in Belastungssituationen: Person- und Situationsfaktoren. In H. W. Krohne (Ed.), *Angstbewältigung in Leistungssituationen* (pp. 94–114) [Coping with anxiety in achievement situations.] Weinheim: Edition Psychologie.

Jürgens, U. (1979). Vocalization as an emotional indicator. A neuroethological study in the squirrel monkey. *Behaviour, 69,* 88–117.

Lamendella, J. T. (1977). The limbic system in human communication. In H. Whitaker & H. A. Whitaker (Eds.), *Studies in neurolinguistics.* Vol. 3 (pp. 157–222). New York: Academic Press.

Laver, J. (1975). *Individual features in voice quality.* Unpublished doctoral dissertation, University of Edinburgh.

Lazarus, R. S. (1966). *Psychological stress and the coping process.* New York: McGraw-Hill.

Malmo, R. B. (1975). *On emotions, needs, and our archaic brain.* New York: Holt, Rinehart & Winston.

Müller, S. (1978). *Bewegungsdauer als Indikator physiologischer Erregung in Abhängigkeit von Persönlichkeitsvariablen* [Movement duration as an indicator of arousal as mediated by personality traits]. Unpublished diploma thesis, University of Giessen.

Robinson, B. W. (1972). Anatomical and physiological contrasts between human and other primate vocalizations. In S. L. Washburn & P. Dolhinow (Eds.), *Perspectives in human evolution* (pp. 438–443). New York: Holt, Rinehart & Winston.

Rudert, I. (1965). Vom Ausdruck der Sprechstimme [Expressiveness of the speaking voice]. In R. Kirchhoff (Eds.), *Handbuch der Psychologie, 5* (pp. 422–468) Göttingen: Hogrefe.

Scherer, K. R. (1979). Nonlinguistic vocal indicators of emotion and psychopathology. In C. E. Izard (Ed.), *Emotions in personality and psychopathology* (pp. 493–529). New York: Plenum Press.

Scherer, K. R. (1981a). Vocal indicators of stress. In J. Darby (Ed.), *Speech evaluation in psychiatry* (pp. 171–187). New York: Grune & Stratton.

Scherer, K. R. (1981b). Speech and emotional states. In J. Darby (Ed.), *Speech evaluation in psychiatry* (pp. 189–220). New York: Grune & Stratton.

Scherer, K. R. (1981c). Wider die Vernachlässigung der Emotion in der Psychologie [Against the neglect of emotion in psychology]. In W. Michaelis (Ed.), *Bericht über den 32. Kongress der Deutschen Gesellschaft für Psychologie in Zürich* 1980. Göttingen: Hogrefe.

Scherer, K. R. (1982). Methods of research on vocal communication: Paradigms and parameters. In K. R. Scherer & P. Ekman (Eds.), *Handbook of methods in nonverbal behavior research* (pp. 136–198). Cambridge: Cambridge University Press.

Scherer, K. R. (1984a). On the nature and function of emotion: A component process approach. In K. R. Scherer & P. Ekman (Eds.), *Approaches to emotion* (pp. 293–318). Hillsdale, New Jersey: Erlbaum.

Scherer, K. R. (1984b). *Toward a dynamic theory of emotion: The component process model of affective states.* Unpublished manuscript, University of Giessen.

Scherer, K. R. (1985). Vocal affect signalling: A comparative approach. In J. Rosenblatt, C. Beer, & M.-C. Busnel (Eds.), *Advances in the Study of Behavior. Vol. 14* (pp. 198–244). New York: Academic Press.

Scherer, K. R. (1986). Vocal affect expression: A review and a model for future research. *Psychological Bulletin, 99,* 143–165.

Scherer, K. R., & Scherer, U. (1980). Psychological factors in bureaucratic encounters: Determinants and effects of interactions between officials and clients. In W. T. Singleton, P. Spurgeon, & R. B. Stammers (Eds.), *The analysis of social skill* (pp. 315–328). New York: Plenum Press.

Scherer, U., Helfrich, H., & Scherer, K. R. (1980). Internal push or external pull? Determinants of paralinguistic behavior. In H. Giles, P. Robinson, & P. Smith (Eds.), *Language: Social psychological perspectives* (pp. 279–282). Oxford: Pergamon.

Scherer, K. R., Wallbott, H. G., & Summerfield, A. (Eds.) (1986). *Experiencing emotion: A cross-cultural study.* Cambridge: Cambridge University Press.

Scherer, K. R., Wallbott, H. G., Tolkmitt, F., & Bergmann, G. (1985). *Die Stressreaktion: Physiologie and Verhalten* [The Stress Reaction: Physiology and Behavior]. Göttingen: Hogrefe.

Selye, H. (1936). A syndrome produced by diverse nocuous agents. *Nature* (London), *138,* 32.

Streeter, L. A., Krauss, R. M., Geller, V., Olson, C., & Apple, W. (1977). Pitch changes during attempted deception. *Journal of Personality and Social Psychology, 35,* 345–350.

Taylor, J. A. (1953). A personality scale of manifest anxiety. *Journal of Abnormal and Social Psychology, 48,* 285–290.

Tolkmitt, F., Helfrich, H., Standke, R., & Scherer, K. R. (1982). Vocal indicators of psychiatric treatment effects in depressives and schizophrenics. *Journal of Communication Disorders, 15,* 209–222.

van Heck, G. L. M. (1981). *Anxiety: The profile of a trait.* Unpublished doctoral dissertation, University of Tilburg.

Wallon, H. (1949). *Les origines du caractère chez l'enfant* [The origins of personality in the child]. Paris: PUF.

Weinberger, D. A., Schwartz, G. E., & Davidson, R. J. (1979). Low-anxious, high-anxious, and repressive coping styles: Psychometric patterns and behavioral and physiological responses to stress. *Journal of Abnormal Psychology, 88,* 369–380.

# PART IV

# Coping and Stress

*Three different analyses of the relationship between coping and stress are presented in the chapters in this section, raising useful questions about the ways in which coping is measured and its relationship to short- and long-term stress is assessed.*

*In Chapter 10, Frese examines the* mediator *and the* moderator *roles of coping. The former occurs when coping "links" the stressors to the stress reaction; the latter, when the relationship is increased or reduced by whether the person is a "good" or "bad" coper (or defender). Studying both conscious (self-reported) and automatic (indirectly measured) coping strategies in a work setting, Frese compares psychoanalytic and cognitive theory predictions of psychologial dysfunction (in this case, psychosomatic complaints). Among interesting findings, he reports little evidence of a mediating role for coping. A moderating role is found, but only for "problematic" coping strategies that are positively related to later psychosomatic complaints. This relation, involving self-reported, conscious, emotion-focused coping, is taken as supportive of the psychoanalytic position. Using over-reporting (an indirect, more objective measure), however, the cognitive position appears to be supported.*

*Krohne carries the analysis of coping processes even further, examining the relationship between situation parameters and "specific characteristics of coping strategies in determining coping efficacy." Using what he calls a* multilevel-multitemporal approach, *Krohne segments stress situations into anticipation, confrontation, and postconfrontation phases, proposing that the effect of* variable controllability *on coping efficacy varies systematically with the phase in which it is employed. Further, individuals can be distinguished according to their comparatively stable (situation invariant) coping modes that link coping dispositions (a function of competencies, plans, etc.) to actual coping behavior. Successful versus unsuccessful copers differ in the degree to which the goals of their coping acts are regulating emotions, behavioral control of the stressor, and/or information control (in relation to phase).*

*Self-presentation provides a transactional perspective on coping behavior, in which individuals (actors) "project identity-related images to others and then*

**181**

*form identities based on the reactions of others to themselves." In his self-presentational view of coping with stress, Laux proposes a "process-oriented assessment procedure," using video-playback of role-playing, in which sequential interdependencies of cognition, emotion, and behavior are examined over time. Such analyses yield defensive strategies of self-handicapping, self-serving explanations and self-deception, and the more constructive (adaptive) strategy of self-extending, as identifiable coping patterns.*

# CHAPTER 10

# Coping as a Moderator and Mediator between Stress at Work and Psychosomatic Complaints

## MICHAEL FRESE

## Introduction

Coping has become a central variable in psychological stress research. The concepts of coping and defense have been introduced to explain phenomena that cannot be explained by a simple stress–strain model. Some people react strongly to minor stressors, whereas others do not react even to major stressors. There are two ways to explain this. Coping or defense may be either a mediator or a moderator. (For ease of presentation, I shall use the term *coping* to stand for both coping and defense

This research is part of the research project "Psychological Stress at Work" in which a group of psychologists from Switzerland (U. Fellmann, I. Udris, and E. Ulich, Technical University, Zürich) and from Germany (E. Bamberg, H. Dunckel, S. Greif, G. Mohr, D. Rueckert, N. Semmer, and D. Zapf, Free University, Berlin), including the author of this chapter, collaborated.

MICHAEL FRESE ● Institut für Psychologie, Universität München, D8000 München 22, Federal Republic of Germany. The research was supported by a grant from the Bundesminister für Forschung und Technologie, Projekttraeger "Humanisierung des Arbeitslebens" to S. Greif and E. Ulich (# 01 VD 177-ZQ-TAP 0016) (Greif *et al.*, 1983). Work on this chapter was supported by a grant from the Deutsche Forschungsgemeinschaft #FR 638/1-1).

in the following presentation.) This distinction, between moderator and mediator, has rarely been made in the literature:

1. Coping serves as a *mediator* when it is related to both the stressors and the stress reaction or, more specifically, when it *links* the stressors to the stress reaction. The causal impact of stressors on the stress reaction works via coping (see Figure 1). Theoretically, this may mean that the stressor situation influences a certain type of coping response that, in turn, leads to psychological health or dysfunctioning. More technically, this can be examined with a partial correlation procedure (Simon, 1954).

2. Coping can function as a *moderator* when the relationship between stressors and stress reaction is dependent on whether a person is a "good" or a "bad" coper (or defender). Here the relationship between stressors and stress reaction is increased or reduced by a third, independent variable. Figure 2 displays this graphically. Theoretically, this may mean that people have learned certain coping strategies (or coping styles) and use them *vis-à-vis* the stressors. Depending on the coping strategies or styles, dealing with the stressors may produce psychological dysfunctioning or positive growth. This moderator function can be analyzed by comparing the correlations between stressor and stress reaction for different subgroups or by using an interaction term in a regression analysis (Zedeck, 1971).

Thus, the moderator or mediator effect of coping may either enhance or disturb psychological functioning. Although most theories seem to agree that problem-focussed coping has positive consequences, there is disagreement on emotion-focussed coping. Here, psychoanalysis has been much more pessimistic than the more cognitive approach of Lazarus (1966, 1982). According to psychoanalysis, emotion-focussed coping is often done in the form of repression. This implies that energy is expended, that this process is unconscious, and that the result of this process may be the development of psychopathology (A. Freud, 1978; Haan, 1977; Vaillant, 1977). In contrast, Lazarus's cognitive approach argues that "repression" does not, of necessity, lead to continuous expenditure of energy, that the process of repressing can be conscious, and that the result is usually positive because the negative emotion has been dealt with, and therefore does not exist any more. Once an emotion has been

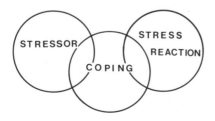

**Figure 1.** Coping as mediator.

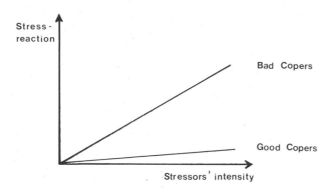

**Figure 2.** Coping as moderator.

coped with, the emotion no longer has a negative impact, as long as other stressors do not trigger the same type of emotion again.

There is still a third approach to the question of the cost and benefit of coping—the action theory perspective (cf. also Schönpflug, this volume). According to this perspective, coping involves effort if the method to cope is not highly practiced and automatic. If a certain coping strategy has been used often enough, it will take very little effort to use it again. This implies that effort is involved only when a coping strategy that has not been highly practiced is used. Moreover, using such a strategy is a conscious process. There is an additional implication within action theory that is of interest here. Human beings turn conscious attention to things only when it is necessary. This necessity arises when a regularly used strategy does *not* work, when one is in a new situation, or when unexpected problems and difficulties arise (Frese & Sabini, 1985). Thus, usually, we use automatic, overlearned strategies. Only when the normal, easy to use, automatic coping strategies do not work do we think of them consciously. This notion has implications for measuring coping. If coping strategies are checked off on a questionnaire, only consciously used strategies will be checked. This means that problematic coping strategies will be reported more often than nonproblematic (i.e., automatically used) ones. Therefore, this theory would suggest that measuring coping with questionnaires (e.g., like the one used by Lazarus and co-workers, cf. Lazarus & Folkman, this volume), leads to reporting problematic coping strategies, although indirect measurement of coping (that includes automatic coping) will have different relations with psychological functioning. Conscious and problematic coping strategies should be positively related to psychological dysfunctioning although automatic coping strategies should be negatively related.

Coping refers to stressors. Stressors can be conceived to be either objective (as seen from an observer's point of view) or subjective (as seen by the subject). Furthermore, a stressor can be a stimulus occurring at only one point in time (e.g., an earthquake) or occurring repeatedly, as in daily hassles (DeLongis, Coyne, Dakof, Folkman, & Lazarus, 1982). Little is known about coping with everyday *objective* "hassles." Stress has been studied either in extreme situations, like disasters, war, or unemployment (thus leaving out the daily hassles), or assessed by subjective questionnaire responses (thus leaving out the objective side).

The study of the moderator effect of coping has looked, for the most part, at the relationship between subjectively measured stress and long-term stress reaction [signified as (a) in Figure 3]. If the objective features of a stressful situation are considered as well, then two additionally interesting effects can be conceptualized. The relationship between objective stressors and stress perception could be mediated or moderated by coping [(b) in Figure 3]. According to psychoanalytic theory, this should occur because defenses influence stress perception (A. Freud, 1978). In a similar vein, modern cognitive stress theories argue that the perception of stress is influenced by coping (e.g., by defensive reappraisal) (Lazarus, 1966). Additionally, coping may have a direct influence on the relationship between objective stress and psychosomatic complaints. This would follow specifically from psychoanalytic theory, because even repressed, or otherwise defended stress situations, may

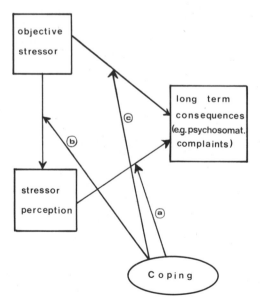

**Figure 3.** Theoretically possible mediator and moderator effects of coping.

have a long-term influence on psychosomatic complaints [(c) in Figure 3]. Stress at work is an area in which both the objective conditions as well as daily problems can be studied (cf. Gardell & Johansson, 1981). Here, it is possible to look at all three moderating or mediating functions of coping.

Thus, in summary, this chapter will argue that it is useful to distinguish moderator and mediator effects of coping and that it is necessary to study not only conscious coping strategies but also automatic ones. This is particularly important if one is interested in the relationship of coping with psychological dysfunctioning, like psychosomatic complaints. Conscious strategies are problematic and are, therefore, positively related to psychosomatic complaints, while automatic coping strategies are negatively related.

## Study Methods and Design

Three studies will be reported, all with blue-collar, male workers from several different firms in the automobile and steel industries in the Federal Republic of Germany (details of these studies can be found in Greif, Bamberg, Dunckel, Frese, Mohr, Rueckert, Rummel, Semmer, & Zapf, 1983). The first and second studies are cross-sectional studies, involving 206 and 841 blue-collar workers, respectively; the third is a longitudinal study, involving a subsample of 90 subjects from the first-cross-sectional study, who filled out questionnaires for a second time, 16 months later, and whose work places were re-observed (for details, see Frese, 1985).

The same measurement design was used in all three studies. Stress at work was measured in three different ways: (1) Subjects were asked to fill out a questionnaire on relevant job dimensions. Wording of the items was as objective as possible. For example, we did not ask whether the subject felt that the work was straining but "Does your work demand quick reactions?" (2) Trained observers observed the subjects at work for 1 hour to 1 1/2 hour intervals and filled out the same questionnaire items as the subjects. (3) The third measure was an aggregate called the "group" level measurement. We had three or more people in the same job (for example, three welders) fill out the questionnaire. The median obtained on each dimension was then used as the measure for each person; for example, if three welders gave the answers 2, 3, and 5 for intensity of work, a 3 was assigned to each of them. This index has two advantages: it eliminates idiosyncratic responses (the same way as the observers' judgments do); and it takes the expertise of the subjects seriously. None of these measures is perfect, but the problems offset each other, those of one method not being the problems of the other.

## Measures of Stress

The following stressors were assessed:

*Psychological stress* (measured on the subjective, observed, and "group" level) is an index of five different scales on stress at work (which were developed by Semmer, 1982, 1984) that correlate with each other. These are "uncertainty" (e.g., ambiguities, conflicts, and small error-big damage), "organizational problems" (e.g., one does not get material to work with on time), "environmental stress" (e.g., noise), "danger of accidents," and "intensity" (speed) of work.

*Physical stress* combined two indices (developed by Semmer, 1982, 1984): physical intensity and one-sided stress of parts on the body, for example, arms, legs, and so forth. These indices were also measured on the three levels.

*Social stress* (developed by the author) was assessed on the subjective level only. A typical item was: "One is always criticized here; and nobody acknowledges it if one does something well."

Additionally, *leisure-time stress* (developed by Bamberg, 1986) was included in the analyses of the longitudinal study because it had been suggested (e.g., Folkman & Lazarus, 1980; Pearlin & Schooler, 1978) that the choices for coping strategies are different for work stressors than for stressors outside work. A typical item was "I have so much to do that I cannot do anything for my hobby."

The dependent variable used in the studies reported was psychosomatic complaints (an adaptation of Fahrenberg's (1975) *Freiburger Beschwerden Liste* by Mohr, 1984). The items ask for reports of headaches, stomachaches, sleeping problems, and so forth.

## Measures of Coping

Before discussing the development of the measures of coping, some theoretical remarks are in order. There is a debate about whether one should measure situationally specific coping strategies or consistent coping styles. There is no doubt that the choice of strategy depends, to a large extent, on the situation. However, if one wants to argue that ineffective coping contributes to long-range problems, like psychosomatic complaints, then it is unlikely that only situationally specific coping strategies play a role. The assumption is that psychosomatic complaints are developed only when one is exposed to ineffective coping strategies rather frequently. Thus, in order for coping to influence the development of psychosomatic complaints, there must be some commonality in type or style of coping strategies.

Further, research on coping should enable us to draw general conclusions about the usefulness of certain coping "strategies" versus others, and since we cannot determine the infinite number of potential coping–situation transactions, the notion of style helps us to make research more manageable. In fact, coping strategies are combined into styles by nearly all researchers, regardless of whether they argue for an idiographic or a nomothetic approach to measuring coping.

The measurement approach chosen here is somewhere between the two positions—style versus strategy. Although a situation-based questionnaire was used, the answers were grouped across situations. Four different stressors were described briefly, as a vignette, on the top of the questionnaire. The four situations were: "When I am under pressure in work, then . . . ," "When something bothers me at work, then . . . ," "When I have an argument with a colleague, then . . . ," and "When I have an argument with my wife or girlfriend, then. . . ." Below each of these four vignettes various alternative strategies were listed, and the subjects were asked to rate each alternative. There were 80 items in all.

## Factor-Derived Scales

Principal component analysis revealed six clear and stable factors all but one of which cut across the different stress situations. Only the factor "socially focussed positive outlook" was specific for the two social situations. Repeating this analysis, with a somewhat reduced set of items in the second cross-sectional study (with different subjects), led to the same stable factors. (The six factors are described in Table 1.)

With the exception of socially oriented coping, all the factors can be described as "emotion-focussed" coping. This is not just the result of the selection of coping alternatives listed in the questionnaire and used in the principal component analysis. Several questionnaire items were concerned with "problem-focussed" coping. (For example: "When I am under pressure in work then . . . I postpone other things and concentrate on the work that I have to do"; . . . "I tell the supervisor that I will not be able to finish this work in time"; . . . "I work not faster but with more care"; or ". . . I tell the supervisor that I do not want to be pressured.") Interestingly, these items did not comprise a factor. On the other hand, the more emotion-focussed items, like "I tell myself consciously: Now be calm," and so forth, easily clustered into factors.

This suggests that there may be an asymmetry between emotion-focussed and problem-focussed strategies or styles. Problem-focussed coping implies that a specific means is used to solve a specific problem. Thus, coping strategies change with problems, since a different solution will be necessary for each problem. Therefore, there can be little in the

**Table 1.** Coping Factors[a]

---

If something bothers me in my work, then . . .
(Pressure, argument with colleague, argument with spouse)
(1) Positive outlook (5 items; $\alpha$ = .68/.75)
    ". . . I say consciously to myself: 'Now be calm.'"
(2) Socially focussed positive outlook (9 items; $\alpha$ = .78/.77)
    ". . . I think that there are better sides to him/her."
(3) Brooding (6 items; $\alpha$ = .81/.84)
    ". . . I think about it for some days."
(4) Socially oriented coping (6 items; $\alpha$ = .70/.62)
    ". . . I ask other colleagues for help."
(5) Attention diverting (5 items; $\alpha$ = .72/.75)
    ". . . I try to divert my attention from this."
(6) Repression (4 items; $\alpha$ = .76/.76)
    ". . . I swallow down my anger."

---

[a] Number of items and Cronbach's alpha for the two cross-sectional studies shown in parentheses.

way of coping *style* in problem-focussed coping. Emotion-focussed coping, on the other hand, can be similar in different situations because the focus (the emotion) is less differentiated. As a small number of emotions have to be dealt with, emotion-focussed coping can be more stylistic and more cross-situationally consistent.

**Additional Scales**

In addition to the six-factor analytically-derived scales, there are four more scales on coping (as displayed in Table 2). Two of these relate to pressures at work, denial and avoidance. Avoidance is related to wanting to leave one's job when under pressure. Denial consists of relatively extreme responses about the positive quality of job pressure. (I do not want to imply that this scale measures denial in a psychoanalytic sense. A more parsimonious explanation would be that it measures a redirection of attention—one looks at the bright side of pressures at work instead of at the negative side.)

All the scales described so far are self-report scales. The final two coping scales used are indirect measures and, like all indirect measures, they hinge on certain assumptions. The theoretical assumption is that coping and defense have an impact on stress perception, a position shared by psychoanalytic (e.g., Haan, 1977; Vaillant, 1977) as well as cognitive theories of stress (e.g., Lazarus, 1966). The assumption is that defenses reduce the perception of stress, and palliative, as well as problem-focussed, coping have an impact on how threatening a stress situation is perceived to be. It follows, then, that the difference between the objective stress situation and the subjective perception of it can be taken as a measure of coping.

Two "objective" indicators of psychological stress were used, each independent of a particular subject's perception, namely, the observers', and the "group" estimates. Two deviation scores were derived by subtracting the observers' (or "group") estimates from the subjects' estimate of psychological stress. In each case, the scales making up psychological stress at work were transformed into z-scores and the subtraction was done separately for each scale. The resulting scales (4 for overreporting/deviation from observers and 5 for overreporting/deviation from "group") were then recombined to make up the two overall deviation scales. In each case, the 4 or 5 deviation scores (items) lead to acceptable Cronbach alphas, despite the brevity of each overall scale. The two resulting scales correlated .52 in each of the two cross-sectional studies.

## Methods of Analysis

In general, a correlational approach was used. The mediator effect was analyzed by partial correlations (criterion—change of .10 between zero order correlation and partial correlation) the moderator effect by subgrouping on the coping variables and comparing correlations between the respective variables (Fischer's z-test).

The analysis of the longitudinal study used a cross-lagged panel

**Table 2.** Additional Coping Scales

(1) Denial (6 items; $\alpha = .73/.78$)
  "When one is under pressure in work, one is able to show what one can accomplish."
(2) Avoidance (3 items; $\alpha = .63/.65$)
  "When the pressure at work is high, I think sometimes about changing my job."
Overreporting:
(3) Overreporting/deviation from observers →
  subject's psychological stress − observed psychological stress (4 scales; $\alpha = .64/.71$)
(4) Overreporting/deviation from "group"-level →
  subject's psychological stress − "group" psychological stress (5 scales; $\alpha = .70/.74$)

[a] Number of items and Cronbach's alpha for the two cross-sectional studies are shown in parentheses.

correlation approach (Kenny, 1979). A difference of the z-standardized cross-lagged correlations of .20 or higher was used as a criterion. Although not extremely stringent, it was deemed sufficient in light of the exploratory nature of the research (in order not to overlook any possible relationships), the relatively small time lag of 16 months (which does not allow for the development of large effects), and the homogeneity of the sample.

The cross-lagged correlation approach has recently been criticized (e.g., Rogosa, 1980). Rogosa showed that differences (and similarities) between the cross-lagged correlations could be produced by differences in stabilities and by lack of "stationarity." These criticisms were taken into account. Partialling out the stabilities did not change the results dramatically, and the principle of stationarity was rarely violated.

In summary, results were based on eight scales on stressors (three on psychological stress, three on physical stress, and one each on social and leisure time stress); and ten scales on coping, six of which were derived from a principal component analysis of a situation-oriented questionnaire. The dependent variable was psychosomatic complaints (see Table 3).

## Results and Discussion

The results are presented in the following steps: (1) The bivariate relationships between stressors and coping, (2) the bivariate relationships between coping and psychosomatic complaints, (3) the role of coping as a mediator and moderator of the relationship between objective stressor and stressor perception, and (4) the mediating and moderating function of coping in the relationship between stressors and psychosomatic complaints.

## Stress and Coping

The bivariate relationships between stress and coping are presented in Table 3. With the exception of avoidance and overreporting, the correlations are relatively small. There is a fair degree of consistency across the two cross-sectional studies. In the main, stressors and coping seem to be largely independent factors.

Longitudinally, one might look for subjective stress to be either mainly determined by coping or to cause coping strategies to develop. However, here too, no consistent relationships of any importance were found between stress and coping in the cross-lagged correlations of the

**Table 3.** Biovariate Relationships between the Variables in the Cross-Sectional Studies

| Coping | Observed psychological stress | "Group" psychological stress | Subject's psychological stress | Observed physical stress | "Group" physical stress | Subject's physical stress | Social stress | Leisure-time stress | Psycho-somatic complaints |
|---|---|---|---|---|---|---|---|---|---|
| Denial | −.13/.04 | −.10/.03 | −.12/.01 | −.01/.05 | −.01/.06 | −.08/.05 | −.06/−.08** | .03/−.01 | −.27**/.03 |
| Socially focussed positive outlook ⎫ | .13*/.04 | .02/.07 | .14*/.14** | .09/−.08 | .17*/.05 | .09/.01 | .05/.04 | .17*/.10 | .16*/.07** |
| Positive outlook | .20**/.07 | .17*/.11** | .16*/.15** | .08/−.08 | .14*/.05 | .07/.02 | .02/.05 | .10/.07 | .03/.10** |
| Brooding ⎫ | .10/−.04 | .04/.06 | .19**/.10** | .06/−.02 | .13/.08* | .10/.14** | .33**/.14** | .19**/.17** | .33**/.36** |
| Socially oriented Coping ⎭ | .15*/.04 | .11/.03 | .09/.12** | .01/−.11* | −.08/.04 | .01/.07* | .22**/.16** | .22**/.12** | .19/.11** |
| Diverting attention | .11/.01 | .04/.08* | .16**/.04 | .10/−.04 | .16*/.04 | .15*/.05 | .08/.05 | .02/.03 | .22**/.11** |
| Repression | −.05/−.12** | −.02/.04 | .07/.10** | .15*/.01 | .21**/.03 | .17*/.10** | .02/.05 | −.05/.06 | .23**/.12** |
| Avoidance | .02/.03 | .09/−.01 | .29**/.12** | .18*/.15** | .10/.10** | .19**/.21** | .40**/.31** | .35**/.18** | .23**/.23** |
| Overreporting 1 (deviation obs./subj.) ⎫ | — | .16*/.12* | — | .18*/−.07 | .23**/.01 | .36**/.19** | .24**/.23** | .08*/.11** | .21**/.11** |
| Overreporting 2 (deviation "group"/subj.) ⎭ | −.14/.03 | — | — | .17*/.05 | .01/.14** | .22**/.28** | .11/.30** | .04/.11** | .17/.23** |

* p < .05; ** p < .01. *Note.* First number from 1st study/second one from 2nd study.

longitudinal study. This is not surprising since most theories describe coping predispositions and stressors as coming from distinct sources that are not causally related.

## Coping and Psychosomatic Complaints

The question of whether inadequate coping strategies cause psychosomatic problems or vice versa is important, both theoretically and empirically. On the cross-sectional level, moderately high and largely positive correlations were found between coping strategies and psychosomatic complaints, as shown in Table 3. With the exception of positive outlook and denial, all coping strategies have consistent, significantly positive relationships with psychosomatic complaints in both studies. This seems to contradict those theories that see the primary function of coping to be its reduction of stress effects.

The same pattern of positive correlations is also found in the longitudinal study (data not shown). Here three of the coping strategies (socially focussed positive outlook, avoidance, and overrating/deviation from observers) show positive causal correlations with pychosomatic complaints that are higher (criterion .20) than the other cross-lagged correlation (the path from psychosomatic complaints at $t_1$ to coping at $t_2$). This would suggest that the measured coping strategies are actually *ineffective*, leading to more rather than fewer psychosomatic complaints. I shall return to this later.

## Coping as Mediator or Moderator of the Relationship between Objective and Subjective Stress

Does coping have a moderating or mediating role in the relationship between objective stressors and their subjective perception? There are two "objective" indices in our studies—group level and observers' level.

No important reductions in the correlations are found after the coping factors are partialled out. An exception is when overreporting/deviation from a group is partialled out, which increases the correlation between subjective stress and observed stress in both cross-sectional studies.

In a second step, the moderator effect of coping was tested. The samples were divided into subgroups of equal numbers (median partition). Two groups (in the first cross-sectional study) and three groups (in the second study) were formed according to their scores in each coping strategy. When the correlations between objective and subjective stress

**Table 4.** Repression as Moderator of the Relationship between Observed and Subjective Psychological Stress

| First study | | Second study | | |
|---|---|---|---|---|
| repression | | repression | | |
| low | high | low | medium | high |
| .48 | .24 | .53 | .29 | .23 |

were then compared, there were some significant differences between the correlations of the subgroups. Repression is the only variable, however, that shows a consistent difference between the correlations in the two cross-sectional studies. As shown in Table 4, the relationship is higher for the low repressors. (This speaks for the scale's validity, because repressors should not be able to perceive stress adequately.)

In the longitudinal study, there are no clear-cut results that point to any moderator effect. This may be partly due to the fact that, at the time of the study, the subjects had been in their particular jobs for a long time and had therefore developed a particular picture of their stress situation that no longer fluctuated over time. (This conceptualization of their stress may have been influenced by coping styles and strategies at an earlier point). Therefore, this nonresult does not necessarily mean that coping styles play no role in the development of stress perception at the beginning of a career or after a job change (cf. Frese, 1982, 1984).

In summary, there is little indication of any important mediator or moderator effects of coping on the relationship between objective and subjective stress in these data.

## Coping as Mediator or Moderator of the Relationship between Stress and Psychosomatic Complaints

Using partial correlation, there is again very little indication of coping mediation between stressors and psychosomatic complaints. The only exception is avoidance, which is a mediator between social stress and psychosomatic complaints in both cross-sectional studies.

The moderator effect of coping was again examined by dichotomizing (first study) and trichotomizing (second study) the subjects, according to their scores on each coping variable, and searching for significant differences between the subgroups' correlations of stressors with psychosomatic complaints. The 7 stressors (leisure-time stress was not

included in this analysis) and 10 coping factors in the two studies allow
for 140 comparisons. Were only the results of the first study to be presented, some interesting moderator effects could be reported. The same
would be true, if only the results of the second study were presented.
However, when we examine both sets of results together, there is no
consistent moderator effect that appears in both cross-sectional studies.
(When using interaction terms "stressor × coping" in moderated regression analyses, the same results prevail. There are no moderator effects
that appear consistently in both cross-sectional studies.)

    In summary, there is no indication for a moderator effect and there
is only little indication of a mediator effect (except in the relationship
between social stress and psychosomatic complaints). The most consistent
findings, so far, are the simple correlations between coping and psychosomatic complaints. These are nearly all positive—meaning more coping
leads to more psychosomatic complaints.

### Longitudinal Findings

    In the longitudinal study, the expectation of similar inconsistent
findings as were found in the cross-sectional studies turned out to be
wrong; there were some interesting and consistent moderator effects.

    In this study, the sample was dichotomized into high and low groups
on each of the respective coping dimensions at time 1 ($t_1$). A cross-lagged
panel design was used again for analyzing the results. There were two
criteria now—the cross-lagged correlations had to be different, that is,
the z-standardized correlation of stress $t_1$ with psychosomatic complaints
$t_2$ had to be at least .20 greater than the correlation of psychosomatic
complaints $t_1$ with stress $t_2$. Second, the difference between high and low
copers (on each dimension) had to be at least .20 in the largest cross-
lagged correlation. (As before, these are not extremely stringent criteria
but, given the nonresults in the cross-sectional studies, I did not want to
miss any effect in the longitudinal study. A stringent significance criterion
would be difficult to reach in a study that does not stretch over a long
time period. Furthermore, the sample gets very small when 90 people
are partitioned into two subgroups.) Third, the criterion of a double
difference is not easily reached. Finally, I think it may be more important
to find consistent results in this type of research than to find significant
results.

    In Table 5, a truly fascinating picture emerges. (For methodological
reasons, the two observed indicators and the group index for physical
stress could not be used, as their stabilities were too low, partly due to
slight differences in the training of observers at the two measurement
points.) The meaning of the numbers in this table can be explained with

**Table 5.** Longitudinal Study: Coping as Moderator of the Correlation between Stress and Psychosomatic Complaints

|  | Correlations[a] | | | | | | | | | |
|---|---|---|---|---|---|---|---|---|---|---|
|  | Subject's psychological stress $t_1$/Psysom $t_2$ | | Group psychological stress $t_1$/Psysom $t_2$ | | Subject's physical stress $t_1$/Psysom $t_2$ | | Social stress $t_1$/Psysom $t_2$ | | Leisure-time stress $t_1$/Psysom $t_2$ | |
| Coping $t_1$ | Coping low | Coping high | Coping low | Coping high | Coping low | Coping high | Coping low | Coping high | Coping low | Coping high |
| Denial |  |  |  |  |  |  |  |  |  | .56 |
| Socially focused positive outlook } |  | .58 |  |  |  |  |  |  |  | .60 |
| Positive outlook |  | .57 |  | .40 | .47 |  |  |  |  |  |
| Brooding |  | .52 |  |  |  |  |  |  |  |  |
| Socially oriented coping } |  |  |  |  |  |  |  |  | .54 |  |
| Attention diverting |  |  |  |  |  |  |  |  |  |  |
| Repression |  | .51 |  | .41 |  | .49 |  |  |  |  |
| Avoidance |  | .56 |  | .45 |  |  |  |  |  |  |
| Overreporting 1 (dev. obs./subj.) } |  | .44 |  | .38 |  | marginally |  | .43 |  | .55 |
| Overreporting 2 (dev. "group"/subj.) } |  | .49 |  | .41 |  | marginally |  | .43 |  | .58 |

*Note.* Psysom = Psychosomatic complaints.

[a] A number appears in a cell only when the double criterion (see text) has been met.

the example given in Figure 4. Here, all the correlations of the cross-lagged panel are displayed. Repression $t_1$ was median-split and then all the correlations were computed for the high and low repressors. High repressors show the highest cross-lagged correlation between stress $t_1$ and psychosomatic complaints $t_2$ ($r = .51$). This correlation is .20 higher than the respective cross-lagged correlations ($r = .31$) for low repressors. Similarly, it is also higher than the other cross-lagged correlation ($r$ = psychosomatic complaints/$t_1$, psychological stress/$t_2$) for high repressors ($r = .20$). The highest cross-lagged correlation ($r = .51$) in the figure is displayed in Table 5 in the respective cell.[1] As can be seen in Table 5, with the exception of two cases, whenever the double criteria are met, the highest paths from stress $t_1$ to psychosomatic complaints $t_2$ are in the "high coping" cells. Moreover, the highest cross-lagged correlations are consistently from earlier stress to later psychosomatic complaints. Most of the moderating effects involve subjective psychological stress, but they are reproduced, for the most part, with the more objective indicator of "group" level psychological stress. The smallest number of moderating effects involve social stress and subjective physical stress. The most consistent relationships are found with the two indices of overreporting.

The fact that, with only two exceptions, the "high" copers show the highest causal paths from stressors $t_1$ to psychosomatic complaints $t_2$, may be taken as a test of psychoanalytic versus cognitive theories. The cognitive position (e.g., by Lazarus, 1982) would predict that emotion-reducing coping strategies, like denial and repression, lead to less negative effects of stress on psychosomatic health. This is obviously not the case (cf. Table 4 and the example in Figure 4). Thus, these data seem to be more supportive of psychoanalytic conceptualizations that presuppose that emotion-focussed coping strategies are not effective and may lead to the development of psychosomatic complaints (Haan, 1977, Vaillant, 1977).

However, this statement is true only for the self-reported coping scales (all except the two indices of overreporting). The indirect indices of overreporting tend to favor a cognitive account against the psychoanalytic one. A cognitive account of stress would predict that overreporters show greater stress-effects because they perceive more stress and therefore develop more psychosomatic complaints. This prediction would not follow from a psychoanalytic account. Since the underreporters are repressors, from a psychoanalytic perspective, they should show the great-

---

[1] Whenever the double criterion applies, the higher cross-lagged path leads from stress $t_1$ to psychosomatic complaints $t_2$ and not from psychosomatic complaints $t_1$ to stress $t_2$.

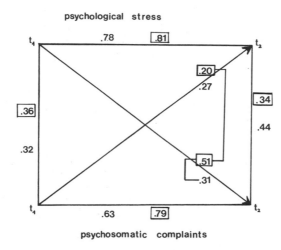

**Figure 4.** Cross-lagged panel for repression (example).

est impact of stress on the development of psychosomatic complaints.[2] However, the data do not support this prediction; there is a higher causal path from stress to psychosomatic complaints for overreporters than for underreporters (see Figure 5 for an example). A cognitive theory of stress seems to be supported here.

Thus, there is an interesting paradox in the data—the coping factors that directly measure coping via questionnaires show a moderating effect, supporting psychoanalytic theory. On the other hand, the indirect and more objective indicators of coping seem to support a cognitive account.

## Interpretation

To interpret these results, it is useful to consider the situation of the subject filling out a questionnaire. To report a coping strategy, the

[2] The psychoanalytic theory by Vaillant (1977) would be somewhat vague in its predictions because overreporting may stem from (positive) suppression or (negative) repression. However, within his system, it is reasonable to argue that underreporters are repressors and they should, therefore, show the highest impact of stress on the development of psychosomatic complaints.

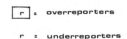

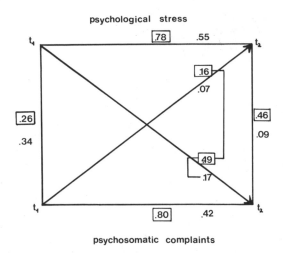

**Figure 5.** Cross-lagged panel for overreporting deviation from "group".

subject has to know, consciously, what kind of coping strategy he uses when he checks a response. As suggested before, only those coping strategies that are "problematic" are consciously represented, and, therefore can be checked on a questionnaire. Ordinarily, we use automatic, overlearned coping strategies. Only when the normal, easy to use, automatic coping strategies do not work do we think about them consciously. Therefore, checking off a coping strategy on a questionnaire may mean that it is a strategy used in a difficult, new, surprising situation—in short, that it is a *problematic* strategy. Therefore, questionnaire studies on coping may produce the result that coping strategies lead to psychological problems or show moderator effects similar to the ones found in this study. Coyne, Aldwin, and Lazarus (1981) reported that out of the seven coping strategies they studied, six had a higher (although not always significant) use by depressed than by nondepressed subjects.

This explanation does not imply that the results derived from questionnaires are methodological artifacts. They may be perfectly valid, but reflect only the correlations between *problematic* coping strategies (those that people think about) and psychosomatic complaints (or depression). It seems that a great impact of stress on psychosomatic complaints, under conditions of high repression or high positive outlook, may mean only that one is uncomfortable enough with these strategies to have been forced to think about them. This uncomfortableness may, in turn, be due to the realization that these coping strategies are not effective, or that the stress situation is high enough to make one think of possible ways to reduce it.

This action theoretic interpretation not only explains the results from the self-reported coping factors but also those with the variable of over-reporting. Since over-reporting is measured indirectly, all of the unconscious, automatic, highly practiced coping strategies are operative here as well. Overreporters suffer from greater stress effects, a finding consistent with cognitive theory of stress.

Therefore, we can conclude that questionnaire studies on coping are only useful if we are interested in this specific problematic type of coping strategies, and that it is more useful to develop indirect measures of coping that include automatic coping strategies. Furthermore (at the time of writing), since daily hassles are emphasized in stress research (instead of singular events with which people do not have any prior experience), it becomes imperative to look at the routinized coping responses that people have learned to use vis-à-vis the daily hassles.

## Some Remaining Problems of Interpretation

There are some potential problems of interpretation that still remain. First, could the indices of overreporting actually be scales of demand characteristics (Orne, 1962) or social desirability? Second, how can the differences in findings between the cross-sectional and longitudinal studies be explained? Third, do methodological problems of the cross-lagged panel design lead to the obtained results? And fourth, how can the findings of other studies (notably the one by Pearlin & Schooler, 1978) be explained in the light of our theoretical interpretation?

The issues of demand characteristics and social desirability are quite complex in the context studied here. Some subjects may have thought that the study was supposed to prove the existence of great stress at work. In such a case, demand characteristics would produce low correlations between stress at work and psychosomatic complaints, since stress reports would be elevated. Also, overreporters (who comply with demand characteristics) would show a *lower* correlation than underreporters. This was not the case.

Other subjects may have reported elevated levels of both stress at work and psychosomatic complaints because they thought that this was in line with the hypothesis of the investigators. However, this is not likely, as such a hypothesis is not really salient when one is confronted with a lengthy questionnaire on all aspects of life at work and outside work. Empirically, there is no evidence for demand characteristics. If these demand characteristics were operative, the variable overreporting should moderate the relationship in the cross-sectional studies. The results of these studies give no hint of a moderator effect—only the longitudinal study does. It is unlikely, further, that demand characteristics would produce effects 16 months later (it is doubtful that the subjects even remembered their answers after such a long time interval). Finally, the results of the variable "group" level psychological stress cannot be explained with the notions of social desirability or demand characteristics. If overreporting were due to social desirability or demand characteristics, it would not moderate the relationship between group psychological stress and psychosomatic complaints, which it does in the longitudinal study (cf. Table 5). Thus, demand characteristics and social desirability cannot explain the results.

Why are there different results in the cross-sectional and longitudinal studies? The former do not lead to clear and consistent results, whereas the latter do. First, let me state that the differences are not due to an artifact. Since the first cross-sectional study and the first portion of the longitudinal study share the same subjects, the latter could have just replicated the results of the first cross-sectional study. However, this is not the case. Of the 16 differences between high and low copers, which were found in the longitudinal study, five also appeared in the first cross-sectional study (leisure time stress was not included in the analysis). Conversely, in the 11 instances in which the correlations of stress with psychosomatic complaints are different between high and low copers in the first cross-sectional study, 5 are replicated in the longitudinal study. There is some overlap, but the overall picture is much clearer in the longitudinal study.

Let me hasten to point out that I did not expect different results between the cross-sectional and longitudinal studies, and my explanations are, therefore, necessarily *post hoc*. In another study, on the effects of unemployment (Frese, in press), we found that hope (for theoretical reasons called "hope for control" in this study) had a negative correlation with depression on the cross-sectional level but a positive correlation in a longitudinal study for those who stayed unemployed. The interpretation was that only after one had experienced unemployment for a certain amount of time does one lose hope. Under such conditions, it is much worse if one had had high hopes in the past. A similar argument might apply for coping. Repeated unsuccessful attempts to cope have a greater impact on the development of psychosomatic complaints than does giving up trying to cope in the first place (cf. Schönpflug, 1985, for a similar argument), or having been able to cope using automatized strategies. Processes of this kind need time to develop. One has to be exposed to the stressors and to (ineffective) coping strategies for a long period of time before psychosomatic complaints can develop. Therefore, the results can be expected to become clearer and more coherent in longitudinal studies. It should be noted that the coping strategies described in this study are considered ineffective only with regard to the development of psychosomatic complaints. They may be very effective in dealing with the task at hand—for example, producing products in the factory (see Schönpflug, this volume).

As already noted, there are several methodological problems in using cross-lagged correlations, mainly the impact of stabilities on such correlations and lack of stationarity. Using a difference of .20 or higher between the correlation of stress and psychosomatic complaints at $t_1$ and the same correlation at $t_2$ as a criterion for the violation of the stationarity assumption, 5 of the 21 correlations shown in Table 5 violate this assumption (among them, the relationship displayed in Figure 5). There are no apparent patterns. To reduce its confounding effect, stability was partialled out (a procedure suggested by Pelz & Andrews, 1964). When this is done, 3 of the 21 differences between the cross-lagged correlations disappear, but 6 additional relationships now meet our double criterion of differences between high and low copers. It seems unlikely that the methodological problems of the cross-lagged panel design lead to the results at hand.

How do the results presented here relate to other studies in the field? There are only a few that look at coping as moderating or mediating the relationship between stressors and a psychological health variable. Coyne et al. (1981), although not really looking at the moderating or mediating role of coping, nevertheless found essentially the same results—people with higher self-reports of coping show more depression. Pearlin & Schooler (1978) reported different results, namely, that coping seems to be an effective shield against the stress effects. However, I think that their study does not really test the moderating effect of coping. Coping should moderate the relationship between stressors and strains, but these, as measured by Pearlin and Schooler, are theoretically and empirically not really different concepts. Stress is measured with questions about whether one feels unhappy, worried, frustrated, and so forth, in daily situations (as in daily life with one's spouse). Strains are measured essentially in the same way. For example, there is a scale on "frustration of role expectations" (strain) and a scale on "nonacceptance of spouse" (stress). The latter includes items such as "My marriage doesn't give me enough opportunity to become the sort of person I'd like to be," which actually seems to be an instance of "frustration of role expectations." It is not surprising, therefore, that, for example, the correlation between strain and emotional stress in the marriage role is .78 (given the unreliability of their scales, this is practically unity). Thus, the moderation of the relationship between stress and strain cannot be tested with this design, since the two concepts, stress and strain, measure practically the same thing.

In summary, our study found only very few mediating effects of coping. A consistent moderator effect was found in the longitudinal study. Our interpretation was that self-report measures assess only problematic coping strategies, and coping strategies of this kind open one up to stress effects. In contrast, the indirect measures, related to normal and automatic everyday coping strategies, show a different picture, one that supports the cognitive theory of stress.

ACKNOWLEDGMENTS

Thanks are due to J. Sabini for criticizing an earlier draft of this paper.

# References

Bamberg, E. (1986). *Arbeit und Freizeit: Eine empirische Untersuchung zum Zusammenhang zwischen Stress am Arbeitsplatz, Freizeit und Familie* [Work and leisure time: Empirical research on the relationship between stress at work, leisure time, and family]. Weinheim: Beltz.

Coyne, J. C., Aldwin, C., & Lazarus, R. S. (1981). Depression and coping in stressful episodes. *Journal of Abnormal Psychology, 90,* 439–447.

DeLongis, A., Coyne, J. C., Dakof, G., Folkman, S., & Lazarus, R. S. (1982). Relationships of daily hassles, uplifts and major life events to health status. *Health Psychology, 1,* 119–136.

Fahrenberg, J. (1975). Die Freiburger Beschwerdeliste FBL [The Freiburg complaint list FBL]. *Zeitschrift für Klinische Psychologie, 4,* 79–100.

Folkman, S., & Lazarus, R. S. (1980). An analysis of coping in a middle-aged community sample. *Journal of Health and Social Behavior, 21,* 219–239.

Frese, M. (1982). Occupational socialization and psychological development: An underemphasized research perspective in industrial psychology. *Journal of Occupational Psychology, 55,* 209–224.

Frese, M. (1984). Job transitions, occupational socialization, and strain. In V. Allen & E.v.d. Vliert (Eds.), *Role transitions* (pp. 239–252). New York: Plenum Press.

Frese, M. (1985). Stress at work and psychosomatic complaints: A causal interpretation. *Journal of Applied Psychology, 70,* 314–328.

Frese, M., & Sabini, J. (Eds.) (1985). *Goal oriented behavior: The concept of action in psychology.* Hillsdale, NJ: Erlbaum.

Frese, M. (in press). Alleviating depression in the unemployed: On the effects of adequate financial support, hope and early retirement. *Social Science and Medicine.*

Freud, A. (1978). *Das Ich und die Abwehrmechanismen* [The ego and the defense mechanisms]. München: Kindler.

Gardell, B., & Johansson, G. (Eds.) (1981). *Working life: A social science contribution to work reform.* Chichester: Wiley.

Greif, S., Bamberg, E., Dunckel, H., Frese, M., Mohr, G., Rueckert, D., Rummel, M., Semmer, N., & Zapf, D. (1983). *Abschlussbericht des Forschungsprojekts: "Psychischer Stress am Arbeitsplatz—Hemmende und fördernde Bedingungen für humanere Arbeitsplaetze"* [Final report of the research project "Psychological stress at work—factors promoting and impeding humane working conditions"]. Universität, Osnabrueck.

Haan, N. (1977). *Coping and defending: Processes of self-environment organization.* New York: Academic Press.

Kenny, D. A. (1979). *Correlation and causation.* New York: Wiley.

Lazarus, R. S. (1968). *Psychological stress and the coping process.* New York: McGraw-Hill.

Lazarus, R. S. (1982). The denial of stress. In S. Breznitz (Ed.), *Denial of stress.* New York: International University Press.

Mohr, G. (1986). *Die Erfassung psychischer Betindenensbeeinträchtigungen bei Industriearbeitern* [Measuring psychological well-being in blue-collar workers]. Frankfurt: Lang.

Orne, M. T. (1962). On the social psychology of the psychological experiment: With particular reference to demand characteristics and their implications. *American Psychologist, 17,* 776–783.

Pearlin, L. I., & Schooler, C. (1978). The structure of coping. *Journal of Health and Social Behavior, 19,* 2–21.

Pelz, D. C., & Andrews, F. M. (1964). Detecting causal priorities in panel study data. *American Sociological Review, 29,* 836–848.

Rogosa, D. (1980). A critique of cross-lagged correlation. *Psychological Bulletin, 88,* 245–258.

Schönpflug, W. (1985). Goal directed behavior as a source of stress: Psychological origins and consequences of inefficiency. In M. Frese & J. Sabini (Eds.), *Goal directed behavior: The concept of action in psychology* (pp. 172–188). Hillsdale, NJ: Erlbaum.

Semmer, N. (1982). Stress at work, stress in private life and psychosocial stress. In W. Bachmann, & I. Udris, (Eds.), *Mental load and stress in activity: European approaches* (pp. 42–52). Berlin (DDR): Deutscher Verlag der Wissenschaften, and Amsterdam & New York: Elsevier-North Holland.

Semmer, N. (1984). *Stressbezogene Tätigkeitsanalyse: Psychologische Untersuchungen zur Analyse von Stress am Arbeitsplatz* [Stress-oriented analysis of work: Psychological studies on the analysis of stress at work]. Weinheim: Beltz.

Simon, H. A. (1954). Spurious correlation: A causal interpretation. *Journal of the American Statistical Association, 49,* 467–479.

Vaillant, G. E. (1977). *Adaptation to life.* Boston: Little, Brown.

Zapf, D., Bamberg, E., Dunckel, H., Frese, M., Greif, S., Mohr, G., Rueckert, D., & Semmer, N. (1983). *Dokumentation der Skalen des Forschungsprojekts "Psychischer Stress am Arbeitsplatz—Hemmende und fordernde Bedingungen für humanere Arbeitsplaetze"* [Scale documentation of the research project "Psychological stress at work—factors promoting and impeding humane working conditions"]. (Available from D. Zapf, Institut für Psychologie, Freie Universität Berlin, Habelschwerdter Allee 45, 1000 Berlin 33, Federal Republic of Germany).

Zedeck, S. (1971). Problems with the use of "moderator" variables. *Psychological Bulletin, 76*, 295–310.

# CHAPTER 11

# Coping with Stress

## Dispositions, Strategies, and the Problem of Measurement

### HEINZ W. KROHNE

## Introduction

In recent years, a controversy has evolved concerning the usefulness of the trait concept for predicting a person's actual behavior (see e.g., Alston, 1975; Bem, 1983; Bem & Allen, 1974; Bem & Funder, 1978; Eysenck & Eysenck, 1980; Mischel, 1968, 1973, 1983, 1984; Mischel & Peake, 1982, 1983). This controversy has also influenced paradigms in stress and coping research. There is an increasing tendency to abandon trait concepts (like "repression-sensitization") and, instead, to adopt concepts like coping process or coping strategy to describe and predict stress-related behavior and behavior outcomes (see Folkman, 1984; Folkman & Lazarus, 1980, 1985; Lazarus & Folkman, 1984).

The present chapter includes an analysis of this controversy and deals especially with the question of how far the concept of trait (or, as I prefer to say, "disposition") contributes to the understanding of coping behavior. The chapter is organized around the following topics:

1. Definition of the terms *coping* and *coping strategy*.
2. The role of the situation in determining the efficiency of coping acts.

HEINZ W. KROHNE ● Psychologisches Institut, Johannes-Gutenberg Universität, 6500 Mainz, Federal Republic of Germany. Preparation of this chapter was facilitated by a grant from the Stiftung Volkswagenwerk (EAA-Projekt, No II/35 461 and No II/37 071).

3. Dispositional antecedents of coping acts and the problem of person–environment fit.
4. Assessment problems related to a dispositional approach.
5. Discussion of the question of whether or not coping strategy and coping disposition really represent mutually exclusive approaches to the measurement of coping.

## Definition of Coping

If one tries to define coping, one first faces the problem of the very broad usage of the concept. In fact, many authors (e.g., Weisman & Worden, 1976; Welford, 1973) tend to call any form of goal-directed behavior coping. Such use of concepts (which has been criticized by Lazarus & Launier, 1978, and Schönpflug, 1983, among others), seems to be an indication of a still serious theoretical deficit in the areas of stress and coping research.

However, several definitions have been proposed that try to avoid the problems of excessive broadness, lack of clarity, and arbitrariness of the concept (see, e.g., Folkman & Lazarus, 1980; Krohne & Rogner, 1982; Lazarus & Folkman, 1984). They have the following characteristics in common:

1. Coping refers to a *process*, not to the goal (of "mastery" or "management") aimed at by an act (see Lazarus & Folkman, 1984).

2. This process encompasses behavioral as well as cognitive (or "intrapsychic," Lazarus, 1966) acts. A majority of authors consider the so-called defense mechanisms, with their tendency to distort reality, to be a subgroup of intrapsychic acts. (I prefer to use the term "act" instead of "response" to emphasize the multiple-response character of coping as well as the active role of the person in coping with stress events.See also the concept of person–environment transaction elaborated by Lazarus & Launier, 1978.)

3. Coping acts focus on (internal as well as external) demands that are experienced by a person as taxing or even exceeding his or her capacities. Internal demands can arise by heightened emotional states, like anxiety, which may interfere with concurrent problem-related behavior. (Lazarus & Launier, 1978, have introduced the term *palliative* for emotion-focused coping.) External demands, like noise, can be coped with by instrumental acts. It is common to all types of demands that a person cannot respond to them by automatic behavior, but only, if at all, by the mobilization of effort.

4. The general aim of coping acts is the removal of an experienced imbalance between demands and capacities. The idea that a balanced

state between demands and capacities is the aim of coping has been proposed so frequently that it has almost acquired the status of an ideology. (For an overview, see Laux, 1983.) However, the problem with this conception is to operationalize an achieved state of balance independently of the predicted behavioral outcome of this state (e.g., a reduced anxiety level). Even intuitively, it is by no means convincing that an achieved balance between demands and capacities is the least stressing state for an individual. Correspondingly, Schulz and Schönpflug (1982) argue that stress will be most pronounced if capacities and demands just match, or if capacities marginally exceed demands. This may be true especially for the problems of work load investigated by this research group (see Schönpflug, 1983), although in social interactions, for example, stress may indeed be created by a perceived imbalance between demands and capacities.

5. Many authors distinguish between the actual coping process, with the strategies employed in it, and the dispositional determinants of preferring certain strategies in stress situations (Höfer, Wallbott, & Scherer, 1985; Krohne, 1978, 1985a; Krohne & Rogner, 1982; Krohne & Schaffner, 1983; Lazarus, 1966). People differ in their degrees of ability (or skill) to realize those strategies most serviceable to the reduction of a state of stress (Krohne & Rogner, 1982; Pearlin & Schooler, 1978). Employing the term *skill* in this context points to an interesting development in coping research, namely, a shift from psychodynamically oriented psychology (Byrne, 1964; Goldstein, 1959), where coping is conceptualized as a more or less unconscious personality process determined by childhood experiences (Freud, 1946), to the area of investigating abilities or skills. This shift has implications, of course, for the field of behavior or cognitive modification (D'Zurilla & Goldfried, 1971; Meichenbaum, 1977; Meichenbaum, Henshaw, & Himel, 1982).

Connected with the definition of coping as a process, a second concept has become important, namely, that of *coping strategy*. Strategies refer to behavioral classes, that is, to theoretical constructions in which single, concrete (i.e., observable) acts are related only on the basis of theoretical assumptions concerning a specific strategy. Viewed in terms of strategy, these acts function as empirical indicators.

A strategy in coping with threat, for example, may be trying not to take notice of cues related to forthcoming dangers. From a theory of the functioning of this strategy, it could be deduced that such acts as "going to the movies the evening before an important exam" or "listening to music instead of monitoring a warning signal" are empirical indicators of such a strategy, which one could label "avoidance by attentional diversion." At the same time, this theory should also determine that acts like "running away after having been confronted with a warning signal" do not belong to this strategy. Of course, empirical confirmation of the validity of these theoretical deductions is needed.

The above-mentioned distinction between coping as a process (encompassing strategies that manifest themselves during this process in the form of concrete acts) and mastery or management as a possible result points to another characteristic of this construction. Except for a few extremely unadaptive ways of coping (e.g., paranoid distortion), one cannot tell *a priori* (that is, without considering the concrete stress situation) whether a certain coping act is efficient (in the sense of mastery or management) or not.

Certain acts assigned to a distinct coping strategy (e.g., increased search for stress-relevant information) can be serviceable (for mastering stress) in one situation (e.g., when preparing for an exam, Houston, 1982; Krohne & Schaffner, 1983), but counterproductive in another situation (e.g., before a surgical operation, Cohen & Lazarus, 1973; Miller, 1980). Quite obviously, the degree of efficacy of a strategy depends on the interaction between specific situational characteristics and the content of the strategy realized.

I do not agree with those researchers associated with ego-psychology (e.g., Haan, 1977) who distinguish between "coping" as an elaborated and mature way of handling stress, and "defense" as a simple and, because of its reality distorting character, less efficient way of handling stress (see also Prystav, 1981). This distinction would lead to an *a priori* evaluation of coping strategies without taking situational requirements into account.

These reflections require a more detailed analysis of the role of the situation in the coping process. How do situational parameters interact with specific characteristics of coping strategies in determining coping efficacy?

## The Role of the Situation in Determining Coping Efficacy

This chapter will not provide a comprehensive classification of stress situations (for more details see Laux, 1983), but, will elaborate those general situation characteristics that may determine whether a coping strategy is efficient or not when applied in a particular situation.

One starting point for this analysis is the characteristic of variable controllability of situations, as analyzed by Averill (1973), among others. A second point is the segmentation of stress-inducing situations into an anticipation phase (with the elements "announcement of a certain event" and "execution of preparatory acts"), a confrontation phase, and a postconfrontation phase (with the elements "feedback" and "processing of this feedback," which are typical of situations of evaluative stress). (For a more detailed analysis of this aspect, see Krohne & Rogner, 1982.)

The characteristic "controllability of a situation" has been dealt with in several studies (see, e.g., Glass & Singer, 1972; Miller, 1979b; Monat, Averill, & Lazarus, 1972). Therefore, I will refer only to the distinction between behavioral control (controllability) and informational control (predictability), which is central to this concept (Averill, 1973; Miller, 1979a; Mineka & Kihlstrom, 1978; Prystav, 1981, 1985).

If one recognizes only two levels of each control mode (control possible versus impossible) and combines those levels, four types of situations with different control patterns result: behavioral control possible, informational control impossible, and so forth (see Krohne & Rogner, 1982). It now becomes obvious that a given coping strategy may have a differential effectiveness in reducing stress, depending on the control patterns of the situations encountered.

For example, the coping strategy described by Miller (1980) as "monitoring" (i.e., attempts to gain information about a stressing event and to exert influence on the stressor) is especially unfavorable when such a situation does not permit behavioral control, as, for example, when anticipating surgical operation (Miller, 1980; Miller & Mangan, 1983). In this case, the person tries to gain information about the stressor without being able to use this information for controlling the event. As attempts to influence or control the stressor fail, the stress load may even be augmented by a monitoring strategy.

On the other hand, monitoring may be a very serviceable strategy if the information searched for increases the controllability of a stressing event, for example, when preparing for an exam (Krohne & Schaffner, 1983). However, it should be kept in mind that, with achievement-related stress situations, two measures of the efficacy of a coping strategy can be applied (Eysenck, 1979): *efficiency,* that is, performance level achieved (e.g., number of problems solved), and *effectiveness,* that is, ratio of number of problems solved to effort invested in a task (e.g., time spent to prepare for an exam or to control solutions). It may very well be that persons who apply monitoring strategies extensively reach a high performance level (efficiency) but, nevertheless, have a comparatively low effectiveness (Krohne & Schaffner, 1983).

The efficacy of a given coping strategy depends not only on the control pattern realized in a situation, but also on the phase of a stress event in which the given coping strategy is applied. In analyzing this relationship, the above mentioned segmentation of stress events into *preparation, confrontation,* and *post-confrontation* phases may be useful.

To mention an example: The so-called palliative coping acts described by Lazarus and Launier (1978) should prove their efficacy by reducing the emotional arousal (e.g., anxiety) elicited by a stressor. This reduction is especially necessary if a problem-oriented behavior has to be carried out shortly afterward, because otherwise an interference between emotion-related and problem-related responses would result.

The general success of coping (e.g., with the stress of an achievement situation), however, will depend on the point in this phase sequence at which the emotional arousal is attacked. In situations with sufficient time to prepare for the confrontation, as in most exam situations, for example, a heightened arousal level at an early stage of the preparation phase may very well be adaptive with regard to an optimal handling of the stressor. In this case, arousal functions, so to speak, as a motive for testing out different, and especially more differentiated coping strategies, thus resulting in a more "modulated" (Epstein, 1967) handling of internal as well as external sources of stress (Krohne & Rogner, 1982). In contrast, immediate attacking of the emotional arousal may result in an inefficient adaptation to the stressor and, hence, a breakdown of the system of organized coping acts when entering into the "real" confrontation.

This relationship has been impressively demonstrated by Epstein and Fenz (1965; Fenz & Epstein, 1967), who investigated the coping behavior of experienced and novice parachutists. Both groups manifested a distinct peak of arousal. However, with experienced parachutists, this peak occurred long before confrontation, which was adaptive for them because it facilitated subsequent organized behavior, although, with novice parachutists, the peak occurred right in the middle of the confrontation, and thus interfered with task-related behavior.

The case is quite different when there is little or no preparation time for the confrontation with the stressor. On such occasions, it is more adaptive to direct coping acts immediately against the arousal (and then to turn to the problem), instead of taking the arousal as a motive for a more differentiated handling of the stress situation. The price for the second strategy could likely be that the heightened arousal level extends into the confrontation phase, thus interfering with problem-related behavior.

Compared with instrumental acts, palliative or emotion-related coping as the primary reaction to a state of stress is more adaptive if the individual must be ready to act quickly, as in the case with short or no preparation time, but may be less adaptive than instrumental coping if there is sufficient time to prepare for the confrontation with the stressor.

A third, and so far rarely investigated possibility in stress situations, is found when there is a combination of the characteristics "control pattern" and "phase of a stress situation." Many real-life stress situations are structured so that the degree of controllability varies systematically with the phase.[1] To refer again to the example of the surgical operation: When anticipating the operation, the patient has practically no behavioral control of the situation. Here, the strategy of monitoring would not serve the goal of reducing stress, although avoiding stress-related information (in Miller's, 1980, terms, using the strategy of "blunting") would be adaptive. After the operation, however, the possibility of exercising control increases gradually, as may be noted, for example, by the fact that the patient is given certain instructions concerning the process of recuperation. In this phase, certain monitoring strategies may be adaptive while continued blunting is less efficient.

Here, then, three variable characteristics of stress situations have been identified, which partly determine the efficacy of a concrete coping act: control pattern, phase, and change in controllability as related to the phase of a stress situation. However, as observed in the Epstein and Fenz studies (Epstein, 1967), there are remarkable individual differences in ability to realize the most serviceable coping strategy in a given situation. Let us look next at those differences and the problems of their assessment.

## Dispositional Determinants of Coping Acts

As already noted, one cannot assign the predicate "efficient" or "inefficient" to a coping strategy (e.g., monitoring or denial) without considering the concrete situation. In characterizing persons, however, the case is different. Here, it is possible to distinguish individuals according to their general, that is, situation invariant, coping efficacy. Thus, it is postulated that individuals have greater or lesser ability to realize the type of coping behavior most favorable in a particular situation.

The existence of such interindividual differences has been nicely demonstrated in an experiment by Averill, O'Brien, and DeWitt (1977):

Subjects could avoid receiving an electric shock if they chose to listen for a warning signal and subsequently performed a control response. However, the effectiveness of this avoidance response varied across trials, being either 100%, 66%, 33%, or 0%. The Ss [subjects] were exposed to each level and were informed about the respective effectiveness probability in advance. As an alternative to monitoring the warning signal and performing the control response Ss could choose to listen to music while waiting for the shock.

[1] The "classical" learned-helplessness design (Seligman, Maier, & Solomon, 1971) can be viewed as an experimental setting representing this type of stress situation: Although no control is possible during the "induction" phase, the S can exercise control during the "testing" phase.

Considering the arguments just presented, an optimal way of coping with this situation would be to listen to the attention diverting stimulus (music) in the uncontrollable situation (0% effectiveness), and then to switch from attention diversion to monitoring at an intermediate level of response effectiveness, and finally to monitor the warning signal with 100% effectiveness of the control response. However, the forementioned authors observed six groups of subjects who differed in their coping behavior across effectiveness conditions: One group of Ss [subjects] was consistently vigilant, monitoring the warning signal even in situations where control responses were inefficient. A second group, on the other hand, was consistently non-vigilant, even in a situation where monitoring the warning signal would have avoided the shock. Members of both groups behaved in a non-optimal way, in the one because they tried to exert control where, in fact, no control was possible, and in the other because they avoided control where such an act would have been successful. The behavior of both groups was not situation-related, but rigid.

Three groups of Ss were characterized by their switching from a diverting (non-vigilant) to a vigilant strategy with increasing response effectiveness. Responses of these Ss followed a Guttman-Scale progression, i.e., if a S adopted a vigilant strategy at one level of effectiveness, he/she maintained that strategy at each higher level. Those Ss behaved in a situation-appropriate manner, and differed only in the effectiveness level at which they switched to vigilant behavior. A last group of Ss showed inconsistent behavior, tending to execute vigilant and non-vigilant behavior regardless of response effectiveness. In contrast to the vigilant and avoidant Ss, however, their lack of reference to situational requirements was not caused by rigidity, but by instability.

The results of Averill *et al.* have been frequently cited as supporting the "preference for information" hypothesis (e.g., Prystav, 1985). However, a statistical reanalysis of their data, carried out by Krohne and Rogner (1985), demonstrated that both vigilant and non-vigilant (avoidant) groups were significantly overrepresented. Additionally, in reviewing a number of experiments purporting to support this hypothesis, Krohne and Rogner (1982) showed that a relatively large group of subjects *always* behaved contrary to expectation, thus challenging the general validity of the hypothesis that the state of being informed about an aversive event is generally to be preferred to the state of being uninformed (see Averill, 1973; D'Amato, 1974).

With this interpretation, the results of the Averill *et al.* experiment can be seen to yield four typical modes of employment of coping strategies:

1. A *rigid vigilant* mode. Without taking into account characteristics of the situation, these persons try to attain informational and

behavioral control. Following Byrne (1964) and many others (e.g., Altrocchi, 1961; Gordon, 1957; for an overview see Krohne, 1978; Krohne & Rogner, 1982), these persons may be labelled as "sensitizers."

2. A *rigid nonvigilant* mode. Without considering situational requirements, these persons try to avoid stress-related information and behavior. This mode may be called "repression."

3. A *flexible* use of coping strategies oriented at situational requirements. This mode may be called "nondefensive." Only with this mode did the different effectiveness levels of the avoidance responses form items in the sense of a Guttman Scale. Perhaps, this observation could lead to a new approach to identifying flexible, yet situation-related coping.

4. A mode characterized by *instable behavior*. Different strategies are applied, though apparently without being related to the situation.

In this presentation, the term *coping mode* is employed to describe the tendency of persons to preferably realize a certain pattern of coping strategies when confronted with a stressor. The coping mode concept represents the link between coping dispositions (as described in terms of competencies, expectancies, plans, etc.) and actual coping behavior.

When comparing the general coping efficacy of such persons, we expect nondefensive individuals to manifest the highest general efficacy (across different situations). Individuals in the two rigid groups (repressors and sensitizers) will be efficient copers only if their strategy "accidentally" matches the situational requirements (as, for example, vigilant subjects in the condition of 100% response effectiveness). It should be kept in mind, however, that, in real life, persons are rarely exposed to situations at random. Individuals with a rigid (i.e., a highly overlearned) use of coping strategies may be expected to select for their functioning those situations that allow them to employ their preferred coping strategies efficiently.

The instable persons are expected to show the lowest level of coping efficacy because, with varying, yet situation-unrelated strategies, the chance of achieving a match between situational requirements and the content of a strategy is again lowered. Therefore, these persons may be labelled "unsuccessful copers."

The distinction between successful and unsuccessful copers raises the question "successful as to which goal?" Several goals of coping acts can be distinguished: regulating emotions elicited by a stressor (e.g., a threat), behavioral control of the stressor, or, if this turns out to be impossible, at least informational control. What is still missing is a conception of how these different goal-related actions form an organized system. For example, regulation of emotions could be a subgoal for achieving improved information control (see Easterbrook's, 1959, hypothesis on the relationship between arousal and cue utilization), and this control, in turn, may facilitate behavioral control of a stressor.

Since a model of the organization of goal-related coping acts has not yet been elaborated, our research group, which is mainly involved in studying coping in threat situations (Krohne, 1978; Krohne & Rogner, 1982, 1985), relies on a more modest definition of success. According to this definition, a person employs coping strategies successfully if, after being confronted with a danger signal, he or she is able to achieve a longer lasting reduction of the anxiety elicited by this confrontation. Correspondingly, it would be an indicator of unsuccessful coping if a person fails to reduce anxiety and, especially during confrontation with a stressor, even manifests an increase in anxiety. (Recall, for example, the course of arousal of experienced and novice parachutists during anticipation and confrontation with a stressor, reported by Epstein, 1972.)

For a descriptive differentiation between persons who act in a flexible and situation-adequate way and those who respond in an instable way unrelated to the situation, the personality construct "anxiety" seems to be suitable, with unsuccessful copers concentrating at the high-anxiety, and nondefensives at the low-anxiety pole of this dimension (see Krohne & Rogner, 1982, 1985).

For a differentiation of persons who react vigilantly in stress situations most of the time and those who manifest nonvigilance (avoidance) in such situations, the personality variable "repression-sensitization" seems to be most appropriate (Byrne, 1964; Krohne, 1978).

If we accept that, in the experiment of Averill et al., a person's responses across different situational conditions (i.e., percentages of response effectiveness) can be viewed as a process (i.e., a sequence of reactions), this interpretation shows that processes and dispositions do not represent contrasting ways of looking at coping behavior, but, quite the contrary, condition each other.

On the one hand, dispositions (like repression-sensitization) can best be operationalized by observing certain ordered sequences of responses (e.g., coping acts, like choosing to monitor the warning signal or to listen to the music) across different situations and, if possible, different indicators. (In the present analysis of the Averill et al. experiment, only one indicator was taken into consideration—the subject's choice of control response. However, other indicators, e.g., physiological reactions, could have been incorporated into the analysis.)

On the other hand, certain typical processes (e.g., pursuing a monitoring strategy even in situations where the coping response is not effective, or switching from avoidance to monitoring with increasing probability of behavioral control) can be understood only by being related to theoretical constructions, such as sensitization or nondefensive coping. Of course, these theoretical constructions do not explain why people behave sensitively or nondefensively in a series of stress situations. (One cannot say a person employs a sensitive coping strategy because he or she is a sensitizer.) In order to explain this behavior, constructions like expectancies, competencies, and self-regulatory systems (Mischel, 1973), as well as theories concerning the developmental conditions of certain competencies, expectancies, and so forth (Krohne, 1980, 1985b) have to be elaborated.

Employment of a given coping strategy is dependent on the situation, to a certain degree. (There is, e.g., generally more vigilance in controllable, and an increased tendency toward avoidance in uncontrollable stress situations. See Krohne & Rogner, 1982; Miller, 1979a.) However, dispositional antecedents partly determine how a situation is subjectively constructed (e.g., the perceived degree of controllability of a situation, see Folkman, 1984) and, hence, what kind of influence situations with varying characteristics can gain on a person's actions. Perhaps a way of assessing coping dispositions could be to register the amount of situational pressure (e.g., aversiveness of a stimulus) necessary to have a person change his or her inefficient strategy (for example, to let a person switch from avoidance to vigilance with 66% response effectiveness).

The dependence of the use of coping strategies on dispositional antecedents is quite obvious with repressors and sensitizers. But even in the case of persons who employ strategies of different quality in different situations (as do nondefensive persons and unsuccessful copers), such behavior can be related to more stable person characteristics, namely, their skills or competencies in analyzing situations appropriately and in choosing that strategy of their repertoire which best fits the situational requirements (see, e.g., Mischel, 1973, 1984).

Some authors object to the concept of disposition (or, as they generally prefer to say, "trait"), believing that a person's behavior in a situation can be predicted better from what he or she actually does in that situation than from dispositions (or "traits"). So, for example, Lazarus and Folkman (1984) state that "the assessment of coping traits actually has had very modest predictive value with respect to coping processes" (p. 288). However, this argument would seem to be open to the following criticisms:

1. One does not predict from "traits," which are theoretical constructions, but from empirical or observable indicators of traits (e.g., scores on the Repression–Sensitization (R-S) Scale, Byrne, 1961), with which they are not identical. Thus, the problem of prediction can be reduced to one of the validity of a given empirical indicator. In coping

research, specifically, one must recognize that the R-S Scale, employed in most prediction studies (e.g., Cohen & Lazarus, 1973), is, indeed, a rather poor indicator of coping disposition, lacking concurrent as well as discriminant validity. Results obtained with this and similar instruments should, therefore, not be cited as evidence for the "weakness" of the trait concept in predicting behavior.

2. Prediction studies in coping research deal with three different variables, which should be kept carefully apart: A. *Disposition indicators* (personality characteristics that can be measured in a comparatively stable manner over time). B. *Actual behavior* (events that may be observed in this form perhaps only once with a given person, as, for example, a special coping act when anticipating a surgical operation). C. The *outcome* of a confrontation with a stressor (a single event, too, e.g., recovery from surgery or grades earned in an exam).

Among these three variables, three different predictions can be realized: *A* predicts *B* (indicators of coping dispositions predict actual coping behavior, e.g., denial or problem-focused coping), *A* predicts *C* (e.g., the indicator of a coping disposition predicts recovery from surgery or the results of an exam), and *B* predicts *C* (the actual coping behavior or the degree of state anxiety predicts recovery from surgery or exam grades). In studies that criticize the usefulness of the concept of disposition, it is generally argued that *B* is the best predictor of *C*, while *A* (disposition indicators) frequently fails to predict either *B* or *C* (see Cohen & Lazarus, 1973).

However, the idea that concrete events can best be predicted from other immediately preceding events is not only a rather trivial one, it is also of comparatively little value for most questions in psychology, especially in applied psychology. Except for clarifying some experimental questions, the goal of psychological assessment procedures cannot be to predict a given single outcome (e.g., grades earned in an exam or course of recovery from surgery) from another (single) event (e.g., amount of state anxiety manifested prior to an exam or coping strategies realized when anticipating surgery). Such event-to-event predictions can hardly be expected to contribute to the solution of problems like, for example, developing intervention programs for the prevention of undesirable outcomes. Efficiency in such prevention requires information about people *before* they enter a stress situation (e.g., an exam or a hospital to undergo surgery). Information about *A* (dispositions) would therefore be critical to predict *B* (actual behavior) and *C* (outcome). Since it is *B* which has to be changed in order to prevent undesirable outcomes, the relation of *A* to *B* is clearly the most important. This leads us to the problem of assessing coping dispositions.

## The Assessment of Coping Dispositions

The traditional unidimensional conceptions of anxiety and repression-sensitization are deficient insofar as they do not specify the relationship between these two constructs. For example, unidimensional measures of the repression-sensitization construct should not, from a theoretical point of view, differentiate between anxious and nondefensive variability (subjects of both groups are expected to score in the medium range of the data distribution), nor should anxiety tests be able to separate sensitive from repressive rigidity (both groups are expected to have medium trait–anxiety scores). Thus, none of the empirical indicators related to these constructs would permit simultaneous distinctions among the four dispositional coping modes, described in the last section.

Empirical results, however, show that tests of repression-sensitization and trait anxiety are highly correlated, thus lacking discriminant validity (Krohne, 1974; Krohne & Rogner, 1985). Very likely, the low-scoring group on both indicators represents a mixture of repressors and non-defensives, high scorers can be sensitizers as well as anxious persons, while intermediates have an unclear status (Chabot, 1973).

Some authors have tried to correct this limitation by proposing a multivariable assessment of coping dispositions. The simplest approach of this kind would be to apply an anxiety test and a test of defensiveness (e.g., a scale of "social desirability").The former would measure the variable tendency of persons to *appraise* situations as threatening, whereas the latter would measure the tendency to *avoid or deny* the threat (especially in evaluative situations), as well as corresponding negative affects like anxiety. (For this interpretation of the defensiveness or social-desirability tendency see Crandall, 1966; Hill, 1971; Krohne & Rogner, 1985; Millham & Jacobson, 1978).

Employing an anxiety test and a test of defensiveness simultaneously, and dividing subject into highs and lows on each test variable (e.g., by use of a median split) would yield four combinations of anxiety and defensiveness data, corresponding to the four coping modes as follows: Nondefensives should manifest low scores in both variables, repressors would be low in anxiety and high in defensiveness, sensitizers would reverse this pattern, and high-anxiety persons should show high scores on both measures (Hill, 1971; Hill & Sarason, 1966; Krohne & Rogner, 1985; Ruebush, Byrum & Farnham, 1963). (It should be noted, incidentally, that the interpretation of the configuration high anxiety/high defensiveness as representing highly anxious persons is not shared by some authors; cf. Asendorpf & Scherer, 1983; Weinberger, Schwartz, & Davidson, 1979).

However, approaches using traditional anxiety or defensiveness scales to assess the coping modes described do not seem very promising. With such instruments, reactions to stressors can be assessed only on a very global level. The items on such scales refer neither to concrete anxiety-arousing situations nor do they require subjects to describe specific coping acts. By such procedures, one learns very little about the strategies preferred by a person in a given situation. Instead, in the manner of attitude measurement, the subject has to comment on certain dangerous circumstances, unpleasant things like conflicts, and highly generalized response tendencies. It should therefore not be surprising that scores derived from such instruments do not allow a satisfactory prediction of concrete behavior. There is still too great a theoretical distance between such inventories and the constructs of coping strategy and coping disposition.

In the following section, some assessment procedures will be presented that are more closely related to the concept of dispositional coping modes than the approaches just mentioned. The measurement of the four forementioned coping modes will be realized in two variants that have the following characteristic in common: persons are no longer identified as repressors, sensitizers, and so forth, by their scores on a uni-dimensional instrument (e.g., the R-S Scale), but are classified according to their results in a profile analysis. Employing a set of theoretically relevant variables, a special data configuration is deduced for each coping mode and subjects are assigned to these "targets" by a search procedure. Persons who do not fit any of the theoretically defined targets are considered to be "unspecific" in terms of the model of the four coping modes.

As a first variant of this procedure, a coping inventory, based on self-descriptive items, will be presented. This inventory, which has been developed according to the theoretical definitions of the four coping modes presented earlier, consists of a repertory of specific, mainly cognitive (intrapsychic) responses to a series of different threat situations.

In this instrument, which follows in its design the idea of stimulus–response inventories (e.g., Endler, Hunt, & Rosenstein, 1962), eight different, potentially threatening situations are presented verbally to the subject. Four of these represent evaluative or ego–threat situations ("when I have to speak in front of an audience"), the other four physical or pain–threat situations ("when I have to see the dentist"). Each situation is combined with a description of 16 cognitive coping responses, half representing repressive ("it doesn't matter to me") and half sensitive ("I cannot think of anything else") strategies. For each situation, the subject is asked to indicate the applicability of each coping response. (For more details concerning this inventory, see Krohne, Wigand, & Kiehl, 1985.)

Unlike Byrne's R-S Scale, this instrument is not bipolar, but separate repression and sensitization scores are calculated for each situation. Subjects are identified as repressors, sensitizers, and so forth, via profile analysis. The procedure can be demonstrated using the four ego–threat situations, with their four repression and sensitization scores. It will be recalled that repressors and sensitizers were both identified earlier as persons who act according to largely predictable modes when coping with different stress situations. Persons who mainly respond to each presented situation with repressive (avoidant) and hardly ever with sensitive (vigilant) coping strategies were labelled repressors, and vice versa for sensitizers. Nondefensive (or low-anxiety) persons should manifest a pattern that is made up of comparatively few intrapsychic, but mainly "overt" responses to stress. Consequently, we expect consistently low repression as well as low sensitization scores with these subjects.

And, finally, since both repressive and sensitive strategies ordinarily cannot be applied to a threat situation simultaneously (efficient coping with anxiety is impossible if one tries to deny a threat and, at the same time, searches for threat-relevant information), persons who nevertheless frequently apply sensitive as well as repressive strategies to the same stressor should be inefficient copers. As already indicated, these "unsuccessful copers" can be considered to be identical with dispositionally anxious persons. The four coping modes described here are defined by the profiles across the four ego-threat situations presented in Table 1. The special configuration of ranks across the eight variables (e.g., for repressors 2 2 2 2 1 1 1 1 , with $2 \geqq 50\%$ and $1 < 50\%$) is defined as a "target" and subjects are assigned to these targets by an *automatized search procedure* (Gediga, 1980a).

Several validation studies, employing verbally presented as well as real life stressors (a surgical operation, sports competition, public speaking), have been and are still being carried out in our research group.

**Table 1.** Theoretically Postulated Score Profiles of the Four Coping Modes across the Four Ego-Threatening Stress Situations

| | Strategies | |
|---|---|---|
| | repressive | sensitive |
| | Situations | |
| Subjects | 1 2 3 4 | 1 2 3 4 |
| Nondefensives | low | low |
| Repressors | high | low |
| Sensitizers | low | high |
| High-anxiety | high | high |

**Table 2.** Significant ($p < .10$) Solutions of the Cluster Analyses

| Boys ($n = 206$) | Girls ($n = 216$) |
|---|---|
| Group   1 ($n = 41$) | Group   1 ($n = 31$) |
| Group   2 ($n = 21$) | Group   3 ($n = 79$) |
| Group   3 ($n = 3$) | Group   5 ($n = 34$) |
| Group   4 ($n = 56$) | Group   6 ($n = 7$) |
| Group   5 ($n = 47$) | Group   7 ($n = 14$) |
| Group   9 ($n = 5$) | Group  15 ($n = 30$) |
| Group 15 ($n = 6$) | Group 21 ($n = 1$) |
| Group 16 ($n = 3$) | Group 80 ($n = 6$) |
| Group 17 ($n = 10$) | Group 89 ($n = 1$) |
| Group 21 ($n = 4$) | Group 93 ($n = 1$) |
| Group 36 ($n = 6$) | Group 108 ($n = 2$) |
| Group 56 ($n = 2$) | Group 110 ($n = 1$) |
| Group 165 ($n = 1$) | Group 121 ($n = 6$) |
| Group 194 ($n = 1$) | Group 177 ($n = 2$) |
|  | Group 209 ($n = 1$) |

Here, data will be presented only on the stability of the assignment procedure. Using the same set of scores, the theoretical way of grouping subjects specified in Table 1 (*heuristic procedure*) is compared with an empirical classification of the same subjects applying the method of cluster analysis (*taxometric procedure*). Serving as subjects were 206 boys and 216 girls from grades 5 to 7 (age 10 to 14 years). Of these, 90 boys and 99 girls could be assigned to one of the four coping groups by the automatized (heuristic) search procedure.[2]

The taxometric analysis (a hierarchical cluster analysis of the four repression and the four sensitization variables, Gediga, 1980b,c) resulted in a significant 14-group solution for boys and a 15-group solution for girls. However, as Table 2 shows, distinct patterns of frequencies could be distinguished among these clusters. In each sample, four clusters attracted the majority of subjects. (For boys: Clusters 1, 2, 4, and 5, with 165 of the 206 subjects. For girls: Clusters 1, 3, 5, and 15, with 174 of the 216 subjects.) These groups were followed by four medium-sized clusters in each sample (containing between 5 and 14 subjects), whereas the remaining groups mainly represented isolated persons.

Considering the frequency distributions across the 29 clusters, one

[2] The author appreciates the assistance of Gerhard E. Kiehl, Carl W. Kohlmann, Paul Schaffner, and Albrecht Schumacher in the collection and statistical analysis of the data.

could expect that the four large clusters in each sample would represent the four coping modes defined above. In order to test this hypothesis, the raw data of each variable were standardized for the total sample, and profiles of the standard scores for each of the four major clusters were calculated. However, as Figures 1 and 2 show, only three of the major clusters in each sample (for boys, 1, 2, and 5; for girls 1, 5, and 15) yielded profiles that could be interpreted as representing the modes of high anxiety (1), repression (2), and nondefensiveness (5) for boys, and high anxiety (1), sensitization (5), and repression (15) for girls. The remaining major clusters represented, with boys, a second (moderate) variant of a repression profile and, with girls, a (very moderate) non-defensive profile. Since the major clusters did not completely manifest the profiles anticipated, the medium-sized clusters were then inspected for correspondence with the theoretically anticipated clusters. Among these clusters, one group could be identified in each sample that almost perfectly matched the still missing profiles (Cluster 17, sensitization, for boys, and Cluster 7, nondefensiveness, for girls; see Figures 1 and 2).

In a next step, the degree of correspondence between the heuristic and the taxometric classification of subjects was tested. For this purpose, all subjects not assigned to a specific coping mode by any procedure were put together into a fifth "mode" (unspecific persons), and a 5 × 5 contingency table was established, using a variant of Cohen's kappa coeffi-

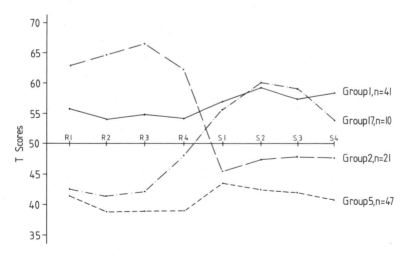

**Figure 1.** Profiles of the clusters representing the coping modes: Group 1 high anxiety, Group 2 repression, Group 17 sensitization, and Group 5 nondefensiveness (boys).

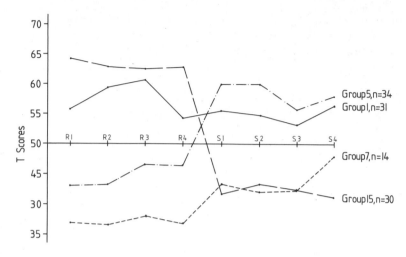

**Figure 2.** Profiles of the clusters representing the coping modes: Group 1 high anxiety; Group 15 repression, Group 5 sensitization, and Group 7 nondefensiveness (girls).

cient to test for degree of correspondence between the two classification procedures (Gediga, 1983).

As Tables 3 and 4 show, the contingency tables yield, for both samples, a high concentration of subjects in the cells of the main diagonal and few persons in those cells that should contain zero frequencies. This distribution of frequencies is highly significant for both boys (kappa = 0.421, $p < .001$) and girls (kappa = 0.464, $p < .001$).

**Table 3.** Association between the Taxometric and the Heuristic Classification of the Subjects for the Sample of 206 Boys

| Heuristic classification[a] | Taxometric classification[a] | | | | | |
|---|---|---|---|---|---|---|
| | S | R | N | A | U | Σ |
| S | 5 | | | | 8 | 13 |
| R | | 8 | | | 8 | 16 |
| N | | | 34 | | 3 | 37 |
| A | | 4 | 1 | 14 | 5 | 24 |
| U | 5 | 9 | 12 | 27 | 63 | 116 |
| Σ | 10 | 21 | 47 | 41 | 87 | 206 |

[a] S = sensitizers; R = repressors; N = nondefensives; A = anxious subjects; U = unspecific subjects.

**Table 4.** Association between the Taxometric and the Heuristic Classification of the Subjects for the Sample of 216 Boys

| Heuristic classification[a] | Taxometric classification[a] | | | | | |
|---|---|---|---|---|---|---|
| | S | R | N | A | U | Σ |
| S | 12 | | | | 7 | 19 |
| R | | 25 | | | 6 | 31 |
| N | | | 8 | | 15 | 23 |
| A | 3 | 1 | | 18 | 4 | 26 |
| U | 19 | 4 | 6 | 13 | 75 | 117 |
| Σ | 34 | 30 | 14 | 31 | 107 | 216 |

[a] S = sensitizers; R = repressors; N = nondefensives; A = anxious subjects; U = unspecific subjects.

Since the heuristic assignment is the stricter one (i.e., it excludes more subjects as unspecific), it is recommended that for the purpose of descriptive analysis, one read the contingency tables horizontally. For boys (Table 3), 5 out of 13 sensitizers (grouped by the automatic search procedure) could be identified correctly, although 8 were assigned to the "unspecific" group. However, no sensitizer was assigned to any of the other three coping modes. The same is true for the groups of repressors and nondefensives (with an excellent result for the latter, where 34 of 37 subjects could be correctly identified). The high-anxiety group turns out to be the least homogeneous. Perhaps our definition of these persons, as frequently applying sensitive as well as repressive intrapsychic coping acts, is too simplistic. Nevertheless, 14 out of 24 subjects manifested the predicted data configuration when classified by the taxometric procedure.

As Table 4 shows, results for the girls' sample are very similar to those for the boys' sample. This time, the highest degree of correspondence between the two grouping procedures was found for repressors (25 out of 31), although the high-anxiety group was, again, the only group yielding misclassifications.

These analyses, of course, do not represent validation studies of the concept of the four dispositional coping modes, but only demonstrate one variant of a procedure to identify these modes empirically. When introducing the automatic search procedure, it was noted that this approach is not only applicable to static variables (like the eight variables of the repression–sensitization inventory), but also to process variables. In the final section of this chapter, some ideas will be presented on how this second variant can be applied to the analysis of processes.

## Coping Processes as Indicators of Coping Dispositions

In the previous section, arguments in favor of the usefulness of the concept of coping dispositions were presented, together with a more sophisticated procedure to assess these dispositions. However, this approach is not completely satisfactory. Stress situations, as well as coping acts, are presented only fictitiously. The subject is neither confronted with real-life stressors nor is concrete coping behavior required. Consequently, measurement is still static and not process-oriented.

Process measurement of coping modes requires not only a multidimensional procedure, as described, but also multilevel and multitemporal assessment. *Multilevel* refers to the fact that coping acts should be assessed on three different levels: on a subjective (self-descriptive) level, as realized in the repression–sensitization inventory, on the level of overt observable behavior (e.g., in analyzing facial expression), and on the level of physiological data. *Multitemporal* means that these parameters have to be measured at different, theoretically relevant points in a time sequence.

In order to develop such a measurement procedure, a theory of the coping process and of the dispositions related to this process has to be elaborated. It must allow to predict which special configuration of data, across variables and across time points, should be expected for a specific coping mode (e.g., repression) in a particular stress situation (e.g., when anticipating a surgical operation).

Such predictions could be based on theories and empirical results in the area of coping research, as, for example, presented by Epstein (1972) or Lazarus (1966) and their co-workers, as well as on the trait–state anxiety model of Spielberger (1966). The discrepancies between subjective and autonomic indexes of anxiety, frequently observed in repressors and sensitizers' being confronted with a particular threat situation (Otto & Bösel, 1978; Weinstein, Averill, Opton & Lazarus, 1968), could be a starting point for such a multilevel-multitemporal analysis.

Figure 3 represents the simplest case of this kind of analysis: two types of situations: nonstress and stress; and two assessment levels: self-reported and physiologically measured arousal. Following Epstein, Lazarus, or Spielberger, typical data configurations are predicted for the four coping modes: discrepancies between subjective and objective data for sensitizers and (especially) repressors, but not for anxious and nondefensive persons. For the latter groups, a differential increase in anxiety from the nonstress to the stress situation is expected. These data configurations are again defined as "targets," with individual subjects' being assigned to these targets by the forementioned search procedure. Needless to say, the validity of these theoretically predicted profiles, as well

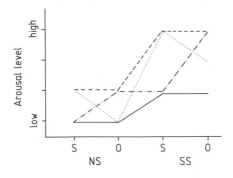

**Figure 3.** Hypothetical profiles for the four coping modes for two data sources across two situations. S = subjective; O = objective data; NS = nonstress situation; SS = stress situation; (——) nondefensive; (----) high-anxiety; (-·-··-) repressor; ( · · · · ) sensitizer profiles).

as the stability of the assignment, have to be investigated by independent studies.

With this presentation, I can summarize my reflections concerning the relationship between coping disposition and coping process. Actual coping behavior, viewed as process, and the concept of disposition do not exclude each other. What is required is the identification of comparatively stable (i.e., reproducible) patterns of actual behavior (as outlined in Figure 3) and the interpretation of these patterns as being indicators of disposition. This interpretation does not exclude a situation's influence on this behavior. A prerequisite of such an interpretation is a theory of how a particular coping disposition manifests itself across these indicators. In the sense of the construct–validation procedure outlined by Cronbach and Meehl (1955), such a theory serves as a starting point for a multilevel-multitemporal analysis, and can be modified by subsequent empirical results.

# References

Alston, W. J. (1975). Traits, consistency, and conceptual alternatives for personality theory. *Journal of the Theory of Social Behavior, 5,* 17–48.

Altrocchi, J. (1961). Interpersonal perceptions of repressors and sensitizers and component analysis of assumed dissimilarity scores. *Journal of Abnormal and Social Psychology, 62,* 528–534.

Asendorpf, J. B., & Scherer, K. L. (1983). The discrepant repressor: Differentiation between low anxiety, high anxiety, and repression of anxiety by autonomic-facial-verbal patterns of behavior. *Journal of Personality and Social Psychology, 45,* 1334–1346.

Averill, J. R. (1973). Personal control over aversive stimuli and its relationship to stress. *Psychological Bulletin, 80,* 286–303.

Averill, J. R., O'Brien, L., & DeWitt, G. W. (1977). The influence of response effectiveness on the preference for warning and on psychophysiological stress reactions. *Journal of Personality, 45,* 395–418.

Bem, D. J. (1983). Further déjà vu in the search for cross-situational consistency: A response to Mischel and Peake. *Psychological Review, 90,* 390–393.

Bem, D. J., & Allen, A. (1974). On predicting some of the people some of the time: The search for cross-situational consistencies in behavior. *Psychological Review, 81,* 506–520.

Bem, D. J., & Funder, D. C. (1978). Predicting more of the people more of the time: Assessing the personality of situations. *Psychological Review, 85,* 485–501.

Byrne, D. (1961). The Repression-Sensitization Scale: Rationale, reliability, and validity. *Journal of Personality, 29,* 334–349.

Byrne, D. (1964). Repression-sensitization as a dimension of personality. In B. A. Maher (Ed.), *Progress in experimental personality research* (Vol. 1, pp. 169–220). New York: Academic Press.

Chabot, J. A. (1973). Repression-sensitization: A critique of some neglected variables in the literature. *Psychologicl Bulletin, 80,* 122–129.

Cohen, F., & Lazarus, R. S. (1973). Active coping processes, coping dispositions, and recovery from surgery. *Psychosomatic Medicine, 35,* 375–389.

Crandall, V. J. (1966). Personality characteristics and social and achievement behaviors associated with children's social desirability response tendencies. *Journal of Personality and Social Psychology, 4,* 477–486.

Cronbach, L. J., & Meehl, P. E. (1955). Construct validity in psychological tests. *Psychological Bulletin, 52,* 281–302.

D'Amato, M. R. (1974). Derived motives. *Annual Review of Psychology, 25,* 83–106.

D'Zurilla, T. J., & Goldfried, M. R. (1971). Problem-solving and behavior modification. *Journal of Abnormal Psychology, 78,* 107–126.

Easterbrook, J. A. (1959). The effect of emotion on cue utilization and the organization of behavior. *Psychological Review, 66,* 183–201.

Endler, N. S., Hunt, J. McV., & Rosenstein, A. J. (1962). An S-R inventory of anxiousness. *Psychological Monographs, 76* (17, Whole No. 536).

Epstein, S. (1967). Toward a unified theory of anxiety. In B. A. Maher (Ed.), *Progress in experimental personality research* (Vol. 4, pp. 2–90). New York: Academic Press.

Epstein, S. (1972). The nature of anxiety with emphasis upon its relationship to expectancy. In C. D. Spielberger (Ed.), *Anxiety: Current trends in theory and research* (Vol. 2, pp. 291–337). New York: Academic Press.

Epstein, S., & Fenz, W. D. (1965). Steepness of approach and avoidance gradients in humans as a function of experience: Theory and experiment. *Journal of Experimental Psychology, 70,* 1–12.

Eysenck, M. W. (1979). Anxiety, learning, and memory: A reconceptualization. *Journal of Research in Personality, 13,* 363–385.

Eysenck, M. W., & Eysenck, H. J. (1980). Mischel and the concept of personality. *British Journal of Psychology, 71,* 191–204.

Fenz, W. D., & Epstein, S. (1967). Gradients of physiological arousal in parachutists as a function of an approaching jump. *Psychosomatic Medicine, 29,* 33–51.

Folkman, S. (1984). Personal control and stress and coping processes: A theoretical analysis. *Journal of Personality and Social Psychology, 46*, 839–852.

Folkman, S., & Lazarus, R. S. (1980). An analysis of coping in a middle-aged community sample. *Journal of Health and Social Behavior, 21*, 219–239.

Folkman, S., & Lazarus, R. S. (1985). If it changes it must be a process: A study of emotion and coping during three stages of a college examination. *Journal of Personality and Social Psychology, 48*, 150–170.

Freud, A. (1946). *The ego and the mechanisms of defense.* New York: International Universities Press.

Gediga, G. (1980a). *Programm RACLUS* [Program RACLUS]. Osnabrück: Fachbereich Psychologie der Universität Osnabrück. (Psychologische Programmbibliothek).

Gediga, G. (1980b). *Ein Abbruchkriterium für hierarchische Clusteranalysen.* [A cutoff criterion for hierarchical cluster-analyses]. (Psychologische Forschungsberichte aus dem Fachbereich 3 der Universität Osnabrück No. 20). Osnabrück: Universität Osnabrück.

Gediga, G. (1980c). *Hierarchische Klassifikation* [Hierarchical classification]. (Psychologische Forschungsberichte aus dem Fachbereich 3 der Universität Osnabrück No. 21). Osnabrück: Universität Osnabrück.

Gediga, G. (1983). *Kontingenztafelanalyse und die Stabilität von Clusterstrukturen* [Contingency tables and the stability of cluster-structures]. (Arbeitsberichte Psychologische Methoden No. 10). Osnabrück: Fachbereich Psychologie der Universität.

Glass, D. C., & Singer, J. E. (1972). *Urban stress: Experiments on noise and social stressors.* New York: Academic Press.

Goldstein, M. J. (1959). The relationship between coping and avoiding behavior and response to fear-arousing propaganda. *Journal of Abnormal and Social Psychology, 58*, 247–252.

Gordon, J. E. (1957). Interpersonal predictions of repressers and sensitizers. *Journal of Personality, 25*, 686–698.

Haan, N. (1977). *Coping and defending.* New York: Academic Press.

Hill, K. T. (1971). Anxiety in the evaluative context. *Young Children, 27*, 97–118.

Hill, K. T., & Sarason, S. B. (1966). The relation of test anxiety and defensiveness to test and school performance over the elementary school years: A further longitudinal study. *Monographs of the Society for Research in Child Development, 31* (2, Serial No. 104).

Höfer, I., Wallbott, H. G., & Scherer, K. R. (1985). Person und Messung multimodaler Stressindikatoren in Belastungssituationen: Person und Situationsfaktoren [Measurement of multi-model stress indicators in stress situations: Person and situation factors]. In H. W. Krohne (Ed.), *Angstbewältigung in Leistungssituationen* (pp. 94–114). Weinheim: Edition Psychologie.

Houston, B. K. (1982). Trait anxiety and cognitive coping behavior. In H. W. Krohne & L. Laux (Eds.), *Achievement, stress, and anxiety* (pp. 195–206). Washington, DC: Hemisphere.

Krohne, H. W. (1974). Untersuchungen mit einer deutschen Form der Repression-Sensitization-Skala [Investigations with the German version of the Repression -Sensitization Scale]. *Zeitschrift für Klinische Psychologie, 3*, 238–260.

Krohne, H. W. (1978). Individual differences in coping with stress and anxiety. In C. D. Spielberger & I. G. Sarason (Eds.), *Stress and anxiety* (Vol. 5, pp. 233–260). Washington, DC: Hemisphere.

Krohne, H. W. (1980). Parental child-rearing behavior and the development of anxiety and coping strategies in children. In I. G. Sarason & C. D. Spielberger (Eds.), *Stress and anxiety* (Vol. 7, pp. 233–245). Washington, DC: Hemisphere.

Krohne, H. W. (1985a). Das Konzept der Angstbewältigung [The concept of coping]. In H. W. Krohne (Ed.), *Angstbewältigung in Leistungssituationen* (pp. 1–13). Weinheim: Edition Psychologie.

Krohne, H. W. (1985b). Entwicklungsbedingungen von Ängstlichkeit und Angstbewältigung: Ein Zweiprozess-Modell elterlicher Erziehungswirkung [ Developmental conditions of anxiety and coping: A two-process model of child-rearing effects]. In H. W. Krohne (Ed.). *Angstbewältigung in Leistungssituationen* (pp. 135–160). Weinham: Edition Psychologie.

Krohne, H. W., & Rogner, J. (1982). Repression-sensitization as a central construct in coping research. In H. W. Krohne & L. Laux (Eds.), *Achievement, stress, and anxiety* (pp. 167–193). Washington, DC: Hemisphere.

Krohne, H. W., & Rogner, J. (1985). Mehrvariablen-Diagnostik in der Bewältigungsforschung [Multivariate assessment in coping research]. In H. W. Krohne (Ed.), *Angstbewältigung in Leistungssituationen* (pp. 45–62). Weinheim: Edition Psychologie.

Krohne, H. W., & Schaffner, P. (1983). Anxiety, coping strategies, and performance. In S. B. Anderson & J. S. Helmick (Eds.), *On educational testing* (pp. 150–174). San Francisco, CA: Jossey-Bass.

Krohne, H. W., Wigand, A., & Kiehl, G. E. (1985). Konstruktion eines multidimensionalen Instruments zur Erfassung von Angstbewältigungstendenzen [Construction of a multidimensional instrument for the assessment of coping tendencies]. In H. W. Krohne (Ed.), *Angstbewältigung in Leistungssituationen* (pp. 63–77). Weinheim: Edition Psychologie.

Laux, L. (1983). Psychologische Stresskonzeptionen [Psychological conceptions of stress]. In H. Thomae (Ed.), *Enzyklopädie der Psychologie: Serie Motivation und Emotion: Vol. 1. Theorien und Formen der Motivation* (pp. 453–535). Göttingen: Hogrefe.

Lazarus, R. S. (1966). *Psychological stress and the coping process.* New York: McGraw-Hill.

Lazarus, R. S., & Folkman, S. (1984). Coping and adaptation. In W. D. Gentry (Ed.), *The handbook of behavioral medicine* (pp. 282–325). New York: Guilford.

Lazarus, R. S., & Launier, R. (1978). Stress-related transactions between person and environment. In L. A. Pervin & M. Lewis (Eds.), *Perspectives in interactional psychology* (pp. 287–327). New York: Plenum Press.

Meichenbaum, D. (1977). *Cognitive behavior modification: An integrative approach.* New York: Plenum Press.

Meichenbaum, D., Henshaw, D. & Himel, D. (1982). Coping with stress as a problem-solving process. In H. W. Krohne & L. Laux (Eds.), *Achievement, stress, and anxiety* (pp. 127–142). Washington DC: Hemisphere.

Miller, S. M. (1979a). Controllability and human stress: Method, evidence, and theory. *Behaviour Research and Therapy, 17,* 287–304.

Miller, S. M. (1979b). Coping with impending stress: Psychophysiological and cognitive correlates of choice. *Psychophysiology, 16,* 572–581.

Miller, S. M. (1980). When is a little information a dangerous thing? Coping with stressful events by monitoring versus blunting. In S. Levine & H. Ursin (Eds.), *Coping and Health* (pp. 145–169). New York: Plenum Press.

Miller, S. M., & Mangan, C. E. (1983). Interacting effects of information and coping style in adapting to gynecologic stress: Should the doctor tell all? *Journal of Personality and Social Psychology, 45,* 223–236.

Millham, J., & Jacobson, L. (1978). The need for approval. In H. London & J. E. Exner (Eds.), *Dimensions of personality* (pp. 365–390). New York: Wiley.

Mineka, S., & Kihlstrom, J. F. (1978). Unpredictable and uncontrollable events: A new perspective on experimental neurosis. *Journal of Abnormal Psychology, 87,* 256–271.

Mischel, W. (1968). *Personality and assessment.* New York: Wiley.

Mischel, W. (1973). Toward a cognitive social learning reconceptualization of personality. *Psychological Review, 80,* 252–283.

Mischel, W. (1983). Alternatives in the pursuit of the predictability and consistency of persons: Stable data that yield unstable interpretations. *Journal of Personality, 51,* 578–604.

Mischel, W. (1984). Convergences and challenges in the search for consistency. *American Psychologist, 39,* 351–364.

Mischel, W., & Peake, P. K. (1982). Beyond déjà vu in the search for cross-situational consistency. *Psychological Review, 89,* 730–755.

Mischel, W., & Peake, P. K. (1983). Some facets of consistency: Replies to Epstein, Funder and Bem. *Psychological Review, 90,* 394–402.

Monat, A., Averill, J. R., & Lazarus, R. S. (1972). Anticipatory stress and coping reactions under various conditions of uncertainty. *Journal of Personality and Social Psychology, 24,* 237–253.

Otto, J., & Bösel, R. (1978). Angstverarbeitung und die Diskrepanz zwischen Selfreport und physiologischem Stressindikator: Eine gelungene Replikation der Weinstein-Analyse [Coping with anxiety and the discrepancy between self-report and physiological stress indicators: A successful replication of the Weinstein analysis]. *Schweizerische Zeitschrift für Psychologie und ihre Anwendungen, 37,* 321–330.

Pearlin, L. I., & Schooler, C. (1978). The structure of coping. *Journal of Health and Social Behavior, 19,* 2–21.

Prystav, G. (1981). Psychologische Copingforschung: Konzeptbildungen, Operationalisierungen und Messinstrumente [Psychological coping reseach: Conceptions and measurement]. *Diagnostica, 26,* 189–214.

Prystav, G. (1985). Der Einfluss der Vorhersagbarkeit von Stress-Ereignissen auf die Angstbewältigung [The influence of the predictability of stress events on coping behavior]. In H. W. Krohne (Ed.), *Angstbewältigung in Leistungssituationen* (pp. 14–44). Weinheim: Edition Psychologie.

Ruebush, B. K., Byrum, M., & Farnham, L. J. (1963). Problem solving as a function of children's defensiveness and parental behavior. *Journal of Abnormal and Social Psychology, 67,* 355–362.

Schönpflug, W. (1983). Coping efficiency and situational demands. In G. R. J. Hockey (Ed.), *Stress and fatigue in human performance* (pp. 299–330). London: Wiley.

Schulz, P., & Schönpflug, W. (1982). Regulatory activity during states of stress. In H. W. Krohne & L. Laux (Eds.), *Achievement, stress, and anxiety* (pp. 51–91). Washington, DC: Hemisphere.

Seligman, M. E. P., Maier, S. F., & Solomon, R. L. (1971). Unpredictable and uncontrollable aversive events. In F. R. Brush (Ed.), *Aversive conditioning and learning* (pp. 347–400). New York: Academic Press.

Spielberger, C. D. (1966). Theory and research on anxiety. In C. D. Spielberger (Ed.), *Anxiety and behavior* (pp. 3–20). New York: Academic Press.

Weinberger, D. A., Schwartz, G. E., & Davidson, R. J. (1979). Low-anxious, high-anxious, and repressive coping styles: Psychometric patterns and behavioral and physiological responses to stress. *Journal of Abnormal Psychology, 88,* 369–380.

Weinstein, J. Averill, J. R., Opton, E. M., & Lazarus, R. S. (1968). Defensive style and discrepancy between self-report and physiological indexes of stress. *Journal of Personality and Social Psychology, 10,* 406–413.

Weisman, A. D., & Worden, J. W. (1976). The existential plight in cancer: Significance of the first 100 days. *International Journal of Psychiatry in Medicine, 7,* 1–15.

Welford, A. T. (1973). Stress and performance. *Ergonomics, 16,* 567–580.

# CHAPTER 12

# A Self-Presentational View of Coping with Stress

## LOTHAR LAUX

## Introduction

Among the many stress situations people encounter, those involving social stress seem to be the most frequent. Social stress situations refer to the evaluation of personal adequacy (e.g., being interviewed for a job or giving a speech). The interpersonal evaluation inherent in these situations is usually appraised as a *threat to self-esteem*. To cope with such threatening situations, people often attempt to present themselves in a particular way. Consider the following excerpt of an interview from my own research on test anxiety. A young female teacher described her coping efforts in an examination, in which she had to teach in front of the class and the examiners, as follows: "Compared to the written examination this performance was much more important to me since I could present my personality. I attempted to appear self-confident. The examiners should not notice my weaknesses. I wanted to save my face."

This example nicely illustrates the view that people manage their *self-presentations* to influence the impressions that others receive of them. It is the aim of this chapter to look at stress and coping from a self-presentational or dramaturgical perspective, thereby utilizing the "life as theater" metaphor. Recent theory and research on stress and anxiety

LOTHAR LAUX • Lehrstuhl Personlichkeitspsychologie, Universität Bamberg, 8600 Bamberg, Federal Republic of Germany. Preparation of this manuscript was facilitated by a travel grant of the Deutsche Forschungsgemeinschaft.

have failed to consider systematically the contributions of *self-presentation* approaches. For the most part, these areas have developed independently, though their issues are quite similar. In this chapter, I highlight the need for a joint consideration of both fields and suggest some new avenues for future research. In the first section, self-presentational approaches are introduced. I then attempt to build a bridge between recent stress and self-presentation approaches. The third section deals with coping processes viewed from a self-presentational perspective. Defensive strategies (e.g., self-handicapping) and self-extending strategies are described in some detail. In the fourth section, I focus on a self-presentational interpretation of anxiety. Individual differences in self-presentation is the topic of the fifth section. Finally, I recommend the use of an individual-centered method for the investigation of stress and self-presentation.

## Self-Presentation

In the theater of ancient Rome, the actors wore masks, called *persona*. It is probably no mere accident that *persona* became the source of the words *personality, personalité,* and *Persönlichkeit*. According to Allport (1937), the Latin word, not long after its first appearance, had many different meanings, including *mask* (as one appears to others, but not as one really is), *role* (the part one plays in life), and *true self* (the actor himself as an assemblage of personal qualities). The contradictory meanings of persona, and of the contemporary term personality, call attention to the differences between our private selves and our public appearances. It is especially the dramaturgical approach of the sociologist Goffman (1959) that has made clear that people sometimes create discrepancies between their private selves and the characters performed. In his book, *The Presentation of Self in Everyday Life,* he extensively used the "life as theater" metaphor, describing social interaction as a theatrical performance.

The view that people engage in performances, like actors, is also at the core of most recent psychological approaches of self-presentation and impression management (e.g., Schlenker, 1980, 1985; Schlenker & Leary, 1982; Tedeschi, 1981):

> *Impression management is the conscious or unconscious attempt to control images that are projected in real or imagined social interactions.* When these images are self-relevant, the behavior is termed *self-presentation.* We attempt to influence how other people—real or imagined—perceive our personality traits, abilities, intentions, behaviors. . . . In so doing, we often influence how we see ourselves. (Schlenker, 1980, p. 6)

The term self-presentation, for some writers, connotes deception and dissimulation. As a matter of fact, research on self-presentation has, to a large extent, been preoccupied with studying how people, more or less consciously, present nonveridical information about themselves, even including deceptive information. However, people often also engage in accurately communicating actual emotional states or habitual traits to control the impressions formed by other people. Many writers agree that the veridical conveying of self-related information should also be placed within the rubric of self-presentation.

Recently, Tetlock and Manstead (1985) have identified basic questions of the "Impression Management Research Program": What types of impressions do people seek to create on others? What motives underlie impression management? Whom do people seek to impress? What behavioral tactics do people employ to achieve desired identities? How effective are people as impression managers? How aware are people of engaging in impression management?

Needless to say, it is not yet possible to answer these questions with regard to the special field of stress. The main goal of this chapter is rather to demonstrate—in a first preliminary step—that it is fruitful and intriguing to view stress and coping from a self-presentational perspective.

## Stress and Self-Presentation

In psychological stress theory, Lazarus and his associates (e.g., Lazarus & Folkman, 1984; Lazarus & Launier, 1978) have suggested that stress can be most adequately described in terms of a transaction between person and environment (cf. Laux & Vossel, 1982). According to Pervin (1968), who proposed a distinction between transaction and interaction, *transaction* focuses on reciprocal causation, although *interaction* denotes unidirectional causality. Following the logic of the analysis of variance model, interaction is defined in terms of interactions of two independent variables (person and environment factors) that influence behavior in a unidirectional way. Transaction, on the other hand, does not only mean that the environment influences behavior, but also that the behavior of an individual is an active agent in affecting the environment. This distinction corresponds to the one proposed by Magnusson and Endler (1977) between *mechanistic* and *dynamic interactions*. Lazarus adopts Pervin's distinction for stress theory:

> most or perhaps even all adaptive transactions involve two-way cause-and-effect relationships via a complex set of feedback processes. The environ-

ment is perceived and interpreted—or as we would put it, appraised—leading to adaptive or coping processes arising out of the person's own personal agendas; the effects of these processes on the environment are also appraised and reacted to in an interplay whose status is constantly changing in a continuous flow. (Lazarus & Cohen, 1978, p. 114)

Psychological self-presentation approaches employ the same basic paradigm. Schlenker (1980), for example, argues strongly against Goffman's emphasis on the role of social rules in determining behavior, which he regards as an example of *unidirectional determinism*. Advocating Bandura's (1978) *reciprocal determinism*, Schlenker also adopts a transactional perspective. Accordingly, he emphasizes that the environment, cognitive scripts, and goals interact to influence behavior that, in turn, changes the environment. Information about these changes is fed back to the persons, changing their goals and scripts, and subsequent behaviors.

More specifically, I would like to take the view that the definition of self-presentation itself implies a transactional perspective, because people project identity-related images to others and then form identities based on the reactions of others to themselves (cf. Tedeschi, 1981). In other words, people use their social behavior as a means of communicating information about images of themselves and thereby attempt to influence the way audiences perceive and treat them. In doing so, they often influence the way they see themselves. Thus, creating a desired impression permits them to receive self-defining feedback that may help them to assess whether they *really* possess a particular attribute or not (Schlenker & Leary, 1982).

Because both areas of research use the transactional paradigm, it should not be too difficult to analyse self-presentational problems as a special instance of stressful transactions. For Lazarus, stress occurs when environmental or internal demands tax or exceed adaptive resources. Thus, whether or not transactions are stressful depends on the balance of power between perceived demands and perceived response capabilities. Lazarus distinguishes three kinds of stressful appraisals of person–environment transactions: *harm-loss, threat,* and *challenge.* All three involve a more or less negative evaluation of a person's present or future state of well-being, with challenge providing the least negative one. Harm-loss refers to damage that has already occurred; threat to harm or loss that is anticipated; and challenge to the possibly risky and difficult-to-attain but probable mastery of an imbalance between environmental demands and response capabilities (cf. Lazarus & Launier, 1978).

Obviously, harm-loss, threat, and challenge are very broad categories of primary appraisal, and each could be further subdivided into a variety of forms. A self-presentational appraisal may constitute an important subtype in each category, because stress very often occurs in front of a real or imagined audience. Thus, there is a *threat* to people's identities whenever they anticipate that they will not be able to generate a particular type of image that will lead to satisfactory reactions from the audience. The appraisal is called *challenge,* when people see the risk of not creating the preferred impression but at the same time emphasize the possibility of positive mastery. Finally, one can speak of *loss* of self-esteem (harm-loss) when the preferred impression has not been created (e.g., one fails a test designed to measure abilities central to one's identity).

## Coping and Self-Presentation

The concept of coping has grown to such an extent that it now occupies a central place in current theoretical models of stress and emotion. Lazarus even argues that stress as a concept pales in significance when compared with coping: "How people cope with stress is even more important to overall morale, social functioning and somatic health than the frequency and severity of the stress episodes themselves" (Roskies & Lazarus, 1980, p. 38). A simple but useful classification scheme of coping acts was offered by Lazarus (1966). His distinction of two main modes of coping—direct actions and intrapsychic modes—has been adopted by many authors. Within the framework of his transactional model of stress, Lazarus has recently reorganized and expanded the former classification scheme (see Lazarus & Launier, 1978). Of prime interest is the emphasis on the two main functions of coping: *altering the troubled transaction* (instrumental) and *regulating the emotion* (palliative). The intended effect of the instrumental or problem solving aspect is the alteration of the stressful person–environment relationship. Palliative coping, on the other hand, consists of efforts to manage the somatic and subjective components of the stress emotions (e.g., anxiety, anger, depression), without changing the actual person–environment relationship. Examples of palliative coping include attention deployment, taking drugs, or engaging in relaxation techniques.

Now, what can we gain when we view coping strategies from a self-presentational perspective? We should begin our analysis by raising these crucial questions: Do persons, at least occasionally, employ forms of coping with the purpose of manipulating impressions? Do they generate coping acts to influence the way audiences perceive and treat them? Imagine, for example, people who drink alcohol to cope with situations in which their competence is going to be tested. One possibility might be that they are drinking to reduce their uncomfortable feelings prior to or after the threatening performance. Another possibility, however, can be derived from a self-presentational view: People might drink alcohol—which they expect to impair their performance—in order to attribute their supposed or real failure to the drug rather than to their lack of ability (Snyder & Smith, 1982). In presenting their "drinking problems" they deflect from their supposed or real deficit in abilities. Such a strategy has been called *self-handicapping,* and is an example of the broader class of *defensive strategies* of self-presentation.

# Defensive Strategies

## Self-Handicapping

According to Jones and Berglas (1978), a self-handicapping strategy is a form of defense mechanism whereby the individual reduces a threat to self-esteem. This is achieved by creating an impediment to performance in evaluative situations, so that the individual has a ready explanation for potential failure, other than a lowered standing on an important self-dimension. In case of success, however, the handicap serves as a source of augmentation of highly valued personal dimensions, since it was possible to do well despite the impairing effects of the handicap.

By using such a strategy, individuals attempt to control attributions made by others concerning their performance. Self-handicapping avoids the implications of failure for central, highly valued dimensions. Individuals create impediments in order to "protect their conceptions of themselves as competent, intelligent persons" (Jones & Berglas, 1978, p. 200). Because many invoked handicaps have negative implications in the handicapper's eyes and in the eyes of others (e.g., being an alcoholic), self-handicapping is only useful when that which is lost is not as highly valued as that which is protected (cf. Snyder & Smith, 1982). As Snyder and Smith (1982) point out, milder forms of self-handicapping are surely adaptive. Without them, life would consist of frequent unpleasant encounters exemplifying one's insufficiencies. However, the more extreme forms of self-handicapping must be regarded as ineffective and even pathological coping strategies, because they involve "(1) being socially disturbing, (2) indirectly and over time creating as much if not more personal distress than they avoid, and (3) limiting the individual's range of available responses to the demands of everyday life" (Snyder & Smith, 1982, p. 114).

## Self-Serving Explanations

Given the potential costs of self-handicapping, people attempt to use more attractive self-protective strategies, such as *self-serving explanations* (Schlenker & Leary, 1982). These are employed to maintain images that are central to one's self-esteem; for example, students, who failed in an examination, may attribute their performance to aspects of the situation ("There was great time pressure") or to temporary internal conditions ("I have had too little sleep"). These are attempts to convince the audience that the bad performance should not be regarded as a fair representation of what the actor is normally like as a person (Schlenker, 1980). If the actor is successful in influencing others, his standing on important personal dimensions, for example, intellectual abilities, is not questioned; self-esteem and public esteem are maintained. Self-serving explanations can be offered after damage has already occurred (harm-loss), or in advance, when self-esteem is jeopardized by an upcoming event (anticipatory coping with threat).

As Schlenker and Leary (1982) point out, self-serving explanations are not always viable, because they can be contradictory to other facts that the audience knows about the actor or the situation. (Members of the audience know, e.g., that the actor has often performed poorly in the past.) If self-serving explanations are unavailable, self-handicapping strategies may be the only alternative. In sum, when the actor's identity vis-à-vis an audience is endangered, he tends to find self-serving explanations not involving potential costs to his identity. Self-handicapping is employed only when attractive alternative explanations are not available.

The conception of an ordered use of self-protecting strategies resembles, in some respects, Appley's model of *stress thresholds* (Cofer & Appley, 1964). In attempting to differentiate between stress, frustration, and related terms, Appley proposes a step-ordered series of thresholds, beginning with the *instigation threshold*, a point of change from habitual to new coping behavior. At the *frustration threshold* "a shift in pattern of response occurs, from exclusively task-oriented, problem-solving behavior to the inclusion of ego-oriented, self- or integrity-sustaining behavior". The *stress threshold* is characterized by "the dropping out of all task-oriented behaviors, and the exclusive preoccupation of the organism with ego protection" (Cofer & Appley, 1964, p. 452). At the final *exhaustion threshold*, ego-defensive behaviors give way to inactivity. The core of Appley's idea is that people try to maintain their self-integrity when confronted with events that threaten it, and that ego-defensive responses are intensified when the individual moves up the "stress ladder". Thus, it should not be too difficult to accommodate the proposal of an ordered use of self-protecting strategies to Appley's model.

## Self-Deception

The importance of self-deception, as sometimes necessary for psychological and physical health, has been emphazised in the writings of Lazarus (Lazarus, 1983; Lazarus & Launier, 1978). He has elaborated, especially, the principles concerning costs and benefits of self-deception in the form of denial, which he defines as the negation of something. For example, denial can have positive value at an early state of coping when the resources of a person do not yet allow the use of problem-focused coping. Denial may, however, prevent mastery when actions that are necessary to protect people against serious illness are delayed. For example, denial of breast lumps as a possible indication of cancer may result in metastasis and poor medical outlook.

If denial involves real or imagined audiences, a self-presentational analysis might be appropriate. Snyder and Smith (1982) point out that self-handicapping appears, in many cases, to be a conscious and intentional process. For optimal functioning of self-handicapping, however, the awareness of its purposive nature has to be avoided. If we consider the self-defining feedback process in projecting images to other people, even intentional employment of a handicap can finally result in self-deception. According to Schlenker, exaggerated self-presentations start with the goal of impressing an audience and end up, under certain conditions, with private beliefs. The internalization of these self-presentational tactics

> is most likely to occur when cues in the situation prevent people's labeling their tactic as a lie, such as when an account is accepted by a significant and knowlegeable audience and the account does not blatantly contradict the facts as known by the actor. (Schlenker, 1980, p. 195)

Stated negatively, self-presentations do not only fool the audience, they also may deceive the actor himself.

## Self-Extending Strategies

Although people often attempt to convey veridical images of themselves, they sometimes create a discrepancy between the "real" selves and the images as "projected" selves. In these cases, the conveyed images are inconsistent with the way people believe they "really" are. As was described above, an individual may pretend to feel anxious while giving a speech in order to provide the audience with an "explanation" for a (possible) bad performance (self-handicapping). Another individual, who feels anxious, may attempt to appear self-confident while giving a speech and thus disguise or inhibit the expressive display of anxiety. In both instances, an attempt is made to cope with the threatening situation by conveying nonveridical information about the private self. Both individuals use a protective screen of "make believe." Although the self-handicapper's use of a protective mask may involve, in the long run, more personal distress than it avoids, the employment of a protective mask in the case of the second individual may result in growth and mastery, if the self-concept is extended by a process of internalizing the role of a self-confident person. I will call such a form of self-presentation a *self-extending strategy*. The intended effect of self-extending strategies may be to alter a stressful person–environment relationship, as well as to control the emotional reaction arising from that relationship (cf. Lazarus & Launier, 1978).

The full protection of "make believe" is the core idea of Kelly's (1955) *Fixed-Role Therapy*, which can be considered as a prime example of a self-extending strategy. This therapy offers the client a mask behind which one can try out new forms of behavior:

1. At the beginning of the procedure, the client is asked to write a character sketch of himself from the view of a third person. Kelly used this form of self-characterization to urge the client to describe himself as a coherent whole and not as a list of faults and virtues.

2. The therapist then studies this sketch, in consultation with colleagues and, with their help, writes a new personality sketch suitable for enactment by the client. This *fixed-role sketch* invites the client to explore sharply contrasting behaviors. For example, if the client has presented himself as "cautious," the new personality may be described as "bold." An even better solution is to suggest a new dimension, one that has never before occurred to the client. Thus, an attempt is made "to loose him from the semantic chains with which he has bound himself" (Kelly, 1955, p. 371). The sketch should also provide a basis for a new role relationship, by introducing concepts that enable a person to subsume the principles under which other people are operating.

3. After the client has accepted the sketch, he is asked to act as if he were that new person: "You *act* like him! You *think* like him. You *talk* to your friends the way you think he would talk! You *do* the things you think he would do! You even *have his interests* and you *enjoy* the things he would enjoy! (Kelly, 1955, p. 385).

4. Meeting the therapist at least three times a week, the client is given help, by a series of rehearsals and checks of enactment effectiveness. The enactment is usually terminated after two weeks.

It is not the goal of the therapy to replace the personality of the client with some kind of new one. The self of the client is not questioned or criticized. He is not even asked to change himself. In offering him a protective screen, fixed role therapy provides the opportunity to try out new ways of living without posing too much threat to the integrity of the present self. Kelly points out, however, that for individuals who have ceased to discover themselves, threats cannot be entirely avoided when fixed role therapy is used: "To present these individuals with the responsibility of actually *being* anything additional to what they have already encapsuled in their self-concept is to confront them with a threat" (Kelly, 1955, p. 384).

The therapy is said to be making progress when the client regards the role as no longer strange or artificial and gradually begins to internalize aspects of the role as part of the self-concept: "I feel as if this were the real me" (Kelly, 1955, p. 416). It is a well-known fact that such a merger of self and role also takes place in stage actors. For professional actors, however, it is a serious handicap when role and own self are not clearly separated. They even might confuse role and self, as is the case in the so-called *histrionic syndrome* (Yablonsky, 1976). Actors tend to avoid this form of "occupational disease" by devoting their attention not only to the role they play but, at the same time, attempting to maintain a watchful and critical attitude on the part of their own self. This *double consciousness* has been described by many actors (cf. Metcalf, 1931). In fixed role therapy, on the other hand, the merger of "real self" and role is a desired process.

There is no doubt that role-playing is also employed by naive persons outside therapeutic intervention. Imagine, for example, an applicant for a job who anticipates an upcoming speech in front of influential executives. He or she appraises the situation as threatening because there are many competitors and only the best one will be hired. Being motivated to get the job, most candidates will attempt to convey the desired impression of a competent and self-confident candidate, even if they regard themselves as anxious or only moderately self-confident. They act as if they were nonanxious and self-confident and may, after frequent enactment, internalize the role. That people can "become" the roles they play may also be seen with individuals who often use handicapping. (For example, the frequent strategic employment of anxiety may become incorporated into the individuals' self-concept.)

What are the implications of using protecting screens for the assumption of a "real" or "true" self? If people act in ways that violate our conception of them, we often describe their behavior as superficial or "phony." There is a longstanding commandment that people "be themselves." They should not "wear masks" that hide their "real" selves. In contrast to such evaluative statements, the position advanced here is that "projecting inauthentic identities" (Schlenker, 1980) may serve as a protective screen, sometimes aimed at maintaining central conceptions of self, sometimes even aimed at extending a narrowly defined "real" self.

## Self-Presentation and Anxiety

Emotions constitute a further topic for a dramaturgical analysis. Averill (1980), for example, has proposed a general role model of emotion in which he defines an emotion as a "transitory social role (a socially constituted syndrome) that includes an individual's appraisal of the situation and that is interpreted as a passion rather than as an action" (p. 312). Following Averill, the experience of passivity (of being "overcome" by emotion) is an interpretation of behavior, it is not intrinsic to emotion. Such a role-theoretical point of view, with its emphasis on the reflective quality of emotion, nicely fits in with a self-presentational analysis of emotion in which the strategic use of emotional expression is stressed. A variety of stress emotions, such as anxiety, anger, and depression, are possible candidates for such an analysis, but I limit the discussion here to anxiety.

There are some statements in the anxiety literature that are concerned with the self-presentational nature of anxiety reports. In reviewing studies stimulated by Trait-State Anxiety Theory (Spielberger, 1972), Glanzmann, for example, comes to the conclusion that high levels of state anxiety, expressed by high trait-anxious persons after confrontation with ego threat, might be interpreted as instrumental to the prevention of blame: "The specific line of reasoning in a high anxious person might be as follows: 'It is possible that the experimenter will be disappointed by the way I have performed on this task. Therefore, I'll show him how miserable I felt. This will explain why I didn't do very well' " (Glanzmann, 1985, p. 15). Using such a strategy of "cautionary justification" might lead to a self-produced elevation of anxiety levels in high anxious persons, especially if instructions emphasized the importance of one's performance.

The strategy of self-handicapping may serve as another example for the self-presentational nature of anxiety reports. Snyder and Smith (1982) have argued that complaints of anxiety can be used as a strategy for discounting the image-related implications of poor performance in tests and examination. The reports of anxiety symptoms (e.g., "I feel so panicky when I take an important test that I forget what I know") may deflect from the true meaning of real or imagined poor performance. In using anxiety reports strategically, the standing on highly valued personal dimensions, such as ability and competence, is obscured. If the handicapping strategy is incorporated into the self-concept, individuals may typically use their reports of anxiety in this self-protective manner.

Smith, Snyder, and Handelsman (1982) demonstrated the self-protective strategy of high test-anxious persons. Their subjects were told that they would be administered a two-part intelligence test. In the evaluative condition, they were told that the test was widely used and that they would be given feedback after the second part of the test. In the nonevaluative condition, they were informed that the test was one the researchers were developing, so that no feedback would be given after the second part. All subjects then completed the first part of the test.

For students in the evaluative condition, three different instructions were delivered to investigate the effects of self-handicapping. They were told either that (1) anxiety interferes with performance on the test (explicit self-handicapping condition), or that (2) anxiety seemed to have no effect at all on test performance, or (3) they were given no information about the influence of anxiety. Before the second part of the test was administered, the subjects filled out a shortened version of the A-State scale of the State-Trait Anxiety Inventory (STAI) (Spielberger, Gorsuch, & Lushene, 1970), indicating how they had felt during the first part of the test. Level of state anxiety served as the major dependent variable in this study. The results showed that subjects in the nonevaluative condition reported the lowest level of anxiety. The authors concluded that these subjects experienced no threat to self-esteem. Within the evaluative condition, however, results showed that the "anxiety inhibits performance" condition and the "no information condition" lead to higher anxiety than the "anxiety has no effect" condition. Thus, reported anxiety levels were reduced when anxiety was not a usable excuse for poor performance, although they were elevated whether or not the debilitating effect of anxiety was explicitly described. Based on these findings, the authors concluded that test anxious subjects may employ their anxiety states as self-handicapping strategy.

The self-handicapping interpretation of test anxiety is not considered in current theories of anxiety (e.g., Sarason, 1980; Spielberger, Gonzales, Taylor, Algaze, & Anton, 1978). In these theories, reported state anxiety reactions are basically conceived as expressions of the actual emotional experience. Spielberger *et al.* (1978), for example, define state anxiety as subjective feelings of tension, apprehension, nervousness, and worry, and recommend the A-State scale of the STAI to assess these qualities. According to Spielberger, scores on the A-State scale increase in response to physical danger or psychological stress, and decrease as a consequence of relaxation training. Thus, A-State scores correspond to the intensity of the actual anxiety experienced. In Spielberger's model, defensive maneuvers are considered to be evoked by state anxiety, but state anxiety reports themselves are not interpreted as reflecting the operation of defensive maneuvers such as elevations of anxiety as a self-handicapping strategy.

How can we integrate the self-presentational view of anxiety in Trait-State Anxiety Theory? It will help to refer to the differentiation of worry and emotionality in recent test anxiety approaches. Briefly stated, worry describes the cognitive component of the anxiety experience, such as concerns about one's performance or its consequences. Emotionality, on the other hand, refers to the self-perceived autonomic-affective arousal of the anxiety experience (Liebert & Morris, 1967). Adopting this important differentiation, I would like to argue that the experience of self-centered worry cognitions aroused by a threat to individuals' self-esteem constitutes the antecedent condition for the employment of self-presentational strategies. If attractive self-serving explanations or other alternatives are not available, the individuals employ a self-handicapping strategy, such as the strategic use of anxiety (see Schlenker & Leary, 1982), to deflect from an imagined or real deficit of abilities. It must be emphasized that, in this case, anxiety refers to the autonomic-affective arousal component. The state anxiety results in the study of Smith *et al.* (1982), which supported the assumption of the self-handicapping use of anxiety, are based on the A-State-Scale of the STAI, which measures primarily the emotionality component of anxiety. Therefore, self-handicapping individuals tend to elevate the self-reports of their feelings of tension, nervousness, and arousal.

Unfortunately there are no studies that have been concerned with the influence of self-handicapping on measures of the worry component. It can be hypothesized, however, that self-handicapping implies a strategic reduction of the worry scores, because self-handicapping subjects are motivated to conceal the concerns about their abilities.

It is evident that the appearance of anxiety in evaluative situations cannot be understood only in terms of a self-protective strategy. It is necessary, therefore, to differentiate between high test-anxious subjects who use their anxiety reactions strategically and those who do not. The differential impact on worry and emotionality scores is supposed here only for the group of strategic users of anxiety. The validity of the foregoing interpretation has to be demonstrated in future studies.

## Individual Differences in Self-Presentation

A wide variety of motives have been proposed to describe individual differences in self-presentation. Baumeister (1982), for example, distinguishes between two main self-presentational motives, the motive to please the audience and the motive to construct one's public self congruent to one's ideal. Tedeschi and Norman (1985) view the self-presenting individual as primarily concerned about social power and influence. They differentiate between *tactical* and *strategic* forms of impression management. Tactical self-presentations refer to short-term objectives, whereas strategic self-presentations have long-range consequences over time and situations. Strategic forms are undertaken to establish some reputation or identity for the individual (sometimes referred to as traits or personality). Such reputational characteristics serve as power resources for multiple audiences and are effective across various situations. Many other motives and personality variables have been proposed, including desire for personal control, needs for social approval, Machiavellianism, self-consciousness, and self-monitoring (see Schlenker, 1980, for a comprehensive overview). I will concentrate on Snyder's (1979a) *self-monitoring* approach, because some interesting ideas for coping research can be derived from his conception.

Presenting oneself in a desired way requires extensive expressive management, as there is always the danger of considerable "leakage" from desired interpretations. The actor may want the audience to form one particular impression, but it is possible that the audience will form an entirely different impression. An individual who attempts to appear self-confident in giving a speech, for example, must disguise or inhibit the expressive display of anxiety. On the other hand, for an individual who attempts to appear anxious in an examination in order to provide the audience with an "explanation" for his bad performance, it is not sufficient to verbally claim anxiety. He must also convincingly communicate the nonverbal displays of anxiety. Snyder's construct of *self-monitoring* relates to the ability to manage one's expressive behaviors. He proposed that people differ in the ability to monitor and control their expressive behaviors.

> Self-monitoring individuals, out of a concern for the situational appropriateness of their social behavior, are particularly sensitive to the expression and self-presentation of relevant others in social situations and use these cues as guidelines for regulating or controlling their own verbal and non-verbal self-presentation. (Snyder, 1979a, p. 183)

The goals of self-monitoring may be to communicate accurately one's true emotional state, to communicate an emotional state that is not necessarily congruent with the actual emotional state, or to conceal an inappropriate emotional state. Snyder's conception reminds us that successful self-presentation involves the ability to control expressive behavior.

What might be of interest for the assessment of coping strategies is his conception of mental images. According to Snyder (1979b), a hypothetical high self-monitoring individual asks the question "Who does this situation want me to be and how can I be that person?" The individual then constructs an image of a person who best exemplifies the type of person called for by the situation in question. The image serves as a guideline for monitoring the actions and expressive behaviors of the high self-monitoring individual. By contrast, a hypothetical low self-monitoring individual asks the question "Who am I and how can I be me in this situation?" This individual uses an enduring self-image that represents knowledge of behaviors in situations most relevant to the situation at hand. This self-image is used by the individual as a guideline for monitoring actions.

Snyder's hypothetical analysis may well be applied to the issue of coping. Imagine, for example, an individual who intends to cope with the situation of giving a speech in front of an audience by presenting himself as an assertive, nonanxious subject. The question arises, how is this plan actively translated into corresponding behavior? The candidate may use knowledge of his behavior in similar, though less threatening, situations in the past as a guideline for controlling his actions. Another possibility might be to refer to an image of an acquaintance who is usually successful in such situations and to use this person's prototypical behaviors as detailed guidelines for coping with the situation. Still a third possibility is the use of abstract rules or generalized images, for example, of behaving in a nonanxious and assertive manner, which are not exemplified by images of concrete persons. Coping research would definitely profit from an analysis of mental images along these lines.

No systematic attempt will be made here to evaluate Snyder's theoretical contribution and his attempts to assess self-monitoring by a self-report scale. One could seriously question, for example, whether it is reasonable to conceive of self-monitoring as a single dimension. According to Snyder, high self-monitors possess both the *ability* to successfully control their expressive behaviors and the *motivation* to seek and use cues that indicate what is appropriate in social interactions, whereas low self-monitors are less concerned with the social appropriateness of their behavior and are also less skilled than their high self-monitoring counterparts. I would argue, however, that the motivation and the ability to present oneself may be completely independent. Based on the independence assumption, it is possible to conceive of persons who are consistently motivated to accurately communicate their true emotional states, attitudes, and traits, and who also have a well-developed repertoire of self-presentational skills.

# An Individual-Centered Approach to the Assessment of Self-Presentation and Coping

In the preceding sections, appraisal and cognitive coping processes have been mentioned frequently. Stress and self-presentation approaches rely heavily on cognitive processes. In describing coping strategies, such as self-serving explanations and self-handicapping strategies, the authors usually cite one or two short sentences to exemplify such cognitive strategies, for example, "I feel so panicky when I take an important test that

I forget what I know." Given the importance of cognitive processes in these approaches, it is rather surprising that only rare attempts have been made to assess the continuously changing stream of cognitions when people engage in self-presentation. Frequently, the investigators do not tap the actual intrapsychic processes but only present inferences derived from their experimental manipulations, that is, they report, for example, what thoughts subjects might have had during an experiment. In the study of Smith *et al.* (1982), the self-handicapping strategy of high anxious subjects was inferred from the impact of the differential threat manipulation on state–anxiety scores. The investigators started with the presupposition that their subjects adopt the attributions presented in the instructions, for example, "anxiety inhibits performance" (self-handicapping condition), and think and act accordingly. The results indicated that subjects who were given no information about the influence of anxiety also reported high anxiety scores. Did they also employ self-handicapping? Are there other reasons for their high anxiety scores? How did the subjects in the self-handicapping condition interpret the instruction? It is possible, for example, that the instruction "anxiety inhibits performance" involves a greater threat to self-esteem than the instruction "anxiety has no effect". Thus, even in this carefully designed study, a more stringent interpretation would have been possible if the experimenter had assessed the actually occurring cognitions and emotions of their subjects.

The tapping of the streams of cognitive and emotional experience is at the core of Lazarus's transactional stress approach. He also recommends that investigations focus on the description of appraisal and coping processes as they actually occur in stress. Even within a short period of time, coping can involve a complex amalgam of continuously changing intrapsychic and behavioral acts that demands a process-oriented assessment procedure. To tap the streams of cognitive and emotional experience in social stress situations, the method of *videotape reconstruction* can be employed (Meichenbaum & Butler, 1980). The procedure involves two phases. In the first phase, the subject is videotaped while being confronted with stressful situations in the laboratory or in real life. In the second phase, the subject watches the videotape and is asked to remember all thoughts and emotions in the earlier taped experience, and to reconstruct them as accurately as possible.

I would like to recommend an *individual-centered* version of the general procedure of videotape reconstruction, in order to permit the assessment of the subjective world of experience in as unrestricted and undistorted manner as possible. The participating individuals are informed prior to the video-playback that they are considered as active colleagues who are experts on themselves. Every attempt is made to relax them in the situation and to minimize the pressures that arise from trying to impress the experimenter.

During playback of segments of the videotape, the subjects are asked to verbalize spontaneously what they were thinking and feeling. In addition, they are requested to report their thoughts and feelings at fixed points. The aim of this video-based form of open interview is to enable the subjects to describe their rich world of personal experiences, without the restrictions usually imposed by self-report measures with fixed response categories. Only after the subject has completed the description does the interviewer ask prepared questions pertaining to topics with which the subject has not dealt. At a later date, the typed responses of the subjects are content analysed (Krippendorff, 1980).

Using videotape-aided recall, one cannot meaningfully expect that all people are able to report whether they employed self-presentational strategies or not. But, they can tell us what they thought or felt, for example, while approaching the speaker's podium; whether they attempted to appear calm or whether they engaged in negative rumination. Furthermore, I do not expect that all subjects in the video-playback phase attempt to convey self-images that are, from their point of view, veridical. The video-playback phase constitutes a state of self-awareness, and some subjects may consciously engage in some kind of "nonveridical" self-presentation (e.g., failing to reveal or even concealing personal information). From a self-presentational perspective, such a strategy is completely legitimate, since subjects might, for example, attempt to protect highly valued personal dimensions. A careful analysis of subjects' expressive behaviors may provide leakage cues (Ekman & Friesen, 1974; Lippa, 1976) that would help identify such a strategy. Also Grawe's (1982) *Vertical Behavior Analysis* is very useful for studying self-presentation, because this observation system aims at inferring the actual goals subjects pursue in the interaction process, even if these goals are unconscious.

In general, it would be important to measure behavior in stress situations objectively, because discrepancies between cognitions assessed by video-aided self-reports and expressive behaviors could serve as a source of information about coping. Expressive behaviors should therefore be measured by naive raters for each segment of the videotape. Form and extent of behavioral acts should then be compared with the occurrence of particular cognitions for each segment of the tape. One might also include measures of actual autonomic arousal. In processing along these lines, one attempts "to capture the flow of the streams of cognition, emotion, and behavior and examine the sequential interdependencies between these streams of experience over time" (Meichenbaum & Butler, 1980, p. 151). The discussion of various statistical treatments for such a serial, multimethod analysis is beyond the scope of this chapter. It might suffice to note that the logic of a multitrait–multi-method paradigm can be applied (cf., Laux, 1976).

Based on the proposed method, future research should not focus only on descriptions of how self-presentation is used to cope with stressful encounters. Videotape reconstruction can also be employed as a procedure to teach coping skills, as has been summarized by Dowrick and Biggs (1983). In *interpersonal process recall* (Kagan, Krathwohl & Miller, 1963) clients are videotaped while interacting in a social situation. During playback of the videotape, the participants are encouraged, at significant points, to verbalize what they were thinking, feeling, imagining, or doing. The aim is to make clients conscious of their behaviors while interacting, and to enhance the effectiveness of their behavioral and intrapsychic forms of coping.

As Biggs (1983) has highlighted, video playback allows actors to "step outside." The distance between the viewer and the object (the self as actor) leaves room for "free play" around the object of attention. The self can be viewed and described from different perspectives, leading to the awareness of alternatives to the status quo. Video playback, as a stimulant to self-extending, might be especially useful for clients who—to use Kelly's (1955, p. 383) words—"devote their efforts so exclusively to *being themselves* that they have no time left for *discovering themselves*."

ACKNOWLEDGMENTS

I would like to thank J.R. Averill, R.S. Lazarus, B.R. Schlenker, C.D. Spielberger, and J.T. Tedeschi for their thoughtful comments on an earlier version of this manuscript.

# References

Allport, G. W. (1937). *Personality: A psychological interpretation.* New York: Holt, Rinehart & Winston.

Averill, J. R. (1980). A constructivist view of emotion. In R. Plutchik & H. Kellermann (Eds.), *Emotion: Theory, research, and experience* (Vol. 1, pp. 305–339). New York: Academic Press.

Bandura, A. (1978). The self-system in reciprocal determinism. *American Psychologist, 33,* 334–358.

Baumeister, R. F. (1982). A self-presentational view of social phenomena. *Psychological Bulletin, 91,* 3–26.

Biggs, S. J. (1983). Choosing to change in video feedback: On common-sense and the empiricist error. In P. W. Dowrick & S. J. Biggs (Eds.), *Using video. Psychological and social applications.* (pp. 211–226). New York: Wiley.

Cofer, C. N., & Appley, M. H. (1964). *Motivation: Theory and research.* New York: Wiley.

Dowrick, P. W., & Biggs, S. J. (Eds.) (1983). *Using video. Psychological and social applications.* New York: Wiley.

Ekman, P., & Friesen, W. V. (1974). Detecting deception from the body or face. *Journal of Personality and Social Psychology, 29,* 288–298.

Glanzmann, P. (1985). Anxiety, stress, and learning. In B. D. Kirkcaldy (Ed.), *Individual differences in performance* (pp. 89–113). Lancaster, England: MTP Press.

Goffman, E. (1959). *The presentation of self in everyday life.* New York: Doubleday.

Grawe, K. (1982). *Implikationen und Anwendungsmöglichkeiten der vertikalen Verhaltensanalyse für die Sichtweise und Behandlung psychischer Störungen* [Implications and possibilities of use of the Vertical Behavior Analysis for the interpretation and treatment of emotional disturbances]. Research Reports from the Department of Psychology, University of Bern.

Jones, E. E., & Berglas, S. (1978). Control of attributions about the self through self-handicapping strategies: The appeal of alcohol and the role of underachievement. *Personality and Social Psychology Bulletin, 4,* 200–206.

Kagan, N., Krathwohl, D. R., & Miller, R. (1963). Stimulated recall in therapy using video tape—A case study. *Journal of Counseling Psychology, 10,* 237–243.

Kelly, G. A. (1955). *The psychology of personal constructs* (Vol. 1). New York: Norton.

Krippendorff, K. (1980).*Content analysis. An introduction to its methodology.* London: Sage, 1980.

Laux, L. (1976). The multitrait-multimethod rationale in stress research. In I. G. Sarason & C. D. Spielberger (Eds.), *Stress and anxiety.* (Vol. 3, pp. 171–181). Washington: Hemisphere.

Laux, L., & Vossel, G. (1982). Paradigms in stress research: Laboratory versus field and traits versus processes. In L. Goldberger & S. Breznitz (Eds.), *Handbook of stress. Theoretical and clinical aspects* (203–211). New York: The Free Press.

Lazarus, R. S. (1966). *Psychological stress and the coping process.* New York: McGraw-Hill.

Lazarus, R. S. (1983). The costs and benefits of denial. In S. Breznitz (Ed.), *The denial of stress* (pp. 1–30). New York: International Universities Press.

Lazarus, R. S., & Cohen, J. B. (1978). Environmental stress. In J. Altman & J. F. Wohlwill (Eds.), *Human behavior and the environment* (pp. 89–127) New York: Plenum Press.

Lazarus, R. S., & Folkman, S. (1984). *Stress, appraisal, and coping.* New York: Springer.

Lazarus, R. S., & Launier, R. (1978). Stress-related transactions between person and environment. In L. A. Pervin & M. Lewis (Eds.), *Perspectives in interactional psychology* (pp. 287–327). New York: Plenum Press.

Liebert, R. M., & Morris, L. W. (1967). Cognitive and emotional components of test anxiety: A distinction and some initial data. *Psychological Reports, 20,* 975–978.

Lippa, R. (1976). Expressive control and the leakage of dispositional introversion-extraversion during role-playing teaching. *Journal of Personality, 44,* 541–559.

Magnusson, D., & Endler, N. S. (1977). Interactional psychology: Present status and future prospects. In D. Magnusson & N. S. Endler (Eds.), *Personality at the crossroads: Current issues in interactional psychology* (pp. 3–35). Hillsdale, NJ: Erlbaum.

Meichenbaum, D. T., & Butler, L. (1980). Cognitive ethology. Assessing the streams of cognition and emotion. In P. Blankstein, P. Pliner, & J. Polivy (Eds.), *Assessment and modification of emotional behavior: Vol. 6. Advances in the study of communication and affect* (pp. 139–163). New York: Plenum Press.

Metcalf, J. T. (1931). Empathy and the actor's emotion. *Journal of Social Psychology, 2,* 235–238.

Pervin, L. A. (1968). Performance and satisfaction as function of individual-environment fit. *Psychological Bulletin, 69,* 56–68.

Roskies, E., & Lazarus, R. S. (1980). Coping theory and the teaching of coping skills. In P. Davidson (Ed.), *Behavioral medicine: Changing health life styles* (pp. 38–69). New York: Brunner/Mazel.

Sarason, I. G. (Ed.) (1980). *Test anxiety: Theory, research, and applications.* Hillsdale, NJ: Erlbaum.

Schlenker, B. R. (1980). *Impression management; The self-concept, social identity, and interpersonal relations.* Monterey, CA: Brooks/Cole.

Schlenker, B. R. (1985). *The self and social life.* New York: McGraw-Hill.

Schlenker, B. R., & Leary, M. R. (1982). Social anxiety and self-presentation: A conceptualization and model. *Psychological Bulletin, 92,*641–669.

Smith, T. W., Snyder, C. R., & Handelsman, M. M. (1982). On the self-serving function of an academic wooden leg: Test anxiety as a self-handicapping strategy. *Journal of Personality and Social Psychology, 42,* 314–321.

Snyder, C. R., & Smith, T. W. (1982). Symptoms as self-handicapping strategies: The virtues of old wine in a new bottle. In G. Weary & H. L. Mirels (Eds.), *Integrations of clinical and social psychology* (pp. 104–127). New York: Oxford University Press.

Snyder, M. (1979a). Cognitive, behavioral, and interpersonal consequences of self-monitoring. In P. Pliner, K. R. Blankstein, & I. M. Spigel (Eds.), *Perception of emotion in self and others: Vol. 5. Advances in the study of communication and affect* (pp. 181–201). New York: Plenum Press.

Snyder, M. (1979b). Self-monitoring processes. In L. Berkowitz (Ed.), *Advances in experimental social psychology* (Vol. 12, pp. 85–128). New York: Academic Press.

Spielberger, C. D. (1972). Anxiety as an emotional state. In C. D. Spielberger (Ed.), *Anxiety. Current trends in theory and research* (Vol. 1, pp. 23–49). New York: Academic Press.

Spielberger, C. D., Gonzales, H. P., Taylor, C. J., Algaze, B., & Anton, W. D. (1978). Examination stress and test anxiety. In C. D. Spielberger & I. G. Sarason (Eds.), *Stress and anxiety* (Vol. 5, pp. 167–191). Washington: Hemisphere.

Spielberger, C. D., Gorsuch, R. L., & Lushene, R. E. (1970). *Manual for the State-Trait Anxiety Inventory.* Palo Alto, CA: Consulting Psychologists Press.

Tedeschi, J. T. (1981). *Impression management theory and social psychological research.* New York: Academic Press.

Tedeschi, J. T., & Norman, N. (1985). Social power, self-presentation, and the self. In B. R. Schlenker (Ed.), *The self and social life* (pp. 293–322). New York: McGraw-Hill.

Tetlock, P. E., & Manstead, A. S. R. (1985). Impression management versus intrapsychic explanations in social psychology: A useful dichotomy? *Psychological Review, 92,* 59–77.

Yablonsky, L. (1976). *Psychodrama: Resolving emotional problems through role playing.* New York: Basic Books.

# PART V

# Psychosocial Aspects of Stress

*The psychosocial aspects of stress are now coming into focus as the instant impact stressor is replaced by life events and recognition of etiological factors. Dohrenwend's analysis of life events as stressors involves life processes as influenced by recent events, ongoing social situations, and personal disposition. His objective is the determination of "the extent to which personal dispositions and social circumstances predict ways of coping with life events" and relate to adverse health conditions, especially psychopathology. This is his chosen path to the "evaluation of the role of environmentally induced stress." He presents five models of life stress processes related to health loss—victimization, vulnerability, additive burden, chronic burden, and event proneness—to explore further the relationships between life stress and psychopathology. He finds promise in increased understanding of "the individual's network of potential supporters and the conditions under which it is activated to help or hinder when specific events occur" (p. 290).*

*Brown, too, recognizes the role of social support in reducing clinical depression and other forms of psychopathology. Having determined that most depression is provoked by critical life events, he finds that vulnerability to these situations involves lowered self-esteem and/or reduced ability to draw upon someone close. Indeed a major thesis is "the mutual interdependence of the image of ourselves as worthy of support and the actual support offered by those around us" (p. 258). This vulnerability leads to increased generalization of hopelessness which, in turn, is more likely to occur during feelings of low self-esteem. His study supports the thesis that most vulnerability tends to be specific rather than general and available for study through "contextual" measures. A significant finding is that stressors work in terms of meaning, representing the human potential for symbolism and having negative implications for use of life events, per se. Further, prediction of depression is possible when a severe event matches an ongoing conflict of roles and relationships, such as between the domains of motherhood and work.*

*Breznitz's thesis that "the work of hoping has positive impact on the health and morale of people under stress" is a natural extension of Brown's "hopelessness" concept and seeks the "manipulation" of hope in a positive context. His studies of qualitative information of individuals under serious threat have resulted in the "work of stress" emphasis and how to achieves its effect. Using five metaphors of hope, such as a protected area, a bridge, intention, performance, and end in itself, he seeks an objective, experimental format for its analysis. Believing that "hope can thrive even in situations of total hopelessness," his goal is "the ability to mobilize cognitions of hoping to aid perseverance." Brown would also like the answer. For him "hope may prove to be the critical intervening experience between experiencing loss, failure and disappointment, and clinical depression."*

# CHAPTER 13

# Social Support and Depression

## GEORGE W. BROWN and BERNICE ANDREWS

### Introduction

Social support may act to reduce the chances of a major stressor provoking clinical depression, or, for that matter, other forms of psychopathology or illness. Interest in this possibility increased in the 1970s with several influential reviews (Caplan, 1974; Cassel, 1974, 1976; Cobb, 1976). In discussing this protective or buffering role, we will take largely for granted that there is now good evidence that most instances of depression are provoked by a critical life event or difficulty. As a rough guide, our argument will turn on two specific themes and one general theme. First, if the link between such events and difficulties and depression is to be understood, the meaning of stressors will need to be dealt with. In our view, this is best done not by asking our subjects directly, but indirectly, using the investigator as a measuring instrument—and by considering an event or difficulty in the light of the context of a particular individual's life.

Second, consideration of meaning will not be enough. As noted by a 17th-century commentator, "If you estimate it correctly there is a shipwreck everywhere." Only a minority develop depression, even following the severest of life's crises. The sources of vulnerability to depression are

**GEORGE W. BROWN AND BERNICE ANDREWS** • Department of Social Policy and Social Science, Royal Holloway and Bedford New College, University of London, London, WC1BV 3RA, England. This chapter formed the basis of the first Gerald Caplan lecture given by George W. Brown at Harvard School of Public Health, Boston, Massachusetts on October 25, 1984. The research in Islington was supported by the Medical Research Council.

doubtless many. However, whatever its origin, depression will often involve either a lowered self-esteem, or a reduced ability to draw upon support from someone seen as close, or both together. In fact, one of our themes will be the *mutual interdependence* of the image of ourselves as worthy of support and the actual support offered by those around us.

Third, and most general, there has been too great an emphasis on personal responsibility, in the sense that the depressed have overreacted to circumstances that it would have been more natural to shrug off or play down. It will be argued that it is often more appropriate to see depression as a "natural" consequence of adversity.

## Stressors and Their Meaning

The meaning of an event or difficulty can never be entirely divorced from its context and from the individual to whom it occurs. However, this need not lead to despair about achieving the generalizability required by science. There is no unbridgeable gap between the intensive case–history method, rich in biographical detail, on the one hand, and the epidemiological approach, on the other. In attempting to bridge this gap, we have developed a system of "contextual" measures, based on precedents collected over the last 16 years. Such ratings reflect the spirit of the 19th-century German social science idea of *Verstehen*, or understanding, and enable the ideographic and nomothetic traditions of the social sciences— the interpretative and positivistic, the soft and the hard—to be brought together (Brown, 1983).

In using such contextual ratings, a person's biography and current circumstances are taken into account, in so far as they reflect likely plans and aspirations. In this sense, a birth is never merely a birth—to be given some kind of standard rating—but an event to be judged in context (e.g., Is the woman unmarried? Is her husband in prison? Was the pregnancy planned?) (Brown, 1981). Therefore, after taking into account that, say, a woman is unmarried, is a practicing Catholic, and is in the middle of studying for a medical degree in which she has done well, we ask ourselves, as investigators, the degree of threat most women would feel on discovering an unexpected pregnancy in such circumstances. Thousands of examples of prior ratings have been collected to help us in this task.

One strength of the approach is that any correlation between such ratings of threat and onset of depression must be minimal, so long as certain procedures for controlling possible bias are followed. The most important of these is to rely on a team of consensus raters who are blind to whether or not the subject is depressed. The basic assumption is that respondents will be able to supply us with sufficient material with which to make such a rating, but will not necessarily be able to tell us about the meaning of an event when asked directly; or, if they can, their accounts will be open to bias, since, when one is depressed, one may describe things in more negative terms than they were actually experienced. Therefore, our approach is deliberately investigator-based, giving the job of measurement to the interviewer and his or her team of colleagues and not to the subject (Brown, 1983). It is necessary, in this way, to take into account both life events occurring at a point in time, and ongoing difficulties (such as poor housing, or a husband who is a heavy drinker). Such ongoing difficulties are measured in terms of threat, in a similar way as events (Brown & Harris, 1978). Although they may not always give rise to life events in the period of time covered by a research inquiry, they may nevertheless raise the risk of depression (Pearlin, Lieberman, Menaghan, & Mullan, 1981).

There is now good evidence that certain stressors play a major etiological role in the broad range of depressive conditions. But it is only events with severe long-term threat (such as discovering that one's school-age daughter is pregnant), or difficulties that are distinctly unpleasant (such as a husband who has a markedly handicapping schizophrenic disorder), that are capable of this. The terms *severe event* and *major difficulty* refer to the stressors or provoking agents that the early research in Camberwell showed were capable of bringing about depression. It is now clear that such stressors work in terms of their *meaning* rather than through change as such (a notion which was central in the development of early life-event instruments). The words *loss, failure, abandonment, rejection* and *disappointment* probably sum up well the meaning that is critical for depression.

In dealing with the onset of affective disorders, we seem to be involved with meanings of such profound evolutionary significance that they have been reflected in psychobiological response patterns (Gilbert, 1984). This biological foundation probably helps to explain the surprising success of recent efforts to extend life–event research to a range of cultures. For example, the work on depression has been replicated with women attending psychiatric services in Nairobi (Vadher & Ndetei, 1981). It is clear, at the same time, however, that simple-minded attempts to link events and meaning are unlikely to be successful. The symbolic capacity of human beings is so great that it is essential to move beyond the simple checklists that have dominated life–event research. In the Nairobi ratings, for example, it was necessary to take into account the context of a man taking a second wife. Although polygamy is a traditional practice and still quite common, it appears today often to be entered into in a spirit akin to taking a mistress in Western society. In these circumstances, severe threat to the first wife was rated, and the event emerged as highly predictive of depression.

The experience of such women was judged as involving loss (often not so much loss of a person but loss of an idea or an aspiration). If the term loss is seen, in a broad sense, to include deprivation of a cherished idea about oneself or someone close, some 90% of all depressive conditions in the general population are brought about by something akin to a critical loss. The comparable proportion for psychiatric patients is less clear—although, if we leave aside the small group of bipolar depressive conditions, it is unlikely to be much less than two-thirds (Brown & Harris, 1978). The size of these effects may be a surprise, given how common it has been to quote a statistic that can be highly misleading, namely, that life events explain only some 10% of the variance of onset of depression (Andrews, 1978; Kessler, Price, & Wortman, 1985; Tennant, 1983). Although this is technically correct, the same use of statistics would have heavy smoking explain far less than one percent of lung cancer. This is a simple consequence of the fact that most heavy smokers do not develop lung cancer and a measure of association based on variance explained (i.e., $r^2$) takes this into account. It is more informative to formulate the matter in two stages—that is, depression rarely occurs *without* a major loss or disappointment; but, as with heavy smoking and cancer, losses of this order do not always lead to depression (Brown & Harris, 1986). It is these exceptions that point to the central question of vulnerability. Why do only some persons develop depression?

The most common explanation of the fact that apparently comparable stressors may lead to clinical depression in only a minority of instances has been to see the person who becomes depressed as in some way *distorting* experience by maladaptive thoughts; that is, by overreacting in terms of how most people would have responded. Beck has documented, in fascinating detail, some of the ways in which this may be done (Beck, 1967; Beck, Rush, Shaw, & Emery, 1979). An alternative perspective underlines the *naturalness* of depression, emphasizing that it is understandable, given an evolutionarily based propensity to react in a specific way to a particular type of experience, and given the degree of adversity inherent in the person's life. It is, in fact, usually fairly easy to present the same data in terms of either perspective: that is, as a cognitive distortion, or as a natural response. One woman's "clinging maladaptive personality" can be turned into an emphasis on the way women are encouraged to serve and live for others, and how, to a much greater degree than men, they are caught up in axiomatic relationships that cannot be broken, except at the greatest cost. Similarly, a so-called catastrophing response can be turned into a recognition of the real-life implications of the loss.

We do not suggest that it is a simple matter of choosing one perspective rather than the other. Both undoubtedly play an etiological role. In any case, there is bound to be a two-way influence between them. Nevertheless, we believe that not nearly enough weight has been given to a naturalistic interpretation.

## Vulnerability to Depression

In the research in Camberwell, in 1970, the quality of a woman's tie with her husband was emphasized as a vulnerability factor, and many studies have now suggested its key role (e.g., Brown & Prudo, 1981; Campbell, Cope, & Teasdale, 1983; Costello, 1982; Murphy, 1982; Paykel, Emms, Fletcher, & Rassaby, 1980; Parry & Shapiro, 1985). The definition we have used for such factors is that they relate to a higher risk of depression *only* in the presence of a stressor, but have little or no association otherwise.

In interpreting the link between a woman's lack of intimacy with, and confiding in, a husband and increased risk of depression, it was postulated that the role of such vulnerability factors was to increase the risk of generalization of hopelessness in response to a particular stressor. Following Samuel Johnson, "The natural flights of the human mind are not from pleasure to pleasure, but from hope to hope." (See also Breznitz, this volume.) Given the stressor, the average person would feel some hopelessness specific to it, but the more vulnerable would be more likely to generalize these feelings, applying them to life as a whole. Further, such generalization of hopelessness is more likely to occur in the presence of ongoing feelings of low self-esteem, where a person is less able to imagine emerging from the privation. It was finally postulated that other factors, such as lack of intimacy with one's husband, also play an etiological role, because they relate to ongoing feelings of low self-esteem, and this is what links vulnerability factors to depression. Of course, the naturalistic and cognitive distorting perspectives tend to converge if self-esteem is seen in these terms, namely, that low self-esteem leads *to* a kind of distorted view of the future. But here it is necessary to emphasize how natural it can be to have low self-esteem given the key role of the social milieu in determining it, and how it can be entirely realistic to feel hopeless in some circumstances.

However, some doubt has been thrown on such a view of depression. Lewinsohn, for instance, in an influential large-scale investigation using questionnaire measures in a prospective inquiry, failed to show that those who went on to become depressed had differed in self-esteem before onset (or, indeed, differed in any other of a number of negativistic cognitions), although once depressed they did show differences (Lewinsohn, Steinmetz, Larson, & Franklin, 1981). Other research has indicated that self-esteem may play a role (Hobfall & Walfisch, 1984; Pearlin *et al.*, 1981), but, in general, it has proved difficult to establish that the distortions posited by a cognitive perspective exist before the onset of depression. Since self-esteem is involved, this is equally threatening for our own (naturalistic) perspective.

At Bedford College in London, we carried out a prospective inquiry designed to look at the question of vulnerability: that is, why only 1 in 5 of the women who experience a major loss or disappointment go on to develop a depressive disorder. In planning this research, it was essential to recognize the danger that attempts to answer this question can become self-fulfilling, if the depression colors the subject's retrospective accounts of herself and her contacts (e.g., that she will, perhaps, look back and describe herself quite misleadingly as just as lonely and worthless before onset as she feels now she is ill). In order to avoid this possibility, information was collected about the womens' self-esteem and social support at a time prior to the onset of any depression.

Figure 1 gives an overall view of the study. An interview dealing with self-esteem, social support, and the like (SESS: Self-Evaluation and Social Support), and a semi-structured psychiatric interview (the PSE: Present State Examination), were carried out (Cooper, 1978; Brown,

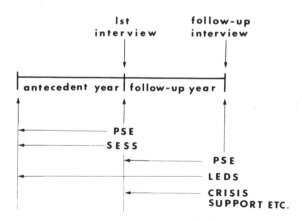

**Figure 1.** Basic design of the Islington Prospective Survey: PSE = present state examination; LEDS = life event and difficulty schedule; SESS = self-evaluation and social support schedule.

Craig, & Harris, 1985; Finlay-Jones, Brown, Duncan-Jones, Harris, Murphy, & Prudo, 1980; O'Connor & Brown, 1984; Wing, Nixon, Mann, & Leff, 1977). At a second contact a year later, the same psychiatric interview was repeated. The onsets occurring during the year between interviews were used to test hypotheses about support. At this second interview (the follow-up), the Life Event and Difficulty Schedule (LEDS), with its contextual ratings, was also given, in order to establish the presence or absence of stressors before any onset. In addition, women were questioned in detail about support received for any of these stressors (whether or not they were followed by depression). There are, therefore, two distinct sources of data about support. The main material, on which most weight will be placed, was collected *before* any onset of depression; the second, dealing with support with any stressor, had, of necessity, to be collected retrospectively—that is, *after* any onset had occurred. Fortunately, the two approaches agreed remarkably well, on the whole, and the possibility of serious bias seems low.

The site of the research, Islington, is an inner-city area in North London. A random sample of some 400, largely working-class, women with a child living at home was selected. A fifth of the sample turned out to be single parents, a proportion far in excess of the national average, and one indicator of the kind of adversity to be found in inner-city areas today. Indeed, 22% of the women experienced a psychiatric disorder at a case level in the period of a year; one half of these were "chronic" in the sense of lasting continuously for a year or more (Brown, Craig, & Harris, 1985).

Experience with the PSE over the last 15 years, by our own and other research teams, leaves little doubt that most of such cases are at the level of severity of conditions treated by psychiatrists in outpatient practice (Brown *et al.*, 1985; Dean, Surtees, & Sashidharan, 1983). The great majority were depressive (see Figure 2 for the criteria for *caseness* of depression). In addition to that of depressed mood, at least four *core* symptoms were required to be present (Finlay-Jones *et al.*, 1980). In all instances, many other symptoms were also rated. On average, those with depression had a total of 19.06 symptoms. A recent epidemiological inquiry in Edinburgh has indicated that, if anything, the criteria used for caseness of depression are more strict than both the Index of Definition system of other PSE users and the "major depressions" of the Research Diagnostic Criteria system used in the United States (Dean *et al.*, 1983).

As with the life–event schedule, all measures in the main social interview (SESS) are investigator-based. The tape-recorded, semi-structured interview allowed the women to talk freely, providing many spontaneous comments. Domains covered are shown in Table 1, and include

CASE DEPRESSION: A & B MUST BE PRESENT.

A. Depressed mood
B. Four or more of the following symptoms:

Hopelessness
Suicidal ideas or actions
Weight loss
Early waking
Delayed sleep
Impaired concentration
Neglect due to brooding
Loss of interest
Self-depreciation
Anergia

**Figure 2.** Finlay-Jones criteria for Bedford College caseness ratings of depression.

roles such as marriage and motherhood, and social support from partner and other very close ties. Also included were twelve aspects of self-evaluation; remarks from any part of the 3- to 4-hour interview could form the basis of these "self scales." It is important to note that negative and positive remarks were kept totally distinct. A woman could score highly both on scales dealing with positive *and* those dealing with negative statements about herself. Surprisingly, it was only those scales dealing with negative statements that predicted depression. Measures based on

**Table 1.** Main Domains Covered by Self-Evaluation and Social Support Schedule (SESS)

|                              | Scales     |
| ---------------------------- | ---------- |
| Self-evaluation              | 12         |
| Motherhood                   | 22         |
| Marriage                     | 27         |
| Housework                    | 16         |
| Employment                   | 23         |
| External interests           | 24         |
| "Very close relationships"   | 32 (each)  |
| Sexual relationship          | 14         |
|                              | 170        |

a woman's positive statements about herself, on the meaning she found in her life, and on her general satisfaction were unrelated.

For a factor to be judged in terms of a model of vulnerability, it is necessary for there to be a provoking stressor. This was the case in our Islington study, where 30 of the 32 women with an onset of depression in the follow-up year had a stressor—almost always a severe event involving loss, failure, or disappointment—usually occurring in the few weeks before onset.

Following the Camberwell model, we first considered vulnerability in terms of self-esteem, taking as an index *negative evaluation of self* (based just on negative comments the woman made about herself during the course of the first interview). Table 2 shows that this is a vulnerability factor—that is, there is an increase in risk of depression associated with it *only* in the presence of a stressor. This cumbersome label has been used, rather than low self-esteem, to emphasize that it is based only on negative comments. Depression was over twice as likely to occur following a stressor among those with such negative evaluation. (In all such tabulations, cases of depression at the time of first interview are excluded.)

One unexpected result, emerging from the twelve self-scales completed at first interview, concerned *role conflict*. This rating summarized a woman's expression of conflict in her roles and relationships, and took into account meaning, satisfaction, and sense of duty. The conflict was usually between two domains of her life, such as motherhood and work, but also included conflicting attitudes within relationships such as needs for security and adventure. Such conflict predicted depression, but, and this is the critical point, *only* when the severe event provoking the disorder *matched* the conflict (Brown & Bifulco, 1985). Conflict, occurring in conjunction with a nonmatching event, was *not* associated with increased risk. (The determination of "matching" was entirely straightforward—in most instances it followed directly from a simple comparison of a

**Table 2.** Negative Evaluation of Self at First Interview and Percentage with Onset of Caseness of Depression in Follow-up Period[a]

| Provoking agents | Negative evaluation of self (%) | | Total (%) |
| | No | Yes | |
|---|---|---|---|
| Yes | 13 (12/96) | 33 (18/54) | 20 (30/150) |
| No | 1 (1/126) | 4 (1/27) | 1 (2/153) |
| Total | 6 (13/222) | 23 (19/81) | 10 (32/303) |

[a] Cases of depression at first interview excluded. First row, $p < .01$; second row, not significant.

description of the event and the domain of a woman's life involved in the conflict).

An example may be helpful. It concerns a single parent with one child whose conflict was between work and motherhood. Mrs. Gray, at our first contact, described the long hours involved in her job and how it might be leading her to neglect her daughter. She also said that she did not want to give up the job because of its interest. When we saw her a year later, it emerged that she had developed depression when she found that her daughter had been stealing money from her purse. When seen originally she had no negative evaluation.

About the matching event itself occurring in the follow-up year, she said:

> "I was very disappointed in Sharon. I felt absolutely wretched because I felt helpless. I felt ashamed. It was all my . . . gosh what will people think. I had a daughter who was not a nice daughter any more. I felt a bit of a failure myself. . . . I had absolutely nothing to be proud of any more. It had all been shattered as it were."

Quite a number of the women with role conflict, who developed depression after a matching event, had originally expressed, like Mrs. Gray, little or no negative evaluation. Indeed, the conflict itself often related to an essentially positive set of circumstances. Risk of depression in Islington was not, therefore, only a matter of level of self-esteem—it would seem, in fact, that it was high self-esteem that gave some of the women confidence to get into the conflictful situation in the first place.

The specific area of conflict which is "matched" does not have to be part of the present. At an extreme, on occasions, such an event may reawaken dormant emotional schemata. Depression after death of a mother is rare in urban populations. But one woman in Islington became depressed after her mother died and after estrangement from her much older sister, just before her mother's death, over differences concerning the mother's care. The onset occurred despite a supportive husband and a lack of negative evaluation. Her depression made more sense when we discovered that, at the age of three, she had been looked after indifferently by this same sister while her mother was out of the country for 15 months. In other words, the current events echoed the past loss of her mother and the past rejection by her older sister. Such responses, on the basis of the Islington material, are rare but—given the possible tendency for phenomena to be overdetermined in this area—the significance of such latent emotional schemata may be wider than it appears to be at present. But, leaving the possibility of this kind of hidden mechanism to one side, the fact that women, such as Mrs. Gray, develop depression, despite lack of negative evaluation, demands some elaboration of our theory.

Table 3 summarizes the results of an analysis made with this in mind. The table gives priority to women with a stressor and negative evaluation. The proportion developing depression among them is shown in the top row (also shown in Table 2). By contrast, the next three rows deal with women *without* negative evaluation, and the second and third rows with the fact that certain kinds of severe event are still, under these circumstances, highly related to risk of depression. These are the *matching conflict events*, already discussed, and a handful of *husband events* (that is, severe events concerning the woman's partner, typically involving being let down in some crucial way). Such events usually arose from a situation of tension with the husband: one of the women, for example, was told by her husband that he loved someone else (this occurred in the setting of a long history of tension, but strong commitment on her part to the marriage).

The term "matching," itself, results from an effort to go somewhat beyond our contextual measures to try to link the event and the woman's biography in an even more sensitive way. So far, we have used only the present; but there is no reason why such ratings should not involve consideration of the past, and this would bring a new perspective to the

**Table 3.** Components of the Causal Model, Ordered Hierarchically, Showing Proportion of Women Developing Caseness of Depression[a]

| | | Married (%) | Single parent (%) | Total (%) | |
|---|---|---|---|---|---|
| | | With Provoking Agent | | | |
| | All with negative evaluation of self | 31 (11/36) | 39 (7/18) | 33 (18/54) | |
| No negative evaluation of self | "Husband" severe event | 29 (4/14) | — — | 29 (4/14) | 36 (27/76) |
| | Role conflict and "matching" severe event | 67 (2/3) | 60 (3/5) | 63 (5/8) | |
| | Remainder | 6 (3/48) | 0 (0/26) | 4 (3/74) | |
| | | Without provoking agent | | | |
| | | 1 (1/132) | 5 (1/21) | 1 (2/153) | |

[a] Cases of depression at first interview excluded.

naturalistic/cognitive distorting positions outlined earlier. A response may be understandable in a naturalistic sense, given a person's past. Mrs. Gray illustrates the potential usefulness of this kind of consideration. As it stands, it might be argued that she had "distorted" the significance of her daughter's theft. But it is probably relevant that, while she was pregnant, her fiancé was killed in an accident, and she had lived, since then, very much for her daughter and, in recent years, for her job. We would be surprised if she showed such a response to events in general. (Indeed, a year later, she separated from her boyfriend with very little upset.) Of course, the psychoanalysts' attention to hidden past experiences may extend this naturalistic perspective even further (as in the example of the woman's estrangement from her sister which apparently revived memories of a painful rejection). But social science is perhaps not quite in a position to pursue such insights at present.

However, systematic consideration of either kind of past is a task for the future. The ratings of *matching* deal only with the present, as yet. Returning to Table 3 and to the women with a stressor, it is notable how high the chance of depression was among those with either negative evaluation or a husband or matching event (36%, as shown in the final column), and how very low it was among the remaining women with a stressor and no negative evaluation (4%)—$p < .0001$. The latter hardly differs from those with no stressor at all.

## Social Support

It is now possible to consider how far social support can provide protection. There has been an increasing interest in this possibility, and a literature review is no longer to be undertaken lightly (e.g., Broadhead, Kaplan, James, Wagner, Schoenbach, Grimson, Heyden, Tibblin, & Gehlbach, 1983; Heller, 1979; Henderson, 1984; Price, 1983). The sophistication of theoretical discussion is impressive. But despite this, effects have been surprisingly slight and, on the whole, empirical findings demonstrate an unnerving gap between what seems likely and what has been demonstrated (Kessler & McLeod, 1983). Indeed, one recent important prospective study, carried out in Canberra, concludes that social support, as traditionally conceived (that is, external to the person), plays *no* part in protecting against a depressive disorder (Henderson, Byrne, & Duncan-Jones, 1981).

The weakness of the research can be summarized as failure to focus. Studies tend to utilize *prevalence* of disorder, rather than onset, at a particular point in time; a life–event *score* for a period, rather than the characteristics of particular events' occurring at discrete points in time;

support in terms of a *network* of ties, rather than from particular ties; and attempts to understand the etiology of psychiatric disorder, in general, rather than a particular condition. (Almost all research has been based on questionnaires, and these have almost certainly contributed to this concern about things, in general, rather than, in particular.)

Since we are conceiving of support in terms of vulnerability, we need to consider its role only for the 150 women in Islington who experienced a stressor. We will start with material collected at the first interview and, therefore, as earlier explained, methodologically sound.

For married women, measures dealing with the quality of the tie with the husband or to the cohabitant were, on the whole, quite highly correlated. However, a simple rating of *negative interaction* emerged as the best predictor of depression. This took account of reports about arguing, strain, violence, indifference, and coldness, and ignored anything positive. Indeed, a marriage could be satisfactory in a number of ways, but there still could be sufficient strain in the relationship for negative interaction to be rated.

A second measure of support concerned persons the woman named as very close (excluding a child at home, husband, or a boyfriend). All but one fifth of the women at the first interview named at least one person as very close, with an average of two. However, there was a considerable range in the quality of the relationships. We therefore characterized as "true" very close relationships only those in which there was both confiding about intimate matters and frequent regular contact (O'-Connor & Brown, 1984).

Table 4 shows two clear results. The left-hand column deals with single parents and the two right-hand columns with the married parents. As shown in many cross-sectional studies, quality of marriage acted as a

**Table 4.** Onset of Depression in Follow-up Period among Those with a Provoking Agent[a]

| Type of very close relationship | Single parent (%) | Married—negative interaction (%) | |
|---|---|---|---|
| | | Yes | No |
| None | 44 (4/9) | 22 (2/9) | 11 (1/9) |
| "Non-true" | 29 (5/17) | 36 (5/14) | 5 (1/20) |
| "True" | 4 (1/23) | 41 (7/17) | 13 (4/32) |
| Total | 20 (10/49) | 35 (14/40) | 10 (6/61) |

[a] By marital status, negative interaction in marriage, and type of very close relationship. (Cases of depression at first interview excluded.)

vulnerability factor, and was related to a threefold greater risk of depression. It is notable (and we will return to the point later) that this effect was, to a large extent, mediated by negative evaluation—that is, negative interaction in marriage and negative evaluation were highly associated; and both can be seen as vulnerability factors. It is impossible to say, with any confidence, which led to which, although evidence to be presented later strongly suggests that difficulty in the marriage often had a direct influence on negative evaluation. Negative interaction within marriage was also associated subsequently with severe events involving the husband. Such events, by their very nature, largely rule out the possibility of support from the person involved. When women with a husband event were excluded, there was an association between high security in marriage and low risk of subsequent depression. (Security was defined in terms of the dependability of the husband, predicted interaction with him, and the duration of the marriage). At this stage, it was not clear in what way high security reduced risk. Twelve percent of those with high security in their marriages subsequently became depressed (compared to 36% without such security).

It was disappointing to find that the presence of a very close tie was associated with a reduced risk *only* for single parents, and, here, those with a "true" very close tie exhibited a particularly low risk.

A wide range of other measures of the social network were made, to try to take account of every potentially supportive relationship, but none were found to be associated with risk of depression.

But these results need to be taken further, as they do not consider what happened during the follow-up year. Here we looked at support entirely in terms of what happened once a stressor had occurred (support was defined stringently, in terms of the presence of confiding, *and* in terms of emotional support from particular persons, as long as this was not accompanied at some point by a negative response. It was also necessary for support to come from a *core* contact—that is, someone named as very close at first interview *or* from a husband or boyfriend). Support, here, was called "crisis support," to distinguish it from the measures made at the time of first contact with the women. Fortunately, with one notable exception, the measures of support made at our first contact were highly correlated with what happened in the follow-up year, that is, to crisis support. This makes the analysis a good deal simpler than it might have been.

The right-hand column of Table 5 shows that crisis support relates to a much lowered risk for both the married and the single parents. Moreover, this held, whether or not there was a negative evaluation of self. Of particular interest is the suggestion that, among the married, crisis support from a tie other than a husband also can be protective.

**Table 5.** Onset of Depression among Those with a Provoking Agent[a]

| Core crisis support | Negative evaluation of self (%) | | Total (%) |
|---|---|---|---|
| | Yes | No | |
| | *Married* | | |
| No | <u>41</u> (7/17) | <u>38</u> (5/13) | <u>40</u> (12/30) |
| Yes: other core but not husband | <u>25</u> (3/12) | <u>11</u> (2/19) | <u>16</u> (5/31) |
| Yes: husband at least | <u>17</u> (1/16) | <u>7</u> (2/30) | <u>8</u> (3/36) |
| | n.s. | $p < .05$ | $p < .01$ |
| | *Single parents* | | |
| No | <u>58</u> (7/12) | <u>17</u> (2/12) | <u>38</u> (9/24) |
| Yes: Very close relationship or lover | <u>0</u> (0/6) | <u>5</u> (1/19) | <u>4</u> (1/25) |
| | $p < .05$ | n.s. | $p < .01$ |

*Note.* n.s. = not significant.
[a] By type of core crises support, negative evaluation of self, and marital status.

The first interview measures, it will be recalled, gave no hint of this wider source of protection. This appears to have been because, for married women, the quality of a relationship failed to predict whether or not support would be received in a crisis; and this was largely due, in one capacity or another, to the failure of a person named as very close to live up to the picture given at the first interview. This fragility did not apply to the ties among single parents, however, and practically all of their true very close relationships gave support. Almost all were of long standing and all had been tested under fire in the sense of providing support in previous crises. However, there was one parallel here with married women: for them high security within marriage predicted very well a husband's support in a crisis, and support in a crisis, as with single parents, related to both duration of the relationship and availability of support in the past. It is clear that support here needs to be considered in context. (High security and negative interaction within marriages made independent contributions to "outcome"—with high security being a much better predictor of crisis support than lack of negative interaction.)

At this point, it is possible to consider an objection to the picture that begins to emerge. This is that lack of support and stressor are confounded, in the sense that the latter often involves loss of a supportive tie (Mueller, 1980). Susan Gore has argued this point particularly well (Gore, 1981), and, as she would have predicted, severe events often involve a crisis in a core relationship (e.g., a child getting into trouble; the death of a close friend; a husband starting an affair).

However, it is still possible to conclude that stressor and support have not really been seriously confounded. For this to occur, it would be necessary for relationships to be involved where, to follow Gore, there is potential for support (i.e., where it would have been reasonable for the woman to have expected to receive it). But stressors only rarely involved such potentially supportive relationships. Most concerned a tie, which it was clear from the previous interview, was very unlikely to prove supportive (e.g., a husband who had been feckless and untrustworthy for several years announcing that he was going to leave home for good). Here, there is no *deprivation* of support (although the incident may brutally remind the woman that she had gone without support for some time).

Our model of depression, therefore, survives this particular objection. Nevertheless, the example does serve as a reminder that variables tend to be interrelated, and this needs to be taken into account. In fact, about half of the severe events arose (as in the case of the feckless husband) from difficulties that had lasted for some time. It is hardly surprising, therefore, to find that the presence of either a long-term difficulty or negative interaction in marriage was highly related to negative evaluation. In Islington, negative evaluation seems in large part to be a reaction to a climate of adversity, disappointment, and failure. Thus, in emphasizing the overwhelming importance of the present, we do not wish to argue that the past plays no part—either in negative evaluation or, for that matter, in support received. There certainly are long range influences at work.

Experience of marked rejection and indifference by key caretakers in childhood appears to be especially important in increasing the chance of premarital pregnancy, which, in turn, is highly related to adult depression. This lack of care in childhood is particularly common after the loss of a mother by death or separation of at least one year. A study, carried out in Walthamstow in North London by Harris and Bifulco, suggests that there are two types of long-range effects following an early loss of a mother (Brown, Harris, & Bifulco, 1985; Harris, Brown, & Bifulco, 1986a,b,c). The first is an easily documented pathway of adverse environmental experience, into which women tend to become increasingly locked. To take the example noted above, the experience of lack of care in childhood and adolescence (particularly common among those with loss of a mother in childhood) is related to a high rate of premarital pregnancy; which is further related to later working-class status and undependability of husband, both of which are highly related to depression. All this, of course, translates into a naturalistic model (shown as Strand 1 in Figure 3).

Strand 2 (in Figure 3) also stems from early childhood. It appears to work through styles of attachment (of the kind documented by Bowlby, 1980) and through cognitive sets that may act to produce distortions of the kind described by cognitive therapists. In the Walthamstow study, negative evaluation of self was not measured; instead, weight was placed on a measure of helplessness; it was felt that the two are linked, in the sense that belief that one can master situations and other people feeds into one's sense of being a person worthy of respect. A long-term disposition toward such cognitions seems to relate to the same crucial social experiences just outlined, in childhood and at the point where a teenager launches into adult roles. Their impact can be considerable. In Walthamstow, women with early loss of mother, who experienced either lack of care *or* premarital pregnancy, had five times more chance of being depressed (Table 6).

Lack of care in childhood was also relevant in the Islington survey.

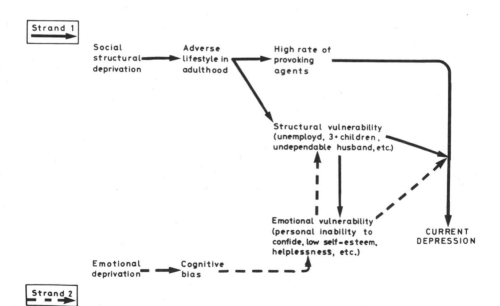

**Figure 3.** Speculative causal model, showing main lines of impact of loss of mother.

**Table 6.** Walthamstow Survey. Percentage of Women with Depression, by Lack of Care and Experience of Premarital Pregnancy

| Premarital pregnancy | Lack of care (%) | | Total (%) |
|---|---|---|---|
| | Yes | No | |
| Yes | <u>50</u> (12/24) | <u>22</u> (2/9) | <u>42</u> (14/33) |
| No | <u>28</u> (13/47) | <u>5</u> (3/59) | <u>15</u> (16/106) |
| Total | <u>35</u> (25/71) | <u>7</u> (5/68) | |

It occurred in 15% of the population, and premarital pregnancy *or* lack of care in nearly half. (The high rates are probably due to Islington's being an inner-city area.) Negative evaluation was twice as common among those with either lack of care or premarital pregnancy. However, and this is the critical point, the association between such past experience and self-evaluation held only for women rated as currently experiencing tension or difficulty in the home.

Figure 4 illustrates that, for those *without* current difficulties or tension, the proportion with negative evaluation is the same, regardless of whether or not there was lack of care or premarital pregnancy. (This is shown by the lines that meet in the extreme left of the diagram.) But *with* difficulties and tension, negative evaluation increases disproportionately among those with premarital pregnancy or lack of care. The important message would seem to be that the past *can* have an influence on negative evaluation, but *only* in so far as it is linked via troubles in the present.

Figure 5 suggests an etiological model and deals with the various interrelationships that have emerged. The middle and bottom sections, dealing with stressors and vulnerability, have already been dealt with. The middle (dashed lines) deals with *general* vulnerability, as this is expressed through negative evaluation. (We call it "general" because no specific link between the meaning of an event and the source of the negative evaluation is assumed.) Risk of depression is raised by negative evaluation (i.e., low self-esteem), regardless of source. (It might be likened to a last-straw-on-the-camel view of vulnerability. Any kind of extra load will break its back—the source being immaterial.) General vulnerability can be contrasted to *specific* vulnerability (shown in the bottom part of the diagram, in solid lines). To simplify matters, we have restricted this to women without negative evaluation. Here, we have in mind a key-in-lock notion of a particular fit between event and prior vulnerability. This is best seen in the notion of matching where a specific link between domains involved in the conflict and the severe event is necessary. With-

out this, conflict does not increase risk. Husband events also have something of this quality. They often arose from a situation of tension with
the husband, and often could be seen to confirm a woman's worst fears
and to echo some prior disappointment or strain.

However (as shown in Figure 5), the distinction between general
and specific vulnerability is intended to be only approximate. There is
no reason why negative evaluation (e.g., deriving from an ongoing marital difficulty) and an event (e.g., a husband's leaving home) should not
be linked in terms of meaning. (There is, to be sure, some ambiguity in
interpreting specificity when a woman also has negative evaluation of
self. If, for example, she has several difficulties, one or all of these may
influence her self-esteem. Whether negative self-evaluation precedes an
ongoing difficulty or arises from it, is also unclear.) Nevertheless, our
present judgment is that, when we have completed the analysis of the
Islington material in these terms, we will find that a considerable amount
of the vulnerability will be specific. For instance, there is evidence that
high commitment to a particular domain of one's life relates to higher

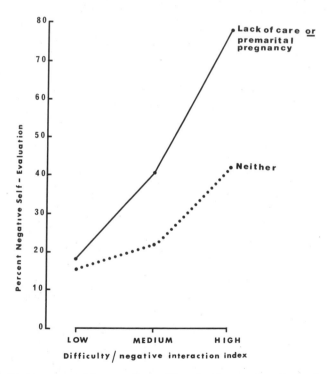

**Figure 4.** Percentage with negative self-evaluation at first interview, by diffi-
culty/negative interaction index and early adversity.

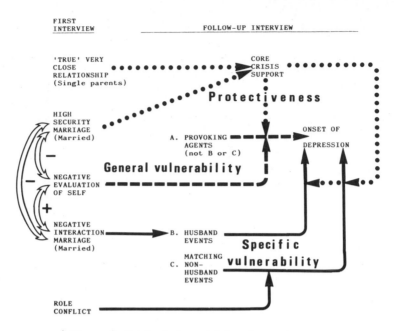

**Figure 5.** Etiological model for depression.

risk of depression when a "matching" severe event occurs. At present the distinction is intended to highlight a theoretical issue that needs considerably more explanation (see Brown, Bifulco, & Harris, 1986).

Figure 5 also shows the dual role of negative interaction in marriage—which relates to negative evaluation and to subsequent severe crises concerning the husband. The top section (dotted lines) deals with the role of support, and more needs to be said about this.

Marriages that have reasonably high security, not unsurprisingly, were associated with a lack of negative evaluation and with receiving crisis support from the husband. (The latter link—that is, between high security and crisis support is shown by the bottom of the two left-hand dotted arrows.) This prompts a critical question. There has been a tendency to see vulnerability as a mirror image of protection. However, it has been possible to demonstrate, with these Islington data, that this is not so—that the two can make independent contributions. The association, for example, between crisis support from husband and lowered risk of depression (i.e., protection) remains statistically significant (using logit analysis), once negative interaction in marriage and negative evaluation (i.e., vulnerability) have been taken into account. Even when a marriage has been relatively good and the stressor does not involve the husband, if he fails to provide support, the wife is more likely to succumb to depression. The converse of this is also true. The presence of crisis support can reduce the risk associated with either negative evaluation or matching events for both married women and single parents (see dotted arrows in Figure 5, starting from crisis support).

However, in spite of this, it is by no means clear what crisis support represents. The fact that there is such a large correlation between it and support at first interview (and, to a lesser extent, with negative evaluation), raises the possibility that support in a crisis is of little consequence by itself. It is rather the long history of support that is critical, acting, in part, through its favorable impact on self-esteem. Support in a crisis may well play a part *only* because it is the latest in a long series of illustrations of love and concern. It is difficult to assess this, however, because the measures of support are so highly correlated. Nevertheless, it has been seen that crisis support is helpful for those with negative evaluation, and the obvious should not be ruled out: that they particularly *need* it—and the reconfirmation of a "secure base," in a Bowlbyan sense, that it represents.

## Discussion

The experience of loss, failure, and disappointment appears to provoke most instances of clinical depression, and loss of hope may be the critical intervening experience. Self-esteem appears to play a central role, and much of what we have termed "negative evaluation" may be the consequence of failure and disappointment in core roles and activities. For a married woman, the dependability of her husband and the quality of her ties with him are of great significance here. This does not rule out influence from the past; but, for the most part, it appears necessary for this to be mediated by current difficulties and tensions. By the same token, good experiences in core relationships can serve to neutralize the past. This has been confirmed in an important recent study by Quinton and his colleagues (Quinton & Rutter, 1984; Quinton, Rutter, & Liddle, 1984). Girls who were first seen when in public institutions in London as a consequence of a complete breakdown of parental care were seen again 15 years later. At follow-up, affective disorder and failure to provide adequate parenting for their own children were found to be very common. However, outcome was far better among those with support from a husband. It was particularly notable that such support was uncorrelated with childhood disturbance.

In contrasting naturalistic and cognitive distorting perspectives, we have argued for a certain change in the center of gravity of our thought; not that either perspective should be preeminent. It seems clear that it will be necessary to struggle with processes reflecting the mutual influence of personality, stressors, position in the social structure, quality of interpersonal relationships, and experience of psychiatric disorder (and, indeed, probably with genetic vulnerability to such experiences once there are satisfactory biological markers). It is also clear that the picture is less complicated than it might at first appear.

On the whole, the past has to be translated into a fairly limited set of current adverse circumstances for depression to develop, and herein lies an element of optimism in the situation so far outlined. Vulnerability stemming from adverse early experience can be reduced by "good" experiences; moreover, though it is difficult to doubt that personality can influence the quality of such relationships, there appears to be nothing inevitable here. It is difficult, further, not to see a role for luck. In Walthamstow, there were many instances of women with early adverse experiences who, nevertheless, flourished once they had escaped from a poor marriage (although it is possible, and even likely, that a characteristic attachment style—say, one of ambivalent dependence and hostility—had played a part in the failure of the marriage). However, whatever handicaps they had experienced in forming a satisfactory marital relationship did not rule out the creation of a successful new one.

On the other hand, a number of women develop depression though they have no negative evaluation (as with the woman whose daughter stole from her). At times, hopelessness appears to be highly specific, and profound depression may develop in a woman who, otherwise, is coping well in most areas of her life. Here, research must move to consider, in finer detail, a person's biography and current commitments in relation to the kind of matching phenomena we have discussed.

As for support in the crisis itself, the mechanisms involved have still to be elucidated. It is possible that it is not much more than unconditional intimacy, love, and affection that is critical—making it possible not to despair completely of a better future.

The effects outlined are considerably greater than those revealed by studies using questionnaire-type instruments. An investigator-based approach is not difficult to apply. All that is necessary, if one has not one's own instrument, is to visit a research center to be trained—and this, as we understand it, is a common practice in laboratory-based sciences. The measures are exceptional only in the sense of the time needed for their development, relying as they do on the compiling of manuals of precedent.

If the current findings are confirmed, we will have reached a stage in the study of affective disorder in which theoretical ideas and findings are beginning to come together in ways that are quite complex; and etiological models and theory are bound to become still more complex. A naturalistic perspective is compatible with recognizing a role for personality (and a great deal remains to be done here) as well, of course, as testing the relevance of the model for other populations. The interweaving and overlap of factors from the past with those from the present mean that intervention studies will be needed to help sort out the interrelationships. However, we believe that it would be wasteful and foolhardy to invest in such demanding and costly work, without the kind of back-up provided by intensive epidemiological research, and the insights into fundamental etiological processes that it can produce.

ACKNOWLEDGMENTS

We are grateful and indebted to the women who took part in the interviewing and who spoke to us at such length and also to the many general practitioners in the area who collaborated with us. We are indebted to our colleagues Zsuzsanna Adler, Toni Bifulco, Julia Brannan, Linda Bridge, Titus Davis, Jessica Meyer, and Eileen Neilson, who participated in the interviewing, to Pat O'Connor, who did much to develop the SESS measures, to Tom Craig for his contribution to the clinical aspects of the research, and to Laurie Letchford for work with the computer.

# References

Andrews, G. (1978). Editorial: Life event, stress and psychiatric illness. *Psychological Medicine, 8,* 545–549.

Beck, A. T. (1967). *Depression: Clinical, experimental and theoretical aspects.* New York: Harper & Row.

Beck, A. T., Rush, A. J., Shaw, B. F., & Emery, G. (1979). *Cognitive therapy of depression.* New York: Wiley.

Bowlby, J. (1980). Loss: Sadness and depression. In: *Attachment and Loss, Vol. 3.* London: Hogarth Press.

Broadhead, W. E., Kaplan, B. H., James, S. A., Wagner, E. H., Schoenbach, V. J., Grimson, R., Heyden, S., Tibblin, G., & Gehlbach, S. H. (1983). The epidemiologic evidence for a relationship between social support and health. *American Journal of Epidemiology, 117,* 521–537.

Brown, G. W. (1981). Contextual measures of life events. In B. S. Dohrenwend & B. P. Dohrenwend (Eds.), *Stressful life events and their contexts* (pp. 187–201). New York: Neale Watson Academic Publications.

Brown, G. W. (1983). Accounts, meaning and causality. In G. N. Gilbert & P. Abell (Eds.), *Accounts and action* (pp. 35–68). London: Gower.

Brown, G. W., & Bifulco, A. (1985). Social support, life events and depression. In I. Sarason (Ed.), *Social support: Theory, research and applications* (pp. 349–370). Dordrecht: Martin Nijhof.

Brown, G. W., & Harris, T. O. (1978). *Social origins of depression: A study of psychiatric disorder in women.* London: Tavistock Publications; New York: Free Press.

Brown, G. W., & Harris, T. O. (1986). Establishing causal links: The Bedford College studies of depression. In H. Katschnig (Ed.), *Life events and psychiatric disorders* (pp. 107–187). Cambridge: Cambridge University Press.

Brown, G. W., & Prudo, R. (1981). Psychiatric disorder in a rural and an urban population: 1. Aetiology of depression. *Psychological Medicine, 11,* 581–599.

Brown, G. W., Craig, T. K. J., & Harris, T. O. (1986). *Depression: Distress or disease? Some epidemiological considerations. British Journal of Psychiatry, 147,* 612–622.

Brown, G. W., Harris, T. O., & Bifulco, A. (1985). Long-term effect of early loss of parent. In M. Rutter, C. Izard & P. Read (Eds.), *Depression in childhood: Developmental perspectives* (pp. 251–296). New York: Guilford Press.

Brown, C. W., Bifulco, A., & Harris, T. O. (1986). Life events, vulnerability and onset of depression: Some refinements. *British Journal of Psychiatry.*

Campbell, E. A., Cope, S. J., & Teasdale, J. D. (1983). Social factors and affective disorder: An investigation of Brown and Harris's model. *British Journal of Psychiatry, 143,* 548–553.

Caplan, G. (1974). *Support systems and community mental health.* New York: Behavioral Publications.

Cassel, J. (1974). Psychosocial processes and "stress": Theoretical formulations. *International Journal of Health Services, 4,* 471–482.

Cassel, J. (1976). The contribution of the social environment to host resistance. *American Journal of Epidemiology, 104,* 107–123.

Cobb, S. (1976). Social support as a moderator of life stress. *Psychosomatic Medicine, 38,* 300–314.

Cooper, B. (1978). Epidemiology. In J. K. Wing (Ed.), *Schizophrenia: Towards a new synthesis* (pp. 31–51). London: Academic Press.

Costello, C. G. (1982). Social factors associated with depression: A retrospective study. *Psychological Medicine, 12,* 329–339.

Dean, C., Surtees, P. G., & Sashidharan, S. P. (1983). Comparison of research diagnostic systems in an Edinburgh community sample. *British Journal of Psychiatry, 142,* 247–256.

Finlay-Jones, R., Brown, G. W., Duncan-Jones, P., Harris, T. O., Murphy, E. & Prudo, R. (1980). Depression and anxiety in the community. *Psychological Medicine, 10,* 445–454.

Gilbert, P. (1984). *Depression: From psychology to brain state.* London: Erlbaum.

Gore, S. (1981). Stress-buffering functions of social supports: An appraisal and clarification of research models. In B. S. Dohrenwend & B. P. Dohrenwend (Eds.). *Stressfull life events and their contexts* (pp. 202–222). New York: Neale Watson Academic Publications.

Harris, T. O., Brown, G. W., & Bifulco, A. (1986a). Loss of parent in childhood and adult psychiatric disorder: The Walthamstow study 1. The role of lack of adequate parental care. *Psychological Medicine*.

Harris, T. O., Brown, G. W., & Bifulco, A. (1986b). Loss of parent in childhood and adult psychiatric disorder: The Walthamstow study 2. The role of social class position and premarital pregnancy. *Psychological Medicine*.

Harris, T. O., Brown, G. W., & Bifulco, A. (1986c). Loss of parent in childhood and adult psychiatric disorder. The Walthamstow study 3. The role of situational helplessness. (Unpublished manuscript).

Heller, K. (1979). The effects of social support: Prevention and treatment implications. In A. P. Goldstein and F. H. Kanfer (Eds.), *Maximizing treatment gains: Transfer enhancement in psychotherapy* (pp. 353–382). New York: Academic Press.

Henderson, A. S. (1984). Interpreting the evidence on social support. *Social Psychiatry, 19*, 49–52.

Henderson, S., Byrne, D. G., & Duncan-Jones, P. (1981). *Neurosis and the social environment*. Australia: Academic Press.

Hobfall, S. E., & Walfisch, S. (1984). Coping with a threat to life: A longitudinal study of self concept, social support and psychological distress. *American Journal of Community Psychology, 12*, 1.

Kessler, R. C., & McLeod, J. (1983). Social support and mental health in community samples. In S. Cohen and S. L. Syme (Eds.). *Social support and health* (pp. 219–240). New York: Academic Press.

Kessler, R. C., Price, R. H., & Wortman, C. B. (1985). Psychopathology: Social approaches. *Annual Review of Psychology, 36*.

Lewinsohn, P. M., Steinmetz, J. L., Larson, D. W., & Franklin, J. (1981). Depression-related cognitions: Antecedent or consequence? *Journal of Abnormal Psychology, 9*, 213–219.

Mueller, D. P. (1980). Social networks: A promising direction for research on the relationship of the social environment to psychiatric disorder. *Social Science and Medicine 14A*, 147–161.

Murphy, E. (1982). Social origins of depression in old age. *British Journal of Psychiatry, 141*, 135–142.

O'Connor, P., & Brown, G. W. (1984). Supportive relationships: Fact or fancy? *Journal of Social and Personal Relationships, 1*, 159–175.

Parry, G., & Shapiro, D. A. (1986). Social support and life events in working-class women: Stress buffering or independent effects? *Archives of General Psychiatry, 43*, 315–323.

Paykel, E. S., Emms, E. M., Fletcher, J., & Rassaby, E. S. (1980). Life events and social support in puerperal depression. *British Journal of Psychiatry, 136*, 339–346.

Pearlin, L. I., Lieberman, M. A., Menaghan, E. G., & Mullan, J. T. (1981). The stress process. *Journal of Health and Social Behavior, 22*, 337–356.

Price, R. H. (1983). Does the social support hypothesis lack support? *Contemporary Psychology, 28*, 450–451.

Quinton, D., & Rutter, M. (1984). Parents with children in care—II. Intergenerational continuities. *Journal of Child Psychology and Psychiatry, 25,* 231–250.

Quinton, D., Rutter, M., & Liddle, C. (1984). Institutional rearing, parenting difficulties and marital support. *Psychological Medicine, 14,* 107–124.

Tennant, C. (1983). Editorial: Life events and psychological morbidity: The evidence from prospective studies. *Psychological Medicine, 13,* 483–486.

Vadher, A., & Ndetei, D. M. (1981). Life events and depression in a Kenyan setting. *British Journal of Psychiatry, 139,* 134–137.

Wing, J. K., Nixon, J., Mann, S. A., & Leff, J. P. (1977). Reliability of the PSE (ninth edition) used in a population study (1977). *Psychological Medicine, 7,* 505–516.

# CHAPTER 14

# Note on a Program of Research on Alternative Social Psychological Models of Relationships between Life Stress and Psychopathology

## BRUCE P. DOHRENWEND

### Introduction

Since the turn of the century and up to about 1980, there have been between 80 and 100 studies in which investigators, or teams of investigators, have attempted to count cases of mental disorders in communities all over the world, whether or not the cases located are people who have ever been in treatment with members of the mental health professions (B. P. Dohrenwend & B. S. Dohrenwend, 1982). These epidemiological investigations have been described as "true prevalence" studies, and the cases they have identified consist of disorders that were in evidence at the time of the study regardless of the time of onset. Very few of these studies have involved successive surveys over time. As a consequence, therefore, by and large, they do not provide data on incidence.

BRUCE P. DOHRENWEND ● New York State Psychiatric Institute, and Social Psychiatry Research Unit, College of Physicians and Surgeons, Columbia University, New York, NY 10032.    This program is supported by grants K05-MH14663, MH36208, and MH30710 from the National Institute of Mental Health and DE05989 from the National Institute of Dental Research.

About 16 of the studies were conducted prior to World War II. These "first generation" studies relied mainly on key informants and records to assess cases. The second generation studies, following the war, relied more on direct interviews with community residents of representative samples of them. Although there are serious methodological problems with these first and second generation studies, they are the basis for a third generation that is just beginning to make an appearance and that promises to be conducted by investigators who will use far more rigorous methodology.

## What We Would Like to Explain

The yield from the first and second generation studies provides the best source of cumulative information in existence, about the amounts and types of disorder in communities, and on the ways these disorders are distributed. From the more complete data of the second generation studies, for example, it has been possible to calculate median rates for several of the major types of psychopathology (B. P. Dohrenwend & B. S. Dohrenwend, 1969; B. P. Dohrenwend, B. S. Dohrenwend, Gould, Link, Neugebauer, & Wunsch-Hitzig, 1980). With a little additional arithmetic, Table 1 shows that it would not be unusual to find 15% or so of the adults in a sample of communities suffering from a diagnosable mental disorder with no known organic basis. On the average, we estimate that only about a quarter of these cases have ever been in treatment

**Table 1.** Functional Psychiatric Disorders Reported in Epidemiological Studies of "True" Prevalence in 1950 or Later

| Type of disorder | Median | Range | Number of studies |
|---|---|---|---|
| Schizophrenia | 0.76 | 0.0023–1.95 | 17 |
| Affective psychosis | 0.43 | 0.0000–1.59 | 12 |
| Neurosis | 5.95 | 0.305–75.0[a] | 25 |
| Personality disorders | 4.19 | 0.23–14.5[a] | 19 |
| Overall functional disorders | 14.05 | 1.25–63.5 | 27 |
| "Demoralization" | 27.5 | 3.4–69.0 | 17 |

*Note.* All percentages adjusted for sex differences except for rates of "Demoralization." Medians and ranges calculated from detailed tables and bibliography prepared to supplement B.P. Dohrenwend and B.S. Dohrenwend (1974; 1976).
[a] Includes Stirling County Study "symptom patterns" that are not necessarily considered "cases" in that study (D.C. Leighton, Harding, J.S., Macklin, D.B., Macmillan, A.M., and Leighton, A.H., 1963).

with members of the mental health professions (Link & Dohrenwend, 1980).

Note that Table 1 records 17 studies based on results secured with symptom scales of a type of nonspecific psychological distress that, we think, is best described by Frank's (1973) concept of "demoralization." In these studies, about a quarter of the adults showed distress as severe as that shown by psychiatric outpatients. We estimate that in about half of these, the distress coincides with diagnosable mental disorders of the kinds shown above in Table 1, but that the remainder, about 12% or 13%, show severe distress unaccompanied by a major, diagnosable mental disorder.

When these 12% or 13% distressed are added to the 15% or so with diagnosable disorders, we see that serious psychopathology is shown by between 25% and 30% of the adults, on the average. Note, however (in Table 1), that some of the important subtypes of psychopathology are extremely rare; the current prevalence of schizophrenia, for example, averages a bit less than 1%, as counted in these community studies.

My aim, together with that of my colleagues at Columbia University and the New York State Psychiatric Institute, is to evaluate the role of environmentally induced stress in the occurrence and distribution of the various types of symptomatology and disorder counted in these studies. As is evident from the results in Table 1, such psychopathology, in the aggregate, is not rare in the general population. In addition, there are major differences in how the various types are distributed according to gender, social class, and rural and urban location that raise questions and issues about why they occur (B. P. Dohrenwend & B. S. Dohrenwend, 1982). All these differences could involve environmentally induced stress, although there are other plausible explanations.

Against this background of what we would like to explain, let me turn to how we view life stress processes as they may be involved in the occurrence and distribution of these disorders in communities.

## Components of Life Stress Processes

We see life stress processes as consisting of three main components.

### Recent Events

By recent, I mean any relatively brief period in which you want to observe the events. If you want to observe the events with some hope of accuracy of recall, it had better not be more than a year, and preferably less; if it is too much less, you will not get an adequate sample. So, the term *recent* is any period from two or three months to about a year. The events that occur within this time interval can range from extreme situations, such as combat and natural disasters, to more usual life events that most of us experience at one time or another, such as birth of a child, marriage, death of a loved one, getting a new job, losing a job, and so forth. For some purposes, especially when it is possible to take multiple measurements at brief intervals over time, they can include smaller events, such as some of those that Lazarus and his colleagues describe as daily "hassles" (Kanner, Coyne, Schaefer, & Lazarus, 1981).

### Ongoing Social Situation

Here, the origins of the various elements of the situation antedate the observation period for recent events, but have an impact within that period—that is, a current impact. The kinds of things we look at under this heading include the presence or absence of what we call supportive social networks, a noxious or hazardous work environment, the presence of a chronically ill relative in the home, and so on. We include the kinds of things that Brown and Harris (1978) refer to as "ongoing difficulties" and that Pearlin and Lieberman (1979) refer to as role strains.

### Personal Dispositions

Under this third component we include genetic vulnerabilities, insofar as we can measure them (the only way I know is ambiguous and involves finding the rates of disorder in first-degree relatives), and the residues of remote events such as early childhood bereavement. With regard to the last of these, although we do not know what the current dispositional residue of such a remote event might be, we would measure whether there was bereavement, and we would assume that if it has a current impact it would have it via personal dispositions, because its effects would have been internalized long since. We also include personal assets in the form of physical stamina, health, intelligence, and personal liabilities, such as blindness, deafness, a game leg, and so on. And, of central importance, we consider a set of normal personality variables, which range from attitudes of mastery to helplessness, and include locus of control, masculinity–femininity (especially with regard to depression), sensation-seeking, and denial.

## Alternative Social Psychological Models of Life Stress Processes

Barbara Dohrenwend and I have extracted from the theoretical and empirical literature five alternative models of the possible nature of life stress processes as they may be related to adverse changes in health. We have called these *victimization, vulnerability, additive burden, chronic burden* and *event proneness* (see B. S. Dohrenwend & B. P. Dohrenwend, 1981a,b,c).

I will describe the models primarily in terms of my interest in various types of psychopathology. They could be referred to other adverse health changes thought to be related to stress as well. The five models are summarized in Figure 1.

The first model, which we call *victimization,* indicates that cumulations of stressful life events cause psychopathology. This model was developed empirically in studies of extreme situations, such as combat and concentration camps. I have generalized some of the ingredients of extreme situations to normal civilian life in terms of a pathogenic triad of

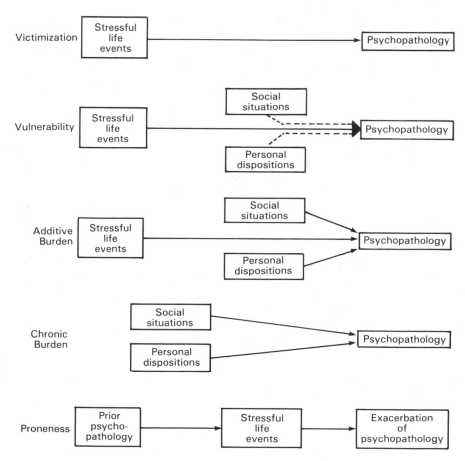

**Figure 1.** Five hypotheses about the life stress process (B. S. Dohrenwend & B. P. Dohrenwend, 1981b).

concommitant events and conditions involving physical exhaustion (resulting often from severe physical illness or injury); loss of social support (as a result, for example, of geographical relocation); and the fateful negative events other than physical illness or injury over whose occurrence the individual has no control (such as death of a loved one) (B. P. Dohrenwend, 1979).

The second model describes how preexisting personal dispositions and social conditions mediate the causal relation between stressful life events and psychopathology. This hypothesis underlies much of the literature on vulnerability and makes strong use of conceptions such as coping ability and social support. We call it the *vulnerability* model. The third model contrasts with the second in that, rather than mediating the impact of stressful life events, personal dispositions and social conditions are portrayed as making independent causal contributions to the occurrence of psychopathology. This we characterize as the *additive burden* model.

The fourth model is another and further modification of the second. It denies any role to recent life events, suggesting instead that stable personal dispositions and social conditions alone cause the adverse health changes. In contrast to the previous one, this is called the *chronic burden* model.

The final model enables us to confront directly the crucial issue of the direction of the causal relation between life events and psychopathology. It indicates that the presence of a disorder leads to stressful life events, which, in turn, exacerbate the disorder. We call this the *proneness* model in the sense that proneness to stressful events is the central mechanism posited.

These models are neither exhaustive nor mutually exclusive. They provide, nevertheless, a framework for designing research to advance our understanding of relations between life stress and psychopathology.

## An Underlying Social Psychological Issue

In investigating these models, there is an underlying theme or issue. This is the problem of determining the extent to which personal dispositions and social circumstances predict ways of coping with life events. In the context of our focus on social and psychological factors, the ways of coping to be predicted include perceptions of various dimensions of an event and the situation related to it (e.g., whether occurrence of the event is seen as within or outside the control of the individual). The key question we ask is whether these perceptions are determined by the objective characteristics of the event and the situation by contrast with personal dispositions (e.g., locus of control as a personality variable) or some complex interaction of the two. These distinctions require that we be able to designate and measure the important objective characteristics of the events and the social situations related to them; the individual's perceptions of these events and situations; and the relevant personality variables.

## Methodological Problems

As is so often the case in the behavioral sciences, research in this area is severely hampered by the lack of adequate solutions to key measurement problems. These problems have made many of the results from much previous research on stress and psychopathology difficult to interpret. The problems are especially severe when one deals with events that, unlike natural and manmade disasters, have occurrences that are not clearly outside the control of the individuals affected. It is all too easy to confound measures of events, personal dispositions, characteristics of the on-going social situation, and psychopathology with one another. For example, is the stressful life event of divorce independent of a vulnerable personal disposition to psychopathology? Does failure to obtain social support result from *a priori* defects in the external social situation, or is the failure a consequence of the individual's psychopathology? When it occurs, such confounding guarantees results that, at best, are uninterpretable and, at worst, can lead to erroneous conclusions.

Lazarus and Folkman (this volume) refer to a study that my colleagues and I have done to try to show how seriously contaminated some leading measures of stressful events and social supports are with other variables in the life stress process (B. S. Dohrenwend, B. P. Dohrenwend, Dodson, & Shrout, 1984). In this case, we took the extreme example of contamination with an adverse health change in the form of symptoms of psychological disorder. One of the measures that we tested was the *Hassles Scale,* developed by Lazarus and his colleagues and focussing on small, frequently occurring negative events (Kanner, Coyne, Schaefer, & Lazarus, 1981). As we showed, a large percentage of items in this scale were judged by a sample of clinical psychologists more likely than not to be symptoms of psychological disorder. I now think, upon further examination of the actual instructions to respondents contained in the *Hassles Questionnaire,* that even hassles judged unlikely to be symptoms by our clinicians on the basis of item content alone will tend to be symptoms, given the way that they are presented to the respondents (Kanner *et al.,* 1981, p. 25). Each respondent is told that there are "a number of ways in which a person can *feel hassled*" (emphasis added) and that these are listed in the questionnaire pages that follow. The respondent is asked to circle whether each "hassle" (not event) happened to him or her in the past month, and then go back and judge its "severity." Although, earlier, hassles are defined as "irritants that can range from minor annoyances to fairly major pressures, problems or difficulties," the only response categories provided for "severity" opposite the list of hassles are: (a) Somewhat severe; (2) Moderately severe; and (3) Extremely severe. There is no response category for anything that is less than "somewhat severe."

The implication of these instructions, and the response categories provided, must be that, if it is not at least somewhat severe, it is not a hassle. If so, positive responses on the items—whether scored as "occurrence" only, or by degree of severity—are limited to those subjects experiencing difficulty coping. There is no provision for our learning about respondents who experienced the events but did not consider them at least "somewhat severe." Positive responses are highly likely, therefore, to indicate the presence of maladapting behavior that overlaps extensively with symptoms of psychological distress and disorder. In addition to the symptom-like content of so many of the hassles items, these instructions and response alternatives seem to me to be a major way in which the items in the measure become confounded with psychological symptoms. It seems likely to me that this is why even the less "confounded" hassles items, according to our clinical psychologist judges, were found by Lazarus and Folkman to be so highly correlated with their measure of psychological distress.

Several approaches to these problems in measurement provide leads on how to resolve them: The work of Brown (1981) on the context in which life events occur, and some of our earlier work on *a priori* categorization of events in terms of the likelihood that they would prove to be independent, are examples (B. S. Dohrenwend, Krasnoff, Askenasy, & B. P. Dohrenwend, 1978). Our more recent research involves testing *a priori* categorization of lists of life events against data elicited by detailed probes about the nature of those events as actually experienced by a respondent (B. P. Dohrenwend, 1983).

With regard to social supports, we think that a promising way to approach the problem of confounded measurement lies in distinguishing between the individual's network of potential supporters and the conditions under which it is activated to help or hinder when specific events occur (B. P. Dohrenwend, 1983). Inferences are drawn about the presence of social support only in terms of how network members become, or fail to become, involved in events that occur to the individual. The determinants of this involvement or the lack of it can then be investigated with reference to the structure of the network, the nature of the events, and the personal dispositions of the individual.

## On-Going Studies

Our own approach focuses mainly although not exclusively (e.g., B. P. Dohrenwend & B. S. Dohrenwend, 1981; B. S. Dohrenwend & B. P. Dohrenwend, 1981c) on the alternative models shown in Figure 1. Investigation of these models is central to three on-going studies in which we are now engaged. It should not be surprising, since particular types of disorders tend to be rare in the general population, that we rely heavily on case–control designs.

The first study (and the one that is furthest along) is a retrospective case–control study of major depression, schizophrenia, and schizophrenia-like disorders in the section of New York City surrounding the Columbia-Presbyterian Medical Center. The second is a large-scale epidemiological study taking place in Israel; one of the main reasons for choosing Israel as the research setting is the existence of a Population Register that makes it possible to select samples from the general population on the basis of characteristics set down prior to the age of risk for developing such disorders as schizophrenia, major depression, and antisocial personality. Finally, we are conducting a prospective study of stress and myofascial pain in a sample of patients and controls; in this study, we are taking monthly measures of variables in the life stress process along with the monitoring of pain experience. This is the only prospective study in which we are engaged, and it gives us a chance to look at life stress processes in much higher magnification than in the other two studies, although it is not focused on one of the major mental disorders.

## Conclusion

In these studies, we look to major life events, small events, and aspects of the on-going social situations as sources of environmentally induced stress that may be causally related to adverse health outcomes, especially various types of psychopathology. Yet it is a fact that some life events, some small events, and some types of social support are themselves consequences of personal dispositions in general, and psychopathology, in particular, whereas others are independent of such characteristics. It seems to us that the development of measures of these life stress variables, in the context of theoretical formulations that explicitly take these facts into account, offers the best chance for incisive evaluation of the role of environmentally induced stress.

# References

Brown, G. W. (1981). Contextual measures of life events. In B. S. Dohrenwend & B. P. Dohrenwend (Eds.), *Stressful life events and their contexts* (pp. 187–201). New York: Neale Watson. New Brunswick, NJ: Rutgers University Press.

Brown, G. W., & Harris, T. (1978). *Social origins of depression: A study of psychiatric disorder in women*. New York: Free Press.

Dohrenwend, B. P. (1979). Stressful life events and psychopathology: Some issues of theory and method. In J. F. Barrett, R. M. Rose, & G. L. Klerman (Eds.), *Stress and mental disorder* (pp. 1–16). New York: Free Press.

Dohrenwend, B. P. (Chair). (1983, August). *Measurement innovations in the study of life stress processes*. Symposium conducted at the meeting of the American Psychological Association, Anaheim, CA.

Dohrenwend, B. P., & Dohrenwend, B. S. (1969). *Social status and psychological disorder: A causal inquiry*. New York: Wiley.

Dohrenwend, B. P., & Dohrenwend, B. S. (1974). Social and cultural influences on psychopathology. *Review of Psychology, 25*, 417–452.

Dohrenwend, B. P., & Dohrenwend, B. S. (1976). Sex differences and psychiatric disorders. *American Journal of Sociology, 81*, 1447–1454.

Dohrenwend, B. P., & Dohrenwend, B. S. (1981). Socioenvironmental factors, stress and psychopathology—Part 1: Quasi-experimental evidence on the social causation-social selection issue posed by class differences. *American Journal of Community Psychology, 9*(2), 129–146.

Dohrenwend, B. P., & Dohrenwend, B. S. (1982). Perspectives on the past and future of psychiatric epidemiology. *American Journal of Public Health, 71*, 1171–1179.

Dohrenwend, B. P., Dohrenwend, B. S., Gould, M. S., Link, B., Neugebauer, R., & Wunsch-Hitzig, R. (1980). *Mental illness in the United States: Epidemiologic estimates*. New York: Praeger.

Dohrenwend, B. S., & Dohrenwend, B. P. (1981a). Life stress and illness: Formulation of the issues. In B. S. Dohrenwend & B. P. Dohrenwend (Eds.), *Stressful life events and their contexts* (pp. 1–27). New York: Neale Watson. New Brunswick, NJ: Rutgers University Press (1983).

Dohrenwend, B. S., & Dohrenwend, B. P. (1981b). Life stress and psychopathology. In D. A. Regier and G. Allen (Eds.), *Risk factor research in the major mental disorders* (pp. 131–141). National Institute of Mental Health (DHHS Publication No. ADM 81–1068). Washington, DC: U.S. Government Printing Office.

Dohrenwend, B. S., & Dohrenwend, B. P. (1981c). Socioenvironmental factors, stress and psychopathology—Part 2: Hypotheses about stress processes linking social class to various types of psychopathology. *American Journal of Community Psychology, 9*(2), 146–155.

Dohrenwend, B. S., Dohrenwend, B. P., Dodson, M., & Shrout, P. E. (1984). Symptoms, hassles, social supports, and life events: Problem of confounded measures. *Journal of Abnormal Psychology, 93* (2), 222–230.

Dohrenwend, B. S., Krasnoff, L., Askenasy, A. R., & Dohrenwend, B. P. (1978). Exemplification of a method for scaling life events: The PERI life events scale. *Journal of Health and Social Behavior, 19,* 205–299.

Frank, J. D. (1973). *Persuasion and healing.* Baltimore: Johns Hopkins University Press.

Kanner, A. D., Coyne, J. C., Schaefer, C., & Lazarus, R. S. (1981). Comparison of two modes of stress measurement: Daily hassles and uplifts versus major life events. *Journal of Behavioral Medicine, 4,* 1–39.

Leighton, D. C., Harding, J. S., Macklin, D. B., Macmillan, A. M., & Leighton, A. H. (1963). *The character of danger: Psychiatric symptoms in selected communities* (The Stirling County Study of Psychiatric Disorder & Sociocultural Environment, Volume III). New York: Basic Books.

Link, B., & Dohrenwend, B. P. (1980). Formulation of hypotheses about the ratio of untreated to treated cases in the true prevalence studies of functional psychiatric disorders in adults in the United States. In B. P. Dohrenwend, B. S. Dohrenwend, M. S. Gould, B. Link, R. Neugebauer & R. Wunsch-Hitzig (Eds.), *Mental illness in the United States: Epidemiologic estimates* (pp. 133–149). New York: Praeger.

Pearlin, L. K., & Lieberman, M. A. (1979). Social sources of emotional distress. In R. G. Simmons (Ed.), *Research in community and mental health,* Volume I (pp. 217–247). Greenwich, CT: JAI Press.

CHAPTER 15

# The Effect of Hope on Coping with Stress

SHLOMO BREZNITZ

## Introduction

My studies on hope and its effects on coping are still in their initial stages, and, consequently, this presentation will be a highly speculative one. It consists of an attempt to delineate some common foci pertaining to hope that can be found in a variety of stressful situations. These foci are abstractions based on qualitative information obtained in interviews with people under a serious threat, such as awaiting the results of biopsy testing for breast cancer, waiting for surgery, anticipation of a major oral exam, and so forth. Because the purpose of these interviews was hypothesis-generating, rather than testing, some clear notions about the role of hope, the samples are by no means representative, nor were they meant to be.

Toward the end of this chapter, I shall describe the way we try to manipulate hope in field and laboratory studies. To some extent, the experimental paradigm that we use is related to my theoretical speculative discussion, which is the main thrust of this presentation.

Considering its role in the lives of many individuals, the psychology of hope is an almost totally neglected area of study. Searching the *Psychological Abstracts*, one finds references to Hopi Indians where hope should have been. Hope, as a separate concept, does not appear there at all. In view of scientific preference for new terms rather than ones

**SHLOMO BREZNITZ** ● Roy D. Wolf Center for Study of Psychological Stress, University of Haifa, Haifa, Israel.

taken from ordinary language, it was possible that scholarly analysis of hope appears under a different name. However, this does not prove to be the case. In spite of a few sporadic attempts to deal with hope (e.g., Mowrer, 1960; Stotland, 1969), its neglect as a valid research theme is a genuine one.

The strong bias toward predominantly negative psychological experience and negative emotions might be seen as a plausible explanation for the absence of interest in what is clearly a positive experience. While working on the concept of worry (Breznitz, 1971), I discovered that, in spite of its being an obviously negative phenomenon, worry, too, received hardly any attention at all in traditional psychological research. The main reason for the neglect of hope and worry probably lies in their subjective nature that poses major obstacles to systematic scrutiny. The highly intimate cognitions that take place when one worries or hopes discourage programmatic venture into what is rightly perceived as a high risk area of study.

> Hope is the thing with feathers
> that perches on the soul
> and sings a song without a tune
> and never stops at all.

This quotation, from one of Emily Dickinson's poems (Life, 32, from *Part I, Life* XXXII), adequately describes the subtle and sensitive elements involved in the attempt to describe this songless tune called "hope." This chapter does not deal with the content of hoping but with its format. I suggest that the structure, pattern, and rhythm of the cognitive processes that take place when we engage in hoping transcend specific thematic constraints and are, to a great extent, content free.

## The Work of Hoping

The distinction ought to be made between hope and the work of hoping. Whereas the first relates to a fleeting thought, or to a description of a cognitive state, the work of hoping implies an ongoing process. In order for hoping to have a serious impact on adjustment to stress and on the health status of the individual, it must consist of a process that is sufficiently intense and persistent to stimulate any of a serious of potential physiological changes that may account for its effects. Thus, for instance, a brief thought such as, "Everything is going to be all right," has less of a chance of inducing substantial hormonal changes than the more active and time-consuming investment in the cognitive work that takes place during what I suggest be labelled *the work of hoping*.

For the hoping process to cross the psychophysical barrier and initiate the physiological changes necessary for its impact, it must consist of a major investment of time and energy. Karl Menninger in *Love against Hate* writes, "There is no such thing as idle hope." Although he probably meant that hope is never idle in the sense that it always works, I submit that in order for it to work it must not be idle, but active.

My initial working thesis, to be challenged subsequently, is that the work of hoping has positive impact on the health and morale of people under stress. Anecdotal evidence to this effect abounds, primarily in the medical context. Particularly frequent is the classical story of the physician telling the patient, "We have done everything we could, now it all depends on you. If you have the will to live and fight this out, you might recover, If you give up, however, all is lost."

What is this vitality, this *élan-vital*, that is needed for a miraculous recovery to occur? Could it be that the work of hoping plays a significant role in these extreme situations?

Recently, there have been several studies that ventured beyond the anecdote, and in many ways point out the direction for more systematic efforts in this area. Thus, the work of Hackett, Cassem, and Wishnie (1968), as well as that of Gentry, Foster, and Haney (1972) on modes of coping of patients in the intensive care unit following a heart attack; studies by Schmale and Iker (1971) on hopelessness as a predictor of cervical cancer; and the by now classic report by Cousins (1976) are all precursors of a potential opening of this complex area of study to programmatic research.

## Metaphors of Hoping

The following five metaphors of the work of hoping are abstracted formats of cognitive imagery. They are all content free and can be found in a variety of different contexts. There is, of course, no claim that they are either exhaustive or, even, the most important ones. They can serve, however, as initial approximations of processes that provide a bounty of potentially researchable questions.

### Hope as a Protected Area

This metaphor indicates a situation in which everything is threatening, with the exception of a small area of experience that still maintains its positive features. Thus, for instance, one's health may be lost, all financial security gone, and everything falling apart, with the exception of one's family life. In this case the individual reports images of a small island of peace surrounded by storms and disasters. The work of hoping concentrates on efforts to protect the island from being overwhelmed by the surrounding calamities. The images often contain attempts to erect a protective fence around the remaining positive elements in order that they not succumb to the onslaught of misfortune.

The English expression of "clinging to hope" reflects this imagery in a beautiful manner. As in the case of a mountaineer surrounded by the danger of falling, who clings to the rock that embodies the single remaining source of safety, so do people in disaster cling to whatever is left of their world.

The metaphor of the protected area can be viewed as complementing the traditional view of repression. In the case of repression, there is an isolated idea that must be protected from reaching consciousness. This often leads to what has been termed the "spread of repression." Thus, if idea B is associated with the repressed idea A, it, too, must be repressed. Likewise, if idea C leads to B, its fate is similar. This can be seen as an attempt to protect one's relatively positive self-consciousness from the disturbing intrusion of negative thoughts, images, and memories. When overwhelmed by stress, the problem of defense is almost an opposite one, namely to protect the remaining positive foci from the predominantly threatening thoughts, images, and feelings. This is cognitively expressed in the metaphor of hoping as a protected area.

The wisdom of language, as a symbolic product of lengthy cumulative experience, is often quite striking. The Oxford English Dictionary lists many variations of the word "hope" as it refers to the anticipation of a positive future. To my surprise, the very same word, that is HOPE, is listed as having the following meanings:

1. A piece of enclosed land, e.g., in the midst of marshes or wasteland.
2. A small enclosed valley.
3. An inlet, small bay, haven.

It is quite impressive to observe that all three of these definitions actually describe the metaphor of hoping as a protected area, and I find it hard to believe that this is purely a coincidence. Furthermore, English is apparently not the only language in which this happens. In Hebrew, too, the words for hope and for a small enclosure also derive from the same root.

Within the highly speculative mode of this analysis, I venture to suggest the hypothesis that the protective embrace of a parent, when the child is distressed, may well serve as the prototype for this metaphor. The child experiences, in concrete terms, that even though everything "out there" is frightening or dangerous, all is still fine within the protective embrace of the parent.

## Hoping as a Bridge

When in darkness, one searches for light. When faced with a major misfortune, one seeks ways out. However, the bridge from darkness to light is not easy to find, and the work of hoping is sometimes perceived as that bridge. In using this metaphor, people often report that they find it easier to solve the problem of the bridge backward. Although, in the midst of darkness, one does not know in which way to search for the light, rather than finding the route to the light, one attempts to bring the light to the present situation. This is not very different from the often-documented finding that mazes are solved easier backward, taking advantage of the proximity of the reward. The need to weave a complex cognitive scenario for the transition from a stressful situation to a more pleasant one is essentially a problem-solving task, made particularly difficult because of the detrimental impact of powerful negative emotions, such as fear, anger, or anxiety.

When the bridging route is particularly long and difficult, subjects report taking advantage of more or less permanent transition points, which may subsequently provide the opportunity for cognitive short-cuts.

The metaphor of the bridge lends itself to experimental simulations, which we use as another method of investigating the complex patterns of directed cognition. The following illustrates one promising variant of the class of simulated tasks. The subject is presented with two words, a START word, and a GOAL word, taken from two unrelated contexts. One of the words has a clearly positive connotation, and the other a clearly negative one. The task of the subject is to start from the START word and, by a process of associating, reach the GOAL word in a minimum number of steps. For every task that starts from a specific positive word to a specific negative goal word there is a symmetrical opposite task presented to a paired subject. Initial results indicate that adult subjects are more efficient in the process of worrying, that is, transiting from positive to negative, than in the process of hoping, which requires the transition from negative to positive. The finding that it takes significantly more associative steps to cover the distance from negative to positive than the other way around suggests, I believe, that many individuals have little experience with the work of hoping. More about this later.

The above task allows us also to study the degree to which the problem of the bridge is solved backward as well as forward. When starting from a positive word, the initial associations are all positive until, at some point, there appears a word with a clearly negative connotation, which continues as such until the goal is reached. By evaluating the connotation of each single association, independent judges help us find the emotional transition point in the sequence of the subjects' association.

I have dwelt on the above simulation to indicate that, in spite of the highly speculative nature of the metaphors, they can be translated into explicit experimental paradigms.

## Hoping as Intention

As aptly pointed out by Spinoza, "Fear cannot be without hope, nor hope without fear" (*Ethica,* Definition XIII). One of the reasons why the two are so intertwined is that both worry and hope use basically the same tools. The ability to project into the future, to plan, to use imagery, to elaborate scenarios, and to use verbal capacity for internal storytelling serve the process of worrying and the work of hoping. Thus, when one embarks on internal cognitive preoccupation with one's problems, there is no guarantee which way the process will develop. Our control over the stream of consciousness is, to say the least, very limited. Thus, the cognitive preoccupation itself is an obviously high-risk "package deal," with the chances of a particular outcome being, at best, ambiguous.

*In order to increase the changes that hoping, rather than worrying, will take place, there is need to bias the information processing itself in favor of positive thoughts and images.* This can be achieved if the search process is under the control of an overriding intention. The intention, in this case, consists of preferences for alternatives that promise to lead to positive rather than negative thoughts and images. The metaphor of hoping as intention indicates that, at least to some extent, people are aware of the biasing factor itself.

## Hoping as Performance

Intention, although perhaps a necessary condition for some complex cognitive process to take place, is clearly not a sufficient one. The discrepancy between intention and performance is a major source of individual differences in areas where ability and experience both play central roles.

Considering our specific interest in the work of hoping, language behavior can illustrate the issues at stake. Thus, for instance, in trying to communicate an idea to a listener, we do not typically use ready-made sentences that were learned by rote memorization, but, rather, construct the sentences during the speech itself. This poses a major problem: how to ensure that the intended idea will be effectively communicated without being sidetracked in the process. In view of the multitude of associations that can tempt the speaker to follow this or another direction, this is by no means an easy task to accomplish. Thus, the ability to inhibit most of the associations and carry on the original intention to its meaningful end plays a central role in effective communication. Lack of experience, or certain pathological sources of interference—as in the case of the schizophrenic "word salad"—may disrupt the expression of the intended idea.

In the same vein, hoping may fail because of one's inexperience or because of direct interference in the carrying out of its intention.

### Hoping as an End in Itself

The fifth, and last, metaphor is almost self-evident, but its potential clinical importance requires its mention. If, as we assume, the work of hoping reduces fears and worries, this reduction in the intensity of negative emotion should act as a reinforcement. Thus, *hoping is rewarded and its intensity and probability increase with successful usage*. At this point, hoping stops being a means for coping with the ongoing stress and becomes an end in itself. As such, it may acquire some addictive features, not unlike daydreaming, in general.

## Hope as an Illusion

A sobering antithesis to the initial assumption—that hope always has positive outcomes—suggests that, in the absence of objective environmental changes for the better, hope is, by necessity, unwarranted. This is adequately formulated by Nietzsche who wrote that "hope is the worst of all evil for it prolongs the torment of man" (Nietzsche, 1974). The argument about the need to come to terms with negative reality carries, of course, great weight within the context of dynamic psychology.

In Greek mythology, the story of Pandora's box gives expression to the above concern: When Pandora, in spite of all warnings to the contrary, opened the box, and all the evils escaped free to visit humankind, she managed to shut the box at last, but, by then, it was too late. All the evils were set free, with the exception of Hope. The key question is, of course, what was Hope doing in that box in the first place. Ancient Greeks viewed human life as entirely at the mercy of haphazard fate; thus, hope was indeed an illusion.

We are now faced with an obvious dilemma: There is, on the one hand, the central thesis of this chapter, suggesting that hoping has beneficial impact on health and morale. On the other hand, there is the antithesis concerning the illusory basis of human hope. Is there a way to reconcile the two? Is there a synthesis?

## Hope versus Denial

In difficult situations, there are basically two ways of defending or promoting one's morale. On the one hand, one can deny the negative aspects of the situation by not hearing, not seeing, and not thinking about it. On the other hand, it is possible to concentrate selectively on the few remaining positive elements and to amplify them and their potential impact. The first mode of coping is denying, and the second is hoping (Breznitz, 1983). The two are not necessarily mutually exclusive, and all combinations of the two are feasible. Table 1 presents the extreme response types based on the above dimensions.

The basic distinction, which I believe makes clear the synthesis between the opposing views on the benefit of hoping, is the one between Type A and Type C responses. In the case of Type A, hoping goes hand in hand with denying. It is precisely for that reason that there is a temptation, perhaps a necessity, to base the comforts of hope on the denial of the negative elements in one's situation. Such a basis, although providing fruitful ground for unrestricted hope, is continuously challenged by new information to the contrary. Hoping, which is based on denial of reality, must be delusional in its main components, and thus unrealistic and short lived.

Type C, on the other hand, implies hoping in the absence of denying. The person is aware of the negative situation and yet tries to invest cognitive effort in the few remaining positive elements. This kind of hoping will typically be more restricted in its scope than the Type A kind, but, for the same reason, is based on a more realistic appraisal of the situation. *I submit that the Type C response pattern represents hoping at its best.* This kind of "mature hoping" produces the positive outcomes described earlier in this chapter.

**Table 1.** Denial versus Hope

| Denial | Hope | |
| --- | --- | --- |
| | Yes | No |
| Yes | A | B |
| No | C | D |

Consider, for a moment, the case of a person who was told that he has terminal cancer. Type A coping may maintain for some time the notion that eventually everything will be fine and that he will get well. As new information from a variety of sources challenges this notion, it may eventually collapse, with far-reaching consequences to the person's adjustment. The same verdict will express itself in an entirely different way when dealing with a Type C reaction. The person may select a positive event sometime in the not-too-distant future, such as the birth of a grandchild, a major anniversary, and so forth, and concentrate all his cognitive efforts to prepare for that event and try to turn it into a particularly beautiful occasion. Thus, although not denying the threat of the proximity of personal death, he may, at the same time, attend more to the positive and thus deny to the negative images a monopoly over his consciousness.

Type B implies denial in its most extreme forms, sometimes called "blanket denial." One may postulate that, in this case, hoping is absent because one is not allowed even to think about the impending threats. Since hoping requires cognitive preoccupation, this is not possible when denial is complete. Perhaps it is not too far-reaching to suggest that one of the main costs of denial is its exclusion of hope.

From the clinical point of view, the Type D response pattern is probably by far the worst. The absence of both denial and hope suggests that the individual is not engaged in attempts to boost his morale or defend against the stress. Such "giving up" bodes ill for the future and is clinically associated with depression and death. Thus, a closer analysis of the data reported by Hackett *et al.* (1968) indicates that all of their subjects who died in the intensive care unit belonged to this category.

Hoping and denying are psychological "vital signs," indicating that the individual is fighting against the sometimes overwhelming implications of stress. In this perspective, even an ineffective coping mode is better than none at all. Thus, the opposite of hope is not despair, but the absence of hope. Whereas, in despair there is nothing to lose; in the absence of hope, there is nothing to gain. Despair may yet act as a motivating force for acts of despair, whereas, in the absence of hope, there is no energy left. In his *Paradise Lost*, Milton (1957) wrote: "What reinforcement we may gain from hope, if not, what resolution from despair."

## Hopelessness versus Helplessness

The theory that helplessness and, particularly, learned helplessness may play a major role in the etiology of depression has received serious impetus recently (Seligman, 1974; 1975). These formulations are natural extensions of longstanding efforts to explicate the correlates of "locus of control" as a central personality variable (e.g., Rotter, 1966; 1975). These research paradigms are well grounded in what I view as a predominantly North American bias toward control and attempts at active mastery as the most adequate, and perhaps the only adequate, mode of coping with stress.

Our research suggests that hoping can thrive even in situations of total helplessness. Furthermore, its importance as a potential factor in adaptation grows in direct proportion to objective helplessness. One can be in a stressful situation in which there is nothing that can be done to reduce the impending threat, and yet hope that, somehow, things are going to turn out all right after all. Surely, not everyone can remain hopeful in helpless situations, particularly if one's mode of coping is monopolized by the overriding need for control. This is particularly problematic when faced with a major life crisis that does not lend itself to manipulation, and requires the capacity for accommodation and acceptance.

In my view, the importance of the distinction between helplessness and hopelessness cannot be overestimated. The following description, from one of our studies with children, illustrates this point.

After establishing good rapport with the subject (ages 7 to 9), the experimenter, who is an experienced clinical psychologist working with children, presents the subject with a hypothetical threatening situation. Thus, for example, the child is told to imagine that he or she is alone and lost in a forest. The subjects are then encouraged to tell the experimenter what they are thinking and what they will do. At first, the subject may suggest some simple coping behavior, such as, "I will shout." To this the experimenter replies, "You have already tried to shout many times, but nobody heard you." Next, the subject may come up with the idea of climbing a tree and looking for a way out of the forest. The answer to this is once again, "You have climbed a tree and saw nothing but the forest all around." In this way, all of the subject's efforts to deal with the situation by active coping are systematically frustrated, until the point is reached when the subject realizes that he or she is entirely helpless, and there is nothing more that he or she can think of doing. From the viewpoint of research on helplessness, this is the end of the story; from our point of view, concentrating on hoping, the experiment proper is just about to start. Thus, when the point of helplessness is reached, some children quickly and confidently resort to hoping, "I shall wait here until my dad comes to pick me up," although others may start to panic. The individual differences are quite remarkable and I only wish we could better understand their correlates and antecedents.

## Manipulation of Hope: A Research Paradigm

Some psychological phenomena are easier to manipulate than to measure, and hoping appears to be one of them. Our attempts to develop valid and sensitive measures of individual differences in the tendency and capability for hoping are still in a very preliminary stage, but the obstacles we are facing are already quite obvious. At the same time, however, we discovered one particular paradigm that suggests a relatively simple way to investigate the impact of different objective features of stress of high relevance to the issue of hoping. Although several studies using this paradigm are already in progress, they are clearly beyond the scope and the focus of the present chapter. At the same time, however, I wish to describe the paradigm itself, since it directly relates to our previous analysis.

In an important chapter in *The American Soldier,* Janis (1949) describes the intense stress that crews of American bombers were exposed to during their nightly missions over Germany in World War II. Many planes and crews were lost each night, and had to be replaced by new ones. At some point, many members of these crews developed major symptoms of stress and often could not continue to fly.

The psychological analysis of these soldiers indicated that they felt caught in a "no hope" situation. Each night brought new casualties, and, from their point of view, *it was only a matter of time until their turn would come.*

The U.S. Air Corps dealt with this situation in a very elegant and effective way, psychologically. The crews were informed that their tour of duty consisted of forty missions, after that they would be relocated to a safer theater of operation. Although forty missions were not fewer than they were flying before, and although planes were still being downed by enemy action just as before, psychologically the situation altered dramatically, with excellent results in terms of symptom reduction and prevention. Instead of counting forward (e.g., "Today it was this friend, tomorrow it can be me"), the airmen started to count backward (e.g., "Thirty nine to go, thirty eight to go," etc.). Thus, with each new mission, their subjective probability of coming out of the experience alive was augmented. *Stated differently, by telling the airmen when the danger would be over, hope was introduced into the situation.*

In spite of the success of the "tour-of-duty" intervention, and in spite of its subsequent usage as standard policy in many areas of conflict, the underlying psychological mechanisms were never systematically studied. In view of their direct relevance to hoping and its role in alleviating the impact of stress, our first attempts to manipulate hoping are focusing precisely on this paradigm. Therefore, we are investigating the role of information about the duration of stress on individuals' ability to mobilize cognitions of hoping to help them persevere.

It is of some interest to note that the work of hoping can often be affected by such simple and often inexpensive means as an item of information. Our initial results, in both field and laboratory experiments, are highly promising in helping us to better understand this "undiscovered country" of human existence.

# References

Breznitz, S., (1971). A study of worrying. *British Journal of Social and Clinical Psychology, 10,* 271–279.

Breznitz, S., (1983). *Denial of stress.* New York: International Universities Press.

Cousins, N. (1976). Anatomy of an illness (as perceived by the patient). *New England Journal of Medicine, 295,* 1458–1463.

Dickinson, E., (1937). *The Poems of Emily Dickinson.* Boston: Little Brown and Company.

Gentry, W. D., Foster, S., & Haney, T. (1972). Denial as a determinant of anxiety and perceived health status in the coronary care unit. *Psychosomatic Medicine, 34,* 39–44.

Hackett, T. P., Cassem, H. H., & Wishnie, H. A. (1968). The coronary care unit. *New England Journal of Medicine, 279,* 1365–1570.

Janis, I. L. (1949). In S. A. Stouffer *et. al. The American soldier: Combat and its aftermath.* (Vol. 2, pp. 362–410). Manhattan, KS: MA/AH Publishing.

Menninger, K. A. (1959). *Love against hate.* New York: Harcourt & Brace.

Milton, J. (1957). *Complete poems and major prose by J. Milton.* M.Y. Hughes (Ed.). Indianapolis, In: Bobbs-Merrill.

Mowrer, O. H. (1960). *Learning theory and behavior.* New York: Wiley.

Nietzsche, F. (1974). *Human all too human.* New York: Gordon Press.

Rotter, J. B. (1966). Generalized expectancies for internal versus external control of reinforcement. *Psychological Monographs: General and Applied, 80,* (Whole No. 609).

Rotter, J. B. (1975). Some problems and misconceptions related to the construct of internal versus external control of reinforcement. *Journal of Consulting and Clinical Psychology, 43,* 56–67.

Schmale, A. H., & Iker, H. (1971). Hopelessness as a predictor of cervical cancer. *Social Science and Medicine, 5,* 95–100.

Seligman, M. E. P. (1974). Depression and learned helplessness. In R.J. Friedman & M. M. Katz (Eds.)., *The psychology of depression: Contemporary theory and research.* Washington: Winston-Wiley.

Seligman, M. E. P. (1975). *Helplessness.* San Francisco: W.H. Freeman.

Spinoza, B. (1927). *The philosophy of Spinoza, selected from his chief works.* New York: The Modern Library.

Stotland, E. (1969). *The psychology of hope.* San Francisco: Jossey-Bass.

PART VI

# Overview

*In the chapter that follows, an attempt is made to identify, in the contributions to this volume, those elements that contribute to a generalized view of the dynamics of the stress process. The chapters in which such elements are discussed are indicated by use of the chapter numbers in brackets, wherever appropriate. For quick reference, chapter numbers, authors, and beginning page numbers are reiterated here.*

| Chapter | Author | Beginning Page Number |
|---|---|---|
| 1 | Appley & Trumbull | 3 |
| 2 | Trumbull & Appley | 21 |
| 3 | Singer & Davidson | 47 |
| 4 | Lazarus & Folkman | 63 |
| 5 | Schönpflug | 81 |
| 6 | Frankenhaeuser | 101 |
| 7 | Scheuch | 117 |
| 8 | Guttmann | 141 |
| 9 | Scherer | 157 |
| 10 | Frese | 183 |
| 11 | Krohne | 207 |
| 12 | Laux | 233 |
| 13 | Brown & Andrews | 257 |
| 14 | Dohrenwend | 283 |
| 15 | Breznitz | 295 |

*What is presented in Chapter 16 is by no means intended to be a summary of the rich and varied contributions to this volume, but is rather a sampling of common elements and concepts, which, despite differing perspectives and terminology, it seems to us, are shared by a surprisingly large number of the authors.*

# Dynamics of Stress and Its Control

MORTIMER H. APPLEY and RICHARD TRUMBULL

## Introduction

The chapters presented in this volume have offered some fifteen current perspectives on the nature of stress. They give evidence of the significant maturing that has occurred in stress study—and particularly stress theory—since the mid-1960s, when we reviewed the field in a somewhat similar manner (Appley & Trumbull, 1967). Despite some remaining points of contention, we believe that an increasing consensus has been developing among investigators about the factors that contribute to the dynamics of the stress process.

There is general agreement, for example, that the early focus on pathology—and on the systemic level—was too limiting, and, as a consequence, misleading. The history of research on stress shows shifting emphasis on various systems and types of stressors. The early work on physical stimuli and physiological detriment was followed by psychological conflicts and, finally, social patterns or life events. The growing awareness that other response systems were involved—as the role of perception became known and the importance of the social history and present milieu came into play—has brought us to the recognition of a three-system function [Chapters 1, 2, 3, 4, 6, and 7]. True, unique physical assaults on the physiological system might represent simple stimu-

MORTIMER H. APPLEY ● Department of Psychology, Harvard University, Cambridge, MA 02138, and Clark University, Worcester, MA 01610. **RICHARD TRUMBULL** ● Former Research Director, Office of Naval Research, Washington DC, and 4708 N. Chelsea Lane, Bethesda, MD 20814.

lus–response (S-R) relationships, but the majority of stressors to which persons must adjust inevitably involve some combination of the three systems in immediate or delayed responses.

Stress is clearly a broader concept than at first considered. Although it *may* lead to pathology, it is recognized that such outcome is by no means a certainty. Thus, the early interest in the *diseases* of adaptation has expanded gradually to interest in the *processes* of adaptation—in all their complexity—at biological, psychological, and social levels, and the interactions among them.

Selye (1973), among others, has acknowledged that stress is not, in itself, a negative state, to be avoided, as he earlier seemed to hold, but a necessary condition for the functioning of the living organism. "Complete freedom from stress is death" he wrote (p. 693). And Lewis Thomas (1980), in an amusing though serious comment in his "Late night thoughts on listening to Mahler's Ninth Symphony," expressed a similar view, concluding that "what people mean by stress is simply the condition of being human" (p. 77).

Additionally, stress is now recognized as involving the *totality* of an individual's transactions with his or her environment; and, importantly, such *transactions* must be understood both in their *context* and *over time*. In short, the dynamics of stress, as now beginning to be comprehended, have become virtually as encompassing as the dynamics of life!

As the chapters in this volume illustrate, stress studies use a variety of methods and address questions covering a range of levels and phenomena. The diversity of approaches, initially seeming to confuse the issue of the nature of stress, have now begun to fill in the mosaic, and to yield a more comprehensive view of the processes involved. More importantly, these diverse approaches, and the findings that they are generating, have begun to provide clues to the ways in which stress processes may be interconnected.

Although not agreeing in detail, virtually all stress investigators now seem to accept a *relational, interactional,* or *transactional* view of stress, to describe stress as *process* rather than state or outcome, to acknowledge its *multilevel, multitemporal* nature, and to recognize the need for *multidisciplinary* and *interdisciplinary* approaches to its study.

In the sections that follow, we shall examine what we believe are the major elements of the stress process, the role or roles they play in stress dynamics, and the ways they may be seen to contribute to stress control.

## Predisposition

Twenty years ago, we wrote "A man is not a man is not a man" to emphasize the role of individual differences in stress vulnerability (Appley & Trumbull, 1967). Today, of course, we would say "A person is not a person is not a person." In either case, it is evident that any analysis of a stress situation must begin with what the individual *brings to* the situation and not with the demand characteristics of the situation alone.

Our own predilection has been to use the concept of *carrying capacity* to describe the biological, psychological, and social variables operating in the individual at the time of stressor onset or exposure [Chapter 2]. Perhaps a more generic term would be *predisposition,* defined as the state or degree of susceptibility (to a potential stressor) that exists in the individual at any given time as a function of prior determinants. It is a complex matrix of factors that interact with each other, as well as with environmental events, to determine individual reactions to (and in) sequential stress situations.

Although certain relatively short-term factors (e.g., diurnal sensitivities) can influence predisposition, we ordinarily distinguish predispositional from precipitating (or triggering) factors, the former generally being longer term (i.e., more permanent), and contained within the individual rather than the situation.

At the physiological level, predispositions affecting carrying capacity derive from genetic, prenatal, developmental, and nutritional histories of the individual, the history of illness, short- and long-term cyclicities, inherent strengths and predetermined weaknesses, and so forth, though modifiable by such factors as fatigue, drugs, training, or habituation [Chapters 2, 3, 6, 7, and 8]. Good health is a continuing influence on the carrying capacity of the physiological system, most evident when illness, fatigue, or other stressor imposes demands. The presence of this "on call" capacity determinant may go unrecognized and its value unappreciated—until or unless it is needed and is not available.

Psychological predispositions affecting carrying capacity would be found in motivational propensities (e.g., achievement or power needs), personality patterns (e.g., level of self-esteem), response styles, intelligence, timeliness of capability development within the life cycle, feeling of success or failure arising from previous exposure, and so forth [Chapters 2, 3, 5, 7, 8, and 11]. Hope, like health, may be a latent factor in sustaining carrying capacity, either in specific situations or, more broadly, as in generalized hopefulness or even cheerfulness despite severity of event or seeming disparity between demand and carrying capacity [Chapters 2, 13, 14, and 15]. Sociocultural factors influencing predispositions would include the nature and strength of social support systems, cultural (including religious) values and norms, social class, and so forth [Chapters 3, 12, 13, 14, and 15]. The perception of social support predisposes to successful coping in situations that might otherwise result in depression [Chapters 13 and 14].

Predispositions, as we have noted, are what individuals bring to a (potential) stress situation, as opposed to what they find there. It is the interaction of predisposition and situational or demand characteristics that determines the patterns of responses and thus the degree of stressfulness of any particular situation [Chapter 1, 2, 3, 4, 5, 6, and 7].

We have tried to characterize predisposition as acting on (as well as forming) a continually changing load or carrying capacity [Chapter 2]. Chronic fatigue, low self-esteem, or poor social support would serve to lower carrying capacity—or resistance—at the physiological, psychological, or social level, respectively (though each can contribute to lowered capacity in an adjacent level, as well). "Good" experiences (e.g., in early life) can help establish "higher," more resistant carrying capacities, as can good health, a supportive family, and so forth [Chapters 2, 13, and 14].

Predisposing factors continue to be present over time, though their influence may not come into play unless the discrepancy between a new demand and capacity exceeds a limit, or unless there is a "match" between a precipitating or provoking agent and the source of a predisposed (stress-related) response, thus triggering such a response [Chapters 2, 5, 6, 9, and 13].

It would be impossible, except perhaps in extreme situations, to determine the "stress potential" [Chapters 1, 3, and 4] of a situation or the "stress vulnerability" [Chapters 1, 3, 4, 7, 8, 11, 13, and 14] of an individual in a stress setting without assessing predisposition. Susceptibility or vulnerability to stressful (life) events may be mediated by the interaction of preexisting personal dispositions and social conditions [Chapters 2, 4, and 14], affected when "the satisfaction of needs is endangered . . . and it is necessary, and difficult, for the individual to act" [Chapters 1 and 7], influenced by feedback from one's own responses [Chapters 1, 8, 9, 11 and 12], caused by "overload" of system capacity, either at a particular time or cumulatively [Chapters 2, 3, 5, 6, 7, 9, and 14], or determined by other factors contributing to ongoing carrying capacity.

Although we know that general states of hopefulness or depression [Chapters 13, 14, and 15], good or ill health, high or low self-esteem [Chapters 2, 12, 13, and 14], task- or ego-orientation [Chapters 1, 3, 4, and 12], and "felt" social support [Chapters 13 and 14], among other factors, affect the level of carrying capacity, we do not know how such levels are sustained over time [Chapters 2 and 3]; nor are we able, as yet, fully to relate such general levels of resistance to those instances of particular event proneness [Chapters 13 and 14], clearly also determined by predisposition, perhaps in combination with emotional memory of some sort [Chapters 1 and 9].

Thus, although it is indisputable that the state of the individual—

biologically, psychologically, and socioculturally—at the time of "stressor onset," is the key determinant of stressfulness, we have much to learn about the mechanisms of system interaction [Chapters 2, 3, 4, 6, 7, and 9], of "counting" or cumulation (across stresses and/or time) [Chapters 2, 3, 6, 7, 13, and 14], of "matching" and release [Chapters 2, 3, 4, 6, 7, 8, 9, and 13], and so forth.

We describe *psychosomatic processes* as resulting from physiological-psychological system interactions, but are as yet unclear as to the ways subsystems influence each other. Of the various physiological systems, it now appears that glandular and immunological systems are two of the triggers that produce measurable heart rate and other changes. However, these well may be second- or third-order derivatives, with biochemical and neurological intermediaries. The same is true of the psychological systems involved in psychosomatic processes. Which traits, characteristics, and/or other predispositions have the physiological triggers at their disposal, through either "original design" or conditioning? And, further, what are their relative conditioning potentials as we seek means to reduce or modify stress reactions? Control of one's cortical activation level [Chapter 8] may be but one of the rewards that awaits us as a clearer picture of the dynamics of psychosomatics emerges from further study of the interrelations of physiological and psychological systems.

It is to a careful examination of how these psychoimmunological processes operate that we believe the energy of stress investigators should next be concentrated. Not only first order effects, such as those produced by moods in the psychological system, but second- and third-order effects, arising from their interaction with physiological and social systems, remain to be illuminated.

## Context and Meaning

An event occurs in a situational *context*, defined only in part by real time and geographic space. Although such coordinates help determine the characteristics of a particular event or process, its *meaning* derives largely from more subtle aspects of the setting in which the event takes place. The individual experiencing an event is, of course, part of the setting. Thus, individual predispositions, already present at the time an event begins, for example, form part of the context of that event and give it meaning [Chapters 1, 2, 3, 4, 13, 14, and 15]. Some predispositions, as previously noted, have origins in the early development of the individual's biosocial systems, whereas others are more recent. In any case, where an event is located in the personal life history of individuals—in historic (sociocultural as well as developmental) time, in the life cycle, life space, symbolic setting, social situation, and so forth—serves to define context, allowing a determination of the *relevance* and *significance* of the events' being experienced [Chapters 1, 4, 8, 13, 14], and the responses to them.

The load characteristics of a situation change with context [Chapters 2, 8, and 9], as do interpretations of degree and nature of potential threat, danger, or benefit [Chapters 1, 2, 4, 8, 9, 14, and 15], and determinants of controllability [Chapters 3, 5, 6, 7, and 11], choice of strategy [Chapters 1, 4, 10, 12, and 15], and even phase of the event that one is in [Chapters 1, 11, and 15]. One's own actions, and/or feedback from them, also form part of context [Chapters 1, 2, 4, 5, 8, 9, 12, and 15].

The significance of context, as should be clear, inheres not in the situation, as such, nor in the individual, but in the *interaction* (or *transaction*) between person and event.

Of importance to our understanding of stress dynamics is the recognition that measurement contexts, to the extent that they differ from performance contexts, may reflect entirely different relationships among variables. The "training champion" concept and comparing performance under "load" and "no load" conditions [Chapter 8] addresses this, as do attempts to develop systems of "contextual measures" [Chapter 13] to identify situationally specific coping strategies [Chapters 10 and 11], and to use "individuals themselves as measuring rods" [Chapter 6], among other examples.

The controversy over the use of subjective responses—and especially retrospective questionnaires [Chapters 4, 6, 13, 14]—raises several critical issues that will have to be resolved. Do after-the-fact questionnaires invite the invention of rational answers to explain, in the measurement situation, what might have been emotional (nonreflective) responses given in an earlier stress context? Even questionnaires sampling present and "what if" future conjectures cannot posit context—either demand or dispositional factors, let alone their interaction—in an intensity or extensity approximating reality. It is argued that this is true for "daily hassles" as well as more critical stress situations [Chapters 4 and 14].

# Feedback

Feedback is a necessary element in the maintenance and activation of all three systems: physiological, psychological, and social. There still is much to be learned about the relative and differential sensitivity to, desire for, need for, and response to feedback, as it represents inter- and intrasystem functioning.

The physiological-psychological loop in proprioception has been recognized in human factors study for a long time. That arising between the psychological and social in establishing a sense of familiarity, if not security, was noted by Notterman and Trumbull (1959), in positing a "radar Robert" type of personality, characterized by an active seeking of feedback from a social environment. The requirement of "perceived social support" [Chapter 13] is similar. It is at this interface that one also finds the need for approval, in which approval for a deed or action may be translated into approval of self, a support for self-esteem [Chapters 12, 13, and 14]. The converse is equally likely, in which disapproval of action is interpreted as disapproval of self. The genesis of such tendencies, which may reduce or produce stress, is part of the developmental picture that still awaits clarification (see pp. 325–327).

Unfortunately, feedback has not been as active a research interest as one might have thought. It has suffered the fate of many concepts, in which the mere naming of it is taken as if it provided a sense of understanding. Its recurrence in this book, in many different contexts, is most encouraging. Even as the original concept of stress emphasized physiological processes, so, too, has that of feedback. Thus, for example, there is frequent discussion, in the human factors research literature, of displays and controls designed to accommodate biofeedback. Investigators in the present volume continue this trend, in seeking "suitable biofeedback training" [Chapter 8], calling for programmatic stimulus evaluation checks [Chapter 9], and arguing that "organisms constantly scan their environment and evaluate events, including internal stimulation" [Chapter 9].

An important role for feedback is implied when appraisal and coping processes are described as continuously changing, and "recursive, in that outcomes can influence antecedent variables" [Chapter 4]. Feedback is further implied in describing coping as involving "a complex amalgam of continuously changing intrapsychic and behavioral acts that demand a process-oriented assessment procedure" [Chapter 7], and in suggesting the need for an "iterative computer program" for future stress research [Chapter 3].

Psychological and social interactive feedback can be seen when low self-esteem, in a circular manner, results in loss of social support [Chapter 13], and reflected in a Proneness scale, with disorder leading to stressful life event, exacerbating disorder, and so forth [Chapter 14]. Here we see larger and perhaps more complex loops than in biofeedback, in which the concept began.

The presence of feedback as a continuing element in all three systems, and in the interactions among them, suggests that such processes may impact on one another (within or across systems), leading to conflict or mutual reinforcement, to exacerbation or reduction of stress. Virtually all of the chapters in this book describe feedback processes operating at one or more levels: from physical performance [Chapters 2, 5, 7, 8, 9, 10, and 11], self-presentation [Chapter 12], social performance [Chapters 12, 13, 14, and 15], or combinations of same [Chapters 2, 3, 4, 6, and 7], and invoke some form of feedback training as a means of control. This may be biofeedback in the world of physical performance [Chapters 8 and 9], or the use of simulators, orientation training, and other devices or procedures [Chapter 12] for familiarizing an individual with feelings and experiences that will be encountered in some real world situation yet to come. The more familiarity one has with one's feelings and perceptions—inside and out—the easier it will be to recognize the sequence of events that have been set in motion, accept them because they never have led to disaster, or something with which one could not cope, and continue the task at hand.

Radar Roberts would actively look for the first cue to get the uncertainty over with and know that the event sequence has been entered. Delay in the arrival of that first cue could be upsetting for someone if that person's radar is set for what is wrong rather than how far are we on schedule. Such orientation differences, and the effects of feedback on them, have been variously described [Chapters 2, 3, 4, 6, 7, 8, 9, 12, 13, 14, and 15]. The different attributes or sets, established by past experience, self-confidence, feeling of control, and a host of other factors about which we speak rather glibly, are part of what one takes into a situation, and form the base against which feedback from situational factors can be "matched" and evaluated. Such evaluations, it is increasingly clear, involve physiological as well as psychological (and social, operating through psychological) levels of comparison and corrective/adaptive response.

## Time and Timing

Although we describe stress as a process, it should not be surprising that time and timing would play multifarious roles in its development, maintenance, and amelioration. We note, first, that effects of successive stress sequences *cumulate* over time. This is true for chronic stress, though in the case of cyclical or episodic stress, such effects may dissipate if sufficient interexposure *recovery time* is available [Chapters 2 and 3]. Similar notions of recovery, latency, and refractory times or periods are used by a number of investigators [Chapters 2, 3, 6, 7, 8, and 9] to describe the cyclic aspects of processes at both biological and psychological levels and as affecting cross-level influence, as well.

Although physiological and psychological processes are relatively independent and have different time courses [Chapters 3, 7, and 9], as have the numerous sub-processes within each [Chapters 2 and 6], more attention could well be paid to the time characteristics of cyclic functions in relation to each other and to the timing of onset of precipitating stressors in relation to particular stages of predisposition, anticipation, refractory state, and so forth. Would degree of *synchrony* across processes be likely to increase or decrease stress vulnerability?

One answer to this question might be sought in the study of *time lag* between systems. The search for simultaneous physiological correlates coincident with stressor onset and psychological response overlooks the normal time or phase delay in marshalling of forces in the physiological system. Such delay might also be reflecting asynchrony in system functioning [Chapter 2].

*Duration* of stress is identified as important [Chapter 7], as are passage of time [Chapter 2], and balancing, involvement, and vulnerability over time [Chapters 8, 10, and 13], in determining the level of stressfulness of a given situation.

Timing of coping is also important [Chapters 1, 10, 11, and 12], as is the phase of the stress sequence in which coping is undertaken [Chapter 11]. It is further suggested that intervening emotion might lengthen the time between evaluation and response, giving more time for choice of coping response [Chapter 9]. On the other hand, the time allowed, whether imposed or inferred, may become part of the stress situation [Chapters 5 and 8]. Many life events have built-in temporal constraints, established by social custom or by biological and/or psychological limitations [Chapters 2, 3, 5, 13, and 14].

Finally, time must be recognized in yet another way, namely, in the reaffirmation of the fact that early childhood patterns establish vulnerabilities that may not become activated until late in life [Chapter 2, 10, 13, 14, and 15]. The need for new lengths of time sampling in stress studies thus becomes evident.

## Appraisal

The key issue in the transactional model of stress has to do with the nature of the appraisal process. That evaluation or appraisal of some form occurs in potentially stressful situations is not in question. What is unresolved is the extent to which appraisal is necessarily and exclusively cognitive and/or necessarily conscious. Although most theorists accept a predominantly cognitive approach [Chapters 1, 3, 4, 5, 6, and 13], some suggest that not all evaluation need consist of cognitive appraisal exclusively. So, for example, the role of perception is acknowledged as important but not necessary [Chapter 2], evaluations of capacity to do harm, of degree of novelty, certainty, and predictability, can be made like iterative computer programs [Chapter 3]. Stress can arise, in the absence of conscious evaluation, when biological needs (e.g., for activity, optimal stimulus level, and biological recovery) cannot be satisfied [Chapter 7]; when actual as well as interpreted level of activation determine stressfulness [Chapter 8]; when phylogenetically evolved physiological and behavioral adaptive mechanisms augment cognitively mediated responses [Chapter 9]; and when (such) emotion-based response systems relate to predispositional factors affecting arousal reduction and not problem-solving [Chapters 2, 5, 10, 11, and 12].

Further, it is suggested that cognitive stress theories require (force?) mental representation of problem states, ignoring the fact that it is the *process* rather than the product (or content) of appraisal that constitutes the psychic load [Chapters 1, 2, and 5], and that stress is measureable in terms of the *discrepancy* between stressor (demand, load) and carrying capacity (both real and/or perceived) [Chapters 2 and 7].

There is general agreement that stress is a *dynamic* process, in that appraisal and coping influence each other (directly and through feedback) and continually change [Chapters 1, 2, 3, and 4].

# Coping

Appraisal and coping are closely related parts of a complex process. When a situation is appraised as potentially harmful—that is, where the discrepancy between load and carrying capacity exceeds acceptable levels—coping strategies are developed and pursued to reduce that discrepancy [Chapters 1, 2, 3, 4, 5, 6, 10, 11, and 12]. Feedback from the coping process becomes part of a successive appraisal or reappraisal [Chapters 1, 3, and 4], leading to modified coping, further reappraisal, and so forth, until equilibrium is restored, a new equilibrium is reached, or the individual is removed from the situation physically or psychologically [Chapters 1, 12, and 13]. The process of coping can very quickly "involve a complex amalgam of continuously changing intrapsychic and behavioral acts" [Chapter 12]. Its effectiveness will depend on the interaction among specific situational characteristics, predispositional variables, and the content of the coping strategy [Chapters 1, 11, and 14].

The results of coping need not necessarily be favorable. Coping may have the effect of decreasing as well as increasing carrying capacity (e.g., via fatigue), increasing as well as decreasing demand (e.g., via using up limited resources), or both [Chapters 1, 2, 5, 10, and 11], thus increasing the stressfulness of the precipitating situation.

Coping may be situation-specific or general (i.e., dispositional) [Chapters 10 and 11], and it may be task- or problem-focussed or defensive (i.e., emotion-focussed) [Chapters 1, 4, 9, 10, and 11]. Analyses of successful versus unsuccessful copers suggest that these may be distinct coping goals, along with information control [Chapter 11]. Further distinction is made between emotional coping as part of the evaluation process (e.g., perceptual defense strategies) versus when it is directed to an emotional reaction *after* appraisal has taken place [Chapter 9]. Finally, it is noted that emotion-focussed coping is less situation-bound, and can thus be more stylistic and cross-situationally consistent than problem-focussed coping [Chapter 10].

## Disparity Control

We have maintained that stress can result from either excessive load (or demand) in the face of normal carrying capacity, or a lowered carrying capacity in the face of normal demand. In any case, or in combinations like these, stress results when the *disparity* between load and capacity exceeds tolerable limits [Chapter 2].

Although the paradigm is clear—and, in our view, eminently sensible—it is equally clear that we are far from being able to "scale"—across systems, let alone time—the values that make up either load or resistance, to know when they are in dynamic equilibrium [Chapters 1, 2, and 3]. (How many units of social pressure are equivalent to $x$ units of physical health or $y$ units of self-esteem?) Equally intriguing issues arise when we ask by what mechanism or mechanisms the organism is able to keep track of the cumulation of stress over time, in long-term or chronic situations, so as to "know" when a threshold has been crossed [Chapter 3]. Related questions have to do with the nature of the mechanisms for "matching" current demand characteristics with earlier established latent predispositions [Chapters 2, 13, and 14], for the actual way or ways in which feedback works [Chapters 1, 2, and 9], and for damping of oscillations in the system that might otherwise cause imbalance [Chapter 2]. (Indeed, as the many variables with which the systems operate, during the processes we call transactional, become known, we shall gain more respect for the capability of the human to solve simultaneous equations [Chapters 2, 3, 4, 6, 7, and 9].)

## Methods and Measurement

One cannot read the chapters in this volume without being impressed by the plethora of technical improvements that have been made in measuring devices and procedures, and by the ingenuity with which they are being applied to stress research. We note, with equal interest, the various recommendations for improved methods of study.

The use of voice and speech cues to measure emotional changes in stress [Chapter 9] and the automatic baseline reset system, devised to eliminate drift in presenting slow cortical potential, and permitting use of the Brain Trigger Design to control presentation of stimuli coincident with maximum cortical negativity [Chapter 8], are two applications of new technology to the stress field. Similarly, ambulatory recording techniques now enable the obtaining of blood samples from human subjects engaged in their daily activities and the study of patterning of hormonal responses, using "radioimmunologic, enzymatic, mass-spectrometric, gaschromatographic and fluorometric techniques" [Chapters 6 and 7].

Computers are now used more routinely for simulation of live situations [Chapters 5 and 8] and for modeling [Chapters 3 and 9]. Videotape-aided recall [Chapter 12] helps retain, for subject analysis, the sequence of cognition-emotion–behavior interactions as they occurred. And applications of new experimental techniques (e.g., use of "Life as theater" metaphor [Chapter 12], of cluster analysis-produced profiles [Chapters 7, 10, and 11], of "ergopsychometry" [Chapter 8]) give promise of new insights into stress processes, as do the more ambitious efforts to spell out comprehensive theoretical models [Chapters 2, 5, and 9].

Attention should be drawn to two major "trends" that we believe are significant developments: first, the increased ease with which investigators can now do rigorous field research, as a result of new techniques that have become available [Chapters 5, 6, 7, 8, 9, 10, 11, and 12]; and secondly, the increasing recognition of and dissatisfaction with the limitations of questionnaires as research instruments [Chapters 3, 6, 10, 11, 12, 13, and 14]. Some procedures have been devised for use of the investigator as the measuring instrument, rather than the subject, to avoid subjective distortions in recall [Chapters 6, 10, 11, and 13]. However, the problems being identified in the use of questionnaires are larger than this. As was noted earlier in the chapter, questionnaires report conscious, problem-focussed coping strategies, ignoring objective indicators, on the one hand, and noncognitive processes on the other [Chapter 10]. Other problems involving questionnaires or scales have to do with the perpetual issues of validity [e.g., see the discussion about the Hassles Scale in Chapters 4 and 14].

## Stress and Adjustment

At the outset of this chapter, we reiterated the current view that stress is not, in itself, a negative state to be avoided. This is because coping strategies and conditioned somatic processes, which occur in the stress process, develop into lasting response mechanisms that serve development and represent the positive facet of the stress mechanism [Chapter 7]. However, chronic stress can lead to physical disease, to psychosomatic problems, and to psychopathology, if unremitting [Chapters 7, 13, and 14]. The difference in outcome is a function of the effectiveness of coping, in the early stages of the stress process, in reducing the discrepancy between demand and capacity [Chapters 1 and 12].

Several factors seem to emerge consistently as serving protective, buffering roles in reducing the chances that a major stressor will provoke depression or other pathology [Chapter 13]. Among these, *social support* (from someone in very close and frequent contact) appears to be the most important [Chapters 3, 13, and 14]. In fact it has been shown that, even in nonstress situations, individuals with social support fare better than those who lack it [Chapter 3], and that *good health*, also a factor in minimizing stressfulness, is positively associated with social support [Chapters 3, 13, and 14]. Conversely, loss of such support (or reduced ability to draw upon it) and/or lowered *self-esteem* or self-confidence increases vulnerability to depression if stress develops [Chapters 3, 12, 13, and 14]. Further, there seems to be a mutual interdependence between self-image as worthy and the actual support the individual is offered by others [Chapter 13].

Recognition of the roles such supportive elements play in establishing the on-going level of carrying capacity is important in development as well as in therapy. However, as the coincidence of events that later might call them into play is somewhat a matter of chance or luck [Chapter 13], the human tendency to believe that ill-fortune is something that happens to others but not to oneself works *against* considered development of such supports and, thus, the raising of carrying capacity to counter such chance demands. Deliberate programs to establish and maintain health, hope, and social support at appropriate levels in the three systems do not fare well, under the circumstances. Understanding the ultimate price of failure to do so—whether in terms of performance failure [Chapters 7, 8, 11, and 12], depression [Chapters 13 and 14], economic costs [Chapter 5], psychosomatic complaints [Chapter 10], hopelessness [Chapter 15] or other criteria—will serve to stimulate greater appreciation for the importance of the role of the carrying capacity that the individual brings into the stressful situations of life.

Ongoing feelings of low self-esteem seem to induce a greater generalization of hopelessness [Chapter 13, 14, and 15]. As social situations may inherently involve evaluations of personal adequacy, people manage their self-presentations in such a manner as to minimize threats to self-esteem [Chapter 12]. Depression is over twice as likely to follow a stressor in individuals with negative self-evaluations [Chapter 13].

A sense of personal *control* or influence over events (e.g., accurate anticipation, accurate information) is a further important modulating or buffering factor [Chapters 2, 6, and 8] in reducing negative emotions, inducing both a lessening of psychic load and an increase in hopefulness [Chapters 6, 8, and 15], and even enhancing "unwinding" after a stressful encounter [Chapter 6]. Control leads to more effective performance, in that increased effort can be expended without increased distress [Chapters 5, 6, and 8]. However, it has been pointed out that this is not always the case. Where action is not possible, for example, and accommodation is necessary, effort to utilize control as a coping mode can be damaging [Chapter 15]. *Hoping,* on the other hand, is most useful as a buffering factor precisely in situations of objective helplessness [Chapter 15]. And, in general, hope, optimism, and positive outlook toward the future all seem to have positive impact on the health and morale of people under stress [Chapters 13 and 15].

Once again, we return to the remarkable parallels among the physiological, psychological, and social systems, by means of which man relates to the world about him. Their cyclical movements provide periods of even flow as well as peaks and valleys, resulting from summations. We recognize them in circadian rhythm and developmental histories in the physiological system as moods and dispositions in the psychological system, and as standards and laws in the social system. We must also recognize the parallels in their dynamics: the ways in which their personal and collective "health" provide the carrying capacity of individuals, their potential for providing a vulnerability which can be lying in wait until coincidence with some stressor results in unusual response, and an equally surprising capability for adjusting and for maintaining health and integrity under assault from abnormal stressors. Our focus on the "stressed" has led us to overlook "healthy" individuals. (We continue to believe, following a medical model, that we can learn how to make the next generation healthier by studying the infirm, when the answer and guidance might well come from those who are the healthiest.)

We have tried to find other dynamics in that world that emphasizes the physiological system for our understanding of the psychological and social systems. We recognize the roles of predispositions and trauma, of chronic and acute, and we try to find their parallel in the psychological and social systems, as well. Even as medicine is discovering the latent weaknesses, the herpes, which are carried without any major disruption of life until an illness or other reduction of immunological protection allows it to become manifest, psychologists and sociologists are discovering that depression, in both the personal and social sense, might have the same latent potential. We have much to learn about the counterparts to immunology and how they are maintained at appropriate protective levels in the psychological and social systems. Of special interest is the nascent understanding of psychological/immunological systems interaction, a key to *mens sana in corpore sano.* The newer studies of psychopathology illustrate this parallel with depression, apparently fostered by, if not arising from, low self-esteem and inadequate social support. What other defeating, if not destructive moods and/or emotions play the role of herpes in the psychological system? What psychological "immune" systems should have been in place to prevent their occurrence *ever*? Will we learn the answers by retrospective case histories and personal recall from analyses of eruption or expression in response to some stressor *at some given time*?

We find cause for hope in recurrent statements about development in current research. Investigators have begun to concern themselves with the developmental histories that brought their subjects to their experimental setting, with or without the carrying capacity to meet the demands. We study coping strategies, of the moment, without enough interest in their etiology, because we focus on the ever-available college student. We could study other age groups, in which "of the moment" is in the beginning or middle of coping strategy development, and reliance on recall could thereby be minimized.

A similar effort to understand the dynamics and development of the social system has barely begun. Social scientists have yet to recognize the parallels, the similarities between perturbations in their system and the physiological and psychological systems, as we are getting to know them. They do have their stressors, their antecedents, their variety of cycles, which are constantly interacting to provide stronger, weaker and/or neutralized standards, laws, ethics, economies, and so forth. (An occasion on which one of the authors was to present a preliminary appraisal of these parallels in Greece was canceled due to a revolution, a *sociopathological* manifestation of coping failure at the social level.) All of the same questions about specific versus general adaptation syndromes can be raised as they pertain to structure of the society, the interactions between its subsystems, and temporal and contextual determinants.

As we continue to appreciate the interactions among the physiological, psychological, and social systems of the individual's world, real and perceived, we shall acquire understanding of the dynamics and the remarkable parallels that will facilitate translation from one to the other. Any framework or paradigm that facilitates this enlightenment will be as rewarding as it is challenging.

## Dynamics of Stress and Its Control

The dynamics of stress are the dynamics of life. We have discussed predisposition, context, time and timing, appraisal and coping, their interrelations, and the ways each contributes to degree of individual vulnerability, disparity control, and adjustment. It remains for us to comment on how these aspects of the stress process relate to the dynamics and control of stress.

Control, and/or its perception, is recognized as important for the prevention and moderation of stress. This includes control of the situation [Chapters 5, 10, and 11], as well as control of the bodily processes associated with the feeling of stress [Chapters 2, 3, 4, 6, 7, 8, and 9]. Now we learn of more subtle controls available through modes of presentation of self [Chapter 12], coping style [Chapter 11], maintaining hope [Chapter 15], and so forth. The situation can be controlled directly or, indirectly, through a changed perception or attitudinal change. Bodily processes can be controlled by medication, meditation and/or feedback, in which greater awareness of pulse rate, blood pressure, breathing pattern, and muscle tension can lead to their alteration for stress reduction. The majority of programs purporting to help one deal with stress rely on some or all of these means of control.

The view of stress from the pathological end of the telescope has made us aware of the weaknesses and vulnerabilities that individuals bring into potential stress situations and not their strengths. Yet any examination of the concept of predisposition will reveal *immunologic systems* in place—at psychological and sociocultural levels as well as physiological—that serve to protect the individual against being overwhelmed by demands. These latent inner resource "reserves" are recognized as being present but not well understood. They clearly *cross* systems, involving good general health, psychological identity, integrity and self-acceptance, and social support and reinforcement systems that give social congruity to the individual. How these factors develop, are sustained, remain latent over time, and come into play to support carrying capacity when demand increases, is not fully understood. Nor, given their nature, are they likely to be better comprehended if we restrict our studies to conscious recall and recognition through questionnaires. The time sample available through a questionnaire is very limited, whether asking for recall, a response of the moment, or a "what if" speculation. If we accept appraisal as a process of evaluating stimulus threat or whatever, and the individual's resources for dealing with same, the "what if" type of sampling is very questionable—primarily because one cannot posit the context, the time or the on-going flow of system processes for some time in the future any more than one can predict or anticipate the "value" of the stressor. Even "what if" situations presented for "right now," asking for appraisals of threat and resources in the present context, leave much to be desired in the absence of actual occurrence and demand for response. The emphasis on cognitive appraisal, like the earlier one on pathology, may have been too narrow, and, therefore, misleading. That there can be perception and response, without the necessity of mediating *cognitive* interpretation, must be accepted, or we will fail to either search for or find the subtle undercurrents brought to events of the present as predispositions from repressed, forgotten, or unrecognized events of the past. Here, the new techniques and approaches now becoming available should permit further blending of field and laboratory investigation and provide new insights as to suspected mechanisms previously unavailable for study [Chapters 3, 6, 7, 8, and 9,].

The stress process provides opportunities for action and for self-development [Chapter 7], for conscious and intentional management of the activation process [Chapter 8], for the development of effective coping strategies and practices to reduce demand by problem-solving measures before it becomes ego-threatening [Chapters 1, 2, and 12].

The best form of stress control is prevention. The adage "if it ain't broke, don't fix it" is too categorical. A dynamic process is not "not broke" one day and "broke" the next. The disparity between demand and capacity is never at a fixed level [Chapter 2]. Thus, any procedures that help keep the two in balance may be construed as beneficial or therapeutic, even—and especially—before pathology has developed. Reinforcing self-esteem, assuring continuity of some source of intimate social support, developing good health maintenance routines, providing opportunities for self-development and the maintenance of positive, hopeful attitudes all contribute to the immunological and psychoimmunological support system.

Stress cannot be avoided, nor should it be. But the negative effects of unsuccessful stress encounters can be avoided or reduced by monitoring (appraising, assessing) the level of disparity and developing coping strategies appropriate to the source.

## Implications

Our understanding of the dynamics of stress improves with our appreciation of the complexities of the systems under study and the subtleties of their interactions. The refinements of physiological measurements now allow a clearer picture of various subsystem interactions at that level as the body responds to different assaults on those systems. Increased recognition of the role that perception plays has brought our attention to the many psychological factors that the individual brings into the situation. This, in turn, has involved us more than ever with the social structure and its influence on both the situation and the nature of the psychological repertoire that is made available. Even as we now recognize the timeliness of development of various physiological systems that can help in dealing with stress, we appreciate that there are psychological and social systems that "have their day" in co-determining the nature and extent of stressfulness over the life time.

A developmental perspective helps us appreciate the appearance of different coping patterns at different stages in life and their age-related appropriateness. How soon, for example, must "kiddie candor"—the naming of things as they really are—rather characteristic of preschoolers, be modified for social acceptance? How do parental and other models produce the coping strategies we collectively call "social veneer" that make it easier to live with others? How does this expand to include coping strategies to deal with peer pressures? and to discriminate, among peers, those worth following?

Where, when, and how does the child develop the sense of values that provides him or her with the various alternatives that must be screened or reviewed during the appraisal process in coping? Much has been said about the appraisal-coping–appraisal sequence and those things that are (situationally) antecedent to subsequent considerations or actions. Here, on the other hand, we are raising questions about *earlier* antecedents, which place the variety of coping strategies and techniques at the individual's disposal. And, as the child goes through life, there is an ever-changing composition or sequence of appraisal acts, representing the continual interplay among physical, psychological, and social systems as the child matures and copes.

Even as we had previously discussed the manner in which certain physiological systems had their appropriate time to influence physical development, so, too, are there appropriate times for psychological developments—for age- or stage-related changes in behavior patterns, attitudes, and so forth, as the child "grows up." And social patterns also influence the nature of the stressors and the capability for coping available as the individual ages.

It might be interesting to place "life events" and even "daily hassles" on a chronological scale, and to examine the likelihood of their being encountered at particular periods of life. Parallel scaling of traits, moods, or other psychological factors, and judgments of how acceptable or tolerated they would be at different stages in the individual's life history, would be most revealing. We would note, for example, the age- or stage-relatedness of our descriptive terminology. Such terms as "shyness," "coyness," "kittenish," "stubborn," "persistent," and "pigheaded" are examples of descriptors acceptable at one period in the life cycle and not at another.

Such patterns of behavior may represent expressions of coping with social stress situations as they occur at different stages of life, and thus be appropriate at one stage and not at others. This has implications for personality study, in which constancy of behavior across time (or circumstance) has often been expected, though inappropriately so, in our view. We have spoken earlier of events having *relevance* to the lives of those experiencing them and *significance* within those lives. *Timeliness* in the cycle should also be emphasized, as a determinant of both relevance and significance.

If we examine events on the chronological scale noted above, we can note "appropriate" and even "optimal" (or, conversely, "disastrous") timing for certain events. Thus, it does make a difference when a sibling or parent is lost. Marriage has an "appropriate" period which, interestingly enough, is determined by social rather than physiological factors. The impact of any life event can be understood only in the context of predisposition of physiological, psychological, and social systems and subsystems. Although we are more accustomed to recognize cyclicity and periodicity in relation to biological processes, it would seem that timing in relation to psychological readiness or social expectation would be equally important in determining stress vulnerability and choice and effectiveness of coping strategy.

In dealing with the vicissitudes of life, then, it matters a great deal what else is occurring in the biological, psychological, and social systems coincident with the impact of a particular event. In a sense, the state of each system at a given moment constitutes an "event" affecting other systems. It would thus be very difficult to conceive of any point in time or life in which coping capability, if not strategy, would not be dependent on the interplay of systems.

The challenge for future stress research will be in the ability of investigators to appreciate the *dynamics* of processes involving mutually influencing changes in interacting systems. It is to be hoped that research at all three levels will proceed to a point in which their interactions can be better understood as well as their individual and collective contributions to the dynamics of stress.

# References

Appley, M. H., & Trumbull, R. (1967). *Psychological stress: Issues in research.* New York: Appleton-Century-Crofts.

Notterman, J. M., & Trumbull, R. (1959). Note on self-regulating systems and stress. *Behavioral Sciences, 4*, 324–327.

Selye, H. (1973). The evolution of the stress concept. *American Scientist, 61*, 692–699.

Thomas, L. (1980). *Late night thoughts on listening to Mahler's Ninth Symphony.* New York: Norton.

# Author Index

**329**

# Subject Index